Market Limits in Health Reform

This volume explores the deep-rooted tensions between publicly funded health care systems and the dynamics of markets in the delivery of privately financed health care. It lays bare the limitations of market-led health reform and argues for the indispensable role of a vibrant public authority in the renewal of modern health care systems. While markets may be back with a vengeance, health care remains a stabilizing instrument of citizenship at a time of economic uncertainty

International authorities in the field examine public–private conflicts in health policy, including cost-containment and privatization strategies in an international perspective, the virus of consumerism, and the role of business and the private sector in setting the agenda for health care reform. Special attention is paid to the restructuring of Anglo-Saxon health systems and the shift in state/market boundaries in Canada, US, Britain and Australia. Finally, *Market Limits in Health Reform* addresses the frontier of health care reform including health and social cohesion as well as the role of patient choice in health care reform.

Market Limits in Health Reform does not simply lay bare current trends in international health provisioning, but also reflects on the challenges facing health care in the advanced economies. More than simply analyzing the organization and financing of health care services, the contributors stress what is at stake is the establishment of social arrangements which produce health. Both as informed analysis and provocative reflection, *Market Limits in Health Reform* will be of great interest to students and researchers in health economics and policy, public economics, politics and political economy.

Daniel Drache is the Director of the Robarts Centre for Canadian Studies at York University, Ontario and Professor of Political Economy. He is the co-editor, with Robert Boyer, of *States Against Markets: The Limits of Globalization*. **Terry Sullivan** is the President of the Institute for Work and Health, Toronto, and is Adjunct Professor in Sociology at York University and in the Department of Health Administration, Faculty of Medicine, University of Toronto.

Innis centenary series: governance and change in the global era
Daniel Drache
Series Editor

Harold Innis, one of Canada's most distinguished economists, described the Canadian experience as no one else ever has. His visionary works in economic geography, political economy, and communications theory have endured for over fifty years and have had tremendous influence on scholarship, the media, and the business community.

The volumes in the Innis Centenary Series illustrate and expand Innis's legacy. Each volume is written and edited by distinguished members of the fields Innis touched. Each addresses provocative and challenging issues that have profound implications not only for Canada but for the 'new world order', including the impact of globalization on governance, international development and national decision-making; interactions among the state, social movements, and the environment; the nature of the 'market' in the future; the effect of new communications technology on economic restructuring; and the role of the individual in effecting positive social change.

The complete series will provide a unique guide to many of the major challenges we face as we enter the twenty-first century.

The Innis Centenary Series is supported by the Robarts Centre for Canadian Studies and York University. Proposals for future volumes in the series are actively encouraged and most welcome. Please address all enquiries to the editor, by email drache@yorku.ca or by fax 1.416.736.5739.

Other titles in the series include:
States Against Markets
Edited by Robert Boyer and Daniel Drache

Political Ecology
Edited by David Bell, Leesa Fawcett, Roger Keil and Peter Penz

Market Limits in Health Reform

Public success, private failure

Edited by
Daniel Drache and Terry Sullivan

London and New York

First published 1999 by Routledge
11 New Fetter Lane, London EC4P 4EE

Simultaneously published in the USA and Canada by Routledge
29 West 35th Street, New York, NY 10001

© 1999 Daniel Drache and Terry Sullivan; individual chapters © the contributors

The right of the contributors to be identified as the Authors
of their Work has been asserted by them in accordance with the Copyright,
Designs and Patents Act 1988

Typeset in Garamond by Pure Tech India Ltd., Pondicherry, India
http://www.puretech.com
Printed and bound in Great Britain by Redwood Books, Trowbridge, Wiltshire

British Library Cataloguing in Publication Data
A catalogue record for this book is available from the British Library

Library of Congress Cataloging in Publication Data
A catalog record for this book has been requested

ISBN 0-415-20235-3 (hbk)
ISBN 0-415-20236-1 (pbk)

Contents

Figures

Tables

Contributors

Barry Appleton is the managing partner of Appleton & Associates International Lawyers in Toronto and New York City. He holds an LL.B. from Queen's University and an LL.M. in International Law from the University of Cambridge.

Peter Botsman is a specialist and authority on public policy and health care and is Director of Health Studies at the University of Western Sydney, Sydney.

François Champagne is a Professor in the Department of Health Administration at the Université de Montréal.

John Church is a political scientist in the Department of Public Health at the University of Calgary with a particular interest in health system organization and policy.

André-Pierre Contandriopoulos is a Professor in the Department of Health Administration and researcher in la Groupe de Recherche Interdisciplinaire de la Santé (GRIS) at the Université de Montréal.

Raisa Deber is Professor of Political Science and Health Administration at the University of Toronto and is a noted authority and researcher internationally in the field of health policy.

Jean-Louis Denis is Associate Professor in the Department of Health Administration and Associate Director of the GRIS at the Université de Montréal.

Gail Donner is a Professor of Nursing in the Faculty of Medicine at the University of Toronto and has been active as a policy consultant and researcher on health care reform in Canada.

Daniel Drache is Director of the Robarts Centre for Canadian Studies and Professor of Political Economy at York University and has published widely on the impact of globalization on state policies.

Robert Evans is Professor of Economics at the University of British Columbia and an international authority on health care. The Syd Jackson fellow of the

Canadian Institute for Advanced Research, he is a prolific writer on health policy issues and has consulted widely for governments and international agencies.

Gina Feldberg is the Director of Centre for Health Studies at York University and is a Professor in the Division of Social Sciences. She is a noted authority on women's health issues and the history of infectious diseases.

Joel Davison Harden is a graduate student in the Department of Political Science at York University and is writing his doctoral dissertation on the impact of neo-liberal ideology on health care restructuring.

John Lavis is a scientist and Manager of Population Studies at the Institute for Work and Health, and also an Assistant Professor at the Centre for Health Economics and Policy Analysis at McMaster University.

Joel Lexchin is a Professor of Family Medicine at the University of Toronto and a practising emergency room physician. He is a leading commentator on pharmaceutical cost issues in Canada.

Jonathan Lomas is the founding Executive Director of the Canadian Health Services Research Foundation in Ottawa. He was co-ordinator of the Centre for Health Economics and Policy Analysis, McMaster University and Professor in the Department of Clinical Epidemiology and Bio-Statistics.

Mike McCracken is president of Informetrica, an independent economic forecasting and policy analysis firm specializing in macroeconomic issues. He is one of Canada's leading macroeconomists.

Ted Marmor is a distinguished political scientist and Professor in the department of Management and Public Policy at Yale University. He has written widely on American and comparative public policy reforms.

J. Fraser Mustard is the founding president of the Canadian Institute for Advanced Research. A distinguished platelet researcher, he has been widely recognized in Canada and internationally for his work on the health of populations.

Tom Noseworthy is an urgent care physician who has been active in medical education and public policy. He is chair of the department of Public Health Science at University of Calgary and was vice-chair of the National Forum on Health.

Mary Ruggie is Professor of Sociology at Columbia University and author of *The State and Working Women: A Comparative Study of Britain and Sweden* (Princeton, 1984) and *Realignments in the Welfare State: Health Policy in the United States, Britain and Canada* (Columbia, 1996), as well as several related articles.

Natasha Sharpe is a graduate student in the Department of Health Administration in the Faculty of Medicine at the University of Toronto.

Carl Sonnen is vice-president of Informetrica and is a specialist in health care reform among other areas of public policy.

Art Stewart is an independent economic consultant who teaches at Queen's University.

Terry Sullivan is President of the Institute for Work and Health, Adjunct Professor at York University and the Department of Health Administration at the University of Toronto. He is active in the field of health and disability policy.

Louise-Hélène Trottier is coordinator, research transfer and communication, in the GRIS and Ph.D. candidate in Public Health at the Université de Montréal.

Robert Vipond is the chair of the Department of Political Science, University of Toronto and has published widely on issues of governance and public policy reform.

Acknowledgements

This volume grew out of a seminar entitled 'Reforming Canada's Health Care System' organized jointly by the Robarts Centre for Canadian Studies, York University and the Institute for Work and Health, Toronto, in April 1996, and supported by York University, Health Canada and Glaxo Canada. Health care reform has been a preoccupation of all levels of government in Canada as it has been throughout the industrialized world, and the rationale for the conference was that government policy-makers and academic commentators needed to take a fresh look at the restructuring process. It was also hoped that the conference would be a kind of policy laboratory where specialists and non-specialists could assess many of the dramatic changes resulting from spending cuts as well as a range of new initiatives to change the way health care services are delivered regionally and health care is provided for patients. Many other issues were also discussed. Papers from that conference were presented in draft form and were subsequently rewritten. They are included in this volume. Subsequently, a goodly number of the chapters, however, were commissioned expressly for this book. We are particularly grateful to all who participated in the original conference and to those authors who responded generously to our comments and criticisms. As well, we would like to thank Vincy Perri for her exceptional secretarial support in working on the manuscript and her managerial skills in keeping track of the many different drafts of individual chapters. Alison Kirk, the senior editor at Routledge deserves a special thank you for expediting the volume as well. We also would like to thank York Vice-President Michael Stevenson for his support for the original conference and his encouragement to publish this volume. Finally, we would like to thank York President Lorna Marsden for her continued encouragement for both the Robarts Centre for Canadian Studies and the Institute for Work and Health.

Daniel Drache and Terry Sullivan
June 1998

1 Health reform and market talk

Rhetoric and reality

Daniel Drache and Terry Sullivan

INTRODUCTION

Less than a decade ago the notion that a publicly financed health care system would be competing with a privatized alternative would have been unthinkable. A previously inconceivable idea has now found its champions (Herzlinger, 1997). Governments everywhere, including the social market economies of Western Europe, have a new-found interest in privatizing services and redrawing the boundary between the public and the private (Boyer and Drache, 1996). The assumption that private markets somehow on their own could foot the bill for a comprehensive delivery system for most countries deserves a strong but careful rebuttal. This volume takes up the challenge and sets out to explore the deep-rooted tensions between publicly funded health care systems and the dynamics of private markets to deliver privately financed systems of health care.

The intent of the contributors is to offer a compelling, practical analysis of these difficult issues of health care reform. The volume is written for an informed public who want to comprehend the attraction and limitations of market-led health reform and the indispensable role of a vibrant public authority in the renewal of modern health care systems. Significantly, the health care reform agenda has been dominated by economists and policy-makers narrowly focused on deficit reduction and spending controls. At the forefront of comparative reform efforts have been the OECD analyses. In many of its publications, the OECD points to an enlarged role for markets in health reforms as though efficiency was the primary reform objective (OECD, 1994; World Development Report, 1993). This is clearly inadequate.

Every industrial nation has had to cope with a range of issues as diverse as the urgency of fiscal restraint, the pressure to decentralize, increased citizen participation in health care decision-making, the need for harmonization of health arrangements across jurisdictions, partial or wholesale privatization, the rationing of expensive technology and drugs, the downsizing of the hospital sector, constraining the growth of doctors' incomes, the regulation of non-medical practitioners and democratic initiatives to strengthen public health. All advanced economies now admit some role for markets in their financing and delivery systems. Recent reforms in Western Europe have generated competition between doctors within Germany and Britain, among pharmaceutical products in Germany and The Netherlands, between hospitals in Germany, the UK and The Netherlands, and insurers or fund-holders in the UK and The Netherlands (Saltman, 1995). By contrast, no country other than the US relies primarily on private markets to meet a comprehensive range of health needs, and the US system is the most expensive in the world (Kuttner, 1997). None the less, throughout the OECD, states continue to support publicly funded systems as a matter of principle and are steadfast in their commitment to shared responsibility in the field of health. But the fact remains that public authority in every kind of market-based economy has had to confront three essential health policy challenges driven by the new era of global competition.

HEALTH REFORM OBJECTIVES DEFINED

The first and the most important policy imperative remains how to sustain a public commitment to a comprehensive range of health services for all citizens. This is not easy to do. The public policy domain is now dealing with citizens who are increasingly suspicious of state-sponsored health schemes that have gone awry, doctors and drug companies whose livelihoods depend on expanding market opportunities, and the chronically ill who demand better and more compassionate therapies. What then remains of the legacy of universal health care in an era of global markets? It is this question that dominates the health reform agenda in advanced economies and so far states have discovered that they have to make trade-offs if they are to maintain affordable coverage for all. Government authorities have had to choose between the cost of expensive technology and the benefits of better primary care; between critical life-saving interventions and the need for spending more on effective public health programs; between expensive measures to extend life and an increase in resources on perinatal care; between more effective planning by central governments and increased reliance on devolution and decentralized organization of health delivery systems; and between an enhanced role for doctors and other medical elites who want to be paid more and the interests of the public for greater public accountability.

Most states are spending their scarce care resources on hospital beds, physician services and fees, community and chronic care as well as drug and biotechnology. The proportion varies markedly between jurisdictions; nevertheless all authorities are wrestling to find ways to promote the development of community and home-based care, reduce reliance on institutional and hospital care, manage the explosive growth of bio-technology costs, and keep physician fees within nationally acceptable limits. Health expenditures will continue to be the big ticket public spending item in all jurisdictions. An ageing population, the growth of biomedical technology and an ever-increasing supply of physicians ensure that competition for public resources will be intense and pre-occupy governments everywhere.

The second policy imperative is to improve the efficiency of health care services at a time of fiscal constraint. Improved health care for millions of people is one of the undisputed achievements of the modern age. More than any other single program of the welfare state, it transformed the way we live, our spending patterns, our gender identity and the structure of the family. Citizens in most advanced economies no longer need to worry about basic medical coverage, and the fact that they have secure access to hospitals, doctors and life-saving drugs for the majority has transformed people's lives in ways that few could have predicted. Despite this, the advances in health care are reaching the point of limited returns in life-extending benefits. Even if more people than ever are receiving expensive body part transplants, life expectancy in the total population is not rising appreciably as a consequence. A sustained rise in GDP is likely to do more to extend the life expectancy of the total population. Seizing on this fact, governments in the advanced economies are cutting spending – sometimes judiciously, but more often than not in an unplanned way. They are relying on privatization and quasi-market mechanisms to strike a different balance between private and public provision and the financing of health care. Here also states have had to contend with growing expectations from their middle classes and their ageing populations for improved quality of care. For policy-makers, this presents a variety of questions from who pays, who delivers and who benefits to what percentage of national resources should be devoted to expenditures for health.

Among the privatization mechanisms that states are looking at are: the divestiture of public assets; contracting out of health services, self-management of hospitals and the privatization in some cases of hospitals, market deregulation and liberalization of delivery systems, and withdrawal of state provision of health services (Bennett *et al.*, 1997).

The third imperative that so far has eluded a ready-made solution is to devise social arrangements which engender healthy populations. Many years ago the Nobel Laureate Gunnar Myrdal articulated the notion of a vicious cycle of poor health and low income for both the developed and underdeveloped world. His point was that people were sick when they were poor; they became poorer when they were sick, and sicker because they were poorer (Myrdal, 1957). He wanted development to promote social arrangements that generated prosperity and radically improved health as a consequence. If socially cohesive populations are healthier and generate a virtuous cycle of prosperity and health improvements, what (non-health care) measures do public authorities need to adopt to improve people's health (Evans *et al.*, 1994; Blane *et al.*, 1996; Wilkinson, 1996)?

Among the measures that governments need to promote are: healthy child development, safe and fulfilling work environments, reducing social distance and social isolation, and promoting neighbourhood and community engagement. These determinants must be matched by a vibrant and sustainable economy to maximize their health effects (World Development Report, 1993). These social determinants of health are often talked about, but governments have found few ways to take real action in these areas that count the most. In the modern era, efforts to constrain health care spending must be met with an equally strong resolve to promote health-enhancing areas of public policy. At the present, governments are preoccupied to make the state smaller with less of a presence in the economy and to cut back on their role as regulators. Promoting social health requires a new activism on the part of the state. Is this going to happen when government appears to be moving in the opposite direction? There may be some room for optimism.

Increasingly governments need to minimize the social dislocation when markets expand beyond the moral and political boundaries within which they are necessarily constrained to operate. The emergence of new policy capabilities for different market economies is a distinct likelihood. The important repositioning of government can only occur with strategic changes in the functioning of the state – having institutions that learn, that effect long-term and strategic change, and that create high quality and crisis-sensitive modes of policy reasoning. Building a strong central capacity for formulating health policy is the first step towards revitalizing decision-making in the public domain. The 'public domain' refers to assets held in common which cannot be bought and sold in the open market. For society to function smoothly, public authority will be increasingly under pressure to exercise its supervisory role 'when there are no other strong social values to compete with that of money and wealth' (Albert, 1993: 104). If Albert's principal assumption is valid, public authority will be hesitant about transferring many of its prerogatives to the private sector including principal responsibility for health.

An 'effective state', to employ the recent terminology of the *World Bank Development Report 1997*, requires rethinking the framework for social health in highly contrasted market-driven economies. Increasingly, health cannot be separated from policies to create employment, promote social trust and generate a productive economy. The reform of health policy in an era of globalization requires not only institutional innovation but shared policy learning based on the actual experience of other states and not just on what happens in some abstract neo-classical economic model.

In practical terms, this appears to be a small step – in reality it is not. There are many stumbling blocks in the way. The first is the widespread misunderstanding of what kind of commodity health care is and the many costly aftereffects arising from unchecked reliance on the market logic in health care. Second, the health reform movement has to come to grips with the widespread disenchantment with public health care bureaucrats and the loss of faith by the public in health care administrators. This brings us logically back to the fundamentals of Beveridge's universal health care scheme as part of modern governance. Does it have any relevance in an age of globalization? Modern health governance has to forge a new relationship between health care programs and the social production of health in childhood development, the workplace and beyond. In order to satisfy this new policy awareness that social health matters, what mix of health reform policies best meets our three policy imperatives? In the post-Beveridge era, health reform is now one of the principal avenues redefining the boundaries between states, markets and civil society (Dahrendorf, 1995). Readers of this volume will quickly discover that somewhere between market USA and social market Europe, the Canadian system provides a valuable prototype or window on reform for other jurisdictions as they struggle with these modern health policy dilemmas. Canada is a hybrid model, with a strong role for public insurance coupled with a diverse private delivery system.[1] It is to these considerations we now turn.

WHAT KIND OF COMMODITY IS HEALTH CARE: THE DEFINING ISSUE

Despite much debate among health economists, there has been little agreement on the core issue: what kind of commodity health care is. Is it a public good that only states can really effectively provide? Is it closer to what Adam Smith described as a non-market 'necessary' for the support of life that no society can afford to be without? Or is it a service to be bought and sold like any other commodity and subject to market rules and discipline (Albert, 1993)?

At the heart of the dispute is a simple idea that divides economists: namely, health care does not 'trade' like other goods and services (Kuttner, 1997; Evans, 1997a). This is because there is no limit to the amount which consumers will pay when it comes to preserving their health or the health of their families. Unlike other goods or services, health care does not have a line of people clamouring voluntarily for gall bladder surgery; it is driven by need rather than want. Also, most purchasers of health care do not pay at the point of provision for the service; they have insurance and it is the insurer who signs the cheques and pays the doctor. It makes little sense to look to universal laws of supply and demand to discipline health markets when there is no apparent limit to the amount of service they can buy under such an insurance arrangement. With such 'imperfect competition' private health care markets become very expensive, particularly when there is indeed a very large asymmetry between what consumers need to know and the information that health-care providers have.

Knowledge about health and illness is closely guarded as a professional commodity. It is the intellectual property of health care professionals and health care vendors. Information flows are not like capital movements and are subject to many non-tariff intellectual property barriers erected by private individuals and organizations. This asymmetry of knowledge drives the growth of health care costs in private markets because of the push from provider-induced demand. At least on theoretical grounds, there is a strong analytical case that the market model cannot be easily applied to the health care domain. In the view of the American health economist Victor Fuchs (1996), a narrow preoccupation with markets fails to acknowledge the diversity of human wants and the difference between what may be technically best and what is socially desirable.

Another reason that there has been so much disagreement on the economic nature of health is that it is always easier to control costs through integrated public payment systems rather than through multiple, privately financed alternatives (Brousselle, 1998). Private insurance markets fail, for instance, because insurers are unwilling to assume the expensive risks associated with genetic anomalies and catastrophic illness such as AIDS. Even private insurance for middle-of-the-road coverage is often expensive and the benefits are capped to ensure limited coverage in the event of serious illness, as many Americans have discovered to their chagrin. The idea that individuals will simply assume co-payments to match their level of risk constitutes 'an example of academic theorizing of breathtaking proportions' (Kuttner, 1997).

After a decade of market-style reforms in the UK and New Zealand, overall health expenditures as a portion of GDP have gone up, not down (OECD, 1994). Privately financed health care is almost always more expensive than publicly financed alternatives. Hsiao (1995) recently provided an evaluation of the systematic attempt to introduce private medical savings accounts as the market solution of preference in Singapore. He concluded that this private financing model led to rapid cost escalation, excess institutional capacity and rapid increases in doctors' incomes. By contrast Stewart (Chapter 4 in this volume) commends the Scandinavians for relying on non-market solutions and quasi-market style reforms to reduce expenditures. Most sensible health economists have argued that competitive contracting for health care services in the hands of a socially responsible institutional purchaser can provide clear incentives for a good performance (Culyer *et al.*, 1990). This is quite a different nuance from Herzlinger's wide-open competitive marketplace. There is no simple market mechanism which will provide health care insurance for all citizens without some direct regulatory intervention from the state. Such market failures are indeed the economic rationale for a continued state presence.

For quite different reasons, the state's presence may paradoxically be understood – not so much because of incipient market failure but because of the market's success, particularly when private interests masquerade as public concern. Markets appeal to rational self-interests and so require regulation to serve collective social objectives such as the broadest pooling of health risk. The unwarranted assumption in *laissez-faire* economies is that physicians can be looked to as disinterested, self-regulating groups who can be guardians of the public interest. Nothing is further from the truth. They have a complex and contradictory role in health care reform initiatives in modern economies (Rachlis and Kushner, 1994).

A simple, if not straightforward, example of how the private income needs of professionals masquerade as public concern is found in the debate regarding the de-listing of so-called non-essential services. In every province in Canada, for example, there has been constant pressure by organized medicine to remove public compensation for services which are regarded as not medically necessary, such as hair removal, tattoo removal, torn ear lobes, etc. Physicians' organizations are leading the charge on behalf of private markets when they can exploit the pinch of public restraint for private gain. When organized medicine benefits from each new private revenue opportunity, it is not surprising that this vested interest finds it difficult to embrace compensation based on the effectiveness of procedures rather than complete professional discretion. Many public authorities support such initiatives because they look like cost savings, but with various methods of income capping public spending on physicians, de-listing merely involves substituting one form of public spending for another while simultaneously creating new private market opportunities.

When governments extend an open hand to private health care entrepreneurs as typified in the US, there is a double consequence. They effectively de-insure a range of citizens while charging higher prices to the lucky few who can pay the market rate, and they substitute the sometime inefficiency of public insurance for the unproductive overhead of private profit! US Health Secretary Donna Shalala summed up this sentiment by describing the notion of affordable quality health care for all Americans as an idea which has 'collapsed in ruins' (*Financial Times*, 23 January 1998).

What the public has understood intuitively better than many public policy-makers is that the culprit behind rising health care costs is not profligate governments nor rampant citizen abuse (see Feldberg and Vipond, Chapter 3 this volume). Rather, powerful physician organizations and large corporate actors can always inflate health care needs to meet their private income objectives as governments have slowly and painfully learned. As Evans (1997b) acerbically notes, what is offered by advocates is always some form of managed or regulated market – managed and regulated by and/or in the interests of the advocates.

It comes as no surprise that market-driven health policy has proven disappointing even though the state's role in the organization, financing and management of health care is now broader and more complex than ever before (World Development Report, 1993, 1997). Hayek's belief in the universal perfect market may be back, but Keynes and Beveridge have by no means beaten a hasty retreat! Yet, the Beveridge system is in trouble nonetheless.

THE PRECIPITOUS FALL FROM GRACE OF STATE BUREAUCRATS

In Beveridge's model, the state was to be an enlightened guardian of the public interest. By the end of the 1990s, modern pollsters revealed that in the public's mind nothing could be farther than the truth (Hutton, 1995; Zussman, 1997).

Rising health standards have not granted people greater authority to hold the state accountable for its actions in the health sectors. Beveridge's breakthrough was a macro solution for national management, but many of today's health concerns devolve to the local and community level. For example, a fiscal solution to a health care budget will not provide the equality and recognition demanded by the gay community. Nor can central policies deal easily with the gender politics associated with an oversupply of invasive surgical procedures for women. Only sensitive and local democratic governance can respond to such identity needs expressed as health concerns. Such unmet identity expectations have also turned the public against the best of medical science and the public guardians of the Beveridge system.

This is not a case of 'a wilderness of single instances'. The public feel repeatedly betrayed by government's failure to protect them from avoidable cataclysmic health hazards whether they be defective products, communicable disease or bureaucratic bungling. Many governments have repeatedly failed in their fiduciary and health surveillance responsibilities. Of course, this is an exaggeration because public authority is better informed than ever and dramatic health care improvements have benefited the total population. Yet, it is germane to ask, what have governments really learned from the Thalidomide, contaminated blood supply, injurious vaccines, cyanide-laced Tylenol, legionnaires' disease, Lyme disease and DES (diethylstilboestrol)? It would be comforting to give an unequivocal, positive response that health authorities have learned a great deal from these medical disasters that harmed so many. Unfortunately, it is not so simple (Garrett, 1994).

States have continued to fail to protect the public from avaricious and reckless corporations. Silicone breast implants, asbestosis, and tobacco have cast a long shadow on governments' capacity to protect the public and occupational groups such as miners from unsafe products and unsafe work. Governments too have also harmed the health of the public in more direct ways. We now know that in a disturbing number of jurisdictions ranging from Alberta, Sweden to Norway, states of all political stripes routinely sanctioned sterilization practices on those deemed to be inferior or unfit – a practice that continued well into the 1960s. The public has also discovered that on too many occasions hospitals and hospital administrators have betrayed the public's confidence. Negligent and intentional infant deaths and malpractice have convinced many that the public authority is an ill-suited steward of the sacred trust Beveridge conferred on them. It is difficult to think that these episodes of tragedy could be surpassed by events even more dramatic and damaging to public confidence; but they have.

There are still many unanswered questions connected with the role of government public health administrators in allowing the blood system to be contaminated with HIV virus, hepatitis C, and Creutzfeld Jacob disease (CJD) – the human equivalent of mad cow disease (BSE). Initially, public administrators tried to downplay the seriousness and prevalence of these often lethal blood-borne diseases. In fact, the public record documents a kind of administrative mentality that encourages administrators to lie to protect the public interest. Scientists too have been complicit and withheld information in the public interest. When trusted public officials could no longer hide behind technical obfuscation they were forced to acknowledge the scale of the disaster. It is now admitted in Canada alone, more than one hundred thousand people have been infected with hepatitis C, a potentially life-threatening condition, and not ten thousand – the discredited estimate that public authorities used initially to downplay the seriousness of the tragedy.

It used to be thought that these failures of public surveillance were isolated instances of dereliction of responsibility to incorporate biological science into public health practice. They may well be, but the public mood has hardened because too many systemic failures have called into question the underlying assumptions, principles and organizational arrangements of state-sponsored health care systems. Although it may be tempting for those with means, it would be foolhardy to conclude that a disenchanted public should look to markets for protection, the same markets that produced many of these defective products. Indeed only a more vigilant public health authority with a well-resourced infrastructure can identify problems quickly and provide a stronger national and global surveillance system (Foreman, 1994).

Today, when global markets require all governments to take coordinated measures to reduce global health risks, new initiatives and new practices are needed. The advanced market economies face new policy demands having largely eliminated infectious disease and extended life expectancy. Chronic diseases are costly to treat and require policy solutions which marry health care and labour market attachment. The twin challenges of sustaining solidarity and the collective bearing of risk remain principally the responsibility of national governments

This is why it is important to recall Beveridge's larger vision in which health care was at the epicentre of a national project with international significance. His time was much like our own in which countries were under pressure to co-operate internationally. Like today, Beveridge faced an array of critics who questioned the capacity of the state to administer such a broad and complex program. It is worth briefly revisiting his radical ideas in order to recall the foundation principles of health care and the need for clearly articulated and comprehensive public objectives. In Beveridge's plan, health care was never a stand-alone program. It was linked to the other pillar of the modern welfare state – the full employment imperative. Why was this so important?

BEVERIDGE'S FIRST PRINCIPLES AND THEIR RELEVANCE TODAY

In its original form, his grand scheme called for health care to be provided for all those who needed it. Full employment protected society against the ravages of a crude *laissez-faire* market system. Through a system of progressive taxation, states ensured that there would be an adequate and sufficient level of job creation and when there was a shortfall, unemployment insurance was the fall back. As for income distribution, a universal health care system was designed to give greater discretionary spending to the working classes (Esping-Andersen, 1990).

It is not sufficiently recognized that by removing the financial burden of catastrophic illness from their wage packets, their disposable incomes would rise. No longer would they have to pay doctors from their pockets when their children were born or they fell sick and when they went to hospital; lack of money did not constitute a barrier to good care. These reforms, along with the spread of collective bargaining in advanced industrial economies, enabled people to enjoy the benfits of an expanded notion of social citizenship. Health care and full employment thus constituted a forward-looking framework for social health and not simply clinically provided health care. If, then, Beveridge conceived of full employment as essential to the preservation of fundamental liberty the ancillary question, and one that is far more intriguing, is why did he think of a universal health care system as 'a daring adventure' capable of transforming *laissez-faire* capitalism? (Beveridge, quoted in Williams and Williams, 1987: 78).

What was path-breaking was his visionary idea that health insurance would be obligatory and on a scale sufficient to satisfy the health needs for an entire nation. It was intended to cover all citizens without upper income limits, but was fine-tuned to take into account different ways of life. The scheme would recognize diverse social situations and needs and would also provide coverage for those outside of the labour market, including housewives, the young and the aged. His most radical innovation was the notion of health as a right of citizenship for the industrial working classes rather than a need to be met through charity or overtaxed public facilities. The very idea of universal citizenship entitlement to health care eschewed any need to ration care. But it also assumed a great deal more. In particular, the risks inherent in modern society would be borne collectively (Marquand, 1997). The provision of welfare, including health insurance, would cover a whole population against all the main risks of modern life: industrial accidents, sickness, unemployment, destitution, and old age. This entailed fundamental administrative reform because all existing social welfare schemes would have to be welded into, in Beveridge's words, 'one autonomous system without gaps and overlapping.[2]

If these were the essentials, there was much more to Beveridge's action plan. It required a modern and efficient bureaucracy that did not exist in most countries in order to organize a national health service. All these experts would have to be recruited and become part of the public service. The plan also assumed that the state would be a good manager in the stewardship of public funds and that competing bureaucratic rivalries could be re-channelled to serve the public interest. As well, the scheme presumed that public and private interests would be mutually reinforcing, well-delineated, and balanced. It was further anticipated that initially, health care spending would increase dramatically and then level off as the health of the population improved. So it was the state's principal responsibility to invest in public health and, equally, to be the cost-accountant of the system. In this vision of things, a modern public health system would be the great leveller – the poor and working classes would have access to the same facilities as the wealthy and the elites. Yet Beveridge's vision was, also, about generating new resources for doctors, nurses and those working in the health care sector, and their loyalty would be ensured by the promise of rising incomes and revitalized hospitals.

So, all in all it was a dazzling mix of first principles and organizational arrangements to extend citizen rights and accommodate the professional interests of doctors and health care experts. The genius of his model was that states with very different needs and social and institutional arrangements would be able to adapt it to local conditions. In this way, Beveridge captured the attention of the world with his bright ideas for an insurance plan 'all embracing in scope of persons and needs' (Williams and Williams, 1987).

In an era of trade agreements and market liberalization, there is much that endures in Beveridge's original formulation even if many of the theoretical postulates are now stale-dated. Most advanced economies now possess reasonable health care infrastructures as a function of increased national wealth, even where chronic unemployment is prevalent. As a function of market liberalization, health inequalities have been growing as market income inequality has intensified (Wilkinson, 1996). In all jurisdictions these gaps have widened in the past decades as public policy-makers have embraced market-favouring policies. Many of the new challenges cannot be met within the old health care framework (Vegero, 1995). For instance, with globally competitive marketplaces workers in advanced economies now face not only the health threats posed by unemployment, under-employment, and over-employment but also a speeding up of the pace of work and changes in the organization of work associated with technology and new management practices (Drache and Glasbeek, 1992).

Our understanding of the health effects of work organization has advanced beyond early notions of health and safety (Karasek and Theorell, 1990; Siegrist, 1996). Big occupational class differences in health status were presumed to be largely accounted for by differences in lifestyle – diet, smoking, and exercise. Recent breakthroughs in research on occupational gradients suggest that while these 'lifestyle' factors may be important, by far a greater predictor of differences in heart disease between occupational groups is tied up with structural factors such as individual control on the job (Marmot *et al.*, 1997). The challenge for governments and firms is to abandon a nineteenth-century manufacturing model of occupational health and safety and replace it with one that ensures that job redesign takes into account this new knowledge. These labour market and occupational examples demonstrate that Beveridge's notion that universal access would equalize health disparities was mistaken (Macintyre, 1997).

By contrast, the single best predictor of a country's health status is its long-term economic growth and policies which benefit the poor and reduce disparities. In the words of the 1993 World Bank Report, 'government policies which promote equity and growth together will therefore be better for health than those that promote growth alone' (World Development Report, 1993: 7). Contrary to Arrow's assertion that 'recovery from disease is as unpredictable as its incidence' (Arrow, 1963: 951), the most reliable correlate of disease is none other than social class – a category frequently ignored. It is now recognized that health is not a thing apart which can be studied or understood separate from the general organization of society (Blane *et al.*, 1996). From this perspective, the production of health requires a prosperous economy, a reasonably equitable distribution of wealth, and social cohesion (Evans *et al.*, 1994; Sullivan, 1998; Wilkinson, 1996). These notions may not win the applause of neoclassical economists, but they go a long way in explaining why market models do not produce superior health outcomes in terms of life expectancy, infant mortality or other comparable health status indicators (Evans *et al.*, 1994).

Even so, it is significant to note that few governments have been able to broaden their health schemes to include the dimensions of gender, age, occupational status and class as essential goals in comprehensive health reform. Indeed, health policy specialists have an arcane discourse of treating the social determinants of health as a separate health matter from health care delivery. Health is all too frequently seen as primarily a service provision challenge. For this important reason, mechanisms must be found to ensure that the care and comfort giving elements of the health care system are not in competition with the equity imperatives of a modern health policy. The key seems to be that health authorities have to link macro policy objectives with policies which transform the macro environments in which people live and work. There are numerous instances where this has been the case.

Community programs which serve disadvantaged children can contribute as much to adult health as any other single measure (Blane *et al.*, 1994; Carnegie Corporation, 1994). Top of the line sex education can lead to dramatic reductions in sexually transmitted diseases (STD) which account for 250 million new cases of debilitating and sometimes fatal STDs each year. Improved access to family planning clinics could save many children from dying each year and eliminate many of the 100,000 maternal deaths which occur annually, particularly in developing countries (World Development Report, 1993: 10). Companies which have strong workplace representation and which delegate authority to workplace committees demonstrate fewer injuries and ill health conditions (Shannon *et al.*, 1997). Reining in the power of physicians by reducing their monopoly of knowledge and privilege in the delivery of health would be a major step towards restoring such balance.

Social market economies with stronger equity arrangements appear to be better positioned to take the long view by attending to the social determinants of health. The elites in *laissez-faire* market economies have yet to abandon the rugged individualism inherent in market-driven policies. They continue to think, wrongly, that the old welfare state is exhausted and many of its programs are obsolete. They have not absorbed the important lesson that the significant improvements in health have resulted from the success of public sector health efforts.

CANADA: MORE STATE, MORE MARKET?

Paradoxically, Canada is thought of as the prototype where the tensions between state and market have always co-existed, often uneasily[3] (Tuohy, 1992). The health policy community in Canada remains sceptical about market solutions in health reform (Evans *et al.*, 1994). Nevertheless, Canada's health system combines the efficiency of public payment (72 per cent is publicly financed) with the advantages of private delivery, both profit and not-for-profit. It is the only OECD country which makes no charges for most medically necessary services. Short of crossing the US border, there is no way to 'buy your way to the front of the line'. Virtually all hospitals are publicly regulated. In most provinces, physician salaries are in some way capped, albeit at a generous level. Despite Canada's status as a higher spender in the OECD, the Canadian system is becoming lean and efficient as many of the contributors to this volume candidly describe. Yet Canadians display the highest satisfaction with their system overall, compared to the Americans who display the lowest among ten nations (Blendon *et al.* 1990).

The Canadian story is that Ottawa and the provinces have not simply used persuasive talk of 'managing health care expenditures', they have actually reduced spending as a portion of GDP from 10.4 per cent in 1992 to 9.4 in 1996, despite much public criticism and worry about funding cuts. The fear is that Canada's publicly funded medicare system does not have the funds to survive in its present form. Based on current trends and the size of the existing cuts, the public is worried that Canada seems to be moving towards a US-style system, a dubious notion that is championed by those who stand to gain from such a move and opposed by most Canadians. Even so, its spending record stands in stark comparison to the US, the oddity of the international community currently at over 14 per cent of GDP. The relationships among the amount of money spent on health care, quality of care, and health outcomes remain unclear (Arweiler, 1998; Contandriopoulos, 1998). Not surprisingly, to the outside observer and many Canadians as well, Canadian reforms appear to involve not only a larger role for private finance, but also a larger role for the state! Evidently Ottawa, under the Liberal government, is intent on having the best of both worlds. On the one hand, private payments for pharmaceuticals, long-term care and certain medical services have grown in recent times. On the other hand, there is now significant debate about extending public insurance to include home care and pharmaceuticals (National Forum on Health, 1997). It is doubtful that the compromise between the public and private will remain what it is today without injecting large new resources from Ottawa, a move which is likely to be resisted by some provincial governments. Unless Ottawa is ready to invest heavily in Canadian medicare, Canadians will be facing a more overtly two-tier medical system.

Beyond these short term adjustments, there are more fundamental questions to be addressed. Is Canada moving closer to the market in social policy or strengthening the fundamentals of a publicly anchored system (Drache and Ranachan, 1995)? Has the reduction of GDP spending on health care irreparably harmed the quality of health care in Canada or simply reduced the supply of money for health care? Are the newly evolving regional health authorities bold new experiments in democracy, or a covert exercise to download cost-cutting? By giving markets wider scope, is Canada's health system on the point of being integrated into a more market-oriented North American health market (Appleton, 1994)? Finally, all health authorities are facing the new challenge of reconciling their international trade obligations with the maintenance of a strong, high quality health care system. The lessons derived from the recent Canadian experience in health reform have useful application for academics and policy-makers in other jurisdictions. The National Forum on Health recently conducted intensive qualitative research on whether Canadians continue to value their health care system. Their strong finding was that the Canadian health care system is a fundamental tenet of being Canadian and a majority of Canadians do not wish to see its quality compromised. In a time where markets are relied on more than ever as an adjustment mechanism, Canada stands out as a country that continues to balance market pressures with state activism and a continuing commitment to the social market policies, despite powerful continental harmonization pressures in health policy. Canada, of course, may not be unique. In all market economies there is an active 'residual' of Keynesian public trust nurtured by public commitment to universal health care. Markets may be back with a vengeance but health care remains a stabilizing instrument of citizenship at a time of global instability.

OVERVIEW OF THE VOLUME

The contributors to this volume comprise many leading Canadian experts in the fields of health economics, sociology, political science, medicine and nursing. They are complemented by health policy authorities from our Anglo-Saxon neighbours, the US and Australia.

Part I of the volume, entitled 'Public–Private Conflicts in Health Policy' explores the factors and forces that are causing the Canadian, British and American authorities to re-examine their health policies in response to market liberalization. Health care is not only a matter for doctors, patients and politicians, it is also in Bob Evans's words, 'the business of business'. Business spokespersons have largely been silent on health care policy, but one should not confuse their silence with consensus. Evans demonstrates that health care is big business and the people who like to make it bigger are those whose business interests such as health care vendors, as distinct from the majority of businesses which are purchasers. His most powerful insight is that the mixed model of health care financing now being considered by many governments will result in higher costs with perverse distributional consequences. States have to think carefully about the conflicting economic interests in their health care systems.

In 'The Virus of Consumerism' Feldberg and Vipond tackle head-on one of the most contentious issues in the reform debates – whether consumer abuse is a myth or widespread practice. Little empirical evidence exists to support or refute claims that the Canadian system is systematically abused. The important point is that no taxonomy of abuse exists and the term is used to describe a range of behavior and moral attitudes which should be kept analytically distinct. They go on to explore the twin narratives of citizenship and consumption, which are both ideological flashpoints in health reform debates, and they have distinct meanings in Canada from those in the US. Here too, the Canadian discourse is markedly distinct from its American counterpart. The Canadian Keynesian welfare state and its universal social rights were always more than US-style consumer rights because there was always a redistributional aspect to them. In other ways Canada and the US share parallel experiences.

Concluding Part I, Art Stewart provides us with an international comparison of cost containment and privatization. Stewart challenges the way much of the literature on health care reform is presented as a false dichotomy. He underscores the fact that presenting the issues as markets versus regulation is often motivated by ideology and that there is a very real danger that policy-makers will lose sight of fundamental social policy objectives. He concludes that the introduction of market elements and competition need not result in wholesale privatization if there is a strong commitment to sustaining access and equity and public accountability.

In Part II, 'Restructuring Anglo-Saxon Health Systems: Shifting State/Market Boundaries', Barry Appleton examines the impact of NAFTA on health care. Economic integration in North America and Europe is driven by multilateral trade agreements, regional trade blocs and transnational organization. It is notable that the multilateral agreement on investment (MAI) has drawn heavily on the regional North American Free Trade Agreement for investment rights. Significantly, one of the areas in which there is little clarity is the relationship between national health plans and market liberalization in the health sector. Barry Appleton's analysis of this issue represents the first authoritative exploration of the ways in which regional trade agreements affect health care.

Australia's health care system, often compared with Canada's, is not as well known as it should be. For comparative purposes, its system has many incongruous features that appear to work rather well. However, with the election of the Howard Conservative government in 1996, it has given the green light to private for-profit medicine. Peter Botsman's chapter examines the contradictory consequences of relying on markets to restructure Australia's national plan. Overall health costs have been contained compared to their dramatic rise in the US, but the deep cutbacks have raised concerns about the capacity of Australia's delivery system to respond to future demands.

Mary Ruggie, in a wide-ranging examination of the many meanings and implications of privatization, challenges the idea that the state is better off (or worse off) because the private sector has a larger role to play in health care. Although it is commonly thought that regulation is a public sector activity, she makes the important point that it too is subject to privatization. The great value of her chapter is her examination of the contrasting role of the state in Britain, the US and Canada in the social construction of the health care system. She stresses that many of the changes in the health care field are not adequately captured by conventional categories of the public and private domain.

Part III, 'Decentralization and Devolution', examines new institutional forms and practices. The single most dramatic level of change in Canada and other jurisdictions is occurring at the sub-national level of government. Governments everywhere are interested in devolution and decentralization. The question is whether such changes in government practice have more to do with style than substance. Furthermore, it is also important whether these new arrangements actually empower communities with a greater say in decision-making at the local level. Compared to most other jurisdictions, Canada is a unique political and social laboratory and has gone further than most other public authorities in creating an array of regional boards, distinctive province by province.

Part III begins with the chapter by Trottier *et al*. Quebec has been a vigorous supporter of decentralization – not primarily for fiscal reasons but to re-establish an equilibrium between national spending authority and Quebec's desire for greater autonomy. In Quebec the centralization/decentralization dynamic is driven by three different visions of the role of the state – the liberal, the social and the community. As Trottier *et al*. demonstrate, the social vision seeks to maximize the role of state in order to strengthen social solidarity. The community vision tends to minimize the role of the state while increasing freedom of choice for local communities. The liberal vision seeks to minimize the role of state and expand individual liberties. In contrast to the analysis presented by Mary Ruggie, the Quebec tradition has been a strongly social one, designed to enhance a collective sense of identity through the state.

Jonathan Lomas has written a pioneering study examining the evolution of devolution, and documents what kind of authority communities want. Contrary to conventional wisdom, decentralization is not a panacea which automatically empowers people or communities. The community is not always reaching for greater authority, particularly when they are being asked to cut their own budgets as they take on authority.

Church and Noseworthy in 'Fiscal Austerity Through Decentralization' examine the health care reform policies in Alberta and provide another view of market rhetoric and reality. The Alberta reforms have in fact created a weak state presence in the health sector consistent with Alberta's liberal vision of the state.

Significantly, in Ontario with 40 per cent of Canada's population, the politics of local control of health care have been at the centre of a continuous debate for over twenty years, beginning with the *Report of the Health Planning Task Force*, popularly known as the 'Mustard Report'. The election of a Conservative government in June 1995 has meant drastic change in Ontario's medicare sector – numerous hospitals have been closed and others merged. Harden describes how the debate over local control has been hijacked to ensure a reform agenda that offloads cutbacks to local communities.

Part IV, 'The Political Economy of Health Reform in Canada', provides three unique perspectives on the Canadian cost-containment experience. Frequently it is difficult to develop a comprehensive view of the many pressures that are reshaping Canada's health system and the degree to which government policy is capable of responding to them. The central question to be addressed is whether a downsized system will force a re-examination of the principles of The Canada Health Act. Carl Sonnen and Mike McCracken weigh in on this question and provide a detailed overview of the political economy of recent Canadian reforms from a macroeconomic perspective and with a view to a revitalized federal role.

The idea that money can be saved by modifying patient demands is taken on directly by Gail Donner. Her chapter is highly revealing because she challenges the accepted wisdom that cost control is an effective way to implement health reform. She argues that rather than focusing on the limited impacts of demand modification in a system which has global budget caps, primary care reform presents more fruitful possibilities for real structural change.

Ted Marmor provides some straight talk on the 'intellectual acid rain' that drifts northward to Canada from US health interests. President Clinton's failed health reform provides Marmor with ample material to analyse the politics of cross-national claims in health policy. He urges Canadians to steer a prudent course away from a privately financed alternative.

Part V, 'On the Frontier of Reform', addresses four unique health policy problems. The problem of patient choice and decision-making, the unique challenges of constraining the drug industry and the special challenge of overcoming our policy legacies in health are addressed in turn. Deber and Sharpe begin with an important empirical look at patient preferences in decision-making. The economic argument that health care can be bought and sold and that consumers behave like shoppers faced with competing choices is worth testing. They employ original data from people facing health information choices for problem-solving in angiography and those facing surgery decision making options arising from prostate problem. One of their chief conclusions is that patients do wish to be involved in decision making when they have the necessary information. The relationship between the providers and the recipients of care is not one structured on the market but in their view is better conceived as a partnership of mutual respect. Genuinely shared decision-making does not necessarily threaten doctor–patient relations.

The single fastest growing expenditure item in health budgets has been pharmaceuticals. Relatively little is known about why drug costs have risen so dramatically. Joel Lexchin documents the cost effects of new drugs, changes in drug pricing and the patent conflicts between Canadian generic drug manufacturers and their multinational brand name competitors. His chapter can be profitably read alongside Appleton's analysis of the patent protections which are a key feature of the NAFTA.

Lavis and Sullivan explore the role of interests in shaping and hindering policy reform in the health sector. They argue that new institutional arrangements are required if states are to consider the social determinants of health in decision-making. In particular they single out the important roles for multi-stakeholder bodies and policy entrepreneurs. Economic integration has produced large scale adjustments for many countries. Coordinating social and health care programs with neighbouring states appears, in principle at least, a reasonable and attractive objective. Cross-national diffusion of health care practices is not simply a North American issue but requires close scrutiny because many European countries are also facing similar prospects

The final word belongs to Fraser Mustard in 'Health, Health Care and Social Cohesion'. He examines the new realities which face health policy-makers. In much of the debate on health policy throughout the OECD, there has been intense focus on the concept of community and social organization and the role of communities in solving social problems. Terms like 'social capital' and 'social trust' have been frequently invoked, particularly in relationship to the hollowing out of the state and polarized labour markets. Mustard contributes to the long tradition of medical practitioners in contributing to our understanding the determinants of health. His chapter concentrates on the role of social trust in promoting human development in the health domain. He is highly critical of government reform efforts that sacrifice social capital objectives in the rush to implement short-sighted cost-cutting measures.

NOTES

1   With respect to health care delivery, there is no universal model but only different public–private mixes reflecting institutional arrangements. At one end is Sweden with largely public providers; in the middle is Australia and New Zealand with a mix of public and private providers; Canada has a unique niche with its largely not-for-profit private delivery system. The US completes the spectrum with a private, for-profit delivery system. Even the US, however, has a significant not-for-profit component. Most OECD nations have predominantly publicly financed systems, with the US as the main outlier (OECD, 1994).

2   Prior to the Beveridge reform in the UK and social market economies, the principle of social insurance – the operative premise of Beveridge's reform zeal –

had already been accepted by public authorities for industrial accidents and old age pensions (Stone, 1986). Social welfare legislation made modest but uneven progress between the wars in most jurisdictions.

3 Canada has never produced a social reformer of the stature of Beveridge, but Norman Bethune, who hailed from Gravenhurst, became a Canadian hero of the Chinese revolution for his work in promoting the barefoot doctor as a model of primary care. He brought medicine to people without professional affectation, self-interest or profit motives. The Canadian political landscape has always been home to radical political figures like the early feminists, trade union activists, the Co-operative Commonwealth Federation (CCF), the forerunner of Canada's modern social democratic party, the NDP, political leaders like former NDP parliamentary leader Tommy Douglas, Monique Begin, and radical liberals like her who have made health care reform a central political goal. These reform movements and state-sponsored health innovations have long interested practitioners and policymakers the world over.

REFERENCES

Albert, M. 1993. *Capitalism versus Capitalism*. New York: Quadrangle Books.

Appleton, B. 1994. *Navigating NAFTA: A Concise User's Guide to the North American Free Trade Agreement*. Toronto: Carswell.

Armstrong, P., A. Glynn and J. Harrison. 1991. *Capitalism Since 1945*. London: Blackwell.

Arrow, K. 1963. Uncertainty and the Welfare Economics of Medical Care. *American Economic Review* 53: 940–973.

Arweiler, D. 1998. International Comparisons of Health Expenditures. In National Forum On Health, *Health Care Systems in Canada and Elsewhere*. Volume 4, *Canada Health Action: Building on the Legacy*. St Foy, Quebec: Editions Multimondes.

Bennett, S., B. McPake, and A. Mills, 1997. The Public Private Mix Debate in Health Care. In Sara Bennett *et al.* (eds) *Private Health Providers in Developing Countries*. London: Zed Books.

Birch, S. and J. Eyles. 1993. Needs-Based Planning of Health Care: A Critical Appraisal of the Literature. *Canadian Journal of Public Health* 84: 112–117.

Blane, D., M. Bartley, G. Davey-Smith, H. Filakti, A. Bethune and S. Harding. 1994. Social Patterning of Medical Mortality in Youth and Early Adulthood. *Social Science and Medicine* 39 (3): 361–366.

Blane, D., E. Brunner and R. Wilkinson. 1996. *Social Organization and Health*. London: Routledge.

Blendon, R., R. Leitman, I. Morrison and K. Donelan. 1990. Satisfaction with Health Systems in Ten Nations. *Health Affairs* 9 (2): 185–192.

Boyer, R. and D. Drache. 1996. *States Against Markets: The Limits of Globalization*. London: Routledge.

Brouselle, A. 1998. Controlling Health Expenditures: What Matters? In National Forum On Health, *Health Care Systems in Canada and Elsewhere*. Volume 4, *Canada Health Action: Building on the Legacy*. St Foy, Quebec: Editions Multimondes.

Carnegie Corporation of New York. 1994. *Starting Points, Meeting the Needs of Your Youngest Children*, Report of the Carnegie Task Force on Meeting the Needs of Young Children.

Contandriopoulos, D. 1998. How Canada's Health Care System Compares with Other Countries: An Overview. In National Forum On Health, *Health Care Systems in Canada and Elsewhere*. Volume 4, *Canada Health Action: Building on the Legacy*. St Foy, Quebec: Editions Multimondes.

Culyer, A. J., A. K. Maynard and J. W. Posnett, eds. 1990. *Competition in Health Care: Reforming the NHS*. Basingstoke: Macmillan.

Dahrendorf, R. 1995. A Precarious Balance: Economic Opportunity, Civil Society, and Political Liberty. *The Responsive Community* (Summer): 13–38.

Drache, D. and H. Glasbeek. 1992. *The Changing Workplace*. Toronto: Lorimer.

Drache, D. and A. Ranachan, eds. 1995. *Warm Heart, Cold Country: Fiscal and Social Policy Reform in Canada*. Ottawa: Caledon Institute.

Esping-Andersen, G. 1990. *The Three Worlds of Welfare Capitalism*. Princeton, NJ: Princeton University Press.

Evans, R. 1997a. Going for Gold: The Redistributive Agenda behind Market Based Health Care Reform. *Journal of Health Politics, Policy and Law* 22(2): 427–465.

Evans, R. 1997b. Coarse Correction – And Way Off Target: A Response. *Journal of Health Politics, Policy and Law* 22 (2): 503–508.

Evans, R., M. Barer and T. Marmor. 1994. *Why are Some People Healthy and Others Not?* New York: Aldine de Gruyter.

Foreman, C. H. 1994. *Plagues, Products and Politics: Emergent Public Health Hazards and National Policymaking*. Washington, DC: Brookings Institute.

Fuchs, V. 1996. Economics Values and Health Care Reform. *American Economic Review* 86 (1): 1–24.

Garrett, L. 1994. *The Coming Plague: Newly Emerging Diseases in a World Out of Balance*. Harmondsworth: Penguin Books.

Government of Ontario. 1974. *Report of the Health Planning Task Force*. Toronto: Queen's Printer.

Herzlinger, R. 1997. *Market-Driven Health Care: Who Wins, Who Loses in the Transformation in America's Largest Service Industry*. Reading, MA: Addison-Wesley.

Hsaio, W. 1995. Medical Savings Accounts: Lesson from Singapore. *Health Affairs* 14 (2): 260–266.

Hutton, W. 1995. *The State We're In*. London: Jonathan Cape.

Karasek, R. and T. Theorell. 1990. *Healthy Work: Stress Productivity and the Reconstruction of Working Life*. New York: Basic Books.

Kuttner, R. 1997. *Everything for Sale: The Virtues and Limits of Markets*. New York: Knopf.

Macintyre, S. 1997. The Black Report and Beyond: What Are the Issues? *Social Science and Medicine*, 44 (6): 723–745.

Marmot, M., H. Bosma, H. Hemingway, E. Brunner and S. Stansfeld. 1997. Contribution of Job Control and Other Risk Factors to Social Variations in Coronary Heart Disease Incidence. *Lancet* 350, 26 July, 235–239.

Marquand, D. 1997. *The New Reckoning: Capitalism, States and Citizens*. London: Polity.

Myrdal, G. 1957. *Economic Theory and Underdeveloped Regions*. London: Cambridge University Press.

National Forum On Health. 1997. *Canada Health Action: Building on the Legacy*. St Foy, Quebec: Editions Multimondes.

Organization for Economic Cooperation and Development (OECD). 1994. *The Reform of Health Care Systems: A Review of Seventeen OECD Countries*. Health Policy Studies No. 5. Paris: OECD.

Rachlis, M. and C. Kushner. 1994. *Strong Medicine: How to Save Canada's Health Care System*. Toronto: HarperCollins.

Rice, T. 1997. Can Markets Give Us the Health System We Want? *Journal of Health Politics, Policy and Law* 22 (2): 383–426.

Saltman, R. 1995. *Applying Planned Market Logic to Developing Countries Health Systems: An Initial Exploration*. Forum on Health Sector Reform, Discussion Paper No. 4. Geneva: WHO.

Shannon, H., J. Mayr and T. Haines. 1997. Overview of the Relationships between Organizational and Workplace Factors and Injury Rates. *Safety Science* 26 (3): 201–207.

Siegrist, J. 1996. Adverse Health Effects of High-Effort/Low-Reward Conditions. *Journal of Occupational Health Psychology*, pp. 27–41.

Stone, D. 1986. *The Disabled State*. Philadelphia: Temple University Press.

Sullivan, T. 1998. Commentary on Health Care Expenditures, Social Spending and Health Status. In National Forum On Health, *Health Care Systems in Canada and Elsewhere*. Volume 4, *Canada Health Action: Building on the Legacy*. St Foy, Quebec: Editions Multimondes.

Tuohy, C. 1992. *Policy and Politics in Canada: Institutionalized Ambivalence*. Philadelphia: Temple University Press.

Vegero, D. 1995. Health Inequalities as Policy Issues – Reflections on Ethics, Policy and Public Health. *Sociology of Health and Illness*, 17 (1): 1–19.

Wilkinson, R. 1996. *Unhealthy Societies: The Afflictions of Inequality*. London: Routledge.

Williams, K. and J. Williams. 1987. *A Beveridge Reader*. London: Allen and Unwin.

World Development Report. 1993. *Investing in Health*. New York: Oxford University Press.

World Development Report. 1997. *The State in a Changing World*. New York: Oxford University Press.

Zussman, D. 1997. Do Citizens Trust Their Governments? *Canadian Public Administration* 40 (2): 234–254.

Part I

Public–private conflicts in health policy

2 Health reform

What 'business' is it of business?

Robert Evans

IN PURSUIT OF INTERNATIONAL STANDARDS

Canadians are justifiably proud of Medicare. This national (strictly, federal-provincial) program is not merely a mechanism for reimbursing hospital and physicians' services. It is one of the (few) institutions expressing the unity and distinctness of the Canadian people, and our commitment to each other both symbolically and in hard cash. But in fact all (but one) of the major industrialized countries have established universal public payment systems for health care, and most are similarly proud, or at least highly supportive, of them. National systems differ in important details but in broad outline all share the characteristic features that White (1995: 271) labelled the 'International Standard':

- universal coverage of the population, through compulsory participation;
- comprehensiveness of principal benefits;
- contributions based on income, rather than individual insurance purchases;
- cost control through administrative mechanisms, including binding fee schedules, global budgets, and limitations on system capacity.

All have also developed the physical and technical capacity, and the personnel, to make appropriate and up-to-date health care available to their whole populations without financial barriers – though some do impose such barriers. And in all these systems 'the state' is either the principal source of finance, or a powerful force regulating the behaviour of other, quasi-public funding organizations (Abel-Smith, 1992; Abel-Smith and Mossialos, 1994). Where market-like mechanisms exist, they are typically 'managed markets' (Ham, 1994), manipulated to further public (or sometimes private, professional) objectives. They are never the free competitive markets of the economics textbooks.

The great exception, the United States (Abel-Smith, 1985), demonstrates the potential consequences of failing to achieve the international standard. The alternative – it is deceptive to speak of a 'system' *or* a 'free market' – that evolves in the absence of comprehensive public intervention turns out to be extremely expensive, monumentally inefficient, and heartbreakingly inequitable and inhumane.

Nor is this merely 'America-bashing' by a mean-spirited foreigner. Prominent American analysts (on both sides of the political spectrum) have expressed similar views:

> The U.S. health care system is the most inefficient, costly, and inhumane attempt at health care in the Western industrialized world today.
>
> (Navarro, 1992)

> It would be, quite frankly, ridiculous ... to suggest that we in the United States have achieved a satisfactory system that our European friends would be wise to emulate.
>
> (Enthoven, 1989: 49)

The American approach to financing (though not the care delivered) is also highly unpopular with the general public that it serves, as reflected in a large-scale public survey by the Consumers' Union (1996; see also Blendon *et al.*, 1990, 1995).

No serious observer tries to refute this characterization. Most Americans, if not engaging in vapid rhetoric about 'the world's best health care system', prefer to pass over it in embarrassed silence. And indeed they have good reason to be embarrassed. But what seems much more puzzling is the behaviour of those in other countries, and especially those in Canada, who respond to the clear international evidence of public success and private failure by advocating 'rolling back the frontiers of the state' and expanding the scope of private modes of organization and payment. The military maxim is 'Abandon failure and expedite success.' The privatizers in health care seem to have got this backwards.

THE INTERESTS OF BUSINESS

Particularly puzzling, indeed paradoxical, is the attitude of 'business', as reflected in statements by leaders of major corporations and trade associations, and the consistent rhetoric of the business press. Among the messages from international experience is one that is particularly obvious in North America. Health care systems in which government is the sole source of funding have a better (in North America, much better) record of control of overall costs. When funding comes from a multiplicity of public and private sources, overall costs are higher. Moreover, such multiple sources typically include direct contributions from business, in the form of employer-paid private insurance premiums and other fringe benefit costs.

One might then expect that private businesses would recognize their direct economic interest in both keeping overall health care costs down, and shifting them from private premiums to government payment. They might conclude that Canada's Medicare system gives them a significant competitive advantage relative to firms in the United States, where payments for employee health insurance make up a significant component of operating cost. And some do. At a National Health Care Policy Summit, Red Wilson, CEO of Bell Canada Enterprises, remarked: 'I believe that Canada's health care system represents a real source of comparative advantage, particularly *vis à vis* our U.S. competitors. There is a very compelling business case for preserving and strengthening our system' (Wilson, 1996).

In general, though, business spokesmen have been at best silent on health care policy. More commonly they have been among, or have provided financial support for, the advocates of private funding. Can the 'Captains of Industry' simply not recognize their own economic interests? Perhaps. But as Marmor reminds us: 'Nothing that is regular, is stupid.' Their behaviour may have more complex origins.

The apparent paradox arises, I think, because we adopt what Nelson (1977) calls the 'steersman metaphor' of public policy. We are all in the same boat, and we all want to get to the same place. The task of public policy is to steer the boat so that we come as close as possible to our shared objectives. Disputes over appropriate policies are then disputes over means, not ends. They can, at least in principle, ultimately be resolved by more information or better analysis.

The shared objective that people hold for their health care systems would appear to be effective health care, efficiently provided, available to all who need it, and at a reasonable cost shared equitably among citizens. These are, at least, the sorts of things most people say when asked; there is little explicit support for inefficiency, ineffective care, or unreasonable costs. And most people, even in the United States, seem to believe that those in need should not be denied care that they cannot pay for (Taylor and Reinhardt, 1991). If such a health care system *is* the objective that the steersman is to make for, the evidence to date is pretty clear. It must be a universal system with public funding and control, in which access to care does not depend upon ability to pay, but contribution does.

In fact the evidence is now so clear that it may even have convinced American economists and physicians – both groups with the most deeply ingrained ideological hostility to state action. Fuchs (1996) questioned a wholly non-scientific, 'convenience sample' of health economists, general economists, and physicians, and found that in each group, about two-thirds supported universal coverage, and over half favoured tax finance.

But the briefest familiarity with the history and nature of disputes over health care policy is sufficient to demonstrate the inadequacy of the steersman metaphor. One of the most striking features of these disputes is that they are *not* resolved by experience, data, or analysis. The same arguments come forward year by year, decade by decade, in every country, and in virtually the same forms of words, regardless of how many times they are refuted. The term 'zombies' has been suggested to describe such ideas, that are intellectually dead but will not stay in their graves (Evans *et al.*, 1994a; Barer *et al.*, 1998).

The arguments for private markets and private financing presented to (and rejected by) the Royal Commission on Health Services (Canada, 1964) were brought forward in the early 1970s to support high deductible, high coinsurance private coverage in the United States (Feldstein, 1971), and have resurfaced as the 'medical savings accounts' of the 1990s. The labels change, but the 'new' ideas – haven't.

Arguments for private markets in health care are not only persistent, and resistant to both analysis and evidence, but they also come forward from the same groups of people (Barer *et al.*, 1994). Again over the decades, and across countries, one finds the same arguments for private organization and funding coming from spokesmen for private practitioners' associations – physicians, dentists, pharmacists – as well as from private insurance companies and drug manufacturers. In addition they tend to come, as noted above, from representatives of 'business' and, more recently, from 'ideological entrepreneurs' that support themselves and their organizations by championing the interests of the wealthy, cheerleading for the private marketplace. Indeed, they are simply taking advantage of the general ideological climate, currently more favourable, to re-open old issues.

This pattern of persistence reflects fundamental and permanent conflicts of economic interest among the 'us' that are expressed in any country's health care system. Bluntly, in economic terms alone, what is good for some is bad for others. The steersman metaphor disguises this conflict, and thus misrepresents as technical debates over *means*, what are in fact political choices over *ends*. The real difficulty in steering is that we do not agree on where we want to go, and we differ on how best to get there.

Interestingly enough, the assumption commonly made in economic theory, that people can be treated as identical and interchangeable, has exactly the same consequence. It adds greatly to mathematical tractability, while making political conflicts and choices not merely obscure but impossible to discuss because they are literally inexpressible. Of course much disagreement over health policy arises because people are simply confused, misinformed, or misled. Moreover economic interests are not the only, or necessarily the strongest, forces that motivate our political choices. But the groups mentioned above, that over time and across countries are so predictably the supporters of private funding and private 'markets', are generally informed advocates for their members' interests. That is, after all, their job.

There are three principal axes along which conflicts of economic interest in health care systems can be arrayed. Each underlies some part of the 'public–private' debate, and corresponds quite closely to the actual individuals and organizations that are grouped on the different sides of the policy debate.

The three axes of conflict are:

1 The progressivity or regressivity of the health care funding system: who has to pay, and how much?
2 The numbers and relative incomes of providers: who gets paid, and how much?
3 The terms of access to care: can those with greater resources buy 'better' services?

These conflicts emerge from a fundamental accounting identity, that in every society links the *Total Revenues* raised to pay for health care with the *Total Expenditures* on health care, and each of these in turn with the *Total Incomes* earned from the provision of health care. Each of these must, as a matter of accounting logic, be exactly equal to the others. But each can be divided into components, as shown in the following equation:

$$T + C + R / P \times Q / W \times Z$$

Total revenues for health care may be raised through taxes (T), direct charges to users (C), or private insurance premiums (R). Total expenditures are the product of the total quantities of the different types of health care goods and services supplied (Q), multiplied by their respective average prices (P). Total incomes earned are similarly defined by the total quantities of inputs or resources employed in health care, (Z), multiplied by their average rate of reimbursement (W). (Roughly speaking, jobs times average incomes, though the Z includes other forms of income.) Each component of this identity is the setting for a particular axis of conflict.

HOW SHALL THE HEALTH CARE BILL BE SHARED AMONG PAYERS?

Modern health care systems are all collectively financed. Nowhere does out of pocket payment by patients cover more than a small portion of total system costs. The existence and/or level of user charges is a focus for continuing and often bitter controversy, for reasons explored below. But most health care expenditures are made from public funds or reimbursed from private insurance. Nor could it be otherwise, since in all countries a very small proportion of the population, often with the least resources, accounts for so large a share of the needs and the care. Apart from what many of us would regard as the unfairness of requiring ill and injured people to cover the full costs of their own care, most simply could not do so. Modern health care is as expensive as it is sophisticated; it must be purchased collectively if it is to be available at need to more than a wealthy and privileged few.

Less widely recognized is the fact that, with the possible exception of Switzerland, modern systems are now all predominantly financed from *public* sources – either directly from government budgets or through non-profit social

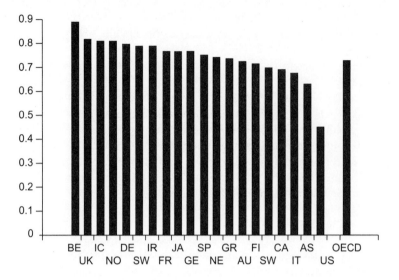

Figure 2.1 Public share of total health spending, selected OECD countries, 1995.
Source: OECD datafile, 1995.

insurance systems under close public regulation (Figure 2.1). Whether countries have adopted or rejected 'socialized medicine' (and whatever that loaded
term may mean), health care *reimbursement* has been socialized – everywhere
(OECD/CREDES, 1997).

The United States is typically offered as the counter-example, with a system
of predominantly private insurance. And indeed the majority of Americans do
rely on private insurers as their primary *source of coverage*. But private insurers
are not the primary *source of funding*, for two reasons.

First, the highest users of care, the poor and the elderly, are covered by
the public plans known in the United States as Medicaid and Medicare. Private
insurers do not cover people who have high risks and few resources; it is more
profitable to insure healthy people. Public plans therefore cover a small share of
the population, but pay a large share of the bills.

Second, most private insurance is provided by employers, and receives a
substantial subsidy from the United States government. Employer-paid premiums are deductible from the employer's taxable income as a business
expense, a labour cost like wages. But unlike wages, they are not taxable as
income in the hands of the employee. This subsidy, hidden in the tax system
but very real, is now worth about $100 billion per year. The reported
expenditure data understate public contributions by this amount, and correspondingly overstate the net contribution of private insurance. Adding the
tax-expenditure subsidy to direct public outlays takes the public contribution
to health expenditure to well over 50 per cent.

The United States is not the only country with private coverage for health care; most, if not all, industrialized countries have some form of private insurance. But the extreme case highlights the general rule. Private coverage nowhere predominates. Private insurers always try to avoid covering the people with the greatest needs, and even so they require direct or indirect public subsidies to maintain a significant market share.

There is none the less considerable scope for adjustment in the mix of funding sources, the relative sizes of the T, C, and R in the accounting identity on p. 29. This mix remains highly contentious because it determines, for any given level of total outlays, who will pay more and who will pay less. Nor is the logic in any way mysterious. Tax systems differ in their progressivity or regressivity, but in general people with more money pay more in taxes – at least up to a point. Thus wealthy people, whether they use care or not, will contribute more to a health care system financed from general public revenues. On the other hand use of health care is strongly correlated with illness. In a system wholly financed from user charges – if such could exist – the principal contributions would be made by the unhealthy, whether they are rich, poor, or in between.

It follows that, if one holds total health outlays – and everything else – constant, and shifts the mix of revenue sources by raising user fees and lowering taxes, the effect is to transfer income from the unhealthy and unwealthy to the healthy and wealthy. Of course these are polar cases; almost everyone is to some extent both a taxpayer and a user of care. But it is straightforward to show that (so long as tax contributions are positively correlated with income) the gainers will be those whose share of total income (percentage, not dollar amount) exceeds their share of total health care outlays (Evans *et al.*, 1994b). This includes the sick but very wealthy, and the poor but very healthy. Their savings in reduced taxes more than offset their costs from increased out of pocket payments for *their own* health care. The rest, all whose share of health expenditures exceeds their share of total income, lose.

Conversely, of course, the past shift from out-of-pocket to tax-based finance had the opposite effect of transferring income from the healthy and wealthy to the unhealthy and unwealthy. The express intent was to ensure access for those with inadequate resources; but the income transfer was an inevitable concomitant. As health expenditures have grown over time, the size of that transfer has also grown. It is thus not difficult to understand why wealthier people tend to express greater enthusiasm for out of pocket charges; and why the issue refuses to die. Fallacious arguments about general advantages from user charges continue to be recycled like zombies, because the real objective – the transfer of income – might not command widespread political support.

The third major potential source of revenue for health care is private insurance.[1] While there is an academic literature as to the relative merits of private insurance versus user charges, this has little practical significance. In active policy debates both private insurance and user fees are advocated or opposed as complementary alternatives to public funding.

Private insurers attempt to offer coverage to groups of individuals at premium rates that match their risk, i.e. their expected outlays for health care. Indeed, a competitive insurance market forces insurers to do so if they hope to stay in business. Since (expensive) illnesses tend to be highly correlated over time – if you had a chronic condition yesterday you will probably have it tomorrow – the simplest way to relate premiums to risk is through experience rating. High outlays today; higher premiums tomorrow.

One would therefore expect the costs of private coverage to be distributed over the population in proportion to their expected use of care, which in practice means in proportion to their actual use of care. To a single individual it may matter a great deal, whether or not she has private coverage for a particular expensive episode of care. But when one looks across income classes, the fact that private premiums are based on expected use, and not at all on income, means that they should distribute the burden of paying for a health care system in very much the same way as user charges do – much more heavily on the unhealthy and unwealthy.

And indeed they do. Empirical confirmation comes from studies in both the United States and the European Community. Rasell, *et al.* (1993) and Rasell and Tang (1994) have shown that in the United States the share of health spending that comes through public budgets is progressively distributed, taking a larger share of the incomes of people at higher income levels. But both user fees and private insurance are strikingly regressive, taking a much larger share of the incomes of lower income people (Figure 2.2).[2] Moreover this pattern is particularly apparent among those over sixty-five, who are virtually all enrolled in the national Medicare program for the elderly. The various deductibles, coinsurance rates, and exclusions in that program, and the corresponding private 'Medigap' insurance market, produce a highly regressive financing structure even for this universal public program.

Similar findings emerge from the large-scale EC equity project directed by van Doorslaer *et al.* (1993), a detailed empirical study of the pattern of distribution of health, health care, and financing burdens across income classes in the countries of the European Community, as well as the United States. They conclude:

> The two countries with predominantly private financing systems – Switzerland and the US – have the most regressive structures overall. This is scarcely surprising in view of just how regressive private insurance and out-of-pocket payments are when used to finance such a large proportion of health care expenditures for such a large proportion of the population. The group of countries with the next most regressive systems are the countries operating the so-called social insurance model,...countries

which . . . rely mainly on tax-finance . . . have the least regressive financing systems.

(Van Doorslaer *et al.*, 1993: 44)

But while 'out-of-pocket payments tend to be a highly regressive means of financing health care' (ibid., 42), the impact of private insurance is more nuanced. Private insurance that is purchased as supplementary cover in a more or less universal public system appears to be a 'luxury' that is more commonly bought by people with higher incomes; such payments are thus progressively distributed. But if, as in the United States, private insurance is purchased by a large proportion of the population because public coverage is restricted or non-existent, the distribution of its costs is highly regressive. Private coverage for deductibles or co-payments in the public system tends to be progressive or regressive depending upon the scale of such charges. In general the larger the user charges and the more people who must pay them, the more regressive are the costs of private insurance to cover them.

The continuing support for 'privatizing' the financing of health care thus makes perfectly good sense as a way of trying to shift a part of the burden of payment from the wealthy and healthy to the unhealthy and unwealthy. Some, at least, of the advocates *would* be better off, at least economically, even if the overall system were to be more expensive, less effective/efficient, and less equitable.

Indeed precisely this issue has arisen in the discussion, in Canada, of the recommendation by the National Forum on Health (1997) to extend universal

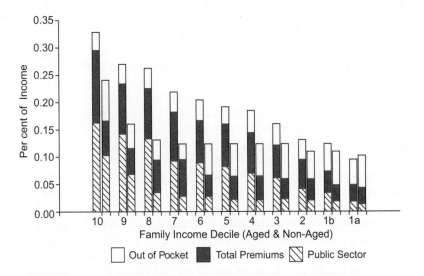

Figure 2.2 Share of income spent on health care: family income decile and payment form.

Source: Rasell *et al.*, 1993.

public coverage to prescription drugs. The Forum argued, partly on the basis of experience with Medicare, that a universal system would not only be more equitable, and reduce barriers to needed care, but would actually be less costly than the present mixed funding system. Opponents have of course questioned this claim. But they have also argued that a universal plan should be rejected *simply because it would require higher taxes*, even if the overall cost to Canadians were lower.

From the point of view of the 'average Canadian' this argument makes no sense at all. If taxes go up, but private premiums and out of pocket charges go down by more, then total costs fall and Canadians are saving money, full stop. Why should the size of the individual components matter? But that is only true *on average*. An individual who is above average in income, and relatively healthy, might well pay more in extra taxes than s/he saved in (direct and indirect) costs of drugs (see Lexchin, Chapter 16 this volume). Such people may then try to convince the rest of us that more taxation is simply bad in itself, unthinkable, regardless of whatever net savings or other benefits might follow. And that is one of the messages that we are now hearing.

HOW BIG SHOULD THE HEALTH CARE BILL BE?

These arguments do not, however, come only from 'taxpayers' associations' and other spokesmen for the wealthy. The Pharmaceutical Manufacturers Association of Canada (PMAC) has also weighed in against a universal plan, but for quite different reasons. In the previous section it was assumed, implicitly or explicitly, that total outlays on health care could be taken as given, a fixed quantity $P \times Q$. Alternative choices of funding systems then determine how the burden of paying for this total will be distributed across the population. PMAC's interest, however, is not at all in how the total cost of health care is distributed, but rather that the total (or at least the amount of it spent on their products) be as large as possible. These expenditures, as expressed in the accounting identity above, are the income of pharmaceutical manufacturers. From their perspective the great danger inherent in a universal public Pharmacare program is precisely that it very well *might* reduce the total cost of prescription drugs in Canada.

Needless to say, PMAC does not make this concern explicit. Instead they offer various versions of the argument that any restriction of expenditures on their products would jeopardize the health of Canadian patients, now or in the future. The merits of these arguments are not our concern here, although it is important to keep in mind that pharmaceutical manufacturers are private, for-profit corporations. Their responsibility, which is both fiduciary and market-enforced, is to generate the highest possible level of income for their shareholders. Industry public relations may tend to create the impression that they are charitable educational and research foundations, primarily concerned with advancing knowledge and improving the health of the Canadian population (PMAC, 1996, 1997). This is not so, but the illusion has a long history. Twenty years ago, *Fortune* wrote:

> Around the headquarters in Rahway, New Jersey, there is so much high-minded talk about Merck's life saving mission that one might consider the company an eleemosynary outfit. But this mis-impression is never conveyed in conversation with [the president] who is as devout a disciple of the bottom line as ever there was.
>
> (Robertson, 1976: 136)]

The essential point, however, is one that applies to all those who make their living directly or indirectly from the provision of health care. Every dollar of expenditure is a dollar of someone's income. This relationship is not 'approximately true', reflecting the fact that health is a labour-intensive industry. It is *exactly* true, part of the accounting identity above. Income is received in various forms – wages, salaries, income from independent practice or unincorporated business, rent, interest and dividends, etc. But in total it must add up to total expenditure, unless an arithmetic error has been made.

It follows that providers of care, *qua* providers, have an economic interest in maintaining and expanding expenditures on their services. That interest is in direct conflict with payers' interests. And payers, ultimately, are not the intermediaries – governments, private insurers – but all those of us who contribute more to financing the health care system than we receive from it as income.

We are, of course, not only payers; we are also actual and potential patients. In those roles we have an obvious interest in the availability of appropriate health care services – the Q in the equation. Those services must be paid for. But as patients we want effective services. We derive no benefit from the expansion of servicing *per se*. And as payers we want to pay lower, not higher, prices for the services that are effective. Our concerns for effectiveness and reasonable cost generally translate in practice into cost containment; in direct conflict with providers.

A salary increase for hospital workers, for example, raises the W term in the accounting identity, and unless matched with loss of jobs, becomes indirectly an increase in P, the implicit price of hospital services. A fee increase for physicians, raising P for medical services, becomes also an increase in W, the incomes of physicians. Either will be passed forward as increased Ministry of Health expenditures, which in turn must lead to one or more of higher taxes, lower expenditures on other public programs, or increased net borrowing. Conversely, a reduction in budgets may lead to hospital mergers or closures, and a loss of jobs. Z falls, although the distribution of the reduction between P and Q will depend upon whether productivity changes.

More indirectly, increased patent protection for drug manufacturers permits them to charge higher prices without fear of competition. The increased expenditures of drug purchasers, and corresponding increased company earnings, will pass through more diverse channels. But eventually it will all emerge as increased incomes for company staff, suppliers, or shareholders – somewhere in the world. (Political compromises may also require that a portion be diverted to the biomedical research community.)

Provider representatives accordingly tend to support the forms of organization and payment they believe to be most favourable to the growth of their prices and sales, or wages and jobs.

Hospital workers, whose patients/clients tend to be very ill and/or have very limited resources – the unhealthy and unwealthy – are generally very supportive of public payment systems. Their opportunities in a private marketplace would be quite limited. But they do *not* support hospital 'downsizing' or cost containment more generally; their ideal policy would be more money from public sources, to hire more highly trained and better paid staff. Expand the T term in the accounting identity so as to support increases in W and Z, and correspondingly P and Q.

The loud voices for privatization, by contrast, come from those who believe that they *could* do better, in the form of increased sales of or higher prices for their products and services, in a more entrepreneurial environment. It is not clear how many, if any, of these would support a *truly* private system, with no direct or indirect contribution of public funds. (T goes to zero, and the other components of the identity adjust accordingly.) The economic mayhem among providers would be truly awesome. Instead what seems to be contemplated is a continuation of public support on a large scale, but without limits on private fee setting or delivery, or private insurance – rather like the United States, in fact, before widespread 'managed care'.

The logic of this objective is clear from the basic accounting identity above (p. 29). If governments continue to be effective at containing costs, growth in incomes must come from private revenue sources. But the objective is to increase the total flow of funds into health care, not merely to replace one source with another. Encourage fiscally pressed (or ideologically sympathetic) governments to shift their focus from containing overall system costs, to containing their own budgetary outlays. Just get rid of the associated restrictions on access to private funds, and let the total costs go where they will, i.e. where they should, i.e. where we want them to, i.e. up. T may stay level – though ideally it should rise too – but C and R should be permitted, indeed encouraged, to rise.

Several provincial governments in Canada, Alberta and Ontario in particular, now appear sympathetic to this line of argument, although they seem to hear less clearly the part about maintaining their own expenditure levels. Cuts have, however, been heaviest in the hospital sector, and these could be interpreted (and have been) as deliberate encouragement of a privately funded medical sector.

Providers' *economic* interests, however, are best served by a continuing high level of government contribution, particularly for those who cannot pay their own bills. But governments should not only permit but subsidize private insurers of hospital and medical care, as they do now in the United States and in Canada for employer-paid dental and pharmaceutical insurance. Physicians could then set their own fees, and operate private clinics alongside the public hospital system, while continuing to have access to the public system for patients without either private insurance or their own resources. But patients who could afford private care might find access to the public hospital system more difficult, if the physician who controls that access also owns a private clinic, and profits from its use.

Subsidized private insurance, plus the absence of any form of effective market competition among physicians, would permit fee escalation similar to that in the United States. In Canada public bargainers have over the years had much more success, holding fees at or (more recently) below general inflation rates. Meanwhile private diagnostic and surgical clinics would remove any limits on overall volumes of activity (or questions about appropriateness). Both P and Q would rise, the increased expenditures being funded from increased user fees and private insurance payments. The public insurance systems would probably find that they had to pay higher fees, to ensure that patients without private insurance could get timely access to care. And maybe not. This is obviously a hypothetical scenario. But it is exactly what did happen in the United States, prior to the current 'managed care' phase. Moreover, each of its components has a counterpart in Canadian experience.

From the beginning of Medicare, physicians tried to preserve or expand their scope for extra-billing, charging patients directly for their services over and above the fees paid by the public plans. This 'safety valve' or 'loophole' – depending upon one's perspective – was explicitly justified as a way of increasing fees and incomes, both directly and through the threat that it posed to insufficiently generous governments. In other words, extra-billing was intended to, and did, transfer income from patients and taxpayers to physicians. P, C, W, and presumably T were all increased

The Canada Health Act of 1984 largely (though indirectly) removed this mechanism for cost expansion. The response has been two-pronged. Physicians have supported provincial governments in their efforts either to repeal the Act or to make it unenforceable. At the same time they have tried to open other, more indirect avenues through which to bill patients directly.

Both de-listing of services and the establishment of private surgical and diagnostic clinics offer such opportunities. De-listing, or removal of services from coverage by the public plans, gives their providers full discretion over their prices. Conceivably in an entirely user-pay 'market' prices could rise or fall. But in fact they have risen – not surprisingly since otherwise why would providers support de-listing?

Second, however, de-listed services can be marketed much more freely since their sales no longer cut into either provincial budgets or the amount available to pay other physicians. All provincial governments now try, with greater or less success, to 'cap' the total amount they pay to physicians. More for some means less for others. But de-listed services, paid privately, are outside the cap.

Private clinics offer another way to expand billings. Physicians are restricted in extra-billing; so the clinic charges a 'facility fee' to the patient. This fee bears no necessary relation to actual costs of facility operation; the clinic is a private business. The fee can include a profit for its physician owners. Furthermore, such clinics permit physicians to increase their volume of activity and billings, outside any efforts to manage patterns of care through the public hospital system.

If patients are to be induced to pay these extra prices, however, they must face the impression, and perhaps the reality, of inadequate access to public facilities. Physicians who work in both the public sector and in their own private, for-profit clinics are in an obvious conflict-of-interest situation; denigrating or impeding access to public facilities increases the demand for their private care (Decoster and Brownell, 1997).

Advocates for private clinics argue that they enhance access and supplement an over-strained public system. The evidence for such claims is mixed to dubious; they tend to reduce to 'more is always better'. If government cannot or will not pay for more, then private individuals must. Our concern here, however, is to emphasize that whatever the effects of 'more' on the health of Canadians, all the privatization initiatives and supporting arguments involve a transfer of income, through higher prices as well as higher volumes of care, from payers to providers.[3] But even if there were no restrictions on extra-billing or private facilities, there are likely to be limits on 'what the market will bear' in private charges, particularly in the presence of a free public system. Denigrating or inhibiting access to that system can assist in recruiting private patients, but could also trigger a political backlash if people begin to see 'their' system as being sabotaged. For really significant increases in total system costs, and incomes, it is probably necessary to introduce private health insurance. Increases in C and R are thus complementary; out of pocket charges provide something for private insurers to cover, and that coverage permits increase in the level of such charges. Private medicine and private insurance are symbiotic.

Thus we find that proposals for privatization in Canada include both freedom to bill *and* removal of the ban on private coverage for services now included in the public programs. Not stated, but implicit, is extension of the public subsidy now enjoyed by private dental and pharmaceutical insurers.

To develop a significant market in Canada, private insurance companies must surely go beyond insuring 'fringe benefit' services. The real money is in hospital and medical care. But if people are to be induced to buy private insurance there must be something to insure – private charges for (actual or perceived) preferred service. More timely or 'better quality' services might be purchased through extra-bills or double bills by physicians, or 'facility fees' in private clinics. Private insurers could cover 'de-listed' services. Whatever the service, private charges and private insurance go hand in hand.

But private insurance, as the American experience shows, brings in a whole new group of very powerful income claimants – a major expansion in the Z term. Large-scale private coverage is a horrendously expensive way to pay for health care. A huge private bureaucracy must be established to assess risks, set premiums, design complex benefit schedules, and review and pay (or refuse) claims. A corresponding financial apparatus is then required in hospitals, nursing homes, and private practices to deal with this system, in a form of 'administrative arms race' (Woolhandler and Himmelstein, 1991; Himmelstein *et al.*, 1996).

Far from trying to minimize the cost of administrative overhead, and match premiums as closely as possible to benefit payments, private insurers refer to the rate of benefit payment as the 'loss ratio' and try to *maximize* the difference between premium revenue and payout. That difference is the income of the insurance sector.

Yet, as we know from the experience of the single-payer system in Canada, all this financial paper-pushing turns out to be as unnecessary and wasteful as the old Soviet planning apparatus. These are not functions that *anyone* needs to perform once a decision has been made to cover the whole population. In the United States, bureaucratic waste by and in response to the private insurance industry now adds more than a hundred billion dollars per year, over 10 per cent, to total health care costs.

It may of course be just scare-mongering to suggest that such a situation could develop in Canada. It would require not only that private insurance for hospital and medical care be permitted and subsidized, but that people begin to withdraw in significant numbers from the public system. That would be formally impossible, so long as that system remains tax-financed; but it could be brought about indirectly if the public system were to deteriorate through continued reductions in government funding or through the actions of providers with competing private interests. And people who rely primarily on private insurance become a constituency not for improvement but for further deterioration – if you do not use it why pay taxes for it? Hirschman's (1970) downward spiral could set in.

This is not going to happen next year, nor probably next decade. But the American system took a generation to reach its present form. The key point to keep in mind is that what to payers and users are the excessive costs of a private insurance system is income to the insurance industry. And it is the normal, expected, and indeed highly rewarded behaviour of private enterprises to seek constantly to expand their incomes. They will, and do, promote political and institutional changes to make that possible.

These strategies might be focused inside Canada, or work through international agreements such as NAFTA, the WTO, or the MAI (see Appleton, Chapter 5 this volume). The pharmaceutical industry has used international pressures with great skill to undermine the authority of national governments, and to transfer income from their citizens to its shareholders. Whatever the channel, the fundamental logic of commercial enterprise guarantees that these pressures will be brought to bear; and the international insurance industry has deep pockets, and plenty of time. Once in, as President Clinton found, they are too powerful to remove.

WHO GETS WHAT CARE, WHEN, AND HOW?

The explicit answer, in a universal public system, is that everybody gets all the care they need, when they need it, on 'equal terms and conditions', and without financial barriers. But this is a statement of principle or an aspiration; in practice people speak of 'reasonable access' in which proximity and information, among other things, inevitably have an influence. The major debates, however, arise from disagreements about need and timeliness. What services does a patient *really* need, and what, if any, is an acceptable delay in providing them? An extreme position might be that patients need, or at least should receive, whatever they and their physicians believe they need, with no delay. But a bit more thought, and familiarity with actual health care systems, reminds one that what patients want, and even are willing to pay for, is often not at all what they should have, or what a responsible health care system should provide. Moreover there is significant variation in the recommendations that different physicians – or other professionals – will make for any given patient and problem. They cannot all be correct.

In fact there is abundant evidence that for many types of problems recommended care depends upon available capacity. Any attempt to provide enough capacity to meet all demands instantly, therefore, will simply result in increased demands. Some physicians have suggested that a system with *no* waiting lists for elective care would be quite dangerous for patients.

That said, however, there is nevertheless an implicit conflict among patients as to who gets cared for, how, and especially when. If some patients, and particularly their physicians, believe that 'the system' is not adequately meeting their needs, either because it is inadequately resourced or because of managerial failures, what then? How are priorities for available care assigned? And over the longer run, how is an acceptable overall level of care determined and maintained?

There are essentially two lines of response, administrative and market. The former involves determining priorities on the basis of relative need or capacity to benefit; the latter on the basis of willingness, which in practice means ability, to pay. Over the longer run, administrative approaches require managerial feed-back loops to identify and eliminate access problems that are a consequence of inadequate management rather than sheer lack of resources. But a responsive political system must also find an acceptable balance between the public's fears that the health care system may, in fact, be under-resourced, and their reluctance to pay further taxes. The market solution permits resources to continue to flow into the health care system so long as individuals are willing to pay, or more accurately so long as various private and public institutions can extract from them the necessary money.

To date, Canadians have accepted the administrative approach, relying primarily on physicians and hospital administrators to set priorities, and trusting that governments are in fact funding the overall system adequately.

Waiting lists exist, but when offered faster service in another jurisdiction, or questioned about willingness to pay for priority, patients have been reluctant to consider such options (Katz *et al.*, 1991; Anderson *et al.*, 1997). The general view seems to be that emergencies and urgent care will be provided immediately, and that the management of elective care is reasonably fair and adequate.

Throughout the history of Medicare, providers and their representatives have claimed that 'the system is underfunded', but these claims have borne no relation to the actual level of funding in the system. They simply reflect the inevitable and permanent conflict between providers and payers.

Since 1992, however, health spending has grown very little (Canadian Institute, 1997). In real (inflation-adjusted) dollars per capita it has actually fallen slightly. And in the hospital sector it has fallen quite markedly. This is not necessarily a bad thing; most observers agree that, historically, in-patient care has been overutilized in Canada. It is now falling in a number of countries (but see Reinhardt, 1996). But the decline has led to increasing claims, particularly from the hospital workers who are traditional supporters of the public system, that 'the system is falling apart'. Certainly hospital use *is* falling surprisingly rapidly, and some of them are losing their jobs.

This environment tends to strain the confidence of the general public. If many people conclude that the public system really cannot meet their needs, a natural response by those who can is to try to buy their way to the front of the public queue, or to seek a private alternative. And for the economic reasons spelled out above, there will be providers only too willing to reinforce any concerns that they may have about the public system.

Indeed, as noted at the outset, there is an obvious confluence of interests in private funding from all three of the axes above. It permits an expansion in total health care costs, meeting the interests of providers whose patients can afford their services. It shifts the burden of payment from taxes to direct charges, to the benefit of upper income taxpayers. And it reassures those with the means that care will be there *for them*, if and when they need it. If there are to be shortages, queues, and 'rationing', any twinges of conscience or sense of social solidarity can be assuaged by the argument that private purchasing actually adds to total system capacity. Private markets *benefit* the unhealthy and unwealthy. Everybody wins – why cannot more people understand that?

It is not difficult, therefore, to understand why so many loud and powerful voices predict the imminent collapse of Medicare, and call for private markets in medicine. Ideological hostility to 'Big Government' is icing on a solid cake of economic interest; indeed it is often difficult to distinguish principle from interest.

BUT WHAT BUSINESS IS IT OF BUSINESS?

Amid this array of embedded but in the end relatively narrow interests, 'business' would seem to be the dog that has not yet barked. User fees, extra-billing, private clinics, can all be highly profitable for a relatively few providers, but most of their supporters profit little. As emphasized above, a really big shift from public to private funding sources requires large-scale private insurance. And that, in turn, requires public subsidy. (As the American experience shows, that does not really get governments off the hook. They still pay the lion's share of the bills, but lose control of the system.)

But the established form of subsidy, sustainable because largely invisible to the general public, is through the tax treatment of employer-paid premiums. In other words, a really serious expansion of private funding means business will have to pay. As Willie Sutton said about banks, 'That's where the money is.' So why doesn't the dog bark?

Most obviously, 'business' is not a monolith with a single interest, as actual or potential payer, in holding down health costs. Businesses sell, as well as pay for, health care. For-profit health corporations in particular – drug and equipment manufacturers and private insurers – are indistinguishable from 'business' in general; just part of the group. Having a very clear understanding of their own interests in health care policy, however, they tend to be the best informed and most motivated on health matters.

For other businesses, containing fringe benefit costs is simply one concern among many, and well down the priority list. Management attention is scarce. As for thinking about the details of public health insurance, or the possible consequences ten or more years out of apparently minor changes in funding details, this rarely happens. But for those businesses that sell health-related goods and services, cost expansion – sales growth – *is* their business. And they take care of it, now and for the future. In the process they appear to exert a disproportionate influence over the attitudes and voice of 'business' as a whole. It is a commonplace of political science that narrow but concentrated interests tend to outweigh broad but diffuse ones.

Moreover, to the extent that businesses do address these issues, they are the concern of specialized benefits managers whose loyalties are inevitably divided. In the firm's interest, they will try to manage the benefits package so as to keep its costs down. But a transfer of functions from private insurance to government, as would follow for example from a universal public Pharmacare program, would eliminate the need for many of their skills and services. Benefits managers, whether employed by or contracted to private firms, are part of the bureaucracy needed to administer private health insurance; their careers are linked with that industry. Will they (if asked) advise management to support the public alternative?

Finally 'business', as Toronto entrepreneur Honest Ed Mirvish pointed out, 'is people'. Senior management, mostly men in middle or late middle age, are into the heart attack zone. Probably a few associates have already died, or suffered major health crises. Allegations that 'the system is falling apart' take on personal significance. To the extent that they meet providers of care socially, these are likely to be physicians or members of the drug or insurance industry who will assure them that their fears are justified. 'You could die waiting for cardiac surgery. In a better system, people like you and I could buy the care we need, when we need it (without going to the United States).'

Thus one need not invoke any general anti-government bias on the part of businessmen – though that may be a factor too – to find reasons why they might be unsupportive of, or hostile to, universal public health insurance, even though it would seem to be obviously advantageous to their businesses.

Another way of putting this argument, however, is that in supporting private health care funding, business leaders in Canada may be putting their perceptions of their personal interests ahead of those of their companies, or shareholders. A competitive business environment is supposed to penalize such behaviour, in either the product or the capital markets. If one manager does not maximize the company's profits, maybe his replacement will. Whatever their personal views and interests, Canadian business cannot afford to overlook or abandon the competitive advantage in lower labour costs that they derive from Medicare.

Or can they? A peculiar feature of this competitive advantage is that while it is easy to understand, and widely referred to, there seems to be a consensus among economists that it does not exist. The argument has two components.

First, the total compensation package, wages and benefits, offered by profit-maximizing firms in a competitive labour market tends to match the employee's contribution to a firm's revenues. If fringe benefit costs go up, wages will go down, or at least be lower than otherwise. Contrary to general belief, employers do not pay for fringe benefits. Workers do. An extension of this logic can be used to argue that the wage–benefit mix offered will be the one that workers want most, so if health costs rise and wages fall, that must be what workers want.

This argument is certainly valid under an assumed set of market conditions. If firms are perfect profit maximizers, fringe benefit costs must either be offset by wages, or passed forward in higher product prices, or passed back in lower stockholder returns. If all markets are perfectly competitive (and large), only the former can occur. Workers *will* pay for their own benefits, and management should be indifferent to their level. The question is, do these market conditions obtain in the real world of Canadian business? *Are* businesses indifferent to the overall level of benefit payments, as this framework predicts?

The second strand of the argument, however, points out that countries as a whole *cannot* price themselves out of world markets. With flexible exchange rates, a country whose exports are not competitive will find the value of its currency falling. Conversely, if Medicare gave Canadian business as a whole a competitive advantage, the Canadian dollar would rise to compensate. Comparative advantage in particular products or services can exist, and has been understood since Ricardo's day. But general competitive advantage is a mercantilist myth. Again this follows logically in a world of static equilibrium. But what proponents of competitive advantage seem to have in mind is a more dynamic world of new technologies and products. Competitive advantage permits the capture of new, high return markets and specialization in forms of production that expand the national stock of both physical capital and 'know-how'. Personal incomes can thus keep growing, without triggering a

trade imbalance. Holding down unnecessary expense in health care – or anywhere else – may then free up resources that business can use for more
productive investments.

FORWARD TO THE PAST?

The persistence of old ideas and the ambiguity of business interests are clearly
illustrated in the discussions following the recommendation by the National
Forum on Health of a universal public Pharmacare program. Employers have
been struggling unsuccessfully to contain the rapid increase in their outlays for
drug benefits; one might expect them to welcome with enthusiasm a proposal
to take this burden entirely off their shoulders. At the same time, the clear
evidence of the success of Medicare, sustained over more than a quarter-century,
should make the fundamental structure of that public program easy to choose –
a 'no-brainer' – although there would be plenty of work in the details.

Yet the Canadian business community has been surprisingly non-commital
on Pharmacare. Meanwhile the pharmaceutical and insurance industries are
promoting a totally different approach to 'universality' through the compulsory extension of employment-based coverage, supplemented by public coverage (with substantial out-of-pocket charges) only for the residual population.

Such a system, already in place in Quebec, is a version of the mixed public–
private approach to universality recommended by the insurance industry to the
Royal Commission on Health Services nearly forty years ago – and rejected. It
was, however, adopted in the United States where it has led to incomplete
coverage, spectacular cost increases, and a heavy cost burden on employers. So
why is this old, bad idea back again, and why is business so quiet? This
approach places employers squarely in the gun-sights of the pharmaceutical
industry, yet they have not taken a firm stand in opposition.

Answers become clear once we escape from the steersman metaphor. The
mixed funding model is back precisely *because* it leads to uncontrollable costs.
The strongest promoters are private insurers and drug manufacturers, for
whom those costs are incomes. They receive a wider hearing because
the mixed funding structure is also more regressive – less taxation, more
private pay – and thus bears less heavily on people at higher income levels
(and more on those at lower). And it permits debt-burdened governments to
offer the shadow of universality without the substance. (The principal effect of
the Quebec program has been to lower government expenditures, by transferring costs onto private individuals and employers.)

Whatever its intrinsic significance, Pharmacare in 1997 is thus a case study
in the conflicts of economic interests in health care finance. It presents, in a
particularly transparent form, the underlying motivations for (and against)
'reform' of health care funding more generally, in every country. Narrowly
based, concentrated economic interests have brought back, yet again, funding
proposals that will on all previous experience lead to a more costly, less

efficient, and certainly more regressively funded system. As they always have. As they always will.

NOTES

1   Some analysts, particularly in Europe, draw a distinction between tax and social insurance finance (though national income accountants do not). The latter distinction is, I believe, unimportant in principle, but matters in substance. Social insurance premiums are in fact a relatively regressive form of tax, both because they have contribution ceilings, and because they tax only wages and salaries, not investment income. Analysts who emphasize the distinction on distributional grounds have a point. It is therefore understandable that wealthier people, and their representatives argue for social insurance over 'taxation' although social insurance is merely a particular form of taxation.

2   Both the accounting and the observations are point-in-time snapshots of people moving through a life cycle. Wealth and health change over time; being healthy or wealthy today provides no absolute guarantee for tomorrow. In theory, then, one could imagine that point-in-time status differences might be evened out over the life cycle. But in reality they are not, these states are highly autocorrelated. If you are healthy (or wealthy) today, your chances of being in that state tomorrow are a good deal higher than if you are unhealthy (or unwealthy) today. And the strength of the autocorrelation increases with age. Illnesses become chronic, and wealth becomes predominantly financial assets. Moreover the two states are cross-correlated. The wealthier (healthier) you are today, the more likely you are to be healthy (wealthy) tomorrow, and this correlation appears to reflect causality in *both* directions. Life does not even out over time.

3   It has now been determined, however, that facility fees charged to patients are in fact user fees within the scope of the Canada Health Act. One consequence, or at least sequel, has been increased efforts by provincial governments to render that Act unenforceable. The new strategy is to convince the federal government, in the name of 'co-operative federalism' to give up its unilateral authority to interpret and enforce this federal statute. If these could be made matters for federal-provincial negotiation, individual provincial governments could in effect do whatever they wish. There seems general agreement that this would mean the end of Medicare in Canada (Canada, National Forum on Health, 1997).

REFERENCES

Abel-Smith, B. 1985. Who Is the Odd Man Out?: The Experience of Western Europe in Containing the Costs of Health Care. *Milbank Quarterly* 63: 1–17.

Abel-Smith, B. 1992. Cost Containment and New Priorities in the European Community. *Milbank Quarterly* 70: 393–416.

Abel-Smith, B. and E. Mossialos. 1994. Cost Containment and Health Care Reform: A Study of the European Union. *Health Policy* 28: 89–132.

Anderson, G., C. Black, E. Dunn *et al.*, 1997. Willingness to Pay to Shorten Waiting Time for Cataract Surgery. *Health Affairs* 16 (5) (September–October): 181–190.

Barer, M. L., V. Bhatia, G. L. Stoddart and R. G. Evans. 1994. *The Remarkable Tenacity of User Charges*. Toronto: The Premier's Council on Health, Well-Being, and Social Justice.

Barer, M. L., R. G. Evans, C. Hertzman and M. Johri (1998) *Lies, Damned Lies, and Health Care Zombies: Discredited Ideas That Will Not Die*. HPI Discussion Paper #10, Health Policy Institute, University of Texas-Houston Health Science Center, Houston, Texas.

Blendon, R. J., R. Leitman, I. Morrison and K. Donelan. 1990. Satisfaction with Health Systems in Ten Nations. *Health Affairs* 9 (2): 185–192.

Blendon, R. J., J. Benson, K. Donelan, R. Leitman, H. Taylor, C. Koeck and D. Gitterman. 1995. Who Has the Best Health Care System? A Second Look. *Health Affairs* 14 (4): 220–230.

Canadian Institute for Health Information. 1997. *Drug Costs in Canada*. Ottawa: CIHI (March).

Consumers' Union. 1996. How Good Is Your Health Plan? *Consumer Reports* 61 (8): 28–42.

Decoster, C. and M. D. Brownell. 1997. Private health care in Canada: saviour or siren. *Public Heath Reports* 112 (4) (July–August): 298–305.

Enthoven, A. C. 1989. What Can Europeans Learn from Americans about Financing and Organization of Medical Care? *Health Care Financing Review* (Annual Suppl.): 49–63.

Evans, R. G., M. L. Barer, G. L. Stoddart and V. Bhatia. 1994a. *Who Are the Zombie Masters, and What Do They Want?* Toronto: The Premier's Council on Health, Well-being and Social Justice (June).

Evans, R. G., M. L. Barer and G. L. Stoddart. 1994b. *Charging Peter to Pay Paul: Accounting for the Financial Effects of User Charges*. Toronto: Premier's Council on Health, Well-Being, and Social Justice.

Fuchs, V. R. 1996. Economics, Values, and Health Care Reform. *American Economic Review* 86 (1): 1–24.

Ham, C. 1994. *Management and Competition in the New NHS*. Oxford, England: Radcliffe Medical Press for the National Association of Health Authorities and Trusts.

Himmelstein, D. U., J. Lewontin and S. Woolhandler. 1996. Who Administers Who Cares? Medical Administrative and Clinical Employment in the United States and Canada. *American Journal of Public Health* 86 (2): 172–178.

Hirschman, A. O. 1970. Exit, *Voice and Loyalty*. Cambridge, MA: Harvard.

Katz, S. J., H. F. Mizgala and H. G. Welch. 1991. British Columbia Sends Patients to Seattle for Coronary Artery Surgery: Bypassing the queue in Canada. *Journal of the American Medical Association* 266 (8): 1108–1111.

National Forum on Health. 1997. *Canada Health Action: Building on the Legacy*. Ottawa: National Forum on Health (February).

Navarro, V. (ed.) 1992. *Why the United States Does Not Have a Universal Health Care Program*. Amityville, NY: Baywood Publishing.

Nelson, R. R. 1977. *The Moon and the Ghetto*. New York: Norton.

OECD/CREDES. 1997. OECD Health Data 97. Software for the Comparative Analysis of 29 Health Systems. Paris: OECD Health Policy Unit.

PMAC. 1996. Prescription Medicines and Canada's Healthcare System. A Submission by the Pharmaceutical Manufacturers' Association of Canada to the National Forum on Health, May.

PMAC. 1997. A response by the Pharmaceutical Manufacturers' Association of Canada to the National Forum on Health Synthesis Paper entitled *Directions for a Pharmaceutical Policy in Canada* (March).

Rasell, E. and K. Tang. 1994. Paying for Health Care: Affordability and Equity in Proposals for Health Care Reform. *Working Paper No. 111* (December). Washington, DC: Economic Policy Institute.

Rasell, E., J. Bernstein and K. Tang. 1993. The Impact of Health Care Financing on Family Budgets. *Briefing Paper* (April). Washington, DC: Economic Policy Institute.

Reinhardt, U. E. 1996. Spending More through 'Cost Control': Our Obsessive Quest to Gut the Hospital. *Health Affairs* 15 (2): 145–154.

Rice, T. 1997. Can Markets Give Us the Health System We Want? *Journal of Health Politics, Policy and Law* 22: 383–426.

Robertson, 1976. Merck Strains to Keep the Pots-a-boiling. *Fortune Magazine* 168 (70): 134–139.

Taylor, H. and U. E. Reinhardt (1991) Does the System Fit?, *Health Management Quarterly* XIII (Third Quarter): 2–10.

van Doorslaer, E., A. Wagstaff and F. Rutten (eds). 1993. *Equity in the Finance and Delivery of Health Care: An International Perspective*. New York: Oxford University Press.

White, J. 1995. *Competing Solutions: American Health Care Proposals and International Experience*. Washington, DC: Brookings Institution.

Wilson, R. 1996. Opeing Remarks, in *Access to Quality Health Care for all Canadians*. Proceedings of a Natural Health Care Policy Summit. Making a Good Health Care System Better: Public–Private Partnering. Ottawan Canadian Medical Association, March 18–19, 1996, p. 11.

Woolhandler, S. and D. U. Himmelstein. 1991. The Deteriorating Administrative Efficiency of the U.S. Health Care System. *New England Journal of Medicine* 324: 1253–1258.

3 The virus of consumerism

Gina Feldberg and Robert Vipond

It is a symptom of the crisis of citizenship . . . that most political rhetoric, whether of left or right, addresses the electorate not as citizens but as taxpayers or as consumers. It is as if the market were determining the very language of political community.

(Ignatieff, 1995: 71)

INTRODUCTION: THE PROBLEM WITH THE SYSTEM IS ABUSE?

The global restructuring of health care employs and invokes consumerism and consumerist models. In Britain, Sweden, the United States and Canada, consumer 'overutilization' is a frequently cited source of escalating costs, while more informed consumer control and awareness are posited as solutions. As concern about increasing costs grows, and proposals for the reduction of health care spending advocate 'more rigorous control of the supply-and-demand forces that drive health care services', (Bagley, 1994: 1747–1748) the shadow or spectre of 'consumer abuse' looms ominously over discussions of demand.

Our intent is not to settle with unequivocal evidence the question of whether 'consumer abuse' is 'myth or reality'. Instead, we suggest that tales of consumer abuse are cultural legends, with mythical significance. These tales are told by remarkably diverse groups that include patients (who fear an erosion of services), practitioners (who fear a threat to their professional livelihood) and politicians. Through an analysis of selected narratives, we assess the ways in which three key parties – the state, the press, and most frequently, the medical profession – have recounted those myths. This analysis suggests that the debate over consumer abuse is both an economic debate and a symbolic moral debate.

Conceptually, no taxonomy of abuse exists and the term is used to describe a range of behaviours and moral attitudes that should be kept analytically distinct. For that matter it is not even clear that we have the right patient on the examining table. As Michael Rachlis is fond of pointing out, it is unclear why the overutilization debate should focus on 'consumer abuse' when '90 per

cent of the health-care services provided in Ontario are referred by physicians'
(Henry, 1995: 49).

VILLAINS AND VICTIMS: WHAT IS CONSUMER ABUSE?

The possibility that 'consumer abuse' may contribute significantly to spiralling health care costs has attracted attention from governments and physicians
alike for the past several years. Colourful anecdotes abound. In one case
reported in the Canadian Medical Association Journal (CMAJ), an Ontario
man lent his health card to an out-of-country relative who needed medical
attention. After a costly stay in hospital, the relative died, but because he had
been using an assumed identity the wrong person was declared dead, the living
man was de-listed from OHIP, and the dead man's body could not be shipped
home (Williams, 1993: 2003). In another case, a 'patient who needed a
hysterectomy produced a health card that had already been used to bill for
a hysterectomy' (French, 1995: 569). A committee reviewing utilization rates
in Manitoba uncovered numerous instances in which individuals had made
profligate use of health services, including one woman who made 247 office
visits to 71 different physicians over the course of a year (CMAJ, 1994: 939).
And the CMAJ reported in 1995 that a recent investigation undertaken by the
Ontario Ministry of Health had 'uncovered 763 cases of suspected fraud on the
Akwesane Indian reserve near Cornwall', where American Indians living on
the reserve may have been 'receiving their care free of charge in Ontario'
(French, 1995: 569). Nor, of course, is abuse confined to Canada. In the US,
the Missouri-based Task Force on Misuse, Abuse and Diversion of Drugs now
publishes a 'scam of the month', drawing attention to the many and ingenious
ways employed by drug abusers to obtain drugs illegally from health care
professionals (Williams, 1993: 2006).

Yet despite the anecdotal evidence, there appears to be little agreement
about exactly how widespread or costly health care abuse is. The Ontario
example stands out. The Ontario Health Insurance Plan, which gathers data
on health care utilization, remains equivocal. High officials, both elected
and appointed, are more adamant about the problem though no less clear
on its scope. A former Deputy Minister of Health in the provincial government
testified before a legislative committee in 1993 that health card fraud cost the
province between $20 – $100 million annually, and the same government
spent $38 million issuing new health cards designed to make abuse more
difficult (Williams, 1993: 2004). Four years later, the same Deputy Minister,
now a consultant, spoke of the 'small group of physicians and consumers who
are costing taxpayers a great deal of money through fraud and abuse of the
health-care system' (Rusk, 1997: A5). Mike Harris, speaking as leader of
the Provincial Progressive Conservative Party, increased this estimate several
fold. Mr Harris maintained that 'hundreds of millions' of dollars were being
siphoned out of the health care system through abuse (Williams, 1993: 2004).

Yet, once in government, the same Mike Harris cancelled a program to produce new photo identity health cards designed to minimize abuse, and estimates of the costs of abuse settled at $65 million. Two years into their mandate, and confronted with mounting dissatisfaction about their approach to health care restructuring, Harris and the Health Minister have once again raised the spectre of abuse, and they announced in September 1997 that they would implement a number of new measures to deal with health fraud, including the creation of a fraud-control unit.

For its part, the Ontario Ministry of Health carried out a pilot educational project in an attempt to convince the citizens of London, Ontario that physicians could do little for colds and flus, and that visits to a physician in these circumstances 'use up energy and resources that are needed for serious health problems'. The project was supported by the Ontario Medical Association, whose president, Michael Wyman, welcomed the initiative because it focused on factors 'driving demand for services' rather than on their supply. Still, Wyman and others had reservations, both about the project's methodology and its conclusions. As one physician put it: 'It was the feeling of most of my colleagues, who are practising family doctors, that they didn't think the public, in general, was abusing [the system] in terms of colds.' And, indeed, it is hard to draw conclusions about the project that move beyond 'feeling', for follow-up was limited and two other educational projects never materialized (O'Reilly, 1994: 201–202).

If the debate over consumer abuse of health care seems desultory, inchoate and inconclusive it is in part because it is being carried on at two levels simultaneously, so that while the debate is framed in economic terms (i.e. 'over-utilization'), the claims that drive the debate itself are decidedly moral in character (i.e. the problem is 'abuse'). Indeed, the moral element is so powerful in these accounts of consumer abuse that we want to characterize and analyse them as myths – as moral tales that carry cultural messages. From this perspective, we have identified four basic myths of consumer abuse that dominate the current discussion that engages government, health care providers and, at least occasionally, the public. Though different in substance, the myths share some elements: each has a villain or victim, each imparts a moral lesson, and each has economic consequences.

At one end of the spectrum, abuse is used synonymously with fraud and refers to those cases in which patients are using health services to which they have no legal entitlement. Much of the anecdotal evidence, like the examples related above, concerns this sort of 'hard' abuse where a deliberate attempt has been made, as Mike Harris put it, to 'rip off' the system. Fraud involves cheating, but it is something more besides. To be guilty of health card fraud is essentially to be placed beyond the moral community. Like those who are guilty of welfare fraud, health card cheats have effectively forfeited their claim to civic dignity and respect. It is, therefore, no accident that most of the examples of this sort of abuse are either literally outsiders (foreigners and illegal immigrants for example) or those whose loyalty to the community's dominant culture is contested (e.g. drug addicts and native people). Beyond the economic savings to be achieved, cracking down on this sort of abuse is a way of protecting the moral, as well as the physical, boundaries of the community.

Consumer abuse in health extends well beyond legal abuse or fraud, however. In a letter to the CMAJ, two doctors from London, Ontario related the case of a patient who sniffs glue, goes repeatedly to the emergency department of the hospital suffering from methanol poisoning, is admitted and is treated with intravenous injections of alcohol. As the doctors put it: 'Mr. X knows exactly what he is doing, and when discharged he notifies the medical team that he will be back . . . He is a deliberate abuser of health care facilities' (Watson and Boyd, 1994: 11). This is consumer abuse that stems from self-abuse. Like the case of health card fraud, these actions are deliberate and may place 'the health and welfare of other patients at risk' by 'diverting valuable medical resources'. (Watson and Boyd, 1994: 11). And as with health card fraud, they tap a deeper moral vein. The doctors who treated Mr. X were not simply personally indignant and angry (their words) at the patient's behaviour; their indignation, rather, was an expression of collective anger that called for public humiliation (by naming the patient) and public exile (by sending him to jail) as a way of showing that he was unfit to be considered a member of the community. Here the moral tale is plainly stated, although its implications are more difficult to pursue consistently. As subsequent letter-writers to the CMAJ pointed out, this sort of abuse as self-abuse raises a series of tricky moral questions. If access to health services were limited or denied to self-abusers like Mr. X, would we not have to consider rationing access to others, like hang-gliders, who 'abuse' the system by taking calculated risks and who assume that 'society will pick up the pieces' (Emson, 1994: 1378–1379)? And if self-abuse is defined as acting in ways that we know to be unhealthy, would we be willing to withhold health services from smokers who develop lung cancer or from overeaters who develop heart problems?

Quite different from either fraud or self-abuse is the case of those who use scarce health resources frivolously. The sense that too many patients seek medical care for minor problems that really do not require medical care resonates particularly powerfully with physicians. In a recent survey of Ontario physicians, almost one-third of respondents cited this sort of apparently unnecessary health care seeking to be an 'extremely important' cause of increased utilization patterns. What is most striking about this version of consumer abuse is that the guilty parties are not social or moral outsiders. The patients who are wasting resources by acting frivolously are those well-educated patients who 'shop' around until they find a doctor and a diagnosis they like, or the 'worried well' who, encouraged by 'you-can-have-it consumerism' demand endless tests to reassure themselves that they are not ill, or even expectant mothers who want ultrasounds performed even though such scans may be medically unnecessary (Ryval, 1993). The Chair of Saskatchewan's Health Services Utilization and Research Commission recently put the point this way: 'The one thing we should not be doing is an ultrasound because Mum wants a picture of baby in utero...That amounts to a misappropriation of public funds. An ultrasound costs $80 and if it's not necessary, that's $80 that could be spent much more appropriately for someone else's care' (Coutts, 1996). What lies at the heart of the frivolous use of health care services according to these physician accounts is, in short, sophisticated selfishness. Frivolous abusers are 'part of the Me generation', who 'are obsessed with being well' and who 'don't want to suffer in any way' – even if that means using expensive services that could be used more appropriately elsewhere (Ryval, 1993).

This attack on the frivolous use of health services shades into, but is distinct from, the fourth form of consumer abuse – irresponsibility. The patient who wants the doctor to treat a minor ailment is not only selfish, s/he is potentially irresponsible for s/he should know how to treat her/himself or, alternatively, should know how to avoid disease in the first place. As they are quick to react to the frivolous use of medical services, so physicians are said to be especially frustrated by their 'patients' refusal to take more responsibility for their health (Ryval, 1993:111). Of all the forms of consumer abuse of health care, this one seems the most open to remedy. Thus, the underlying purpose of the London flu and cold project discussed above was less to chide patients for using medical services frivolously than to provide them with the information that would allow them to 'start taking more responsibility for their health care' (O'Reilly, 1994: 202). The information contained in the flu and cold pamphlet was not intended to rebuke Londoners for wasting precious health care resources; rather, it was meant to 'empower' them. As one health economist commented: 'Clearly, we have to move in this direction. Putting more and better information in the hands of consumers and encouraging more active consumer participation in the care-delivery process is definitely the way to go' (O'Reilly, 1994: 202).

NARRATIVES OF CONSUMER ABUSE

These, then, are the four basic narratives that most often inform the debate over consumer abuse of health care: fraud, self-abuse, frivolousness and irresponsibility. They flow from a variety of different experiences and point to quite different policy responses. There is, however, one basic moral perception that underlies and unites all four types of abuse; namely, that health care abuse exists because individuals act as if they had no obligations to those around them. It is easy to agree that health card fraud is unacceptable because it is so fundamentally asocial; self-abusers generate such indignation because they force 'society to pick up the pieces'; those who use medical services frivolously think only of themselves and are blind to the possibility that when one person uses scarce health resources unnecessarily someone whose need is greater may be denied proper care; and those who don't take responsibility for their health impose burdens on the rest of us who end up footing the bill. In other words, the debate about health care abuse engages some of the most fundamental issues arising from democratic citizenship – about the nature and extent of our duties, as individuals, to those around us and to our political community, about the balance between the rights we enjoy and the obligations we owe.

It is precisely in this context, in the shadow of citizenship, that debates about user fees, rationing and other policy alternatives can and should be located, for all of them raise important questions about the public good and our contribution to it. But it is precisely for the same reason that it seems strange to carry on a debate that is really about citizenship in terms of consumer abuse. Consumers may buy too much, they may miss the sales, and what they buy may be out of fashion, but it is the individual consumer who suffers the consequences. We don't usually complain that consumers are forgetting their duties to others or acting in a selfish and irresponsible way for the simple reason that consumerism appeals to and is sustained by self-interest. If anything, as a recent display in one Toronto shop rather baldly suggested, consumers owe it to others to spend. Still, when they don't spend, we don't blame consumers for their moral failing but say instead that they simply lacked what is usually called 'confidence' – nothing that low interest rates, secure employment and good sales won't remedy. In short, if abuse means that social duty has failed to outweigh individual desire, then the very notion of consumer abuse is an oxymoron, for consumerism celebrates the sovereignty of individual desires.

Yet the fact remains that the health care debate continues to be framed in the language of consumerism and consumer abuse. Why is it such a powerful force in the health care debate? And what are consequences of conflating consumerism and citizenship in this way?

THE MEANINGS AND POWER OF CONSUMERISM

Health consumerism has a long history – dating at least to the nineteenth century when the Ohio physician Daniel Webster Cathell wrote his renowned marketing piece *The Physician Himself and What He Should Add to his Scientific Acquirements* (Cathell, 1882) – but its most recent form emerges from the United States, in the 1960s. In its current guise, health consumerism reflects the convergence of three streams in American health reform – statist, professional and populist. First, health consumerism forms part of a larger story of the growth of regulatory activism in the US in the 1960s. It was linked to the recognition of medical marketplaces, in which a range of health care providers and product manufacturers were seen to compete for business, and from 'growing public demand for justice and fair play in the marketplace'. (Cornacchia and Barrett, 1989: 5). The health consumer movement benefited enormously from the strategic decisions of various state actors to make common cause with, and to take vigorous action on behalf of, health consumers. The Food and Drug Administration's decision to ban thalidomide fits this description; so too does President Kennedy's sponsorship, in 1962, of a

Consumer Bill of Rights to protect consumers from 'the marketing of goods that are hazardous to health or to life'. For American liberal activism in the 1960s, a consumerist approach to health was ideal. It gave the state a clear mission – to protect consumers from unsafe products, misleading information and monopolistic practices. It allowed the state to forge alliances with citizens against what are now called 'special interests'. Yet it also protected the state from the claim that increased regulation necessarily implied more intrusive government because consumerism simply levelled the playing field. The whole purpose of such initiatives as a consumer's bill of rights was to empower citizens to act in their own best interest. Supporting health consumerism was a way of carving out a more active role for the state while perfecting the operations of the market.

If health consumerism served the interests of the American state and citizenry, it also served the interests of health professionals for a related reason. It was not just consumer choice that advocates of consumerism sought to promote, it was wise consumer choice. The emergence of a broader health culture, fuelled in part by health promotion, the fitness movement and alternative health movements, created a wide array of options for American consumers. Consumerism, as a vehicle for making choices, won approval from health care providers – among these the AMA and other licensing authorities – who saw it as a vehicle for educating patients about how best to spend their health care dollars, ensuring that they did not unwittingly fall prey to hucksterism and quackery. Thus, guides written for health consumers explained that the freedom to choose was something of a double-edged sword. 'Positively,' one put it, 'consumer health involves the information and understanding that enable individuals to make wise decisions about health services and products. Negatively, it refers to the avoidance of unwise decisions based on frauds, fads, fallacies, and superstitions' (Cornacchia and Barrett, 1989: 9). The *Guide* elaborated upon the advantages of health consumerism and the responsibilities of the health consumer: 'The intelligent consumer', it suggests:

> is well informed and knows where to obtain information to make sound decisions . . . seeks reliable sources of information . . . is skeptical about health information and does not accept statements appearing in the media, in advertisement or by anyone, on face value . . . is wary of inept practitioners, pseudopractitioners, and pitchmen in the business and medical worlds and can identify quacks and quackery . . . selects practitioners with great care and questions fees, diagnoses, treatments and alternative treatments . . . speaks out by reporting frauds, quackery and wrongdoing to business establishments, and to appropriate agencies and law enforcement officials.
>
> (Cornacchia and Barrett, 1989: 9–10)

In short, consumerism was a way of consolidating professional authority at a time when that authority appeared under threat.

The third set of origins of American health consumerism are what we will call populist and developed as one aspect of the challenge to professional authority to which we have just referred. In the United States, consumerism in medicine emerged coincidentally with the patient-advocacy/self-help movements and the women's/minority rights movements of the 1960s. These movements identified imbalances and inequities in political power and represented challenges to the authority of medicine, the state and other established institutions (Haug and Lavin, 1983: 16–18). Populist consumerism took hold particularly strongly among women. Healthy women, minority women, and women with disabilities alike demanded improved and more sensitive care, and in publications such as *Our Bodies Ourselves* advanced consumerism as an economic and political weapon. Employed correctly, consumerism would transform vulnerable and passive patients into powerful and active agents. As Marie Haug and Bebe Lavin have suggested, consumerism in this populist version represented an egalitarian, anti-credentialist challenge to the intellectual authority – or expertise – of the physician. Thus, it involved 'challenging the physician's ability to make unilateral decisions – demanding a share in reaching closure on diagnosis and working out treatment plans' (Haug and Lavin, 1983: 16–17). This brand of consumerism was enormously attractive because it reversed the conventional power relationship between physician and patient. It posed

> an authority challenge because it focuses on purchaser's [patient's] rights and seller's [physician's] obligations, rather than on physician's rights [to direct] and on patient obligations [to follow directions] . . . In a consumer relationship the seller has no particular authority; if anything, legitimated power rests in the buyer, who can make the decision to buy or not to buy, as he or she sees fit.
>
> (Haug and Lavin, 1981: 213)

The implications of this critique were as much economic as intellectual. As the women's health movement transformed the relationship between physician and patient within traditional medical relationships, it also broadened the definition of healing to include women's traditional and informal ways of knowing and the services of a wide range of non-medical health care providers. Hence, it contributed to the development of a medical marketplace in which women and minorities had 'choices' in health care that had been largely unavailable even a few years before.

COLONIZATION FROM THE US

We dwell on the origins of American health consumerism because it is impossible to evaluate the Canadian debate about consumer abuse without understanding how Canadians have appropriated and adapted the idea of

American health consumerism. For starters, much of the health consumer literature used in Canada is American; that this is taken by most participants in the health care debate to be perfectly normal or unexceptional reflects the extent to which the framework of debate regarding health consumerism has been globalized. Yet even in Canadian materials – popular literatures, government documents, and medical journals found in the consumer health information section of the Metro Toronto Reference Library for example – the American influence is apparent. The materials we have examined suggest that Canadian health consumers are portrayed in ways that respect and reflect the interests that generated the health consumer movement in the US thirty years ago – albeit adapted for the 1990s. In the current Canadian debate three common images or 'types' of Canadian health consumerism stand out: the empowered individual, the demanding patient or 'tyrantosauras Rex', and the responsible citizen.

The most common representation of the consumer found in Canada is a populist one in which the patient is transformed into a consumer for the ostensible purpose of 'empowerment'; here the rationale and rhetoric of American populist consumerism are adapted in an effort to redress the power imbalances in medicine. Variants of this image are typically found in women's health literatures – including writings on self-help and health promotion. The women's health literature advocates consumerism in three distinct but intersecting ways. First, the consumer is a woman who is widely read. She is knowledgeable about her illness and about options for treatment. Thus, the *Montreal Health Press*, *Healthsharing*, the Toronto Women's Health Network and other feminist collectives have published information that enables women to assume a more equal role in health care relationships. For example, in their article 'Staying Healthy: Constructive Change', contributed to the 'Healthwise' section of *Healthsharing Magazine*, Deborah Clark and Lenny Ashton recount the advantages of knowledge gleaned through 'local health units, public and medical libraries, collectives, self-help groups, health information networks, and other special interest organizations' (Clark and Ashton, 1987: 23). They recount the ways in which 'one woman's knowledge-backed assertiveness made a difference in the health care she eventually received: ... "I confronted my physician with my newly-gleaned information and insisted upon the use of one of these alternatives. Consequently, I was not made to endure a distasteful, uncomfortable and totally unnecessary procedure"' (Clark and Ashton, 1987: 23).

But Clark and Ashton also allude to another feature of this new equality. They engage in a semantic shift, in which the patient is transformed into a client. This shift restructures the intellectual power balance between patient and practitioner but also reshapes therapeutic relationships as business and marketing agreements. 'Ours is a consumer oriented society', they write:

> But while discretionary retail shoppers take precautions, such prudence seldom extends to the purchasing of services offered by medical

practitioners . . . the features of a blender are more often afforded serious consideration than are the attributes of a physician. This complaisance when dealing with doctors results from failure on the part of the general public to perceive medical services as commodities over which selectivity should be exercised . . .

(Clark and Ashton, 1987: 22)

Clark and Ashton now make the shift from referring to people, or the general public, to clients. 'There exists among clients of medical services a sort of vulnerable dependence' they maintain, and they advise their readers to 'Shop around . . . Clients, particularly women, must adopt a more realistic attitude towards the physician . . . It is sensible to suggest that partakers of medical services discriminate in their choice of physician, just as they do in acquiring other consumer services and goods' (Clark and Ashton, 1987: 22).

This shopping around or consumerism in medicine is presented as a form of taking responsibility. 'Clients must assume responsibility for their own health', Clark and Ashton suggest. But though Clark and Ashton emphasize the advantages to the individual inherent in consumerism and newfound 'responsibility', their work alludes to broader, collective goods. The assertive consumer protects herself from insensitive and inappropriate care, but she also reduces the use of expensive and 'unnecessary' procedures that cost the system. What one sees in the references to consumerism found in the women's health literature, then, is a dual appeal to individual and collective responsibility.

Consumerist language is also found in health promotion literatures, where, as in women's health, consumerism is linked to empowerment. Targeted to specific population groups – such as youth or the elderly, but also with the broader public in mind – health promotion encourages individuals to take charge of their health by avoiding those factors or behaviours (smoking, alcohol, fat-laden food, and sedentary lifestyles) that predispose towards disease. Enabling individuals to make 'wise' or 'healthy choices' is one goal of health promotion; reducing public expenditures on medical care is another. The choices advocated are consequently lifestyle choices. In this sense, the very essence of health promotion is consumerism – making wise choices about lifestyle and health-care dollars. And health promotion publications targeted to both users and providers adopt blatantly consumerist terms of marketing, advertising and spending.

Consumerism is also frequently alluded to in materials written by health care providers. The emergence of sub-specialities of women's health, health-promotion, and fitness have created an extensive health marketplace exemplified in magazines like *Prevention* or *Health*, in the proliferation of fitness and health-food stores, and in the emergence of numerous new kinds of health care providers – trainers, massage therapists, dietitians, etc. Clientelism initially became common among health care providers with special interests in women's health issues and broader fitness, health-promotion agendas. By referring to those to whom they provided care as clients, a range of complementary and alternative care providers – such as psychologists, naturopaths, massage thera- pists and others who could not bill publicly financed health plans – demon- strated their willingness to participate in the challenge to medical authority and to establish new kinds of therapeutic relationships. But references to clients, rather than patients, have become increasingly common among all the health care providers who deal with women. So, for example, the publications of Toronto's Women's College Hospital frequently refer to clients, as do those of government agencies such as federal and provincial Women's Health Bureaux. Advocates and purveyors of health promotion measures – whether publicly funded or private counsellors, dietitians, trainers, exercise clinics, etc. – market their services to clients. And clientelism has spread into other arenas of health care; the vision statement of City of North York Public Health Department indicates that some of its 'valued' work in 'health promo- tion, health protection and illness prevention... is done on a one-to-one personal basis with clients' (notice not 'citizens' or 'residents', or the 'public').

OFFICIAL DISCOURSE ON CONSUMERISM

Quite a different portrait of the consumer emerges in medical journals – most notably those of medical organizations such as the Ontario Medical Association or the Canadian Medical Association. Rather than representing consumers as a market ready for the taking, the Canadian Medical Association asks us to 'Shake hands with the patient of the 1990s – patient *triumphants*' (Ryval, 1993: 94). Where the women's and health literature presents consumerism as a means for reducing unnecessary health care spending, the Ontario Medical Association sees it as the very source of 'overutilization'. The problem with Canadian health care, a national survey of physicians suggested, is that 'we're now in an era of naked, "you-can-have-it" consumerism, fueled by an abun- dance of pop medical coverage in the media'. Seventy-one per cent of physicians polled believed that 'patients [were] better informed than five years ago' (Ryval, 1993: 99). And a solid majority believed that this has led to patients 'asking more questions about testing, treatments, drug effects and alternative therapies'. Patients who asked questions represented a challenge to the physi- cian's authority and 'increased consultation time... For doctors in private practice, demanding patients are time-gobblers... They come in with a shopping list... they demonstrate concern and inquisitiveness, [they are] aggressive' (Ryval, 1993: 109). Thus, from at least one medical perspective consumerism increases demand and costs.

The final group of references to consumerism is found in government publications. Here, consumers appear in two forms. One is the taxpayer who is not getting a good return on his/her investment. So, for example, one justification for 'user fees' is an appeal to individual self-interest based on the claim that millions of Canadians are 'subsidizing' others and should only pay for what they use. Provincial governments in Alberta and Ontario appeal to the astute consumer and advocate reductions in spending in order to give taxpayers a 'fairer' deal. Or, in the interests of restructuring and reform, district health councils, such as the Metropolitan Toronto District Health Council (MTDHC), appeal to public opinion. In its recent report on restructuring the MTDHC argued that

> public attitudes to health care are changing as people become more exacting about the quality of care offered, and increasingly demand that it be provided in an efficient and effective manner. The public wants compassionate and personal service. In addition, patients want to be more actively involved in decisions about treatment, are requesting improvements in information they receive, and wanting to become more educated about options.
>
> (MTDHC, 1995: 9)

In still another vein, governments adopt the same sort of language about responsibility that is present in women's health writings, and they encourage citizens to make wiser choices. For example, in the London Flu and Cold project, the Ontario government advised the public to exercise restraint and voluntarily ration its use of health care. Here, governments adopt American consumerist language, but they apply it to very different ends. Whereas Ralph Nader appeals to consumerism in order to increase equity and access and give Americans a fairer crack at the system, Canadian reformers of the 1990s have used it to decrease access, rein in spending, and dismantle universality.

The language of consumerism has consequently served several different Canadian interests – women and other disadvantaged populations who sought more equal standing in health care; health care providers who saw the benefits of pursuing a different kind of practice and cultivating clients; physicians, who found more demanding patients a threat to both their authority and the state-funding they received; and the state, which has appealed to consumers in its efforts to rein in the debt. There are two paradoxes to these uses of consumerism, however. First, all of the appeals to consumer interest conflate the attributes of consumerism and citizenship. As Michael Ignatieff suggests, it is as if all political rhetoric 'addresses the electorate not as citizens but as taxpayers or as consumers ... as if the market were determining the very language of political community' (Ignatieff, 1995: 71). In many different kinds of writings, and in popular discourse as well, the term 'consumer' is used interchangeably with 'patient' and 'citizen' and their distinct roles conflated. For example, the conference session in which this chapter was initially presented was 'Do Citizens Need Choices' and included papers on 'consumer abuse', 'consumer education' and the 'role of patients'. Similarly the Metropolitan Toronto District Health Council reframed concerns about equity, fairness, access and other ideals that have been fundamental to Canadian political communities in consumerist terms. Women's health writings have encouraged 'consumers' to take 'responsibility' and, along with health promotion tracts, appealed to 'community building' and 'empowerment'.

CANADA/US: DIVERGENT DISCOURSES

The second problem is that Canadians have imported the language and uses of consumerism from the United States, where those categories served very specific political purposes and contributed to a uniquely American conception of citizenship. In the United States, the conflation of citizens and consumers makes both conceptual and practical sense. As Judith Shklar has observed, the American understanding of citizenship developed in light of the powerful contradiction between the promise of democracy and the existence of slavery. To be a citizen in the United States meant that one was not a slave. Citizenship meant that one could vote and earn a wage, and those who were denied these rights – most notably women – frequently compared their state to slavery. Voting, of course, has 'always been a certificate of full membership' (Shklar, 1991: 2) in the United States. But as Shklar points out, earning a living (and by extension spending what one has earned) became an equally powerful symbol and determinant of public respect. To earn one's own living became 'the ethical basis' of American citizenship because it was only if one was economically independent that one could be politically free. Neither slavery nor aristocracy could be tolerated in such a system because neither was consistent with economic self-reliance; 'we are citizens only if we "earn"' (Shklar, 1991: 67). To spend what one had earned was, as a result, politically meaningful; to spend freely as a consumer was to remind others that one could be trusted to act freely as a citizen.

This understanding of citizenship as productive earning and consuming carried with it a series of other political commitments. It helps to explain the enormous American allegiance to, and faith in, free education, which was understood as a way of democratizing young people so that they would have control over their destiny. But most importantly, it helps to explain why movements of American consumerism, including health consumerism, blur the line between citizenship and consumerism. For consumer advocates like Ralph Nader, consumerism is explicitly defined as a form of democratic citizenship, for it depends upon (and cultivates) that combination of self-reliance and public concern that have been central to American public philosophy for two centuries. When 'a concerned public shops for value' (Cornacchia and Barrett, 1989: 7) the consumer and the citizen become one.

The problem is that 'consumerist citizenship' does not suit the Canadian context. We did not, after all, frame our public expectations in the shadow of slavery, and the Canadian attitude to aristocratic attitudes and institutions was different than in the US. Canadians have never been as single-mindedly devoted to the virtues of self-reliance as Americans (Risk and Vipond, 1996). Not surprisingly, Canadian public health policy has typically been more 'protective' than comparable American policy, and while education has played a part in the history of Canadian public health it does not dominate as it does south of the line. When it came to controlling diseases, such as tuberculosis, Americans adopted educational measures while Canadians mandated vaccination (Feldberg, 1995).

But most importantly, the existence of a publicly funded health care system in Canada stems from a conception of citizenship that differs in significant ways from the American. The Canadian health care system reflects a sort of civic bargain among citizens who consider themselves equal partners in a common enterprise; for whom being a citizen means in part to accept common obligations, like paying taxes for health care, that extend beyond a strict calculation of what is in one's own interest and around which social solidarity is built. Citizenship was levelling in that it made equals of those who had vastly differing financial resources. This is the foundation of the social welfare state that was developed in post-war federal Canada, and the sense of shared responsibility and obligation also enjoys constitutional status. Section 36 of the Charter of Rights, for instance, constitutionalizes the principle of equalization, and Section 1 tempers the absolutism of individual rights by acknowledging that they can be limited for the democratic needs of the whole.

Canadian health care has been remarkably successful in sustaining this sense of citizenship as obligation in the service of equity. Survey data, for instance, demonstrate clearly that Canadians identify what is distinctive about their country with the health care system, and the 1993 Canada Election Study in particular found a remarkable willingness among Canadians to continue to pay for publicly funded health care, even while they are willing (and in some cases perhaps anxious) to cut other public expenditures. The 1993 Canada National Election Study, which indicates that when asked whether they would personally be willing to pay higher taxes to maintain social programs such as health care many Canadians answered 'yes'. Moreover, when 3,775 Canadians were asked a series of questions about government spending the vast majority opposed cuts to social services: 71 per cent of respondents indicated that there should be no cuts to health spending; 25 per cent indicated that there should be some cuts to health spending; 3 per cent indicated that health spending should be cut a lot; only 1 per cent didn't know (Table 3.1). The study indicated a remarkable willingness to support social spending.

Table 3.1 Canada National Election Study, 1993

	No cuts (%)	Some cuts (%)	Large cuts (%)	Don't know (%)
Health care	71	25	3	1
Education	81	17	2	–
Old age security	80	17	2	1
Defence	15	48	35	2
Foreign aid	16	52	30	2

At the same time, the health care system in Canada, as elsewhere, is under enormous pressure in ways that strain the civic bargain that has sustained it so well and so long. The debate over consumer abuse is one of the symptoms of that strain. Our point, simply put, is that this debate needs to be seen for what it is – a debate about citizenship. Consumerism is relentlessly individualistic, and hence it makes no sense to say to a consumer that s/he is using up or wasting scarce resources. It does, however, make sense to say to citizens that they are using scarce resources frivolously or irresponsibly because citizens are by definition part of a larger community. If the consumer spends too much only s/he feels the effect; if the citizen abuses the system others feel it.

The debate about 'consumer abuse of health care' is thus a debate with at least two levels of meaning. It is about our willingness as citizens to ensure that 'the needs of strangers' are met; about finding the right balance between individual liberty and collective responsibility; and about maintaining social solidarity. Reframing a debate about citizenship in terms of consumer abuse is, therefore, unhelpful because consumerism is simply not the right idea to help us develop principles of justice that will engage that debate. At best, consumerism is connected, as in the United States, with a model of the citizen as an independent and self-reliant individual, a model which, whatever its merits, is not consistent with the common obligations Canadians continue to accept as citizens. The Keynsian welfare state and its universal social rights were always more than consumer rights because there was always a redistributional aspect to them. At worst, consumerism may actually corrode our collective will to sustain universal social programs by making it seem that 'smart shopping' is the best criterion by which to evaluate social programs and that 'niche marketing' will help provincial governments get out of the red.

But the debate is not just about citizen's obligations to each other; it is also about the state's investment in its citizenry. Public health measures, and state-sponsored health care, developed and flourished as vehicles that created a productive citizenry (Feldberg, 1995; Rosen, 1958, 1978; Tesh, 1988). As Rosen suggests, the apparatus for public health emerged with the nation-state's interest in cultivating population. 'This almost fanatical emphasis on a dense population', he argues, 'was justified on political, economic and military grounds... a larger population meant greater production as well as greater consumption' (1978: 19). The Canadian state's concern with public health, as it emerged during the era of the two world wars, was part of an effort to enhance military and civilian economic power. The state invested in health because it saw that investment as part of a reciprocal relationship. Investments in health would both promote citizenship and foster the greater economic good.

In the late twentieth century, broad investments in the health of populations appear less lucrative and rewarding to government than the opportunity to sell health care. For example, Alberta's Tory government reduced spending, limited access to services, and proposed user fees while also proposing that Alberta's hospitals open to 'American business'. That example suggests a transformation in the priorities of the state that has helped to reframe the health care debate in consumerist language.

It is this emerging debate that links the political theory of citizenship with the political economy of health reform. If the state enters the business of selling health care, and seeks to make a profit from that sale, then citizens are most valuable as consumers – their usefulness to the state is predicated on unequal buying power rather than on democratic standards that apportion citizenship equally. But what gets lost in the transformation of citizens to consumers, and by implication in current debates over health care restructuring, is both the greater idea or ideal of citizenship and the contextualized economics that accounts not just for the 'costs of abuse' but also for the costs of consumerism.

REFERENCES

Anon. 1995a. Physician Survey on Health-Care Reform. *Ontario Medical Review* (January): 22–29.

Anon. 1995b. Surprising Returns: Canadians Confound the Conventional Wisdom. *Maclean's Magazine* (1 July): 15.

Bagley, G. 1994. Reorganization of Canada's Hospitals Likely to have Major Impact on M.Ds, Consultant Says. *Canadian Medical Association Journal* 151: 1747–1748.

Cathell, D. W. 1882. *The Physician Himself and Things that Concern His Reputation and Success.* Philadephia, PA: F. A. Davis.

Clark, D. and L. Ashton. 1987. Staying Healthy: Constructive Change. *Healthsharing* (Winter): 22–23.

CMAJ. 1994. Manitoba Patient Sees 71 Physicians, Makes 247 Office Visits in 1 Year. *Canadian Medical Association Journal* 150 (6): 939.

Cornacchia, H. and S. Barrett. 1989. *Consumer Health: A Guide to Intelligent Decisions* (4th edn). St. Louis: Times Mirror/Mosby.

Coutts, J. 1996. Saskatchewan Doctors Urged to Limit Use of Ultrasound. *Globe and Mail* (22 March): A4.

Emson, H. E. 1994. Health Care Abuse. *Canadian Medical Association Journal* 150 (9): 1378–1379.

Feldberg, G. 1995. *Disease and Class: Tuberculosis and the Shaping of Modern North American Society.* New Brunswick, NJ: Rutgers.

French, O. 1995. Concern over Fraud Causes Ontario to Invest $90 million in New Health Cards. *Canadian Medical Association Journal* 152 (4): 569–570.

Haug, M. and B. Lavin. 1981. Practitioner or Patient – Who's in Charge? *Journal of Health and Social Behaviour* 22: 212–229.

Haug, M. and B. Lavin. 1983. *Consumerism in Medicine: Challenging Physician Authority.* Beverly Hills: Sage.

Henry, J. 1995. Debating the Role of Private Funding in Ontario Health Care. *Ontario Medical Review* (March 1995): 48–49.

Ignatieff, M. 1995. The Myth of Citizenship. In R. Beiner (ed.) *Theorizing Citizenship*. Albany, NY: SUNY.

Metropolitan Toronto District Health Council (MTDHC). 1995. *Directions for Change: Toward a Coordinated Hospital System for Metro Toronto*. Toronto: MTDHC.

North York Public Health Department. 1995. *A Strategic Plan for the City of North York Public Health Department*. North York: NYPHD.

Ontario, Legislative Assembly. 1995. Standing Committee on General Government, Hearings on Savings and Restructuring Act, 1995.

O'Reilly, M. 1994. Don't Seek Medical Help for Minor Problems, Ontario Pilot Project Tells Patients. *Canadian Medical Association Journal* 151 (2): 201–202.

Risk, R. and R. Vipond. 1996. Rights Talk in Canada in the Late Nineteenth Century: The Good Sense and the Right Feeling of the People. *Law and History Review* 14 (1): 1–32.

Rosen, G. 1958. *The History of Public Health*. New York: MD Publications.

Rosen, G. 1978. Cameralism and the Concept of Medical Police. In G. Rosen (ed.) *From Medical Police to Social Medicine*. New York: Prodist.

Rusk, J. 1997. Focus Fraud War, OHIP Urged. *Globe and Mail* (30 September): A5.

Ryval, M. 1993. Welcome to Jurassic Practice where the Patient is 'Tyrantosaurus' Rex. *Medical Post*. Special Volume, National Survey of Canadian Doctors: 94–111.

Shklar, J. 1991. *American Citizenship: The Search for Inclusion*. Cambridge, MA: Harvard.

Tesh, S. N. 1988. *Hidden Arguments: Political Ideology and Disease Prevention Policy*. New Brunswick, NJ: Rutgers.

Tuohy, C. J. 1992. *Policy and Politics in Canada: Institutionalized Ambivalence*. Philadelphia, PA: Temple University Press.

Watson, W. C. and D. Boyd. 1994. Health Care Abuse. *Canadian Medical Association Journal* 150 (1): 11.

Williams, L. S. 1993. Fiscal Problems Forcing Provinces to Take Closer Look at Health Care Fraud. *Canadian Medical Association Journal* 148 (11): 2003–2006.

4 Cost-containment and privatization:

An international analysis

Art Stewart

There are four unpleasant lessons to be learned at the institutional level if cost containment is to succeed: Government must be given a strong regulatory hand; there must be some form of universal health care coverage; freedom of choice must be limited; and technology assessment must be superintended by a willingness to apply strict standards of efficacy based on some substantive view of human well-being – and by a willingness to use these standards to reduce or eliminate the use of effective technologies when unaffordable, not just those that are ineffective or marginally effective.

(Callahan, 1990: 98)

INTRODUCTION

This chapter focuses on cost containment and efficiency enhancing strategies that alter the public–private mix in health care financing and delivery in leading jurisdictions. These strategies redistribute the benefits and costs of health care, often through processes of privatization. I argue, in a comparative perspective, that cost containment necessarily involves privatization in some dimension of the health care system, with much of it occurring 'passively' or 'by stealth'. Privatization is largely a by-product of cost containment strategies applied stringently, but may also result as a by-product of strategies that enhance the efficiency of health care delivery.[1] My contention is that if privatization is to occur it should be the result of an explicit, inclusive and informed public debate that generates a set of priorities for the financing and delivery of health care, and that includes an understanding of the full consequences of health care reform. The public debate in industrialized countries has largely treated privatization in the dichotomous terms of markets versus regulation with the more extreme versions of these stories dominating the debate. Privatization in health care is a much more complex and subtle process. So far policy-makers have ignored this fact.

Robert Evans has it exactly right when he refers to 'the ambiguity of any assignment of health care policies to the categories "regulation" or "market-based"' (Evans, 1996: 97). Such debates tend to be ideologically motivated and there is a clear danger that we may lose sight of the myriad policy objectives assigned to health care systems in favour of a blind adherence to purely private, market-based systems or to purely public systems.

Of course, privatization means different things to different people. Muschell defines privatization as 'a *process* in which non-government actors become increasingly involved in the financing and/or provision of health care services' (Muschell, 1995: sect. 1.1), and argues that a distinction is necessary between the process of privatization and the public–private mix in health care. Privatization involves changes in public and private roles and responsibilities, and *may* lead to changes in the public–private mix of health care financing.

Consider the following classification of mixes of private and public responsibility in the predominant parts of health services among the G7:

- public provision with public financing (United Kingdom, Italy, parts of the French and German systems);
- public provision with private financing (France, Italy, Japan and Germany impose user charges for publicly provided services, mainly in public hospitals and health centres);
- private provision with public financing (Canada, Japan, parts of the French and German systems);
- private provision with private financing (United States, except Medicaid and Medicare).

This rough and ready classification does not do justice to the complexities of these health care systems, but does serve to give a sense of the broad range of public–private arrangements in the G7.

The classification also masks the role of citizens as both consumers and providers in the health care system. We must recognize that if all resources devoted to producing health care were to be appropriately valued, *all* health care systems would appear as much more private. For example, Angus *et al.* (1995) report that as much as 94 per cent of elder care may come through family, friends and others in the informal care sector. They also estimate that the value of family care may be as high as $4 billion in Canada. Adding other unaccounted types of informal care, all of which use scarce resources, suggests that the burden of health care is much more private than is commonly held to be the case. It is argued below that one of the ways privatization is being manifest in Canada is through an increasing reliance on the informal care sector, a form of privatization that is placing an undue burden on women as caregivers.[2]

Why then should we express a concern for the public–private mix in health care financing and for processes of privatization that alter the mix? Quite simply, our ability to deliver on the goals of the health care system is affected by the balance between public and private financing. Privatization is first and foremost about the distribution of health care costs and benefits, but may also have efficiency and cost implications. In the latter case, the standard economic argument is that private markets, guided by self-interest and profit maximization, will generate a more efficient allocation of resources than will public sector provision. For well-known theoretical reasons,[3] there is no a priori reason to believe that this is so in health care. The empirical evidence suggests that both those systems that are most 'purely private' and those that are most 'purely public' face significant problems in delivering on efficiency, and that proper 'market-type' incentives in the context of 'public control' is our best avenue to control costs and enhance efficiency. Thus, privatization may see the state using market mechanisms in the pursuit of public goals at the same time that it tries to limit market forces that decrease equity and access to the system (Ruggie, 1996)[4].

EQUITY, ACCESS AND REDISTRIBUTION IN THE HEALTH CARE SYSTEM[5]

The equitable distribution of health care has a variety of dimensions. Notions of horizontal equity figure in the health care debate, especially as it relates to differential access. Horizontal equity refers to the principle that individuals in 'like' circumstances should be treated in 'like' manner. In the context of health care, horizontal equity should be taken as meaning that those with like health care needs should be treated in a similar manner.[6] The reallocation of resources that follows upon the pursuit of cost control and some efficiency enhancing strategies may well violate this principle. In the most general sense, these strategies change the institutional rules of the game, affect provider treatment patterns, and may induce governments to close facilities. The key point is that health care resources are redistributed geographically and across treatments, creating winners and losers among patient groups.

A second element of equity relevant to this discussion is vertical equity. A program that achieves vertical equity should result in a redistribution from those individuals/families with higher incomes to those with lower incomes. The structure of public health insurance in Canada, for example, achieves a number of redistributive purposes. First, the system delivers health care benefits on the basis of need rather than ability to pay. Given that those in lower income groups suffer greater incidence of ill health and access the health care system more frequently than other income groups, there will be progressive redistribution on the consumption side of the health care system. In terms of financing, the provinces have chosen a variety of methods to pay for health care, some of which are more progressive than others. For example, financing health care out of general tax revenues (primarily income taxes) will be progressive provided the income tax system as a whole is progressive, but financing health care via a payroll tax will generally be less so and may be regressive. Ruggeri *et al.* (1996) have recently suggested that Canadian spending on health care is distributed in a progressive manner, especially for lower income groups.

A final notion of equity is an intergenerational one. In per capita terms, the elderly consume health care resources at a rate four times greater than the non-elderly. Individuals tend to have lower incomes when they retire and therefore a reduced ability to pay for health care at precisely the time when health care needs are greatest. The presence of a universal health care scheme can be seen as protecting particularly vulnerable seniors from catastrophic financial burdens due to illness later in life.

THE PUBLIC–PRIVATE MIX IN HEALTH CARE

Basic health care financing data for 1993, including the public–private mix in officially measured health care expenditures, is shown in Table 4.1 for a selection of fifteen OECD countries. The United States devotes the largest fraction of GDP to health care, followed by Canada and Switzerland, while Denmark, the United Kingdom and Japan devote the smallest fraction of GDP to health care. In terms of per capita spending the big three do not change, but the United Kingdom is joined by New Zealand and Sweden as the lowest spenders. The United States ranks lowest in public share of total spending, although the number masks generous tax treatment of employer contributions to employee health plans that may add as much as 8–9 percentage points to the public share. Other low public spenders include Australia and Switzerland, although both are closes to the norm than to the United States, Norway, the United Kingdom and Sweden boast the largest public sector share in total spending, although only Norway is much distanced from the norm. Canada

Table 4.1 Health care financing, selected OECD countries, 1993

Country	Total spending as a % of GDP	Rank of 15	Per capita spending in US dollars	Rank of 15	Public share of total spending	Rank of 15
Australia	8.5	8	1493	10	67.7	14
Canada	10.2	2	1971	3	71.9	10
Denmark	6.7	15	1296	12	82.6	4
Finland	8.8	5	1363	11	79.3	5
France	9.8	4	1835	4	74.4	8
Germany	8.6	7	1815	5	70.2	12
Italy	8.5	8	1523	8	73.1	9
Japan	7.3	13	1495	9	71.8	11
The Netherlands	8.7	6	1531	7	77.7	6
New Zealand	7.7	11	1179	15	77.2	7
Norway	8.2	10	1592	6	93.3	1
Sweden	7.5	12	1266	13	82.9	3
Switzerland	9.9	3	2283	2	69.0	13
United Kingdom	7.1	14	1213	14	83.0	2
United States	14.1	1	3299	1	43.9	15

Source: Adapted from Canadian Medical Association (1995).

ranked tenth, but at 71.9 per cent is close to the norm. In most countries, the public share in total health spending has also been decreasing since the mid-1970s.[7] However, we must exercise caution in such statements because the picture of privatization that is painted depends very much on what is measured. For example, Stewart (1996) argues that, if measured in real per capita terms, private health expenditures as a percentage of total health expenditures fell between 1980 and 1992, and were actually lower in 1994 than in 1975. This is in stark contrast to the story outlined above. However, it is true that both indicators reveal increased privatization in recent years.

Figure 4.1 presents total health spending as a proportion of GDP in selected OECD countries. The public–private split in health care for selected OECD countries is further revealed in Tables 4.2 and 4.3. Table 4.2 outlines the major financing arrangements, including the various services that are excluded from public insurance, and the mix of public and private providers. Table 4.3 focuses on the extent of consumer cost-sharing through co-insurance, deductibles and user fees. Canada is relatively unique among the countries selected in having a health care system that is primarily publicly financed through taxation and delivered by mainly private providers. Private financing arises through exclusions from public health insurance rather than through cost-sharing within the public program. In general, Canadian public health insurance has a narrower coverage base than other public systems within the OECD, with the exception of the United States.[8] At the same time, only the United Kingdom imposes as few cost-sharing charges as Canada. Interestingly, the traditional welfare states of Western Europe and Scandinavia, both corporatist and social democratic, impose significant cost-sharing within their public systems, although most also feature exemptions to protect access to needed services.

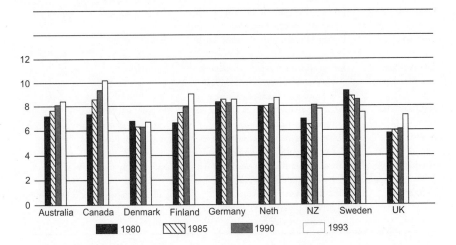

Figure 4.1 Total health expenditure as a percentage of GDP in selected countries, 1980–1993.

Table 4.2   Public–private split in health care, selected OECD countries, 1993

Country	Financing and provision	Exclusions in social insurance
Canada	Financed mainly by taxation with mainly private providers	Sanatoria, out of hospital dental care, non-hospital drugs (some exceptions for seniors), varying degrees for prostheses, spectacles, hearing aids, and treatment in private hospitals
France	Financed mainly by social insurance with mixed public and private providers	Spectacles, dentures and replacement dental treatment
Germany	Financed mainly by social insurance with mixed public and private providers	Virtually none
Italy	Financed almost equally by social insurance with mainly public providers	Virtually none
Japan	Financed mainly by social insurance with mixed public and private providers	Inoculations, health check-ups, private rooms, eyeglasses, and health promotions for the elderly
United Kingdom	Financed mainly by taxation with mainly public providers	Dental care and optical care (except for low income groups), and low-cost pharmaceuticals
United States	Financed mainly by private voluntary insurance with mainly private providers	Medicare excludes long-term home care, out-patient pharmaceuticals, routine eye care and dental treatment
Australia	Financed mainly by taxation with mixed public and private providers	Dental care (limited for specific groups) and pharmaceuticals (some subsidies)
Denmark	Financed mainly by taxation with mainly public providers	Virtually none
Finland	Financed mainly by taxation with mainly public providers	Virtually none
The Netherlands	Financed by a mixture of social and private insurance with mainly private providers	Spectacles
New Zealand	Financed mainly by taxation with mainly private providers	Ambulatory care for higher income groups, dental care and glasses
Norway	Financed mainly by taxation with mainly public providers	Virtually none
Sweden	Financed mainly by taxation with mainly public providers	Low-cost medicines
Switzerland	Financed mainly by voluntary private insurance with mainly private providers	Spa hotel charges, dental treatment, prostheses, glasses and hearing aids

Source: Adapted from OECD Health Policy Study No. 5 (1994:1), and OECD Health Policy Study No. 7 (1995b: Table 17).

Table 4.3 Cost-sharing for health care, selected OECD countries, 1993, US dollars

Country	GP	Specialist	Drugs	In-patient care
United States	20% in excess of $100 deductible, lower deductibles in HMOs	20% in excess of $100 deductible, lower deductibles in HMOs	100%, lower in HMOs	$676 deductible first six days, lower deductibles in HMOs
Japan	Employees 10% of costs, dependants 20%, self-employed 30%	As for GP	As for GP	As for GP
Germany	None	None	$1.25 per prescription (many exemptions)	$3
France	25%, more if extra-billing, many exemptions	25%, more if extra-billing, many exemptions	30–100% depending on the drug	$5–6/day plus 20% of total cost for first 30 days
Italy	None	$7–8	$3 plus 50% or $0	—
United Kingdom	None	None	$4–5 per prescription or $65 per season ticket; many exemptions	None
Canada	None	None	Varies by province	None
Australia	For 25% of bills average of $5	For 71% of bills average of $8	Maximum $11 per prescription	None
Denmark	None except for 3% of population	None except for 3% of population	0/25/50%	None
Finland	$17	$17	60% in excess of $8	$22
The Netherlands	None for publicly covered patients, private patients varies by policy	As for GP	Flat rate per drug with annual selling of $67 per household (public insurance)	—
New Zealand	Extra-billing	Out-patients $3–17	$2–8 with stop loss	None
Norway	$11	$16	25% if on blue ticket, max. $43 per prescription	None
Sweden	$6–19	$17	First drug $15 then $1 each	$8
Switzerland	10%	10%	$7	$7

Source: Adapted from OECD Health Policy Study No. 7 (1995b: Table 18).

COST CONTAINMENT AND EFFICIENCY ENHANCING STRATEGIES

Cost containment and efficiency enhancing strategies in a variety of OECD countries involve four kinds of policy instruments. The policy instruments include:

- *global budgeting* (may be sectoral or system-wide), including the means of allocating budgets (prospective payment schemes, diagnostic-related groups, etc.);
- *direct consumer cost-sharing* through user fees, copayments, deductibles, etc., typically at the point of service;
- *supply-side measures*, including the creation of internal markets or managed competition;
- *other direct privatizations* of health care expenditure (de-listing, de-insurance, introduction of voluntary parallel private insurance, etc.).

Global budgeting

Global budgeting is among the most important supply levers used to control overall budget controls on health expenditures, especially in the hospital sector. All such global policies share one common feature: strong monopsony (single payer) power in dealing with providers (OECD, 1995b; Evans, 1996). The ability to exercise monopsony power depends on the organization of provider–purchaser–payer relationships, especially the degree of centralization/decentralization of spending and the complexities of the flow of funds. The United Kingdom has been successful in controlling costs within the NHS because there is a single payer with strong central control over the budgets of hospital and physician sectors. In recent years, British cost containment has been *relatively* less successful, with the introduction of elements of competition and the attendant reduction in central control of the health care system. This may simply reflect a more costly transition period as players learn in the context of a new institutional structure, or it may be a more permanent manifestation of decreased control.

The massive and unprecedented social and economic experiment in New Zealand since 1984 has included an effort to maintain central control over health care budgets, while introducing greater regional control over health care purchasing and delivery, and increasing reliance on private funding of health care (Kelsey, 1995). Again, the weakening of central control over expenditures has resulted in New Zealand being relatively less successful than other OECD countries in cost containment in recent years. The creation of internal markets may result in spillovers that are difficult to control and enhanced privatization has enhanced the opportunity to spend via alternative funding sources.

In systems where local, county, regional, provincial or state governments are responsible for health care delivery but receive significant funding from central governments, overall expenditure control can be more difficult (OECD, 1995a). In Sweden, which has been remarkably successful in reducing the share of GDP devoted to health care, central government prohibited tax increases by county councils between 1988 and 1994, thus extending central control over costs. In Canada, significant reductions in federal transfers to the provinces, first through the Established Programs Financing arrangements and more recently through the Canada Health and Social Transfer, have played an important role in bringing cost containment considerations to the fore in the provinces.

In social insurance systems, which feature a large number of sickness funds, successful macro-level budget controls require coordinated action on the part of funds, accompanied by restrictions on health insurance premium increases (OECD, 1995b). Germany has enjoyed remarkable success in cost containment since 1977, primarily owing to a series of Cost-Containment Acts (CCAs). In keeping with the corporatist nature of the country, German cost control is the product of negotiated agreements between sickness fund physicians and sickness funds.[9] The 1977 CCA introduced a revenue-oriented approach to health care expenditure regulation, i.e., the growth of sickness fund expenditures is related to the growth of revenues which, in turn, are based on contributions related to the wages of fund members (Schneider, 1994; Ulrich, 1996). The 1977 CCA also created the Concerted Action for Health Affairs, which includes the major stakeholders and makes recommendations to improve the efficacy and efficiency of the health care system. The Concerted Action is the vehicle which lays the basis for ongoing negotiations over the sickness fund expenditures and other global budgeting initiatives. Subsequent CCAs have extended the goal of cost containment and introduced expenditure caps into the hospital sector and on physician expenditures.

Governments have also expressed concern about cost control in the adoption and diffusion of medical technology. White (1995) argues that the American system does not feature any mechanisms to control the 'medical arms race' among hospitals, a factor that many authors believe contributes to the high cost of American health care. Fuchs (1993) suggests that the absence of control over the innovation and diffusion of medical technology means that other cost control measures have, at best, a one-time impact on health care costs. He also notes that:

> In the long run, changes in the rate, or at least the character of technological innovation must play a critical role in slowing the rate of growth of health care expenditures.
>
> (Fuchs, 1993: 181)

Countries that have been relatively successful in cost containment have some measure of control over the diffusion of medical technology. Although a variety of methods are used, all feature a strong role for payers in controlling the adoption and diffusion of technology in the hospital sector. Lassey, *et al.* (1997)

claim that cultural factors may be an important determinant of the spread of medical technology. For example, in The Netherlands, physician conservatism and a reluctance to openly discuss cancer with patients is partly responsible for a hesitation to recommend advanced treatments.

Enhancing the efficiency of health care provision through the elimination of non-beneficial and cost-ineffective technologies frees scarce resources for more beneficial uses. Cost control may result in some costs being privatized if patients and their families are required to travel to regional medical centres for treatment rather than being served in their communities, but these costs are relatively minor. In any event, government support programs can be made available to assist low-income families and others in need to ensure that access and equity are maintained.

In general, global budgeting represents the most effective means of containing growth in health care expenditures, especially if the controls are applied on a system-wide basis. Partial controls may be associated with cost spillovers into uncontrolled sectors or into the private sector. The latter is of special concern because it is often accompanied by calls for increased access to private sources of care and for an increased role for private insurance, at least by those with the ability to pay.

Direct cost-sharing

Direct cost-sharing is the most visible instrument of privatization. Its value in cost containment is based on the assumption that when health care consumers are forced to pay out-of-pocket (typically at the point of service) for services, they will reduce their demand for services. In the process, pressure on health care costs will be eased. The empirical evidence on the effectiveness of cost-sharing in reducing costs is inconclusive. In countries that have experience with cost-sharing, it seems that the user charges must be relatively large in order to have a clear effect in reducing the use of health care resources. Smaller user fees may reduce public health care costs, but do not necessarily reduce total expenditure because direct user charges offer providers an alternative source of financing that maintains service volumes. The OECD (1995b) argues that cost-sharing can have its desired effect in cost containment if (1) the charges are large enough to affect consumer behaviour, (2) private insurance is not allowed to cover the cost-shared component, (3) providers are not able to adjust prices to offset the effects of reduced service volume, and (4) administrative costs do not swamp cost savings that arise.

The major concern about cost-sharing is that it will have a negative impact on equity and access because health status and therefore health needs tend to vary inversely with income. Cost-sharing makes the financing of health care more regressive in countries with social insurance premiums related to income and in countries where health care is financed through progressive taxation. User charges may also result in a transfer of income from the sick and from low-income groups to those who are healthy and in higher-income groups. In intergenerational terms, there would also be a transfer from the sick elderly, who are more intensive users of health care, to the healthy non-elderly.

Cost-sharing might also be used to enhance efficiency within the health care sector. User charges could be imposed on the inappropriate use of certain facilities, providers or treatments in order to improve the allocation of resources. The point is not to reduce costs *per se* by reducing the total volume of services, but to redirect consumers to more appropriate facilities, providers or services. In this context, user charges are unlikely to have a significant impact on equity or access, provided alternative facilities, providers or services are reasonably available. At the same time, we must recognize that the administrative costs will be onerous and may well outweigh the benefits associated with improved resource allocation.

Solid empirical evidence concerning the impacts of user charges is relatively difficult to come by. The most cited study is that of the RAND Health Insurance Experiment, summarized in Newhouse (1993). The key result of the study is that significant cost-sharing in the form of insurance copayments will reduce the demand for health care, with a relatively larger effect on the demand of low-income groups. Although in general health outcomes were not affected in the experiment, there were conditions for which the health outcomes of low-income individuals were adversely affected. In addition, the study revealed that user charges did not encourage greater efficiency, in the sense that both 'needed' and 'unneeded' contacts with health care providers were reduced about equally. Thus it seems that cost-sharing can reduce the demand for health care and therefore potentially the costs of health care, at least in the context of a private health insurance scheme, but the reduction comes at the cost of equity and access. There are, quite simply, far more effective cost containment and efficiency enhancing tools available.

Implicit in the standard economic models of market allocation is the idea that charging a price to consumers will give consumers some power in the market. If a provider does not measure up in terms of price or quality, consumers can redirect their spending to alternative providers. Prices act as signals in the context of competitive markets and are the primary mechanism for rationing goods and services and allocating resources. Thus, direct cost-sharing might be thought of as a means to address the imbalance of power in health care, especially the imbalance between consumers and providers. Clearly, prices can serve this function, but they are not the only means of doing so, nor in the context of the uniqueness of health care are they the best means of doing so. Prior to recent reforms, a Swedish patient presented to a local primary health care centre and was assigned to a provider for treatment. The user charge associated with the visit was simply directed to the appropriate county council and served no purpose other than revenue raising. Patient choice and price were unrelated to resource allocation. Cost-sharing is a mechanism of *privatization* that results in a shift of the financing burden towards private sources of financing and away from public sources of financing, even though it does not necessarily result in a lower total expenditure on health care.

Supply-side measures

Many OECD countries have also tried to grapple with cost containment through improvements in efficiency. They have varied in their approaches, with some opting for 'managed competition' models, others pursuing 'internal market' options, and yet others the more limited 'public competition' options. As Soderstrom (1994) notes, the supply side contains six structural elements: the types of providers, the organization of providers, the payment mechanisms, the regulatory environment, the information available to providers and managers, and the management of the overall supply side itself. Thus, supply side measures may also include actions that are not a necessary part of the creation of managed competition, internal markets or public competition. Such actions might include changing physician remuneration mechanisms to change the incentives faced by physicians, generating better information with regard to the effectiveness and efficiency of different health services, or changing the role of physicians so as to strengthen gatekeeper functions in an attempt to control hospital and/or specialist costs.

In the United Kingdom, cost control was achieved through national global budgeting, with recent NHS reforms[10] being directed to increasing efficiency in the allocation of resources (Glennerster, 1995; Maynard, 1995). The reforms may be thought of as attempting to overcome the negative impact of cost containment on access and choice (Glennerster, 1995), although Maynard (1995) suggests that the reforms have lost sight of these goals and are also in danger of compromising the goal of cost containment. Maynard argues that the British reforms have been poorly targeted and not evidence-based. To date, the evidence seems to suggest that there has been little improvement in access or consumer choice, although administrative costs have increased. The efficiency gains may yet appear and reverse the more rapid increase in British health care costs as a percentage of GDP that has been a feature of the years immediately following the reforms.

New Zealand has also undertaken major supply-side reforms in an effort to increase efficiency, involve the consumer more directly in health care choices, and contain costs. In essence, the New Zealand reform plan, like that in the United Kingdom, was formulated to change a system of public provision and purchase of health care into a system that would feature 'a provider–purchaser split in which public hospitals would become independent, competing businesses and district health authorities (precursors to AHBs) would contract with providers for services' (Anderson, 1996: 78–79). However, unlike the British reforms, New Zealand would also introduce user charges for in-patient services and redefine the role of core health care services. The reforms have generated mixed results. Anderson (1996) reports that the general public are confused by the reforms, which were overly marketed as a means for consumers to have a greater say in the delivery of health care. For most, little seems to have changed except the names of the facilities that deliver care. The reforms have generated needed rationalizations and greater efficiencies in many parts of the health care system and are especially promising in the creation of integrated, community-based care. However, the restructuring of public hospitals into Crown Health Enterprises (CHEs) has not been a particularly successful venture (Kelsey, 1995). CHEs are subject to an expenditure cap, but are expected to contract competitively with suppliers and staff and to compete for patients. In the early 1990s, CHE expenditures exceeded revenues, leading government to cover increasing debts. With local hospital closures and a decline in the number of public hospital beds, the number of private beds increased and CHEs were forced to begin to prioritize patients on the basis of cost considerations.

The New Zealand experiment did have a major impact in terms of privatization. Between 1991 and 1993, the public share in health spending fell from 82 per cent to 76 per cent. Cost-shifting to private sources has occurred. Kelsey (1995) reports that private health insurance coverage, which can include the reimbursement of user charges, increased from 40 per cent of the population in 1991 to 55 per cent of the population in 1995. Increased waiting times for a range of procedures within the public system also became increasingly common, as did decreased access by low-income families.

Health care reform in Sweden was based on an enhanced role for consumer choice, new mechanisms of provider remuneration, and the introduction of public competition within the context of a system of global budgeting and salaried physicians. Sweden has been remarkably successful in containing health care costs when measured as a percentage of GDP. From a position of having health care expenditures approximately the same as those in Canada and the United States between 1960 and 1980 (Rhenberg, 1995), Sweden has moved to become one of the lowest spenders, with further decreases anticipated. Part of this success involves a transfer of health care expenditures on residential care for the elderly to the social envelope, leading to a reduction of approximately 0.6 percentage points in health as a percentage of GDP. Even allowing for this, Sweden's cost containment exercise has been a remarkable success. The primary reason for the success is the degree of control over costs permitted by a single payer system with salaried physicians and the control which the central government has over the local taxes that are used to finance health care. Indeed, from 1988 through 1993, the central administration did not permit any increases in county taxes, thus exercising effective control over all revenue dimensions of the health care system. The majority of this success has come in the absence of public competition or internal markets. However, the nature of the Swedish system is such that productivity is low and there is little consumer choice because patients are assigned to a particular institution for service, including primary care (Rhenberg, 1995). This is the motivating factor behind the introduction of market elements within the Swedish health care system.

Although the reforms vary across jurisdictions, the essence of Swedish health care reforms is the move from a fully publicly administered system with little or no consumer choice to a system that includes consumer choice and competition among public providers. The key elements of the reform package are collective purchasing units, provider competition, contracts and performance-based remuneration, provider autonomy, and consumer choice (Rhenberg, 1995). These changes may represent a move away from an interventionist policy regime in the context of a social democratic welfare state and towards a more integrative policy regime in the sense discussed by Ruggie (1996). To the extent that greater contracting and negotiation among players are part of the introduction of the reforms, and to the extent that this represents a more even distribution of power within the health care system, the reforms may be thought of as contributing to the emergence of an integrative policy regime.

The introduction of market elements on the supply-side of the Swedish health care system has had little impact on access in the sense that the reforms affirm the basic principle of access to health care on equal conditions for all (Jönsson, 1996). However, if access is construed to include consumer choice among providers, then the reforms, which include allowing a patient to enrol with a particular family doctor, may improve access. Saltman (1995) argues that the competition for patients has helped to alleviate the lengthy queuing that has been associated with elective procedures.

It is important to note that the Swedish, British and other Nordic country reforms do not introduce competition on the financing side, nor is there any attempt to privatize financing (other than marginal increases in user charges). The primary concern of supply-side measures is to change the steering mechanism that directs the allocation of resources under a global budget cap (Saltman, 1995). However, public competition does alter the roles and relationships of the various actors. Prior to reforms, the Nordic countries and the United Kingdom are best characterized as interventionist policy regimes with political authority and direction functioning as the primary mechanism for resource allocation. Reforms go some way to altering this balance of power. In all of the aforementioned countries, primary care political boards, institutions and provider groups have been given greater control over large parts of the spending envelope, and the Swedish and Finnish reforms also feature an emphasis on consumer choice and therefore a greater role for patients in the allocation of resources (Saltman, 1995). The relationship between physicians and payers is also changing, moving away from salaried remuneration and towards a system that links remuneration to performance. This will undoubtedly affect the relationship between physicians and their patients, likely in ways that make physicians more responsive to patient concerns. The unifying element in these actions is a fundamental alteration in the distribution of power among the actors, generally in a way that is consistent with a less interventionist policy regime and that heralds the emergence of an integrative policy regime. It seems that the state will play a less interventionist role in the allocation of health care resources, but will continue to play a major role in ensuring that the public values and goals that underpin the health care system are maintained.

The important lesson, within the context of publicly financed health insurance and a commitment to access, is that the introduction of supply-side measures need not lead to increased privatization in financing. However, there is a danger that the increased competition and accountability that accompany such actions may lead to resource rationalizations that reduce needed and effective services and shift the burden of health care to private sources, both formal and informal. This source of privatization is not necessarily detrimental to horizontal equity but may reduce access for all citizens. Supply-side measures that are introduced in a reactive, piecemeal fashion are more likely to generate negative consequences than are those that result from a coordinated plan based on well-defined priorities and guided by a concern that access be protected.

Private insurance

Most OECD nations feature some role for private insurance, either as a supplement to or in competition with publicly insured health care. In France, supplementary private insurance covers 87 per cent of the population and is used primarily to cover the costs associated with user charges and extra-billing. Italy, Germany and the United Kingdom have small, but growing, private insurance sectors. In the UK, private insurance covers treatment received in private facilities and is often used to complement publicly insured services. In Italy, private insurance is primarily the domain of high-income individuals seeking treatment in private facilities, and is perceived to be of higher quality than the service provided by the national health service. Private insurance in Germany is strictly regulated, but may be used to cover treatment in public or private facilities. Norway, Sweden and Finland feature virtually no role for private insurance, while Denmark offers three levels of care through a private non-profit insurer, mainly to reimburse costs not covered under the public health scheme.

Other countries, such as the United States and Switzerland feature a dominant role for private insurers, while in The Netherlands private insurance provided through private sickness funds is a prominent part of the financing landscape. In general, the case against private insurance rests on observations about the system of health insurance in the United States, where many millions of citizens are not covered by any form of health insurance. The United States is an exception in the form of its heavy reliance on private insurance arrangements and should not be the basis for the case against a minor role for private insurance that runs in parallel to the public system. Health care systems that rely primarily on private insurance arrangements are less successful in cost containment than are those that rely on public funding. The major problem with private insurance is *cream-skimming*, which can result in limited access to health care for certain categories of patients. Cream-skimming may also lead to efficient insurers being driven out of the health care market by those who are good at cream-skimming. The practice often results in a social loss because cream-skimming is essentially a process that transfers the costs of health care away from one insurer to other groups in society (Wynand *et al.*, 1995).

The problem can be at least partly addressed through the appropriate structuring of risk premiums on a community basis and regulations that require private insurers to accept all applicants. Many private insurance systems also invoke complex systems of cross-subsidization to ensure that all private operators remain viable.

Several authors have argued in favour of a role for private insurance in Canada. McArthur, *et al.* (1996) argue for a package of health care reforms that would include a much larger private role in health care delivery and financing, including voluntary private insurance that runs in parallel to public health care. The underlying values that drive their recommendations are the primacy of freedom of choice among types of health care provision and financing, and competition as the engine of efficiency. More subtle support for private insurance is offered by Globerman and Vining, who argue that the risks of not introducing private insurance outweigh the risks of doing so. The argument is based on two premises: first, 'that Canadians currently enjoy less than universal access to medical services under Medicare' (Globerman and Vining, 1996: 13), either because services are not covered or because they are rationed through queuing, and second, 'that pressures will increase to further reduce the range (and possibly the quality) of products and services covered under the Medicare Plan and/or accept even longer queues for specific procedures' (ibid.: 14). Together these forces will generate a growing demand for private sector alternatives to Medicare, especially as the perceived limits to access and universality grow. In essence, they argue that the threat to Medicare from the current fiscal situation and from cost containment policies is greater than the threat posed by properly regulated private insurance. Globerman and Vining also carefully address the major concerns that (1) the ability to purchase private insurance will erode citizens' willingness to support Medicare through the tax system, (2) private insurance will lead to a two-tier system with differential access to care by those able to pay for private insurance and those supported by the public system, and (3) competition among private insurers will lead to administrative cost increases, the subsidization of private care and a loss of the advantages associated with a single-payer system. The key recommendation in the Canadian case is an expansion of private insurance to compete with public insurance in the coverage of medically necessary services.

My reading of the evidence from countries that do allow private insurance coverage for core health services is that it serves mainly as an outlet for demand by those with the ability to pay. It is likely that the quality of treatment through private insurance *per se* is not much different, but that access to service is faster and the secondary amenities ('hotel' aspects) of care are of higher quality. In general, those OECD countries (excluding the US and Switzerland) that feature private insurance in competition with public insurance have regulated the role of private insurance to such an extent that private insurance poses little threat to the public system. Therefore, it seems possible to design a role for voluntary private insurance of core health services that would have few impacts on access and equity, but that would relieve some of the cost containment pressure on the public sector. The key element of this privatization is that it is voluntarily assumed and not the result of a process of passive privatization. However, this is a far cry from asserting that such a system could be implemented in practice.

CONCLUSION

This chapter has attempted to explore the consequences of various cost containment and efficiency enhancing strategies on access and equity in health care. The instruments of cost containment are not neutral or equivalent in terms of their impact on access and equity. Global budgeting is the most effective cost containment tool, but can lead to spillovers that privatize the burden of health care financing and increase the burden of health care provision on informal caregivers. As long as cost containment is a major concern of governments, it is essential that the instruments of cost containment be designed so as to minimize their negative impact on access and equity. Direct cost-sharing through the introduction of user charges does little to control the total cost of health care or to enhance the efficiency of resource allocation. It is a process of privatization that directly shifts costs to the private sector. Direct cost-sharing does limit access, especially by those who are most prone to the consequences of ill health and those in low-income groups. It is worth emphasizing that user charges have only a little role to play in overall cost containment because better tools are available. Supply-side measures that introduce market elements into a publicly financed health care system are primarily directed to enhancing the efficiency of health care resource allocation.

The international evidence suggests that the introduction of market elements and competition need not result in privatization if there is a strong commitment to the preservation of access and equity, as in the case of the Nordic countries. By contrast, the New Zealand experience which cedes competitive control to quasi-private sector institutions can have negative impacts on access and equity. The lesson is that access and equity can be maintained in the face of public competition and internal markets if these measures feature a primary role for consumer choice in the allocation of resources while maintaining public accountability and a commitment to access and equity. Parallel private insurance poses few threats to access and equity if it is appropriately regulated and government is strong enough to channel market forces for these social ends.

NOTES

1 Privatization may, of course, be an end in itself for some governments. For the purposes of this discussion and in the absence of knowledge of hidden agendas, I will assume that privatization is a by-product of cost containment only.

2 See Armstrong and Armstrong (1996) for a discussion of this issue.

3 Market failures, especially in insurance markets, frequently justify a public role. See Boadway and Bruce (1994) for an interesting discussion of these issues in the context of health care. It should also be noted that, in the context of a 'second-best' world with pre-existing inefficiencies in one sector, there is no reason to believe that the pursuit of first-order efficiency in other sectors is a desirable policy objective.

4 An integrative policy regime features the state in a health care role that seems less active if measured in terms of expenditure or delivery. However, the state still plays a critical leadership and facilitative role as it attempts to induce other social actors to become more involved in the construction and pursuit of jointly negotiated health care goals. Power is more flexible and more evenly distributed among the players. This suggests that the state's role is greater when there is conflict in the system than when there is not. Roles and relationships are underpinned by more substantive rationality and there is greater reliance on non-market and non-technical criteria in decision-making.

5 This section draws heavily on Stewart (1996).

6 Here treatment does not necessarily refer to the specific procedure delivered by a health care practitioner or institution, but to the fact that individuals should have comparable access to a similar set of treatment options and facilities. Horizontal equity is not about the standardization of practice in relation to the treatment of specific conditions. Rather, it is about access to similar ranges and levels of service.

7 It also appears that privatization in the realm of financing has increased in recent years and is a relatively common phenomenon across a range of countries.

8 The February 1997 Federal Budget provides $150 million over three years for the provinces to experiment with new ways of health care financing and delivery, including pilot projects that would expand the base of health insurance to include drugs and long-term care.

9 Strong central control over funding is a critical element of the German health care system, but for the most part the system relies heavily on self-government or self-regulation. See Stewart and Brown (1996).

10 The British reforms are familiar to most readers and will not be described here. See the OECD Health Policy Studies and authors cited for a full description.

REFERENCES

Anderson, Malcolm. 1996. 'International Experience with Decentralization and Regionalization: New Zealand'. In *How Many Roads . . . ? Regionalization and Decentralization in Health Care*, eds John L. Dorland and S. Mathwin Davis. Kingston: School of Policy Studies, Queen's University.

Angus, D. E., L. Auer, J. E. Cloutier and T. Albert. 1995. *Sustainable Health Care for Canada*. Synthesis Report. Ottawa: Queen's University of Ottawa Economic Projects.

Armstrong, Pat and Hugh Armstrong. 1996. *Wasting Away: The Undermining of Canadian Health Care*. Toronto: Oxford University Press.

Boadway, Robin and Neil Bruce. 1994. 'The Government Provision of "Private" Goods in a Second-Best Economy'. In *Defining the Role of Government: Economic*

Perspectives on the State, R. Boadway, A. Breton, N. Bruce and R. Musgrave. Kingston: School of Policy Studies, Queen's University.

Callahan, Daniel. 1990. *What Kind of Life? The Limits of Medical Progress.* New York: Simon and Schuster.

Canadian Medical Association. 1995. *Canada and Health Care in the Global Village: Basic Facts on International Health Financing.* Ottawa: Canadian Medical Association.

Evans, Robert G. 1996. 'Marketing Markets, Regulating Regulators: Who Gains? Who Loses? What Hopes? What Scope?'. In *Health Care Reform: The Will to Change,* OECD Health Policy Studies No. 8. Paris: OECD.

Fuchs, Victor. 1993. *The Future of Health Policy.* Cambridge, MA: Harvard University Press.

Glennerster, Howard. 1995. 'Internal Markets: Context and Structure'. In *Health Care Reform Through Internal Markets: Experience and Proposals*, eds M. Jérôme-Forget, J. White and J. Wiener. Montreal: Institute for Research on Public Policy.

Globerman, Steven and Aidan Vining. 1996. *Cure or Disease? Private Health Insurance in Canada.* Toronto: University of Toronto, Faculty of Management Monograph Series on Public Policy and Public Administration.

Government of Canada. 1997. *1997 Federal Budget.* Ottawa: Minister of Supply and Services.

Jönsson, Bengt. 1996. 'Making Sense of Health Care Reform'. In *Health Care Reform: The Will to Change,* OECD Health Policy Studies No. 8. Paris: OECD.

Kelsey, Jane. 1995. *The New Zealand Experiment: A World Model for Structural Adjustment.* Auckland: Auckland University Press.

Lassey, Marie L., William R. Lassey and Martin J. Jinks. 1997. *Health Care Systems Around the World: Characteristics, Issues Reforms.* New Jersey: Prentice-Hall.

McArthur, William, Cynthia Ramsay and Michael Walker (eds). 1996. *Healthy Incentives: Canadian Health Care Reform in an International Context.* Vancouver: The Fraser Institute.

Maynard, Alan. 1995. 'Internal Markets and Health Care: A British Perspective'. In *Health Care Reform Through Internal Markets: Experience and Proposals,* eds M. Jérôme-Forget, J. White and J. Wiener. Montreal: Institute for Research on Public Policy.

Ministerial Council on Social Policy Reform and Renewal. 1996. *Report to Premiers.* Ottawa: Intergovernmental Affairs Secretariat.

Muschell, Jeff. 1995. *Privatization in Health.* Geneva: World Health Organization Task Force on Health Economics. URL: gopher://gopher.who.ch:70/00/anonymousftp/tfhe/privatiz.asc.

Newhouse, Joseph. 1993. *Free For All? Lessons From the RAND Health Insurance Experiment.* Cambridge, MA: Harvard University Press.

Organization for Economic Co-operation and Development (OECD). 1994. *The Reform of Health Care Systems: A Review of Seventeen OECD Countries.* OECD Health Policy Studies No. 5. Paris: OECD.

—— 1995a. *Internal Markets in the Making: Health Systems in Canada, Iceland and the United Kingdom.* OECD Health Policy Studies No. 6. Paris: OECD.

—— 1995b. *New Directions in Health Care Policy.* OECD Health Policy Studies No. 7. Paris: OECD.

Rhenberg, Clas. 1995. 'The Swedish Experience with Internal Markets'. In *Health Care Reform Through Internal Markets: Experience and Proposals*, eds M. Jérôme-Forget, J. White and J. Wiener. Montreal: Institute for Research on Public Policy.

Ruggeri, G. C., D. Van Wart and R. Howard. 1996. *The Government as Robin Hood: Exploring the Myth.* Kingston: School of Policy Studies, Queen's University.

Ruggie, Mary. 1996. *Realignments in the Welfare State: Health Policy in the United States, Britain and Canada.* New York: Columbia University Press.

Saltman, Richard B. 1995. 'The Role of Competitive Incentives in Recent Reforms of Northern European Health Systems'. In *Health Care Reform Through Internal Markets: Experience and Proposals*, eds M. Jérôme-Forget, J. White and J. Wiener. Montreal: Institute for Research on Public Policy.

Schneider, Markus. 1994. 'Evaluation of Cost-Containment Acts in Germany'. In *Health: Quality and Choice*, OECD Health Policy Studies No. 4. Paris: OECD.

Soderstrom, Lee. 1994. 'Health Care Reform in Canada: Restructuring the Supply Side'. In *Limits to Care: Reforming Canada's Health System in an Age of Restraint*, eds Åke Blomqvist and David M. Brown. Toronto: C. D. Howe Institute.

Stewart, Arthur E. 1996. 'Crossing the Rubicon? Cost Containment and Privatization in G7 Health Care Systems'. Background paper prepared for National Health Care Policy Summit, Montebello, Quebec, March, 1996. Ottawa: Canadian Medical Association.

Stewart, Arthur E. and Douglas M. Brown. 1996. 'The Federal Role in Health Care: International Perspectives'. Background paper prepared for Health Canada meeting, Kingston, Ontario, July, 1996.

Ulrich, Volker. 1996. 'Health Care in Germany: Structure, Expenditure and Prospects'. In *Healthy Incentives: Canadian Health Reform in an International Context*, eds W. McArthur, C. Ramsay and M. Walker. Vancouver: Fraser Institute.

White, Joseph. 1995. *Competing Solutions: American Health Care Proposals and International Experience.* Washington, DC: The Brookings Institution.

Wynand, P. M., M. van de Ven and F. T. Schut. 1995. 'The Dutch Experience with Internal Markets'. In *Health Care Reform Through Internal Markets: Experience and Proposals*, eds M. Jérôme-Forget, J. White and J. Wiener. Montreal: Institute for Research on Public Policy.

Part II

Restructuring Anglo-Saxon health systems

Shifting state/market boundaries

5 International agreements and National Health Plans: NAFTA

Barry Appleton[1]

INTRODUCTION

Still in their infancy, it is too early to be able fully to appreciate the impact of encompassing multilateral trade agreements, like the North American Free Trade Agreement (NAFTA). At the same time, it may be too late to learn lessons from the NAFTA on new types of international obligations that restrict the policy flexibility of governments as these obligations are being incorporated into future generations of international agreements.[2]

The NAFTA affects health care in two ways. First, it acts as a general limitation on the ways that governments can deal with public policy. Second, the agreement acts to lock in market liberalization in the health sector. In both of these ways, the NAFTA takes a unique, even business like means to accomplish its goals. For remarkably, under this agreement, a government that expands its provision of health services into areas where private enterprises operate will find itself liable to pay compensation to some of those same enterprises for the privilege of entering the field.

At its very heart the NAFTA protects the logic of the free market: an idea which inevitably conflicts with the nature of Canada's health care system. The NAFTA is structured to protect and encourage government measures that increase access to markets. This results in the NAFTA irreversibly protecting the trend towards private health care while eroding the ability of governments to reverse this trend. Its provisions provide unprecedented opportunities for foreign companies to profit from the provision of health care in Canada. In addition, the NAFTA gives these companies the power to protect their new-found rights to these new corporate opportunities.

HOW DOES THE NAFTA AFFECT HEALTH CARE?

There is no single chapter in the NAFTA on health care. The NAFTA deals with health care on a sectoral basis. Health care comprises goods, services, labour and investments, and the NAFTA contains provisions that affect each of these areas: goods (Article 300); services (Articles 1201(1), 1202, 1205, 1210); labour (Article 1603); investment (Articles 1101, 1139).

Health care as a good

Many aspects of the health care industry involve the sale of goods. Pharmaceuticals, medical and laboratory supplies and supplements are all examples of health care goods. The NAFTA created lower tariffs, and in some cases abolished tariffs, on these goods as they are traded in North America. The NAFTA has opened up the government procurement process in the area of health care. As a result, now American or Mexican health care suppliers can enter into contracts with federal government medical institutions such as military hospitals or veterans' facilities.[3]

The NAFTA has also had a significant impact on the price of pharmaceuticals in Canada. When coupled with the passage of Bill C-91 in 1993, NAFTA Article 1709(6) virtually ended Canada's system of compulsory licensing, a system which had a moderating effect on the price of prescription drugs in Canada.[4] In 1991 Canada's health care system paid 13.8 per cent of its budget for pharmaceuticals (Health and Welfare Canada, 1993). The ending of compulsory licensing immediately increased costs to provincial governments, Canada's largest purchaser of prescription medicines. While there are limited exceptions available in the NAFTA that could permit the introduction of a system akin to compulsory licensing, agreements like the NAFTA have politically ended these practices (McKenna and Eggertson, 1997). The Canadian Health Minister adverted to the impact of international trade commitments before the House of Commons Industry Committee during its review of the Patent Act in 1997. He said:

> As Minister of Health, I think we should attempt to do everything we can to try to maintain a reasonable expenditure for the purposes of drugs. But I don't think Canada can walk away from the World Trade Organization. I don't think Canada can walk away from NAFTA. As much as maybe we would want to in some instances, I don't think we can do that.
>
> (House of Commons Standing Committee on Industry, 1997)

Health care as a service

The NAFTA requires governments to provide special treatment to cross-border service providers. The term 'service provider' is broadly defined to mean someone 'that seeks to provide or provides a service' (NAFTA art. 1213). It applies both to persons who currently provide services and to those who wish to provide a service.[5] The NAFTA does not explain what it means when it refers to a 'service' but the term is capable of very broad interpretation. Its only clarification is a list of items that are not services.[6]

The advent of satellite communications and sophisticated computers have allowed medical diagnostic services to be provided remotely. Technology makes it possible to have a radiologist in the United States examining a patient in Canada thousands of miles away. Health care delivery mechanisms have evolved to a point where it is not essential to have direct contact between patient and provider. These changes have both societal and international trade law effects. While services such as surgery will invariably require direct contact, new technologies allow some areas of health care to be provided as a service across national borders. Similarly, laboratory diagnostic services can also be provided on a cross-border basis. Both of these off-site services constitute a cross-border service under the NAFTA.

National treatment

The NAFTA requires governments to provide treatment 'no less favourable than that it accords, in like circumstances, to its own service providers' (NAFTA art. 1202(1)). The implication of this NAFTA obligation is significant. For example, the dispensing of prescription medicines could be a cross-border service. Measures by any NAFTA government that prohibited the cross-border sale of prescription medicines by an appropriately licensed pharmacist could violate this national treatment obligation.[7] A second example could be cross-border laboratory services where tests are administered in one country and processed in another.

Local presence

The NAFTA abolishes government requirements compelling the establishment of a local office as a prerequisite for selling a service (NAFTA art. 1205). This same provision also ends local residency requirements.[8] For instance, rules that require that a health service practitioner be a local resident cannot be maintained.

Professional licensing

The NAFTA contains provisions relating to professional licensing and certification. Under NAFTA Article 1210, Canada is obliged to 'endeavour to ensure' that its licensing and certification requirements and procedures are based on objective and transparent criteria such as professional competence; are no more burdensome than necessary to ensure the quality of the service; and are not a disguised restriction on the cross-border provision of the service. Canada's NAFTA obligation in relation to professional services is very limited. Canada is not required to meet the goals set out in Article 1210; it must only 'endeavour' to meet these goals. In fact, reciprocal recognition of professional licensing is not obligatory under the NAFTA (NAFTA art. 1210(2)).

The licensing of professionals is addressed specifically in NAFTA Annex 1210.5. This annex encourages professional bodies in each NAFTA Party to develop mutually acceptable standards for licensing professionals and reciprocal recognition (NAFTA annex 1210.5(2)) but this is not required. Nor does this annex impose any time limit on this process. The only commitment imposed upon a professional body is the duty to review fairly and answer applications by NAFTA Party nationals for professional licensing (NAFTA annex 1210.5(1)).This is an obligation that is already imposed in Canada under principles of natural justice in administrative law.[9] Thus, under the NAFTA, there is no obligation upon Canadian self-regulating professions to recognize professionals from other NAFTA countries; however, such recognition is permissible.

Labour market mobility for health care professionals

While the NAFTA does not create a free market in labour for health care professionals, it does contain provisions which increase labour market mobility between Canada, Mexico and the United States. The NAFTA provides temporary business entry for professionals and easy access into a NAFTA country for a large number of health care professionals.[10] While physicians are covered by this part of the NAFTA, they are only allowed temporary entry for the purposes of teaching or research.

Temporary entry does not provide the right to apply for citizenship, but it does permit accelerated and extended access to the country. This increases the ability of health care providers to move on a non-permanent basis, accelerating the ability of NAFTA professionals to create investments which provide health services throughout North America.[11]

Health care as an investment

Health care is a business worth over 70 billion dollars every year in Canada.[12] Health care providers are more than service providers, they constitute businesses either as sole practitioners, partners or employees of other entities. Under the NAFTA's broad definition of investment, much of Canada's health care delivery vehicles constitute an investment under international trade law and are covered by the NAFTA (NAFTA art. 1139).

The NAFTA is the most comprehensive investment treaty ever agreed to between developed states. The General Agreement on Tariffs and Trade (GATT) only deals with trade in goods and therefore investments were not covered in a multilateral agreement until the NAFTA. The term 'investment' applies to the widest possible variety of investments, including businesses (incorporated and non-incorporated), shareholdings, loans made to foreign companies for more than three years, real estate, intellectual property and goodwill (NAFTA art. 1139). Simply put, it obliges its members to protect the investments of NAFTA nationals and their business entities. The obligation is contained in a specific investment chapter which contains a powerful tool that allows investors to protect their new-found NAFTA investment rights.

National treatment

The NAFTA requires that national treatment be given in like circumstances for 'the establishment, acquisition, expansion, management, conduct, operation, and sale or other disposition of investments' (NAFTA art. 1102(1)). The national treatment obligation requires governments to grant effective equality of opportunity to investments within its borders. This powerful obligation ends policies that give a preference to Canadians over foreigners in various areas. For example, government policies that impose differential fees based on residency violate this NAFTA obligation. Many provinces currently have such policies, which come into effect whenever an out-of-province patient uses a provincially funded medical facility.[13]

Minimum standards of treatment

The NAFTA provides that its member governments must provide the minimum standard of treatment as established by international law to the nationals and investments of other Parties (NAFTA art. 1105). This minimum standard includes protections regarding due process and fair treatment and it also recognizes important international rights such as freedom of expression and other fundamental human rights.[14]

Performance requirements

The freedom of governments to impose a wide variety of restrictions on business practices is severely limited by the NAFTA.[15] At its very heart, the NAFTA prohibition on performance requirements prevents governments from imposing certain conditions on the 'establishment, acquisition, expansion, management, conduct or operation of an investment of an investor of a Party or of a non-Party in its territory' (NAFTA art. 1106(1)).[16]

NAFTA governments are prohibited from compelling investors to export a certain level of locally produced goods or services (NAFTA art. 1106(1)(a)) or from requiring that investments use local labour or goods (NAFTA art. 1106(1)(b)). Parties are prevented from regulating the distribution of services within its borders. This limits the ability of governments to compel a health service provider to provide a service to a specific region (NAFTA art. 1106(1)(g)).

The NAFTA establishes a special category of obligations in situations where governments offer a subsidy or other benefits made in connection with an investment in its territory (NAFTA art. 1106(3)). These benefits cannot be based on the use of local goods or services. Thus a government cannot require (or encourage) a private hospital to purchase locally produced medical supplies.

The NAFTA has thereby ended the widespread use of performance require-ments as a form of economic development tool.

Expropriation

A fundamental obligation contained in the NAFTA Investment chapter relates to limitations on government expropriations. NAFTA Article 1110 states:

> 1 No Party may directly or indirectly nationalize or expropriate an investment of an investor of another Party in its territory or take a measure tantamount to nationalization or expropriation of such an investment ('expropriation'), except:
>   (a) for a public purpose;
>   (b) on a non-discriminatory basis;
>   (c) in accordance with due process of law and Article 1105(1); and
>   (d) on payment of compensation in accordance with paragraphs 2 through 6.

The NAFTA does not define the term 'expropriation'. Under international law, however, expropriation is any act by which governmental authority is used to deny some benefit of property. This denial can be actual or constructive.

More specifically, for there to be an expropriation under international law it is necessary to establish that a government has interfered unreasonably with the use of private property (*Harza Engineering Co.*, 1982: 504).[17] The expro-priating government need not take formal title to the property. An expropria-tion occurs when the property of an individual or business has been substantially interfered with by a governmental authority.[18]

The terms of the NAFTA itself have broadened the types of activity that will be considered as expropriations by including the words '*a measure tantamount to nationalization or expropriation*'. Any substantial interference with a property right is likely an activity in the nature of expropriation and almost certainly a measure tantamount to expropriation.[19]

The American Law Institute's Restatement (Third) on the Foreign Relations Law of the United States comments upon the obligation to pay compensation for an expropriation.[20] It provides that compensation for an expropriation:

> applies not only to avowed expropriations in which the government formally takes title to property, but also to other actions of the govern-ment that have the effect of 'taking' the property, in whole or in large part, outright or in stages ('creeping expropriation'). A state is responsible as for an expropriation of property under Subsection (1) when it subjects alien property to taxation, regulation, or other action that is confiscatory, or that prevents, unreasonably interferes with, or unduly delays, effective enjoy-ment of an alien's property or its removal from the state's territory.
>
> (712 Sect., Comment (g))

This comment underscores the fact that an expropriation can take place whenever there is a substantial and unreasonable interference with the enjoyment of a property right. The action of a government to provide services in a sector where there is existing commercial competition could well be seen as a government measure harming the property of a NAFTA investor. If governmental action harmed an investor's property (such as market share or goodwill), that investor could make a claim for expropriation under the NAFTA. Thus, whenever government leaves an area of health care to the private sector, its return will invariably be costly.

The NAFTA is a very generous treaty when dealing with the quantum of investor compensation. The Agreement specifically sets out that an investor will receive fair market value for its expropriated property.[21] This valuation basis provides compensation at levels that could be higher than those established under Canadian domestic law. This generous compensation standard augments the broad definition of what constitutes an expropriation under the NAFTA. As governments begin to appreciate their international obligations, and understand the costs of their violation, these two factors will act to limit the range of public policy options available to governments.

Investor–state dispute settlement

The NAFTA contains a powerful remedy that can be used by NAFTA investors where a government has harmed their NAFTA 'investor rights'. The investor–state dispute process allows a NAFTA resident (persons or corporations) to directly bring a compensation claim against another NAFTA government. These claims are heard before a special international arbitration panel that can award financial compensation to investors that have been harmed by governmental action which infringes the NAFTA's investment obligations. The panels cannot strike down NAFTA-infringing measures, but the threat of paying enforceable damage awards can be chastening to government policy initiatives.

NAFTA investors are entitled to dispute government measures. These measures are not limited to legislation but extend to regulations, governmental policies and practices. Not only are the national governments covered by this agreement, but so are state, provincial, territorial and local governments. Actions that these governments do can thus trigger a NAFTA action.

To use the investor–state dispute settlement process, the NAFTA requires that there be some international element involved in a dispute. For example, Canadian investors are not eligible to bring disputes against the Government of Canada; however, American or Mexican investors can. A glaring exception to this rule is that Canadian corporations 'owned or controlled directly or indirectly' by a citizen of another NAFTA country can bring a claim against the Canadian government.[22] The term 'investor' is defined broadly to include an individual or enterprise that 'seeks to make, is making or has made an investment' (NAFTA art. 1139). By the term 'enterprise', the NAFTA means any entity constituted by law and includes companies, partnership, joint ventures or other associations (NAFTA art. 201(1)). Thus an individual or industry association that intended to invest in a NAFTA country would have standing to bring a claim against that NAFTA government that did not meet its NAFTA investment obligations.

The NAFTA investor–state process has been used at least twice since the NAFTA came into force. The first known dispute was brought by a Mexican chemical manufacturer that complained of Canadian regulations which unfairly prevented the sale of its joint venture products in Canada without fair process (Greenberg, 1996). A second case involved an American company that had its imported products banned and domestic distribution business destroyed by Canadian government statements and legislation (Feschuk, 1996).

Governments still do not appreciate the full impact of the NAFTA investor–state process, which creates a new type of international actor that is different from governments or supra-national organizations. The NAFTA creates an entirely new multilateral dispute process, vastly different from the GATT or WTO. The unique ability to allow individuals to bring cases directly against governments (even without the consent of their home government) will result in unpredictable results. What is clear is that the NAFTA creates a speedy and enforceable process to settle disputes with governments. This is likely to result in investors carefully scrutinizing government practices to find a NAFTA provision on which they can base a claim. Thus, policing of the NAFTA will move from governmental channels over to businesses, with enforcement done through the use of international tribunals. With the expansion of investor-state dispute settlement throughout the world's most-developed nations in the OECD's Multilateral Agreement on Investment, this trend will only continue to grow.

What governments can do: NAFTA reservations

Social service reservations

The NAFTA sets out a series of reservations in annexes at the end of the agreement. NAFTA Annexes I, II and III set out measures and sectors that are reserved from certain NAFTA service and investment commitments. These reservations were either finalized when the NAFTA came into force, or over a two-year period thereafter. No additional reservations are permitted under the NAFTA.

Canada made a reservation to deal with the government provision of social services in NAFTA Annex II. Reservations made to Annex II are known as 'unbound reservations' as they allow a government that lists a reservation to have unlimited freedom of action within that policy area. Canada's reservation reads:

> Canada reserves the right to adopt or maintain any measure with respect to the provision of public law enforcement and correctional services, and the

following services to the extent that they are social services established or maintained for a public purpose: income security or insurance, social security or insurance, social welfare, public education, public training, health, and child care.

(NAFTA ann. II-C-9)

A substantially identical reservation has been taken by the United States at II-U-5 and by Mexico at II-M-11.[23]

The NAFTA Social Service Reservation permits governments to maintain existing measures that conflict with specific NAFTA provisions such as national treatment or local presence rules. Because they are 'unbound', the reservations allow governments the freedom to make future inconsistent measures within the specified sectors in regard to the listed NAFTA provisions.

It is essential to note that the NAFTA Social Service Reservation does not permit the continuation of government programs that constitute a performance requirement under Article 1106. Further, no NAFTA reservation of any kind can ever exempt a government from meeting its expropriation or its minimum obligations under the NAFTA.

Unfortunately, the specific wording used to protect the social service sector is ambiguous. Within the Social Service Reservation, sectors have been listed in different ways. Law enforcement and correctional services are listed in an unqualified manner. The other seven subsectors are all covered only to the extent that *they are social services established or maintained for a public purpose.*

The NAFTA does not provide any specific definition as to what is covered by descriptive terms such as 'health' or 'social services'. There are only two other locations where some of the terms used in the reservation can be found. Both the NAFTA Investment chapter and Trade in Services chapter contain similar clauses which mention types of public services. These clauses read:

Nothing in this Chapter shall be construed to prevent a Party from providing a service or performing a function such as law enforcement, correctional services, income security or insurance, social security or insurance, social welfare, public education, public training, health, and child care, in a manner that is not inconsistent with this Chapter.

(NAFTA arts 1101(4), 1201(3)(b))

In neither of these two clauses are any of the specified services limited as they are in the Social Service Reservation.[24] Taken together, none of these provisions provides any definition of the key terms in the Social Service Reservation.

This reservation must have some meaning. The difficulty is in ascertaining it since the wording is clothed in a language more akin to diplomacy than law. Canadians and their governments need to understand the policy powers left within their control. A broad reading of the Social Service Reservation would allow Canadian governments the ability to develop ongoing national health policies without the spectre of international disputes. There is, however, no guarantee that the Social Service Reservation has this broad meaning.

The NAFTA is an international treaty. As an international creature it is not bound by domestic definitions or conceptions of terms. The NAFTA is inter-preted under international law, not domestic law. This international approach makes the meaning of terms such as 'social services' or 'health' very uncertain as there are no set international definitions of these terms. Even within the three nations that comprise the NAFTA, there are very different views on what constitutes an appropriate role for government. What may be a legitimate publicly provided social service in one NAFTA country may very well be delivered entirely by the private sector in another. This problem is com-pounded by the fact that the operative wording of the NAFTA Social Service Reservation is the same for Canada, Mexico and the United States. Thus, the meaning given to its terms applies equally in each of these three different national social service regimes.

We can already see the beginning of this difference. The 29 November 1995 edition of *Inside NAFTA*, a biweekly journal covering the NAFTA, reported that the US Trade Representatives Office had a very different interpretation on the meaning of the NAFTA Social Service Reservation than did Canada. Canada took the position that the reservation should receive 'the broadest possible interpretation' while the US government took a much narrower view, holding that where commercial services existed that sector no longer consti-tuted a social service for a public purpose. Other jurisdictions also expressed differing views on the meaning of this reservation. There is a fundamental lack of a consensus about what is protected here. Yet this is not a new issue (Appleton, 1994: 88).[25]

Coming to a trilateral understanding on the precise meaning of this reserva-tion has not been possible. For example, when the NAFTA Parties met in March 1996 to exchange NAFTA Annex I reservations, they could not come to any mutually agreed-upon meaning for this reservation. It is likely that tribunals will eventually need to sort out the confusion on the meaning of this reservation. In the meantime, the capacity of governments to expand the public nature of health care remains in doubt.

Existing measures

The majority of health care measures in Canada are taken by provincial governments. These governments are not parties to the NAFTA, and did not participate in its negotiation, yet they are subject to its provisions. To accommodate the differing policy goals of provinces the NAFTA permitted these governments to list their non-conforming measures in NAFTA Annex I. Those measures in force on 1 January 1994 remain protected but changes to these measures are not protected if the new measure is less consistent with the NAFTA than the predecessor measure.

These reservations inhibit the development of new delivery mechanisms for social service programs. As a result of the NAFTA, changes to social policy can lead to international trade disputes. An example of the effect that such a change can have can be seen from the 1996 proposed changes to Canada's Agreement on Internal Trade (AIT) regarding health care services. In 1994, Canada's Ministers of Internal Trade signed the AIT to fill in a gap in Canada's constitution and thereby create a complete internal market for goods, services and capital in Canada. In 1996, the Ministers of Internal Trade began considering extensions to the coverage of the AIT. One of the proposed extensions of the agreement dealt with health care. The proposed extension suggested that current regulations regarding the licensing of doctors, dentists and nurses could stay in force but that there would be a free market regarding procurement for all other areas of health care.

The proposed change to the AIT would have affected Canada's international trade obligations regarding national treatment. The NAFTA national treatment obligation for investment granted access to American and Mexican service providers operating in Canada in sectors covered by the AIT. While all measures taken by provincial governments before 1994 were reserved under NAFTA Annex I, any changes to these measures were not.

The NAFTA permitted the reservation of measures that conflicted with the national treatment obligation if they were in existence on the entry into force of the NAFTA. To maintain this NAFTA reservation, this inconsistent measure must remain in force. The changes proposed for the AIT would have changed these NAFTA-inconsistent measures. This would remove existing NAFTA reservations for these otherwise NAFTA-inconsistent policies. Simply put, changing the AIT could have resulted in a change in Canada's current NAFTA Social Service Reservation. This weakening of Canada's reservation could have put Canada's social safety net at risk from aggressive trade attack. This is an excellent example of how domestic arrangements can now have an important international legal impact.

Subsidies

The NAFTA exempts subsidies from the application of several parts of the investment chapter (NAFTA art. 1108(7)(b)). Government subsidies that discriminate on the basis of residency or that require local residency can be continued. Policies that give a preference for the purchase of domestic goods or services (performance requirements) or that fail to provide due process rights (minimum international standards of treatment) are not exempted.

One of the NAFTA's greatest drawbacks is that it does not provide any definition of the term 'subsidies'. Finding a common definition with the United States has been a long-standing goal of Canadian trade policy. When the then newly elected Chrétien government agreed to proceed with the NAFTA in 1993, it committed itself to developing a common understanding on this term. This definition has proved so elusive that a NAFTA working group on this issue could not provide an answer. This lack of an answer affects more than Canadian economic policy. It also affects the scope of the exemption for social policy.

HEALTH CARE REFORM IN CANADA

For many, health care is primarily defined as the types of services covered by the Canada Health Act. However, using this basic definition misses significant health care providers as the Act only applies to physicians and hospitals. Health care consists of numerous specialized providers such as nurses, dentists, dental hygienists, pharmacists, speech therapists, audiologists, physiotherapists, occupational therapists, denturists, chiropodists, chiropractors, midwives, naturopaths and acupuncturists. The traditional Canada Health Act model of service delivery views hospitals and doctors as the primary delivery vehicles and governments as creating extensive structures to deliver health care through these two instruments.

Discussions on the reform of Canada's health care system are pandemic. Often these discussions centre on whether to have a privately funded health care system operating concurrently with a public system. Such a mixed system might reflect the existing American system of health care,[26] or it might deviate from it significantly.

The cumulative effect of recent changes to the funding and delivery of Canadian health care has created the rudiments of a private user-pay health care system. Three important developments have led to the development of this quasi-private system:

1   Constraints on the fiscal capacity of governments. The de-listing of medical procedures covered by government funding schedules has reduced the number of services funded by public health care plans. Provincial health care plans have reduced out-of-province medical coverage and dropped some services, such as dental or chiropractic care. Also, newer procedures have not been listed where existing (and less-costly) procedures exist in the schedule.

2   Reductions on the length of in-hospital patient stays have resulted in important changes to auxiliary services. Reducing the length of patient stays has increased the need for recuperative care facilities and for homecare support.

3   The development of private health care organizations has already begun in Canada. Companies that provide comprehensive in-house patient medical evaluation for life or disability insurance already operate in Ontario and Alberta. These companies offer quick service to those who can afford to pay. By relying upon an exemption contained in the Canada Health Act, these companies have become the prototypes for Canadian health management organizations (HMOs).

De-listing, shorter hospitalization stays and the advent of Canadian HMOs have increased the private component in Canada's health care system. Canada finds itself clearly in the position where private health care exists. Its significance in the health care market will be increased by the needs of Canada's demographically ageing society, which will place greater demands on assisted-care in and outside the home.

International trade will have an impact on the future of Canada's national health plan. Critical changes to Canada's health care system have already occurred. These changes will allow interested parties to force governments to modify their health care policies. In addition, the downsizing resulting from decreasing government spending will result in added NAFTA coverage in the area of health care.

CONCLUSIONS

In the attempt to reduce barriers to trade, globally and domestically, Canada may find itself in conflict with its goal to maintain its distinctive health and social service sectors. Canada's international agreements give certain rights to entities owned by NAFTA investors operating in Canada, and Canada cannot unilaterally alter these rights. Once these foreign investors operate in the Canadian marketplace, it becomes difficult to place controls on their operation. Furthermore, policy changes that are entirely domestic, like the change in the Agreement on Internal Trade, can now have an international effect. This demonstrates just how inextricably linked the NAFTA is into Canada's domestic economic and legal order.

At no time during the extensive domestic debate on NAFTA in Canada or the United States was there any prolonged discussion of health care, the scope of Canada's investment or service obligations, or the investor–state dispute process. In agreeing to a trade deal with Mexico and the United States, Canadians received much more than they expected. Clearly, the advent of the NAFTA will have an important legacy for the citizens of Canada.

A one-way process

It is clear that the NAFTA was always intended to make it difficult for governments to back away from economic liberalization. Gary Hufbauer and Jeffrey Schott reported that the NAFTA Investment Chapter 'strongly reinforces Mexican economic reforms designed to improve the investment climate in that country' (Hufbauer and Schott, 1993: 79). One political scientist examining this issue reported that this ratchet-effect was intended by the Government of Mexico. He writes:

> One of the NAFTA's most important functions, from the Salinas administration's view, is to reduce national sovereignty by binding future

Mexican governments to the privatization and liberalization strategy of the current government. The NAFTA would do this by embedding these policies in an international trade agreement that cannot be unilaterally re-negotiated and would be very costly and disruptive to abrogate.

(Robinson, 1993: 37)

The NAFTA made it difficult for Mexico to backtrack from its process of economic liberalization. However, at the same time, Canadian governments also locked themselves into the same process.

The NAFTA is not the only one-way process at work here. The Agreement's investment obligations, especially relating to expropriation, may have an important effect on the future of Canada's health care system. Despite the desire of future governments to provide health services directly, the NAFTA may effectively prevent such future policy options. Private providers of those services may very well qualify as NAFTA 'investors'. To these investors, government provision of services would be the same as the taking away of their business. Thus the spectre of the NAFTA expropriation claims looms large for any government that might decide to re-enter the field. In essence, when a government now wishes to provide a service, the NAFTA requires it to consider whether its entry will affect existing providers. If existing providers will be harmed, the NAFTA does not prevent governments from returning, it merely makes them pay. Simply put, the broad compensation commitments of the NAFTA ensure that government privatization will be a one-way process.

Governments would rather switch than pay

Governments will shy away from paying for health care services and then paying compensation to business owners who had been providing those services. In essence, the NAFTA will make it too expensive for governments to ever return to providing services. And, while the NAFTA only applies to foreign investors, politically, how could any future government take the position that it will pay foreign owners a fair market price while paying nothing to its own citizens. Thus, the economic impact of the NAFTA and the impact of domestic politics ensures that health care privatization remains a one-way process only. When faced with the choice of paying compensation to the private sector for the privilege of providing social services to the public or switching policies, governments would rather switch than pay. However, with limited policy options available, governments may well not switch to alternative policies but may opt to not participate at all.

NAFTA: an economic constitution

There are no property rights protected in the Canadian Constitution. This omission was a conscious decision of the Trudeau Government to maintain the greatest amount of public policy flexibility. With its stringent protection of private property rights and its unique investor driven compensation process, the NAFTA creates property rights for foreign investors in Canada. In essence, the NAFTA has created a *de facto* amendment to the Canadian Charter of Rights and Freedoms except that these rights treat foreigners better than Canadian citizens. With the first set of NAFTA investment cases coming before international tribunals,[27] there could be new pressures to either change the NAFTA or amend the Charter of Rights and Freedoms to better protect property rights.

Investor enforcement

NAFTA's investor–state dispute system will play a major role in how business will be done in North America over the next decade. In one fell swoop, the NAFTA has broadened the number of entities that can bring trade actions from two (under the Canada–US Free Trade Agreement) to millions. NAFTA investors can have their say without needing to observe the constraints of diplomatic niceties. The impact of allowing investors to police the enforcement of the NAFTA is yet to be seen. There is little doubt that the decisions of NAFTA investor–state tribunals will act to constrain unfettered government action. The cumulative effect of this NAFTA chapter will be to maintain government measures to privatize the delivery of health in Canada.

Future directions

Health care is affected by the NAFTA in a number of areas. Perhaps the most significant impact on the future of Canada's health plan will be the reduction of government involvement. And while, in historic terms, the ink on the NAFTA is barely dry, it is not too early to be able to state that the NAFTA has become one of the most important considerations underpinning future developments for Canada's National Health Plan.

NOTES

1 The author wishes to acknowledge the gracious assistance and comments of the following people during the preparation of this chapter: Daniel Drache, Terry Sullivan, Colleen Fuller, David Kerzner, Mike MacBane, Anthony Macri, John Roberts, Lisa Sinclair, Patrick Westaway and Elana Lipstein.
2 For example, see the OECD Multilateral Agreement on Investment.
3 NAFTA Chapter 10 deals with opening up the government procurement process. It only applies to federal government procurement at this time.
4 It should be noted that there is an exception to this NAFTA provision that could permit a government to reintroduce compulsory licensing in certain limited circumstances.

5 Thus, potential service providers who do not currently provide cross-border services are also covered by the NAFTA service chapter.

6 For example, financial services are excluded as they are covered by another NAFTA chapter. As well, subsidies or grants provided by a NAFTA government, including insurance, are also not covered by the NAFTA services chapter (NAFTA art. 1201(2)(d)).

7 NAFTA Article 2101 sets out exceptions to NAFTA obligations. There is no exception that would allow the American government to prohibit the dispensing of prescription medicines from Canada under that Article. An exception would be permitted to prohibit the sale of Canadian drugs in the United States under NAFTA Article 2101, which reads in GATT Article XX (d) which allows measures 'Necessary to protect human, animal or plant life or health'. However, this exception would have to relate primarily to health and not to protection.

8 It should be noted that provincial and state residency requirements that were in force on 1 January 1994 were allowed to remain in force under NAFTA Annex I. Further discussion of this issue takes place later in this chapter.

9 For example, see the decision of the Supreme Court of Canada in *Re: Nicholson and Haldimand Norfolk Regional Board of Commissioners of Police* (1978), 88 P.L.R. (3rd) 671 (SCC).

10 These include dentists, dietitians, medical lab technologists, nutritionists, occupational therapists, pharmacists, psychologists, recreational therapists, registered nurses, biochemists, epidemiologists, geneticists and pharmacologists.

11 The impact of this trend will be significant. The NAFTA provides protection for foreign investments but not for foreigners without investments.

12 For example, in 1991, Canadian governments spent $68 billion on health care.

13 It is important to note that provincially funded or regulated bodies, such as hospitals or self-governing professional organizations, could be bound by the specific governmental obligations of the NAFTA.

14 In the opinion of the author, this NAFTA provision will become a key provision as it imports a wide variety of civil and political rights into the NAFTA.

15 The performance requirement limitations are the broadest obligations contained within the NAFTA. The obligations apply not only to the investments of NAFTA Party investors, but to all investments made by any national of any country in the world in the territory of a NAFTA Party.

16 This requirement is consistent with the National Treatment and Most-Favoured-Nation standards.

17 This principle was recognized in section 3(a) of the Harvard Draft Convention on the International Responsibility of States for Injuries to the Economic Interests of Aliens which states that:

a 'taking of property' includes not only an outright taking of property but also any such unreasonable interference with the use, enjoyment, or disposal of property as to justify an inference that the owner thereof will not be able to use, enjoy, or dispose of the property within a reasonable time after the inception of such interference.

18 Some commentators, when looking at the customary international law of expropriation, require a higher standard of governmental interference. Professor Brownlie has concluded that: 'The essence of the matter is the deprivation by state organs

of a right of property either as such, or by permanent transfer of the power of management and control' (Brownlie, 1990: 531).

19 The Iran–US Claims Tribunal has come to this same conclusion in a number of cases. In *I.T.T. Industries* (at 351) the Tribunal stated: 'Property may be taken under international law through interference by a state in the use of that property or with the enjoyment of its benefits, even where legal title to the property is not affected.' In *Harza Engineering* (at 404), the Tribunal stated: 'the taking of property may occur under international law, even in the absence of a formal nationalization or expropriation, if a government has interfered unreasonably with the use of property'.

20 The Restatement would qualify as a source of international law under Article 38(1)(d) of the Statute of the International Court of Justice.

21 NAFTA Article 1110(2) states that:

2. Compensation shall be equivalent to the fair market value of the expropriated investment immediately before the expropriation took place ('date of expropriation'), and shall not reflect any change in value occurring because the intended expropriation had become known earlier. Valuation criteria shall include going concern value, asset value including declared tax value of tangible property, and other criteria, as appropriate, to determine fair market value.

22 In essence, Canadian companies owned by Americans or Mexicans have better rights here than do Canadian citizens.

23 It should be noted that the Mexican and American reservations, unlike Canada's, do not extend to reserving against most-favoured-nation treatment.

24 Since the purpose of an exemption clause is to provide a Party with the ability to engage in policy-making, notwithstanding the operation of the NAFTA, these clauses are of little effect. We are of the view that this apparent exemption provides little assistance in the interpretation of the Annex II reservation.

25 This wording certainly raises ambiguity. The meaning of this wording and thus the effect of this part of the reservation will inevitably be determined by the NAFTA Free Trade Commission or a Chapter 20 panel.

26 The American health care system is mixed. Åke Blomqvist reports that up to 40 per cent of the American health care market is supplied by the public sector (Blomqvist and Brown, 1996: 30).

27 See *Financial Post* (1997: 25) and Eggertson (1997: B4).

REFERENCES

Appleton, B. 1994. *Navigating NAFTA: A Concise Users Guide to the North American Free Trade Agreement*. Toronto: Carswell.

Blomqvist, A. and D. Brown (eds). 1996. *Limits to Care: Reforming Canada's Health System in an Age of Restraint*. Toronto: C. D. Howe Institute.

Brownlie, I. 1990. *Principles of Public International Law* (4th edn). Oxford: Clarendon Press.

Canada. Agreement on Internal Trade (1994).

Coutts, J. 1996. Danger to Medicare Seen in Trade Barrier Plan. *Globe and Mail*, 11 June, p. A8.

Department of National Health and Welfare, Health Information Division, Policy, Planning and Information Branch. 1993. *Health Expenditures in Canada, Summary Report 1987–1991*. Ottawa.

Eggertson, L. 1997. Ethyl Sues Ottawa Over MMT Law. *Globe and Mail*, 15 April, p. B4.

Feschuk, S. 1996. Reputation Hurt, MMT Maker Says. *Globe and Mail*, 11 September.

Financial Post. 1997. Ethyl to take MMT Ban to NAFTA Panel. 15 April, p. 25.

Greenberg, L. M. 1996. Mexican Firm Files NAFTA Complaint Against Canada. *Wall Street Journal*, 13 March, pp. A2 and A22.

Harvard Draft Convention on the International Responsibility of States for Injuries to the Economic Interests of Aliens, *American Journal of International Law* 55: 545.

Harza Engineering Co. v. *Iran* (1982), 1 Iran–US C.T.R. 499.

Health and Welfare Canada. (1993). *Health Expenditures in Canada, Summary Report 1987–1991*. Ottawa.

House of Commons Standing Committee on Industry, April 1997. Review of Section 14 of the Patent Act (Chapter 2, *Statutes of Canada* 1993).

Hufbauer, G. and J. Schott. 1993. *NAFTA: An Assessment.* Washington, DC: Institute for International Economics.

I.T.T. Industries v. *Iran* (1983), 2 Iran–US C.T.R. 348.

Klabbers, J. 1992. Jurisprudence in International Law: Article XX of the GATT. *J. World Trade* 26: 63, 90.

McKenna, B. and L. Eggertson. 1997. Committee Backs Liberals' Stance on Drug Patents. *Globe and Mail*, 25 April, p. B5

Re: Nicholson and Haldimand Norfolk Regional Board of Commissioners of Police (1978), 88 P.L.R. (3rd) 671 (SCC).

North American Free Trade Agreement, 17 December 1992.

Robinson, I. 1993. *North American Trade as if Democracy Mattered: What's Wrong with NAFTA and What are the Alternatives*. Ottawa: Centre for Public Policy Alternatives.

Statute of the International Court of Justice, Annex to the Charter of the United Nations Organization. 1949. United Nations, New York.

6   The public–private frontier
The land of Oz

Peter Botsman

There are two problematics of health care reform facing most Western industrialized countries: the conservative problematic involves considering the merits of private and public health care services, even to the extent of revisiting policies that create first and second class health care citizens. The progressive problematic requires rethinking ways to extend community based health care. These problematics represent the two prospective ideological axes for health care reform in the industrialized world over the next twenty years. The best way of describing these ideologies is conservative and progressive, not because they neatly fit with mainstream political models but because conservative health care reformers want to maintain current systems of health care power, be they public or private, and the progressive view is that only through change to both public and private health care is it possible to realize a new set of appropriate health care outcomes that are about improving quality of life and placing sick, disabled or debilitated individuals in charge of their own health care destinies.

In the current political milieu, this debate is supported and promoted by medical interests who want to remain free (US) or be freed (Canada, Australia) from the obligation of universal coverage and cost control. Alternatively, progressives want to build on the foundations of universal access and social insurance and extend it to a new frontier of more appropriate and socially useful health care services that go beyond doctor and hospital based health care and includes support for people with disabilities, long term care, occupational and diversional therapy, podiatry, community-based care, health promotion and alternative medicines. This necessitates extending social insurance, creating a new partnership with private health care providers, restructuring of the health care system around well funded community care and setting up goals, rights and responsibilities for a new frontier of health care services.

THE LAND OF OZ

The Australian health care system (Table 6.1) is an interesting 'laboratory of democracy'[1] in which to consider these issues because of its mix of public and

Table 6.1 Characteristics of the Australian health care system

Insurance	A 'Single (National Public Health Insurance) Payer' co-exists with a large Private Health Insurance Industry (34% of the population hold private cover)
Medical practitioners	Predominantly private with fee based payment schedules
Acute care beds	72% public, 28% private
Overall financing	Commonwealth government 43%, state and local 25%, private sector 32%
Who finances what?	Medical services (Commonwealth 82%, private insurance 3%, co-payments 9%), public hospitals (Commonwealth 49%, state/local 42%, private insurance 5%, co-payments 4%), private hospitals (Commonwealth 8%, private 80%, direct private payments 12%), pharmaceuticals (Commonwealth 46%, private insurance 1%, co-payments 53%), dental (Commonwealth 10%, private insurance 29%, private payment 61%), Community and public health (Commonwealth 23%, state/local 77%), nursing homes (Commonwealth 68%, state/local 9%, private payment 23%)

private health care services. It is the last Western industrialized country to embrace national public health insurance (1974, 1984), and it carries deep within its nerve structure a dependency on private corporations, private practice and private culture that has evolved over most of the post-war period. Australians, like others, have to ask questions without fear of an American outcome. For example, if the best quality private care for a patient with a long term back injury is a family member, or if a private practitioner offers customized, occupational therapy to a developmentally disabled child in a disadvantaged community with no public facilities, then should the community finance these ostensibly private activities? I suspect most of us would answer yes, and in doing so we find ourselves contemplating a new community-based frontier requiring new policy co-ordinates and principles.

To understand the way public and private health care have come to co-exist in the way they do requires a brief sketch of the contemporary evolution of health care in Australia.

In the 1940s when many Western countries moved towards nationalized health care systems, Australia, like the United States, maintained a national health system based on private service delivery and payment. The political influence of private doctors was so strong that Australians passed an amendment to the national constitution which prohibited the 'conscription' of doctors and dentists into any form of national health service, and this remains in force.[2] As a result, in order to achieve equity of access to health care services, Labour governments' have had to spin a web of social regulation around a powerful, self-interested private medical machine. More than once the web has been broken and the diligent Labour spiders have had to start all over again.

For most of the post-war period successive Conservative governments (1949–1972) closely followed the American health care model.[3] Private medicine and 'voluntary' health insurance were the main forms of health care financing and delivery and a considerable government subsidy was provided to private-for-profit hospitals in leafy and affluent suburbs. Until the advent of the Whitlam Labour government's national public health insurance system 'Medibank' in 1974, there were three Australian health care classes: pensioners, the insured and the uninsured. Notably about 17 per cent[4] of Australia's population (outside of the free public health system in the State of Queensland) were uninsured and people in low-income groups were heavily over-represented among the uninsured.[5] After decades out of power, and influenced by the two 'fathers' of Australian public health insurance, John Deeble and Dick Scotton, the Whitlam Labour government established the concept of national public health insurance along Canadian lines. But the Whitlam experiment was short-lived. In 1975 the Conservative leader Malcolm Fraser seized office in a bloodless constitutional coup.[6] Fraser scrapped Whitlam's national health insurance scheme and returned to the traditional private health insurance strategy. This was as disastrous as it had been previously and it was only with the election of the Hawke Labour government in 1984 that 'Medibank' was retagged with the same name as Canada's national scheme, 'Medicare', and re-established with some modifications in 1984. Since that time Medicare's popularity has surged to such an extent that even the incoming 1996 Howard Conservative government would not dare dismantle it.[7]

The legacy of the long unbroken period of Conservative post-war rule is that Australia's current health care system cannot operate without a large private for-profit hospital sector and, to a lesser extent, a large private insurance industry. With 28 per cent of acute care beds controlled by private corporations and over 30 per cent of total health care costs met through private sources, the system would collapse if these services were withdrawn. More importantly, this strong private base is continually agitating for greater involvement and control of the health care system. As Scotton has argued: 'A substantial private sector may be accepted as a necessary component of any national consensus about the shape of the health care system but, in its present form, the lack of articulation between public and private sectors imparts additional incentives for cost-shifting and cost inflation.'[8]

HEALTH CARE COSTS IN AUSTRALIA

If in the health care system of the future there is to be a constructive role for private and public financing and management, how can costs be controlled? The fourteen-year-old Australian Medicare system currently provides some lessons. Australia has managed to do well at combining cost control with public and private sector provision because of the strong role of national public health insurance (and the competitive discipline this imposes on national medical fees) and the national global budget imposed on the public hospital system by the Commonwealth government. Over most of the post-war period the spending levels between the USA, Canada and Australia were comparable; however, since 1987 Australia has maintained a significantly lower health national expenditure as a percentage of GDP and per capita.

Australia's overall health costs have been contained compared to the explosive rise of health care costs in the USA and the steady rise in Canada. In 1960 Australia spent 88 per cent of the USA's health costs as a percentage of GDP, but by 1993 it was 59 per cent. Measured in US dollars per person adjusted for purchasing power, Australia's health care costs were $1,806 less than the USA in 1993. Only Germany and Japan have done a better job of holding health costs steady as a percentage of GDP. All other countries have seen a rise in health care costs of well over 1 per cent of GDP since 1987.

In sectoral terms Australia's health care expenditure is interesting to compare with its international counterparts. Even with its significant private health insurance industry, Australia's health administration expenditures are considerably lower than those of the United States. Because of its predominantly public funding Canada also has a lower level of administrative costs. Australia's very low per capita spending on pharmaceuticals is primarily due to the Pharmaceutical Benefits Scheme created by the Chifley Labour government in 1949. This program allows the Federal government to nationally fix the wholesale price of drugs. Per person spending on physicians' services in Australia rose by 68 per cent between 1987 and 1992 from $185 to $272. This compares with a 73 per cent rise in Canada and a 64 per cent rise in the United States between 1987 and 1993. Since the advent of national public health insurance, investment in medical facilities declined in Australia, falling from $US61 per person in 1987 to $US58 per person in 1992.

The most revealing factor here is the rate of health care inflation net of overall inflation. From 1980–1990 the Australian health care inflation rate net of overall inflation was 0.1 per cent, 27 times less than the USA and 18 times less than Canada. Only France and Sweden had lower rates of health care inflation. If Australia had the same health care inflation rate as the United States it would have lifted health care expenditure by an extra $7.9 billion from 7.8 to 10 per cent of GDP in 1989/90.[9] Also because of higher population growth in Australia, Canada and the United States, higher levels of health expenditure are needed to keep up with population increases. Per person expenditure growth (2.2 per cent) also reveals that health servicing has been increasing at a rapid rate compared with most other countries over the 1980s.

It is possible to combine public and private health care service delivery with effective cost control. The key factors here are the effect of a global budget on public expenditures and monopsonistic price setting of medical

Table 6.2 Health expenditure growth, selected countries, 1980–1990

Growth components	Aust.	Canada	France	Ger.	NZ	Sweden	UK	USA	Unweighted Mean
Share of health expenditure in GDP 1980	7.4	7.5	7.5	8.4	7.2	9.2	5.9	9.2	7.8
Nominal health expenditure growth	12.2	10.7	10.4	5	12.3	8.9	9.8	10.4	10
Health care price deflator	8.2	6.9	5.2	3.4	11.5	7.1	7.6	6.9	7.1
Of which GDP deflator	8.1	5.1	6.22	9.8	7.6	6.1	4.1	6.2	
Of which excess health care inflation	0.1	1.8	−0.9	0.7	1.6	−0.6	1.3	2.7	0.8
Real expenditure growth	3.7	3.5	5	1.5	0.6	1.7	2.1	3.3	2.7
Of which population growth	1.5	1	0.5	0.3	0.7	0.3	0.2	1	0.7
Of which per person real expenditure growth	2.2	2.5	4.5	1.2	−0.1	1.4	1.9	2.3	2
Share of health expenditure in GDP 1990	7.8	9.5	8.8	8.3	7.3	8.6	6	12.2	8.6

Source: Australian Institute of Health and Welfare, *Australia's Health*, Australian Government Publishing Service, Canberra, 1994, p. 130.

services and other inputs. Public finance, as a means of setting price ceilings for new frontier health care services, will clearly be important.

HEALTH SERVICE UTILIZATION

If cost control comes at the price of inequality of access or poor quality health care services then there would be no point in developing a hybrid public/ private system of financing and managing national health care services. In his international quest for solutions to the US health care crisis, White gave Australia the thumbs up in terms of 'the international standard' of universal coverage, comprehensiveness of benefits, contributions based on income and cost control. He wrote: 'While the public and private insurance mix in Australia is not logically neat, one could argue that it is quite equitable. Everyone pays taxes that guarantee a basic level of care. People who want more or better care may buy it. If voters want more convenience in the public system they could vote for politicians who would raise their taxes to pay for it.'[10]

In terms of access to care, Australians enjoy comparatively high levels of service quality. As even one of its chief critics, and one of the major Australian proponents of market based reform says: 'There are few places in the world where a person who is seriously ill will receive better treatment.'[11] It has been observed that Australia has 'approximately 1/6 the number of hospitals over a geographical area that contains 1/15 of the US population.'[12] This high level of capacity affects the rate of servicing and number of consultations per person and Australia has amongst the highest level of consultations with doctors per person of comparable Western countries.

One of the problems of the Australian system lies in the tendency towards over-servicing amongst general practitioners and other professionals. As Duckett has pointed out the national schedule of public insurance based fees creates a visit-based remuneration spiral which has been difficult to control.[13] Scotton and others have argued for case-based capitation payments which would give more precision in prioritizing treatments and values.[14]

Australia's comparatively high intensity admission rates have to be counterbalanced by the short lengths of stay at Australian hospitals. In 1989/90 the average length of stay at an Australian hospital was 5.6 days (7.2 days excluding same day admissions), giving Australia the fourth lowest length of stay at hospitals of OECD countries.[15]

Australia's in-patient treatment levels are also relatively high compared with other countries, ranging from a high of 23 per cent in 1989 to 17 per cent in 1991. In-patient service delivery through public hospitals is potentially a very cost effective way of delivering health services such as skin and breast cancer screening. The drop-off in in-patient services from 1989 to 1991 is an indication of cost shifting from the state to Federal government as hospitals dependent on state financing become more restrictive about services that could be delivered through general physicians and paid for by the Federal government.

One of the most significant perceived weaknesses of the Australian health care system are so-called waiting lists (Table 6.3). Each year in Australia there are 4 million admissions to acute care hospitals. About 3.6 million are admitted directly to hospital without delay. However, about 10 per cent (approximately 390,000 admissions) are for patients who can safely wait at least 24 hours before surgery ('elective surgery') in public hospitals.

Of those 'electing' surgery about 106,094 can be waiting for up to 3 months and about 2,000 people may wait over 12 months before they are admitted to hospital. Many people waiting for elective surgery have postponed surgery in consultation with their doctor or hospital in order to fit in with family or work routines and about 10,000 drop off the list without ever being admitted to hospital.

However, where medical intervention is needed in potentially life threatening situations, even one problem or wasted day is too many. The biggest

Table 6.3 Waiting lists in Australia

State	Numbers requiring elective surgery				Clearance times (months)		Waiting over 12 months
	1993	per 100,000	1994	per 100,000	1993	1994	%
NSW*	34,406	575	42,627	704	1.4	1.8	1
Vic†	28,618	631	29,935	668	1.4	2.6	3
Qld	n/a	n/a	n/a	n/a	n/a	n/a	n/a
WA	10,138	573	10,481	611	3.8	3.3	5
SA	8,775	591	9,364	636	2.7	2.8	3
Tas	6,983	1,492	7,403	1,566	2.7	2.5	6
ACT	3,530	1,161	4,118	1,365	5.7	5.0	n/a
NT	1,683	1,045	2,496	1,476	6.0	9.9	8
Aust	94,730	658	106,094	721	1.8	2.3	2

Sources: AIHW, National Reports on Elective Surgery Waiting Lists for Public Hospitals, 1993, 1994,1995.

Notes: The figures for Australia do not include Queensland.

* Several initiatives undertaken in NSW in 1993/94 resulted in more comprehensive and reliable data collection than existed previously.

† Victoria partitions its register of patients into two – 'unbooked' and 'booked' patients. 'Booked patients' are those who do not have a definite date of admission for six weeks. 'Unbooked patients' are those who do not have a definite date of admission within six weeks. The method used for calculation of waiting time for the Victorian data provided for this report is different from the method used by other States and Territories.

surgery waiting lists are for general surgery where the throughput time is 1.3 months; orthopaedics where the clearance time is about 2.9 months; ear, nose and throat where the admission clearance time is 3.9 months; plastic surgery has a waiting time of 2.7 months; finally, urology has a clearance time of 2.1 months.

REVENUE, EXPENDITURE AND PRIVATIZATION

Given cost control and quality, it would be easy to argue that the Australian hybrid model has a number of advantages for prospective health care reform. However, without a number of caveats that would be an uncritical view. As one of Australia's pre-eminent health care historians Sidney Sax has written, health care policy in Australia is a 'strife of interests masquerading as principles'; this is a useful and cautionary way of thinking about what is at stake in any embrace of such a system. Within a public/private hybrid system there never will be a time when the debates are won and one single model or balance of forces is settled.

In the current context, and for a number of quite complex reasons, private health care provision is coming to the fore. Three forces: slow economic

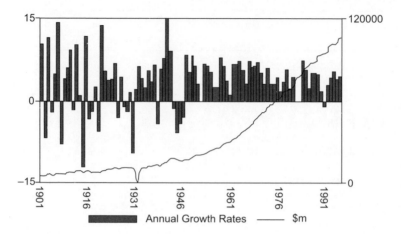

Figure 6.1 Australian national economic growth, 1901–1996.
Source: Australian National Accounts.

growth, the costs of inequality and the ideology of small government are pushing Australia back towards private health care in a mutually reinforcing sequence of events.

The first major problem for the Australian health system is that slow economic growth (see Figure 6.1) has resulted in a low level of general government revenue. Over the past twenty-five years Australia has moved from a period of prosperity to a period of relative misery with all of the concomitant effects, including lost production, slower wages growth, poor government revenues and less home ownership to name but a few outcomes. The downturn in Australia since 1974 has been even more dramatic than that in the United States.[16] The implications for the Australian health care system have been profound.

There is a fairly tight relationship between national economic growth and health expenditure growth. When GDP growth rises, health expenditure tends to follow. The more revenue on hand the more readily the health care system seems to absorb it. However, in the 1991–1993 recession, health expenditure remained relatively stable while GDP returned a negative result for only the second time in the post-war period. In these circumstances health expenditure falls to a safety net level, but not below, due to the inability of health care institutions to operate below a certain floor of costs and because of the higher demands placed on health care institutions in periods of recession and unemployment.

We need some elegant modelling to give us an exact effect of low growth on health care expenditure. However, if we assume a tight relationship between GDP growth and health expenditure growth and calculate health expenditure as a percentage of GDP on the basis of 1950s levels of economic growth, health

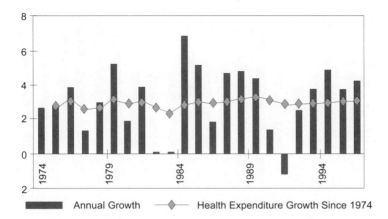

Figure 6.2 Australian national economic growth, 1974–1996.

income has fallen by 1.4 per cent per annum since 1974 due to slower economic growth (Figure 6.2). Cumulatively this represents a 32 per cent shortfall, or a sum of $11 billion in 1993/94 dollars. This is equivalent to 1.3 times the total of the state and local governments' budget for health care each year, equal to the cost of running the entire Australian hospital system for a year or enough to fund the equivalent of twenty of Australia's most needy health care communities for a year. The sum is enough to fund the equivalent of twenty of Australia's most needy regional health services. It is worth observing that any government that tried to impose a budgetary squeeze of this magnitude on the health system would be living dangerously, but because this was achieved gradually, without an ostensible 'razor gang',[17] it has been unconsciously accepted by health administrators, service providers and the general public who have been 'doing more with less' for over twenty years.

The second major climatic effect to befall the health care system is what may be called 'the inequality effect'. On top of the shortfall in funding arising from slow economic growth, the health system must also meet extra health demands resulting from the heightened inequality and economic dependency that is the product of recession and low economic growth.

Slow economic growth causes lost jobs, falling and stagnating wages, eroding markets, closed factories, rising levels of poverty and reduced levels of home ownership. Over the past twenty years Australia has been accumulating these problems in concentrated areas. If economic growth falls below 3.5 per cent the economy is not growing as fast as the workforce. With an average rate of growth of 2.6 per cent since 1974 the net effect is an ever-increasing pool of unemployment and increased economic dependency and insecurity. There have been periods of high growth and new jobs. The last sustained period was Labour's golden period from 1983–1989. In that period,

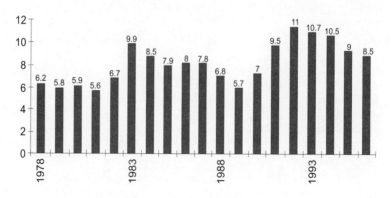

Figure 6.3 Australian unemployment, 1978–1996.

with an average growth rate of 4.5 per cent, it took six years to reduce
unemployment from 9.9 per cent to 6.8 per cent. Conversely, however, it
took only eighteen months of recession from 1990–1991 to push unemployment from 7 per cent to 11 per cent (Figure 6.3).

Colin Mather's work for the Australian Institute for Health and Welfare
from which Table 6.4 has been constructed gives us a broad picture of the

Table 6.4 Health and disadvantage in Australia

	Children 0–14 in low income families	Unemployed young adults 15–24	Unemployed adults 25–64	Disadvantaged older Australians
Increased mortality rates	↑	↑	↑	↑
Propensity for poor health	↑	↑	↑	
Chronic illnesses	↑	↑	↑	
Hospital episodes	↑	↑		
Out-patient and doctors' visits				
Injuries	↑	↑		
Dental visits	↓		↓	
Reduced activity due to illness	↑	↑		
Drug dependency		↑		
Handicap or disability		↑	↑	
Psychological distress		↑		
Motor vehicle accidents		↑		
Overweight		↑		↑
Homicide		↑		
Suicide		↑		↑
Smoker		↑		↑

problems that result from chronically high levels of unemployment. Unemployment and low income create higher mortality rates across all age groups. With them come a higher propensity to ill health and illness. Hospital and doctors' visits increase, as do injuries. In addition, a series of problems become more prevalent, particularly amongst young adults, including drug dependency, psychological distress, motor vehicle accidents, diet, homicide and suicide.

These problems are of course not spread evenly across the Australian economy and society. They are concentrated in newly developing areas, which because of slow economic growth and declining government income, go without established health infrastructure or services. For example, the population of South Western Sydney has high rates of unemployment, more concentrated numbers of single parent families, a population with lower than average educational achievements and large numbers of non-English-speaking background (NESB) new Australians.[18] At the same time it has 2.04 beds per thousand residents compared to 3.81 beds and 3.57 beds per thousand in Central Sydney and South Eastern Sydney and it receives about 50 per cent of the budget allocation of South Eastern Sydney. The problems are so profound that over 50,000 people have to travel outside the area each year to receive hospitalization because of the lack of health care services.[19] There is an equivalent of South Western Sydney in all of Australia's principal cities, and the urban demographic and development pattern of 1990s Australia is very similar to the United States in the 1960s and 1970s except that it is the outer suburbs rather than the inner city that is becoming impoverished.

The third, and most pervasive incentive to privatize the health care system, may be called 'the small government effect'. As *The Economist* has remarked somewhat sarcastically: 'These days fiscal conservatism is espoused by nearly all rich-country leftists',[20] and in an era of slow growth, when government revenues are down and people's demands are up, areas of social spending such as education, health, social security and welfare, housing and community services and recreation and culture are ready targets. The initial introduction of Medicare in Australia in 1983/84 caused Commonwealth health care outlays to rise by 22 per cent for its first two years of operation; after that time Commonwealth health outlays rose at the more modest rate of about 2 per cent per annum. However, over the course of the 1980s and early 1990s Australian social spending became the biggest area of total government outlays (Figure 6.4). In the first decade of Labour government, spending on social security, education and health rose from 52 per cent of all government expenditure per person to over 62 per cent, and health spending rose from $A730 per person to $A1,150.[21]

RAZOR GANGS AND SOCIAL SPENDING

Within this context, even under the former Labour Commonwealth government, politicians made their reputations on 'razor gangs' (see note 17) by cutting down some area of social spending.[22] Under Labour the general

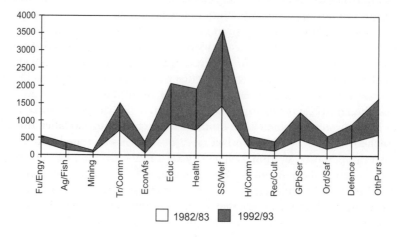

Figure 6.4 Australian government outlays per capita by purpose, 1982/83 and 1992/93.

strategy was to income test every government social benefit as a means of reducing outlays and responsibilities. This created two effects: first, Australians in the bottom three income deciles benefited considerably from 'social wage' spending. The final income of the lowest income groups rose by between 4 and 6 per cent over the 1980s. Second, because of the Wages Accord between the Labour government and the Australian Council of Trade Unions which put a cap on wages claims, and the income tests placed on social benefits, the final income of Australians in the fourth, fifth, sixth, seventh, eighth and ninth income deciles declined by between 1 and 4 per cent over the same period. These two effects created a profound change in political orientation, particularly amongst working class voters. By the time of the 1996 election a political backlash against Labour was brewed up within Labour heartlands and amongst middle income groups who resented the fact that the outlook of the disadvantaged seemed to be improving, while their own was declining in real terms. A symbol of this discontent was the rise of Pauline Hansen, an independent politician, who won a safe Labour seat in Queensland by combining arguments against welfare cheats with overt racism.[23]

Ironically, with Labour thrown out of office, the virtues of small government reached new heights with the incoming Howard Conservative government in 1996. Claiming that Labour left a $A10 billion 'black hole', Howard severely cut back all areas of Commonwealth social expenditure. Because of the vertically imbalanced nature of Australian public finance (76 per cent of Australian taxation is controlled and raised by the Commonwealth), cutbacks across the whole of government are virtually set in train by the Commonwealth Budget and then flow on to the states through reduced general and specific grants. The first budget of the new government targeted hospital funding in particular as an area for 'savings', and the Commonwealth Dental Program which chiefly benefits senior citizens was almost entirely dismantled.[24]

The Labour government's strategy of restricting expenditure growth through income tests and reduced payments to the states and, to a far greater extent, the Howard Conservative government's overt slashing of social spending, caused a pronounced shift back towards a health system dominated by the private sector. With the advent of Medicare, Commonwealth government revenue became the chief financier of the Australian health system.[25] However, from 1983 the government share of total health expenditure has fallen from 71 per cent to 68 per cent and the private sector's share has increased from 29 per cent to 32 per cent.[26] From 1991/92 to 1993/94 the number of private hospitals has grown from 319 to 329 acute and psychiatric hospitals and from 72 to 111 day hospitals.[27] The operating expenditure for private acute and psychiatric hospitals increased from $1.9 billion in 1991/92 to $2.2 billion in the year 1993/94 alone. The operating expenditure for private day hospitals increased astronomically by 57 per cent from $35.3 to $61 million over the three years from 1991/92 to 1993/94.

Privatization in Australia occurs as a ripple-down effect.[28] Affected by Commonwealth cutbacks the states become desperate to find, for example, high levels of capital required for new hospital infrastructure. The frontrunner of the new era of privatization was the privatization of the Port Macquaire Base Hospital in New South Wales. Before the 1991 state election Port Macquarie was promised a new 180-bed public hospital. However, after the election, the Fahey Conservative state government, which retained office, announced it was closing down the 100-bed Public Hospital[29] and replacing it with a privately owned and run hospital. In a bizarre scenario, the private hospital was given a monopoly of care for the area, one of Australia's most significant retirement areas, and was contracted by the government to provide a minimum number of 'public beds'.

The decision to allow a private contractor to build and operate the hospital in Port Macquarie was largely 'based on the argument that private construction ownership and management will be more cost-effective than public construction ownership and management'.[30] However the Evatt Foundation argued at the time that the calculations that the government put forward to prove this were fundamentally flawed.[31] The reality is that the chief motivation for Port Macquarie was that the state government could shift the responsibility for the hospital off its books and into the sphere of private and Commonwealth sponsorship. Despite the previous government's goal of cost effectiveness, through privatization, the Port Macquarie Base Hospital now costs '30 per cent more to run than its own public hospitals'.[32] It could be more. Ironically, the contract signed under the Fahey government does not allow the Department of Health to fully disclose any budget or operating figures of the Port Macquarie Base Hospital due to a commercial confidentiality clause in the contract.[33] However, because privatization has effectively shifted these costs away from state government responsibility they are of no concern to state politicians.

Since Port Macquarie the pace to more fully privatize the Australian hospital system has increased. In the states of Victoria, South Australia and Western Australia governments have moved to shift much of their fiscal responsibility to the private sector, and the South Australian government is reported to have offered a major US health maintenance organization, Kaiser Permanente, a major role in managing its hospital system.

The pace of privatization can be measured by the growth of one of the indigenous private-for-profit hospital proprietors, Mayne Nickless, which entered the 'hospital business' in 1986. Mayne Nickless's biggest move was in 1991 when it acquired the eight hospitals (and 910 beds) of the Hospital Corporation of America for about $A80 million.[34] By June 1994 Mayne Nickless had acquired 22 hospitals on the Australian east coast, with two still under construction, for a total of 2,500 beds, or about 10 per cent of the private hospital sector. The company's turnover for the 1994 year was $A260 million. Earning before interest and tax was $A45 million and annual spending was $A35 million. Analysts expected Mayne Nickless hospitals (which since 1992 operate under the name of Health Care of Australia (HCOA)) to build turnover to about $A300 million in 1996/97 and earnings before interest and tax to $A57 million. The figures imply a healthy improvement in earnings before income and tax (EBIT) of 21 per cent.[35]

POLICY CHALLENGES AHEAD

These developments create some engaging dilemmas. First, the difficulty for supporters of Medicare is that Australia's whole framework of social support and services was never planned to deal with sustained unemployment of over 5 per cent. It was never intended to deal with high levels of inequality, nor was it intended to deal with regions in which unemployment and the problems of inequality are compounded. The original basis for Australia and most other Western welfare systems was Beveridge's UK social contract in which it was assumed that every able citizen worked and made a contribution in the form of taxation to the upkeep of national infrastructure and, accordingly, shared health care facilities equally across the community. The breakdown of the economic and social assumptions of the post-war period: full employment, strong economic growth and shared prosperity have thrown these assumptions into disarray. The health care system and other areas of social welfare system have become shock absorbers for other problems. Hospitals, health care professionals and community workers deal with greater incidence of ill health, violence and crime and a series of spillover effects that result from the inability of increasing numbers of people within our society to fend for themselves. The revenue and resources that could have been expected from taxation and private revenue has been diminished by a smaller workforce and by the need for government to spend more on other economic and social priority areas. Second, and by far the greatest threat to the coherence of Australia's health system, is privatization. As the trends discussed above will suggest, whilst the public/private mix of hospitals has been a feature of Australia's health system for many years, the privatization of health is reaching new heights. Conservative state governments across Australia have embraced privatization strategies as though they held the answer to all financing and budgeting difficulties. Not only is this incorrect, it may in the near future create a fully fledged two-tier health system and threaten the basic right of Australians to fair, equitable and accessible health care through Medicare.

Certainly the economic pressures pushing Australia towards what is in effect a two-tier model of public and private care in Australia are worrying. However, it is interesting to note that, despite a $A600 million per annum effort by the Howard government to subsidize private health insurance costs, Australians are resisting privatization by moving away from private health insurance in droves.

Under the National Health Act 1983 only two categories of private health insurance, one covering hospital care and treatment as a private patient[36] and the other covering health services not covered by Medicare[37] are available. One of the central problems for the private insurance industry is that patients can be left with a very significant payment for private treatment even if they have Medicare and private insurance coverage. There have also been spiralling private insurance premiums.[38] In these circumstances, despite the fact that the Howard Conservative government has offered tax deductions to those who take out private insurance, many Australians prefer to stay with what is, in effect, free public treatment.

Medicare was intended to co-exist with the private health insurance system, and initial estimates of the cost of Medicare assumed that at least 40 per cent of Australians would maintain their private cover. However, as Figure 6.5 indicates, there has been a rapid drop in those covered by private health insurance and in the last quarter of 1997 only 31.6 per cent of Australians have maintained their private cover.[39]

The conjunction of increasing pressure to privatize health care service delivery and increasing preference for comprehensive public insurance, makes the Australian health care system an interesting, though probably not unique, case study. If these two forces continue apace, and Australian Medicare remains unaltered, then it is clear that an expanding private sector must learn to live within a publicly circumscribed budget. In the short term, however, it is possible that the private sector will win the battle for dominance. The Howard government could dismantle the main tenets of Medicare and public control. However, they would do so at their political peril; as the 1975 experience suggests, dismantling Medicare would create an extra and important incentive for Australians to vote Labour at the next election. All things considered, and given strong and wise government, a likely medium term outcome is for the private sector to negotiate a publicly acceptable role and performance goals. What sort of role and performance can we define for private

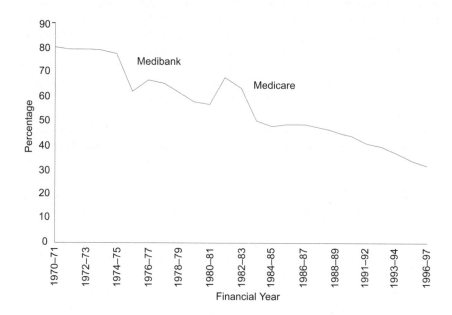

Figure 6.5 Percentage of Australian population with private health insurance.
Source: Industry Commission, 1997.

for-profit and not-for-profit health care? How can public and private constructively co-exist?

The new frontier of health care has a number of dimensions: geographically it is situated in those parts of every nation that have under-developed health care infrastructure, profound social and economic problems, or both; conceptually it is about developing the most effective preventive health care interventions and improving the quality of health care services, and institutionally it is about supplementing and, hopefully, in many cases, supplanting medical models of health care service delivery. All these things come together in the challenges which face health care administrators with restricted budgets in under-developed regions and cities.

A possible way forward is to divide up this new frontier of health care providing for private sector growth and funding in return for the acceptance of agreed population health outcome performance goals and a clear understanding that new modes of service delivery will be rigorously developed and promoted. Using population-based health outcome funding models we could encourage the respective strengths of private and public service delivery.

One of the architects of Australian Medicare, Dick Scotton, has been trying do this through his 'home-grown' Australian managed competition model involving a single funder with public and private budget holders creating competition between public and private service providers.[40] Scotton's model requires a framework for managed competition (budget holders) and a mea-surement system (case payment) in order to achieve efficiencies. Many aspects of Scotton's model are well developed and worthwhile; however, the problem of the managed competition model in general is that it is predicated upon a passive, inward-looking health care system. It creates competition where it is not necessarily needed and relies on budget holders who are not capable or empowered to encourage the development of new, innovative forms of service delivery. (One of the shortcomings of Australia's decentralized area health funding is that area health boards, particularly in the state of NSW, are merely conduits for hospital funding.) Australia's health care system and the systems of most nations, does not primarily need competition amongst traditional medical providers for more money, but rather there needs to be competition for services where money is currently not allocated, in poor and developing areas with inadequate social infrastructure and for illnesses and disabilities that are inadequately covered by social insurance. There is no primary need for a case payment system that tells us that an appendectomy is more expensive in one hospital as opposed to another, when there are no case payments and no cost–benefit analyses available to tell us the savings that would come from more active health promotion and community based care. The better option is to move towards a new set of population health outcomes measures which are not biased towards the approval of medical or hospital models for getting results.

Perhaps the most challenging new frontier health care issue is the health of our ageing Western population. In Australia and many countries, over the next forty years a ripple effect upwards will occur that will see a far larger popula-tion living beyond the age of 85. The numbers of those aged 65+ will increase from 1.9 million to 5.2 million. The peak load in Australia will occur at around 2031 when baby boomers will have turned 80 or over.[41] The budgetary consequences of this phenomena are already starting to be felt. Total recurrent expenditure on aged care services in constant price terms has increased from $A2,181.8 million in 1991/92 to $A2,752.9 million in 1995/96. Expenditure on home and community care (HACC) and hostels increased by over 300 per cent, and nursing homes by 93 per cent, between 1986/87 and 1995/96.[42] The Howard Conservative government's response to this situation was to introduce upfront fees for nursing homes (that for many involved the sale of their family home), de-regulated private provision and underfunding for public institu-tions. Such was the public outcry that the government was forced to back down and to return to the status quo.

As this suggests, leaving long term care to the market is no solution. In addition to the political costs, private long term care insurance is usually limited in coverage of services and timescale, premiums increase markedly when coverage of risks is improved and such policies tend to attract bad risks. The situation demands a social insurance solution where low prevalence, high cost risks are covered by including a large population base in the scheme. Long term insurance would fit neatly under the Medicare public insurance umbrella. Under the model that is being proposed social insurance would be made available to cover a competitive array of public and private health care services. In order to cover basic aged care services for all Australians over 65, it is estimated that the Australian Medicare levy would have to be increased from 1.7 per cent to 2.8 per cent of income per annum. Provision could be made for top-ups to public coverage through extra superannuation or pension fund contributions[43] covering long term care and through private health insurers being given access to selected parts of the market. The price for providing a secure private funding base for long term care would be competition for the right to provide community based aged care according to a charter of aged care rights and responsibilities. An Aged Care Bill of Rights might include the right to self determination of care and independent living, the right of access to high quality and timely medical services, right of access to a system of long term care that includes community-based home, hostel and nursing home support and the right to a co-ordinated and managed plan of retirement.[44]

CONCLUSION

A worrying shift back to the private sector in Australian health care is occurring. 'Single payer' public health care advocates will view what is happening in Australia with dismay. The latest initiatives of the Howard Conservative government may convince them that any hybrid mix of the two North American systems is undesirable because, ultimately, it compromises the principle of universal access and equity to health care services. Alternatively, advocates of market and private models will want to see the Australian health care system as an endorsement of privatization with its apparent cost control and accountability. The lasting lesson, however, is that if we are to move towards a new frontier of health care services the difficult job of balancing public and private modes of delivery and financing will be an ongoing one. In this respect, Australian health care reformers are lucky to be constrained by a problem that must be solved before progress can be made. The right balance cannot be developed theoretically, it will come from devising the financing and service systems necessary to equitably and efficiently meet the increasing health care demands of an ageing population, the needs of those in under-developed areas of our economy and society and the new goals of community health and well-being thrown up by our citizenry.

NOTES

1   The term here is used in the Brandeis sense: 'a single courageous State may, if its citizens choose, serve as a laboratory; and try novel social and economic experiments without risk to the rest of the country'. Supreme Court Justice Louis Brandeis, *New State Ice C* v. *Liebmann*, Dissenting Opinion, 1932. See David Osbourne, *Laboratories of Democracy*, Harvard Business School Press, 1990. Also

see the author's heroic monograph *USACARE: A National Health Insurance Strategy for the USA*, Midwest Center for Labor Research, Chicago, 1991 which argued that a combination of the Canadian and Australian health insurance systems was the stepping stone for US health care reform.

2 In the 1946 referendum the then Chifley Labor government sought Common-wealth power over state administered social welfare, including maternity allow-ances and other benefits. In return for support for the Commonwealth takeover, the Conservatives pushed for the words 'but not so as to allow any form of civil conscription' to be inserted into a new sector 51 (xxiiiA) of the Constitution. These words have subsequently presented a legal and political obstacle for any govern-ment seeking to emulate a British National Health system.

3 'A distinguished British medical visitor to Australia in the early 1960s reported that, in Britain the health system favoured the patient at the doctor's expense, the situation in Australia was the other way around.' R. B. Scotton and C. R. Mac-donald, *The Making of Medibank*, University of NSW, 1993, p. 13.

4 Australia now provides universal health insurance coverage; in the United States over 15 per cent of the population (upwards of 38.9 million people) have no health insurance each year. In most other Western countries less than 1 per cent of the population are uninsured.

5 R. B. Scotton, 'Membership of Voluntary Health Insurance', *Economic Record*, vol. 45, 1969, pp. 69–83.

6 For an authoritative account of the Whitlam government's period of office and demise see Alan Reid, *The Whitlam Venture*, Hill of Content, Melbourne, 1976.

7 When Medicare was first introduced 44 per cent of Australians were in favour of Medicare and the Pharmaceutical Benefits Scheme; by 1991 seven in ten Austra-lians surveyed supported the two programs, and by 1994–95 over 90 per cent of those surveyed supported them.

8 Dick Scotton, 'Managed Competition: Issues for Australia', *Australian Health Review*, Vol. 18, No. 1, 1995, p. 87.

9 Australian Institute of Health and Welfare (AIHW), *Australia's Health 1994*, Australian Government Publishing Service, 1994, pp. 128–129.

10 Joseph White, *Competing Solutions: American Health Care Proposals and International Experience*, Brookings Institution, Washington, 1995, p. 102.

11 John Patterson, 'The Last Picture Show', 1997, unpublished monograph, available from the Victorian Department of Health, Melbourne, Australia.

12 R. B. Scotton and H. J. Owens, *Case Payment in Australian Hospitals: Issues and Options*, Public Sector Management Institute, Monash University, August 1990, p. 241.

13 Stephen Duckett, 'Medicare: Where to Now?', *Australian Health Review*, Vol. 18, No. 1, 1995, p. 122.

14 Scotton, 1995, pp. 93–95.

15 Scotton & Owens, op. cit., p. 162.

16 Jeffrey Maddrick points out that in the century to 1973 real economic growth in the United States averaged 3.4 per cent, but that between 1973 and 1993 the American economy has had its most sustained period of slow economic growth ever, averaging only 2.3 per cent. The lost 1 per cent represents goods and services of $12 trillion. Maddrick argues that if the American economy had maintained its historical levels of economic growth then the US Federal government would have

collected an extra $2.4 trillion in taxes and that state and local government would have collected an extra $900 billion in taxes and charges.

17 In Australia in the early part of the century so-called 'razor gangs', consisting of youths armed with knifes and razors, terrorized the inner city. The term has been re-appropriated and is now the common term for government committees, such as the Australian Commonwealth government's Expenditure Review Committee that has the job of cutting back government revenue to meet the requirements of Finance and Treasury.

18 E. Sullivan, M. Fahey, A. Bassman, G. Close, N. Nash, *Health in South Western Sydney: An Epidemiological Profile*, South Western Sydney Area Health Service, June 1995.

19 South Western Sydney Area Health Service, *Annual Report*, 1995/96, pp. 10–11.

20 Cited in Rudolf Klein, 'Coping with Uncertainty in Hard Times: Political and Social Factors in Health Futures', unpublished paper, June 1996.

21 See P. Botsman, 'Towards Full Employment (The Social Wage)', in P. Botsman, N. Swanscott, T. McDonald, L. Tarrant, R. Archer and P. Robinson, *Unions 2001: A Blueprint for Trade Union Activism*, Evatt Foundation, 1995, p. 229.

22 The most ruthless head of the Commonwealth's Expenditure Review Committee, former Labor Finance Minister Peter Walsh, was proud of his reputation for attacking areas such as child care which he regarded as benefiting middle class 'trendies'. Rising health costs were particularly targeted in the 1991/92 Budget.

23 Hansen has become a favourite media target, and many profiles of her activities can be found in the major Australian newspapers over the period from 1996–1998.

24 Peter Groenewegen, 'The 1996–97 Budget: Fiscal Impact on New South Wales', unpublished paper delivered to a seminar organized by the Evatt Foundation, 22 August, 1996.

25 The Federal government collects an earmarked Medicare levy of 1.5 per cent on taxable income above certain income thresholds; the levy raises about one-third of the costs of the national health system.

26 AIHW, op. cit., p. 122.

27 Day hospitals provide surgery and procedures for patients not requiring overnight accommodation and care.

28 P. Groenewegen, *Public Finance in Australia: Theory and Practice*, Prentice-Hall, Sydney, 1990.

29 A NSW government document in 1992 argued that 'Hastings District Hospital is just not big enough to cope with the growing demands of Port Macquarie area. Expansion of health facilities are now well overdue but the existing hospital is unsuitable for major redevelopment.' New South Wales Department of Health, Port Macquarie: *A New and Secure Approach to Public Health Services*, Circulated Information Booklet, 1992, p. 1.

30 Evatt Foundation, 'Submission to the Select Parliamentary and Public Accounts Committee Inquiry into the Funding of Health Infrastructure and Services in New South Wales', August 1992, p. 34.

31 Ibid., p. 36.

32 *The Sun Herald*, Sydney, 25 June 1995.

33 It is not only increasing operating costs and secret clauses which inhibit public debate which are of concern. There are many failed promises, aspects of the contract which have not been met, and increasing complaints about the hospital. A promised renal unit was not delivered as part of the contract. It was only due to

the efforts of the Port Macquarie Hospital Action Group that the unit was placed back under the management of the regional district health board and is housed back at the old original public hospital site. There have been numerous complaints against the poor quality of service from the Accident and Emergency Department. After receiving 22 stitches in her leg, one elderly women was discharged almost immediately to her apartment which had steps that were difficult for her to mount. A community nurse was supposed to check up on her but never did. The woman was eventually admitted into a public hospital in a nearby town.

34 The price represented $96,000 per licensed bed, about half the industry's previous acquisition cost and well down on the peak price of $250,000 at the height of the 1980s bubble. The market for hospital beds has improved sharply since then to the $100,000–200,000 range.

35 Mayne Nickless management argue that increasing labour productivity is one of the ways it has increased its earnings margins. Nursing staff account for over half the costs of private hospitals. By arranging sharper shifts for nurses, Mayne Nickless has reduced its overall nursing costs. In the public hospital sector overlaps between shifts can be as long as two and a half hours; this is because in some areas (for example, intensive care) incoming nurses are carefully briefed on the changes in status of patients in their care. At Mayne Nickless shift overlaps between nurses average 30 minutes.

36 There are two types of hospital cover: basic and supplementary. Before 1995, the National Health Act allowed the Minister for Health to determine the nature and level of benefits in the basic table. The basic table provides cover for a range of items, including treatment in a public hospital by a doctor of the patient's choice, fees for private patients in public shared ward accommodation, fees for private hospital shared ward accommodation and the 25 per cent difference between the Medicare payment and the MBS provided in hospital for private patients. Supplementary hospital insurance includes all the benefits of basic cover, but pays significantly higher benefits – usually covering the full cost of being treated as a private patient in a public hospital. Private hospital fees usually exceed the benefits provided in the basic table. Consequently, patients using private hospitals need to take out supplementary cover if they are to avoid significant out-of-pocket expenses. Supplementary cover is not regulated by the government other than through the requirement that its premiums are community rated.

37 These are often referred to as ancillary services and include dental treatment, acupuncture, hearing aids and physiotherapy. Ancillary insurance may be held without any hospital insurance.

38 For example, average hospital insurance premiums increased by around 75 per cent (9.8 per cent p.a.) between 1989/90 and 1995/96, while the CPI increased by around 18.7 per cent p.a. (2.9 per cent p.a.) over the same period, leaving a real increase in premiums of around 46 per cent.

39 There have been a number of studies that have highlighted the continuing decline in private health insurance since the introduction of Medicare. Figure 6.10 shows that the introduction of Medibank in 1975 reduced demand for private health insurance by approximately 18 per cent in that year. In October 1976 the Fraser government introduced a contingent 2.5 per cent levy on taxable income, which was waived if private health insurance was purchased; this resulted in a slight percentage point rise in the number of people with private health insurance. Between 1976 and 1981, when free health care services were provided under Medibank,

private health insurance declined steadily. However, this trend was sharply reversed from 1981 to 1982, when the Fraser government abandoned Medibank. When Medicare was introduced, private health insurance fell sharply again. The sharpest reduction over this period was between 1983 and 1984, immediately before and immediately after the introduction of Medicare. In that period coverage declined from around 64 per cent to 50 per cent.

40 Scotton, 1995, pp. 82–104.
41 John McCallum and Karin Geiselhart, *Australia's New Aged Issues for Young and Old*, Allen and Unwin, 1996, pp. 1–14.
42 AIHW, op. cit., p. 1.
43 By law in Australia employers and employees are required to make contributions to superannuation funds.
44 McCallum and Geiselhart, op. cit.

7 The US, UK and Canada

Convergence or divergent reform practices?

Mary Ruggie

Privatization is proceeding in all health care systems despite the fact that national health care is heralded as a triumph over the inequities of market forces and private incentives. There seems to be a widespread willingness, even among the social democracies of Western Europe, to see if privatization perhaps can work to increase efficiency and effectiveness, both economic and administrative. Although privatization is taking a number of different forms (see Stewart, Chapter 4 this volume), most focus on the mechanism of competition to achieve more optimal levels of supply and demand, price and quality. In this experimentation, a more nagging question than the specifics of privatization is the role of the state, and, ultimately, the integrity of public responsibility. By allowing an increase in private sector activities, the state, some claim, is spurning its obligation to promote the common good, a situation made worse when government regulation of the private sector appears to be weak. Every act of regulation, however, restricts the reasons for allowing privatization to occur in the first place. This quandary is testing the capacities of states to govern not only health care, but all areas where privatization is underway.

The purpose of the following discussion is to elaborate the role of the state in the light of increasing private sector involvement in health care. Focusing on recent developments in health care provision and delivery in Britain, the United States and Canada, I present an evolution toward a significantly different state role. Its contours are not well captured by traditional frameworks for understanding the public and private sectors. The state appears to be engaging private actors in the social construction of a health care system that is neither public nor private, but both at the same time. The emerging consequence is not some vague and vacuous mix, however, because of one overriding characteristic–the state has not ceded ultimate authority for the common good to the private sector. While the exercise of public authority continues to function through familiar channels (such as regulations), we are also witnessing a novel, more pragmatic set of responses by the state as called for by different circumstances. In other words, the state is leading the change through privatization policy.

PRIVATIZATION: ITS MEANINGS AND IMPLICATIONS

The term 'privatization' connotes a direction of change in functions and/or activities from public to private auspices (cf. Lundqvist, 1988; Kamerman and Kahn, 1989). The quantitative and qualitative consequences of such a shift must be investigated empirically, one cannot assume that the state is doing less or worse because the private sector is doing more. For example, a full scale transfer in ownership, financing or production would most likely create a net decrease in the public sector and a net increase in the private. But if these functions are separated such that the production of health care is privatized while most financing remains public, the total outcome is ambiguous. When one considers additional government roles, such as regulation, the assessment of net changes in the weight of the two sectors is further confounded. Although we commonly think of regulation as a public sector activity, it too is subject to privatization. Yet, apparent self-regulation by the private sector could be occurring within parameters or goals set by the state or negotiated between public and private sector officials. This type of shift suggests an event that only weakly conforms to the common meaning of privatization or the implication of a reduction in the role or responsibilities of the state.

The process of privatization and the resulting mix of public and private sector functions and activities is complicated by commonly held conceptions of the separateness of these two spheres, each with inherent qualities distinct from the other. Most discussions of the relationship between the public and private sectors and the nature of their intersections tend to imply an opposition in their innate orientations, resulting in interactions characterized by contradictions and tensions. The activities of either sector are thought to counter the other. And, when mechanisms from either sector are introduced to mitigate the excesses of the other, they are considered invasive and distorting. Thus, we use the word 'intervention' to describe state 'regulation'. This understanding informs studies that, for example, are sceptical of the capacity of market forces to achieve efficiency let alone contribute to effectiveness. It also informs studies that seek, for example, to reduce bureaucratic 'gridlock' in national health care systems by introducing market forces (Enthoven, 1985). The prevailing framework within which issues of privatization is discussed conveys a zero-sum conception of resources. Each side possesses its own unique positive and negative attributes (justice is a public sector good, efficiency a private one; overload is a public sector problem, inequality a product of private sector activity). And the benefits of either sector are curtailed and/or its capacity to function improved by the other. Lost in this understanding is the notion of synergism, the possibility that the public and private sectors can deteriorate at the same time or excel together or create new actors or modalities because of the nature of their interactions within a larger context. To put the point differently: is there no interest on the part of the private sector in achieving greater equity in health care aside from the profits that may accrue? Can the public sector pursue cost savings without jeopardizing the well-being of individuals in need? At one level my answer is obvious, only through concerted and coordinated efforts on the part of actors in both sectors to articulate common goals and engage in mutually acceptable means. But at another level, the questions themselves imply a normative stance that is obfuscated by the prevailing conceptual framework: both the public and private sectors are bound and bound together by the ethic of social responsibility. Separating the two spheres leads to the postulation that the burden of exercising and assuring the rule of ethical and normative standards belongs to the public sector and, more specifically, the state. Such an inflation in the concept of the state leaves little room for other actors in society. Are private doctors and private hospitals inherently incapable of ethical behaviour? Is their capacity to act responsibly determined primarily by their location in the private sector? Are they absolved in some way because of their standpoint and the corresponding role of the state?

In adopting a research stance that asks these questions I am trying to formulate an alternative framework for conceptualizing the interrelations of public and private sector activities. Governments in the UK, US, and Canada have allowed competition to enter the health care system but with remarkably different results. Why is this?

Britain

Private sector health care has always existed as a relatively small and mainly separate sphere of activity alongside the National Health Service (NHS). It has consisted primarily of private consultants (specialist physicians), private insurance, and privately paid-for procedures (such as fertilization) that tend to cater to the wealthy. In general, private health care in Britain has been subject to minimal public regulation. Intersections between the public and private sectors have occurred; for example, most private consultants have also worked for the NHS, and everyone has paid small user fees for certain services (dental care, prescriptions). Beginning in the 1980s the intersections deepened and the role of private health care grew. These changes have been explicitly undertaken by the public sector. While they have brought a significant transformation in the delivery of health care and in the workings of the NHS, they have not constituted a clear-cut decline in the public sector.

The first major developments began in the Thatcher administration, which, following groundwork set down by preceding Labour governments, attempted an absolute shift in the burden of health care by selling some public hospitals and facilities to private owners. The result was too small to measure. Other initiatives, however, did bring about a sizeable increase in private sector health care.[1] Incentives for private citizens and groups (employers) to buy private insurance slowly raised the proportion of the population covered in some measure by these subscriptions (it is still less than 20 per cent). However, private coverage remains overwhelmingly supplemental to the NHS, used primarily for private beds, sometimes in public hospitals[2]. Some individuals have purchased private insurance coverage for elective surgeries and for out-patient specialist services, and some privately covered services are provided in public hospitals. But private coverage remains a modest percentage of total health care in Britain (approximately 20 per cent). An increase in user fees for certain prescriptions, for dental care, and for medical devices (such as eye-glasses) has further commodified the NHS. One cannot say that these fees have caused undue strain, especially in light of the many exemptions that continue for low-income groups. Finally, the role of the NHS as a public sector employer has declined with a turn to contracting out for a number of non-health care related services (laundry, maintenance, etc). There has also been a small but significant shift in the number of nurses employed by the NHS and the private sector, reflecting the relative changes in the opportunities offered by these two types of employers.

Offsetting the quantitative picture of change presented thus far are data on expenditures. Privatization has accompanied not a decrease but an increase in NHS spending to well over 6 per cent of GDP; and yet efficiencies and improvements have occurred in the public sector. Some can be directly attributed to privatization, such as fewer prescriptions issued and savings achieved. The cause–effect relationship is more ambiguous in other areas. For example, the number of people waiting for elective surgeries in the NHS has been steadily declining, and the figure is especially significant for those who have been waiting more than one year (Laing and Buisson, 1996). While some claim this is due to competition from the private sector, it may also be the result of other changes in the NHS itself.

Arguably a more revolutionary change has occurred in British health care less from the quantitative increase in the private sector than from the adoption by the NHS of a market-based philosophy. In the 1980s public officials openly proclaimed their goal of making the NHS run like Sainsbury's (a grocery store chain). Trials and errors over the years have shaped a more balanced outcome, one that does not easily lend itself to evaluations of better or worse. But, at the least, we cannot claim that the state has abdicated its role or is a lesser actor, qualitatively speaking, in British health care.

The 1989 White Paper, *Working for Patients*, ushered in the most extensive restructuring in NHS history (Ministry of Health, 1989). Its empirical aim was to transform the three main sets of health care providers (district health authorities, hospitals, and general practitioners) into purchasers. The under-lying expectation was that these health care actors would undergo the appropriate behavioural changes through their activities and the additional incentives offered by the NHS. Ultimately, all of the funds remain within the NHS, but the change in decision-making power over the funds would elicit, it was assumed, a sense of ownership among the new decision-makers and concomitant prudence in spending behaviour. All actors, however, are required to plough any savings back into improvements in health care delivery and provision, instituting a critical bend in how the profit motive operates among providers and purchasers.

District health authorities

Reorganization sought to devolve the hierarchical structure of the NHS by granting more financial discretion to district health authorities (DHAs) – the local jurisdictions that oversee health care delivery. DHAs must still conform to priorities and guidelines issued by the central government's Department of Health and Social Services, and they must include community input in their deliberations. But their new-found freedom to manage the specifics of health care is unprecedented. The NHS now bases DHA budgets on the number of persons in the district, rather than on services provided as before – a formulation that offered no disincentive to spend. It is up to DHA officials to assess needs, decide on services, and form contracts for provision. DHAs can contract with care givers in their own or in neighbouring jurisdictions. The NHS has encouraged DHAs to pool their resources in order to achieve efficiencies of scale; some DHAs have amalgamated, reducing their total number. Because budgets are so tight to begin with, overall savings have resulted more from these efforts to streamline factors over and above the internal health care decisions of DHAs themselves.

Competition is certainly at play in the new management style of DHAs. But one would be hard-pressed to say that this and related market principles characterize the behaviour of DHAs. For example, although larger, more powerful DHAs now have greater financial leverage with providers, a significant factor in their ability to wager agreements has been their lessons in collaborative behaviour. In addition, the new bargaining capacities of DHAs has encouraged greater competition among providers. To say, though, that DHAs have become 'agencies which can challenge providers and hold them accountable for their performance' (Ham and Heginbotham, 1991: 6) is to applaud their normative not their fiscal role.

Self-governing hospital trusts

The 1989 White Paper charted a similar transition in which hospitals would no longer receive funding based on their activities but would instead become self-governing trusts, earning their own revenues based on the services they provide and deciding themselves how to spend their funds. Unexpectedly, the transition to self-governing status was remarkably quick and is now nearly complete. Within the parameters of certain eligibility and operating criteria[3], self-governing hospital trusts enjoy considerable freedom in acquiring and disposing of assets as they see fit; employing their own staffs, including medical personnel, at rates they negotiate[4]; deciding what services to provide; and brokering contracts for their services. The Department of Health monitors these activities; the National Audit office inspects the accounts; and the Secretary of State retains 'reserve powers' over hospital trusts. But this division of labour masks the larger responsibilities that self-governing hospitals have acquired in delivering health care, as purchasing decisions have become more attuned to the demands as well as the needs of patients.

Hospital trusts compete with each other to win contracts with other purchasers (DHAs, GPs, insurance companies) and to attract medical personnel. And while price is an important factor in naming the victor, it has proved to be relatively inelastic. The overarching framework of the NHS as a public service, of hospitals as public trusts, and of most purchasers of health care as public agents, all carry much explanatory weight. So too does the fact that the overall budget of the NHS is very small compared to other countries' budgets. Consequently, competition has introduced other goals into the negotiations between hospitals and purchasers, goals more directly related to health care, such as reduced waiting times for elective surgeries[5]. The principle of competition has worked in its purer market-based form in other ways, such as to identify failing or non-viable hospitals. Some hospitals have formed contracts with each other to achieve economies of scale. Hospital closures have also occurred, especially in urban centres. Although the attempt was to transform accountability into a more widespread function, these tougher decisions that affect the NHS as a whole have been made by central government actors.

General Practitioners

The 1989 White Paper introduced comparable changes for GPs, expanding their managerial duties and promising to raise their professional status *vis-à-vis* consultants by enhancing their referral powers. Approximately one-quarter of GPs have voluntarily chosen to join in small groups of fundholding practices. The NHS allocates fundholders' budgets based on the number of persons on each GP's list and additional practice features[6]. Under the monitorship of public agencies (such as the Families Health Services Agencies and the National Audit Office), GPs have full control of their funds, deciding what level of care they themselves provide, and which services and with whom they should negotiate contracts.

As with any change, and especially one that introduces competition into health care, there is concern about the accountability of GP fundholders–but many of the new developments point to improvements as well as potential problems (Light, 1995). For example, there is some evidence that GP fundholders are performing more procedures themselves rather than referring patients to specialists; but since there was no disincentive to over-refer before, GPs may simply be doing what they could have done all along. Also, fundholding has encouraged participant GPs to be more aggressive in winning preferred treatment for their patients, leaving non-fundholders in a less favourable position; but these results are demonstrating that slow delivery is not endemic to the NHS. In the same vein, because individual GPs have different ideas about needs and arrange for different kinds of contracts, a new strain of fragmentation has occurred in health care for the population as a whole; NHS officials feel that once current changes are more complete, goals for more equitable outcomes can be set. At the same time, multiple fundholders, each with their own administrative costs, have increased total indirect health care expenditures. What the British are learning is that in following the patient, expenditure also follows changing ideas about health care. As long as basic and decent, let alone quality and equitable, health care remain goals, costs will rise. In fact, a general consensus seems to be emerging in Britain that the conception of health care is indeed changing, with more attention being paid to community level care for both acute and non-acute conditions. While enhanced provision of community care services can be evaluated in terms of costs and benefits, their new-found inclusion in the framework of health care is fostering another development, a more general and broader movement away from a medical to a social model of understanding health care.

It is difficult to evaluate the overall impact of these many changes that have occurred across all sectors of the NHS and health care delivery in Britain. Conventional criteria for measuring consequences yield mixed results. For example, overall costs have not been reduced, but providers are now more aware of the costs associated with their health care decisions. Has health care therefore improved or suffered? It seems that while some complaints are new (closing neighbourhood hospitals), others are the same (insufficient kidney dialysis equipment). All of these complaints may ultimately rest less on the particularities of current changes, British health care is well managed, than on the fact that British health care is underfunded, relatively speaking (7 per cent of GNP compared to 10 per cent in Canada and 14 per cent in the United States).

The analysis here has elaborated the changing role of the state within a larger network of interactive processes in order to assess the possibilities for a more synergistic outcome in the future, one that may eventually affect the total level of funding. There is no doubt that the central government is less intrusive now than in the past, and that the NHS directorate is playing a stronger coordinating than supervisory role over the complex web of contracts, purchases, alliances, and so on. However, to say that the public sector has yielded to the private, or even to market forces, is to simplify the story and to miss the point of these changes. The future of British health care rests on the success of this endeavour to expand responsibility for health care beyond the NHS alone.

The United States

Because the private sector has always predominated in the American delivery system, the relative proportion of the two sectors in current privatization initiatives is less important than the corresponding role of government. In the past government agencies have attempted to fill some of the gaps left by the inequities of private sector provision, primarily through the Medicare and Medicaid programs, and to regulate some of the inconsistencies and potential abuses of private provision and delivery systems. Until the 1970s these regulations were generally characterized by their minimum standards on the one hand and laxity in guiding and reviewing compliance on the other. Throughout the 1970s and 1980s the federal government issued more regulations, and they became increasingly more micro-interventionist. For example, the original Medicaid legislation outlined five mandatory programs (Stevens and Stevens, 1974), which subsequent legislation increasingly complexified[7]. Although a canopy of regulations may suggest an active government role, it resulted in this case in a sub-optimum capacity to deliver health care (see also, Ruggie, 1992). State governments felt hampered in their ability to fund additional health care measures, and the will of providers to offer optional and more comprehensive care was strained. This type of regulatory regime is now giving way to a more macro-interventionist one in which private providers are gaining more control over their internal spending and treatment decisions, but within stricter parameters of equitable access and cost containment criteria. These criteria are established either directly by government or through collaboration between public and private sector actors. I elaborate developments in the Medicaid program to illustrate.

The Medicaid program can itself be thought of as a model of integrated public–private sector and central–decentral government relations in health care delivery. But for nearly three decades the model existed on paper only and in practice barely fulfilled minimal expectations. For example, government officials assumed that physicians would incorporate treatment of Medicaid patients into their private practices, but at a reimbursement rate that covered, in some cases, barely half of their normal fees.[8] Such resort to the principle of charity for the poor, even though it had always justified the power of physicians to engage in 'price discrimination' (Bjorkman, 1989), evoked neglect on the part of both public and private sector actors toward health care for the poor and precluded coordination between them. As a result, the Medicaid system has been plagued by problems of inequities in access and treatment, removing health care for the poor from the mainstream. Similarly, the funding arrangements between the federal and state levels of government left a void in leadership. The availability of matching funds was considered sufficient encouragement for the states to embrace their constitutional responsibilities and provide health care for eligible categories of the needy.[9] Although the states in principle enjoyed discretion on eligibility and optional service criteria, pressing needs on the part of an expanding Medicaid population and concomitant growth in Medicaid expenditures brought demands from all quarters for cost containment. Several of these past problems in the implementation of the Medicaid program are now being re-channelled and possibly countermanded by the adoption of managed-care provision for Medicaid recipients. Throughout the late 1980s and into the 1990s many states undertook demonstration projects to experiment with cost-saving measures. Most of these projects focused on enlisting private-sector managed-care providers to enrol Medicaid recipients.[10] Studies were showing that managed-care programs operate at significantly lower costs than fee-for-service provision and with few negative consequences on the quality of care provided (Lute, 1987). In fact, continuing overall declines in the rate of growth in health care costs is still largely attributed to the widespread entry of managed-care into the American health care delivery system (Ginsburg and Pickreign, 1996). States must apply to the federal government for waivers from certain basic requirements in the Medicaid program in order to experiment with the adoption of managed-care programs (PPRC, 1995: 156–162). Because state experiments were proving fairly successful in achieving their goals, the federal government expanded the waivers it allows. Upon federal approval states can now pursue mandatory enrolment in managed-care for all Medicaid recipients as long as full disclosure of terms is provided. Over forty states have received a managed-care waiver. As a result, from a minuscule 3 per cent a decade ago, over one-third of all Medicaid recipients are currently enrolled in some sort of managed-care program in the private sector (Rowland and Hanson, 1996). While in only two states (Tennessee and Arizona) are almost all Medicaid recipients enrolled in managed-care, half of the states will soon have one-quarter of their recipients in such programs.

What is remarkable to watch as these programs evolve is the increasingly more activist role of governments, both state and federal, in pursuing substantive health care goals. Although the states are paying the same rates charged for non-Medicaid patients, overall these rates are less than under fee-for-service reimbursement. As an additional payoff and commensurate with more equitable reimbursement, Medicaid recipients are receiving care comparable to other patients, incorporating them for the first time into mainstream health care. Several states are explicitly utilizing their cost savings to expand eligibility. They requested and received new waivers allowing them to offer Medicaid coverage to previously uninsured persons who do not fall within any of the standard categories of eligibility. One novel waiver occurred in the state of Oregon, which received permission to institute a rationing plan for Medicaid services and is using these and additional savings from managed-care delivery to expand coverage (Brown, 1991; Kitzhaber, 1996). Nine states now boast of achieving a significant increase in the number of persons covered by Medicaid, and one (Tennessee) claims nearly universal health insurance coverage[11]. Even though these developments have centred on the states, the federal government has not abandoned its involvement in the Medicaid program. In fact, federal oversight of state experiments has increased (PPRC, 1996: 339–363). When necessary the federal government has prohibited errant states from proceeding with their projects, and set requirements for reapplication as well as for renewal of projects. The new level of cooperation between federal and state governments, and the more responsive exchanges between them to resolve problems, is unprecedented in the history of the Medicaid program.

Interestingly, relations between public funders and private providers have prospered along with increased public vigilance of private sector trials and errors.[12] In the early days of system change the public sector's oversight role was benign, but over time it has intensified. For instance, the federal Health Care Financing Administration (HCFA), together with the Department of Health and Human Services, developed a Health Care Quality Improvement

System, a quality assurance guidance program that specifies standards, protocols for treatment, quality controls and referral guarantees, and is intentionally similar to systems used in the private sector. The purpose of the program is to foster a joint understanding of care for Medicaid recipients that would replicate the care offered to other patients (PPRC, 1993: 260). To ensure continuing safeguards against under-serving the poor, HCFA has strengthened its annual review procedures, and it has initiated a multifaceted approach to quality assurance, including internal quality improvement programs, external quality review, and standardized quality performance reports.[13] Government officials claim to be 'particularly encouraged by the progress of [these] private-sector efforts' (PPRC, 1995: 339). At the same time, HCFA is entering new areas of collaboration with the private sector to develop new methods of evaluating managed-care in an effort to unify provision for all patients. And some of these projects are being jointly funded with such private sector actors as the Kaiser Family Foundation. While progress is slow, to be sure, HCFA foresees the eventual appearance of national standards and enforcement as well as a shift away from a focus on administrative process in measuring performance toward outcome measures that evaluate health care and health outcome.

Purchasers of health care, especially private-sector employers who have become key actors in defining the future direction of change in health care provision, have begun to rely on HCFA's evaluation measures to help them make better decisions about options for their employees. In addition, employees, as consumers, are becoming increasingly vocal in their demands for more choice and for improvements in delivery and correction of maltreatment. They are calling on legislators at both the state and national levels of government to enact regulations on, for example, grievance procedures, disclosure of clinical guidelines, and financial incentives for under-service (Etheredge *et al.*, 1996: 99). As long as HCFA maintains its vigilance over the achievement and maintenance of equity for Medicaid recipients, we can expect improvements in care for this group.

Studies continue to find mixed outcomes in terms of access, delivery and satisfaction for Medicaid managed-care recipients, compared both to their previous experiences under the fee-for-service system as well as to other managed-care patients (Gold *et al.*, 1996). On the whole, however, the complaints of Medicaid patients seem to be no worse than those of other managed-care patients (Mark and Mueller, 1996). Most researchers and commentators are holding government responsible for leadership, calling on both state and federal levels to sharpen their guard over the fate of Medicaid recipients as well as over the broader transition toward managed-care. The states need to understand the importance of educating clients about enrolment procedures and of building a statewide administrative infrastructure for managed-care; in addition, the inclusion of a well-developed oversight system for all points of the process is critical (Gold *et al.*, 1996: 164–165). States must be willing to learn, both from their own past problems as well as from the experiences of other states, enabling them to adapt successful strategies to their own milieux (Halvorson, 1996; Dallek, 1996). In all this, the role of the federal government remains central, in correcting errors and prodding change, and, together with other actors, in constructing normative and substantive goals for health care.

Driving private-sector managed-care providers to respond to consumer complaints and comply with government directives is a combination of market-based and government-led factors. Now that approximately 70 per cent of the nation's workforce is enrolled in managed-care, organized providers are searching for new clients. They are competing to enrol Medicaid recipients despite the higher start-up costs of caring for this population, because success in these endeavours will pave the way for the next wave of enrollees: Medicare recipients. At the same time, providing satisfactory care for current middle-aged enrollees helps to assure their continued membership once they reach the age of Medicare eligibility. Because Medicare patients are also costly, careful, long-term program planning must precede their entry into managed-care. Incentives for restructuring private sector health care in the United States have come from all quarters, but the role of government in current developments should not be minimized. Government regulations are providing guidance and goals for the gradual switch to managed health care for the majority of Americans. Changes in the Medicaid program are attempting to improve equity in access and treatment for this under-served population, as well as to expand the reach of public insurance to those who are currently uninsured. These developments carry more promise than achievement thus far, but they clearly lag behind comparable developments in other countries. As long as cost containment remains the fundamental goal of change, problems loom. Managed-care organizations already may be reaching the limits of their ability to reduce costs within reasonable criteria of equity in access to quality health care. To continue on the course of reform will require some adjustments in understanding the purposes of change and in articulating acceptable means. Behind the specific innovations in health care delivery that have been discussed here is a new-found mutuality in the goals of both public and private sector actors and in their capacity to achieve them. While cost considerations initially motivated this enterprise, it has not consistently occupied centre stage, nor can it in light of the many gaps in health care provision. It is the linkages themselves that must ground emerging economic, political and social decisions, and shape the future form and substance of American health care.

IMPLICATIONS FOR CANADA

Not so long ago the health care systems of Britain and the United States stood at opposite ends of several spectrums, above all in their reliance on state versus market mechanisms of organization. This is no longer the case. Although the NHS continues to operate entirely under government auspices and private health care remains a relatively small portion of total health care in Britain, the incorporation of market-like mechanisms into the NHS and the rule of legal and ethical constraints over private-sector practices has diminished the analytical utility of spectrums. Similarly, changes in the United States are best understood by looking below the surface of state versus market analogues to find the level where regulation and competition are actually complementary. Witness the state-induced and increasingly state-guided evolution of managed-care organizations. The growing similarity between managed private care in the United States and state sector competition in the British NHS is remarkable.

When Canada is added to the comparison, it is commonly placed between Britain and the United States. Like Britain, Canada's health care system is largely funded through tax revenues. Unlike Britain, much of the delivery has been private, largely not for profit. Although the proportion of private sector expenditure is growing in both countries, its magnitude remains similar, accounting for approximately one-quarter of total health care in Canada and less than one-fifth in Britain. At the level of health care delivery, Medicare in Canada resembles the American Medicaid and Medicare systems in that the government pays private providers without altering their locations or methods of care. However, change is rapidly occurring in the United States with the adoption of managed-care in the Medicaid and Medicare programs.

The innovations in breaking the barrier between public and private ventures that are occurring in Britain and the United States have thus far largely eluded Canada. A relatively substantial private health care sector in Canada is growing alongside the public system, but the dialogue between the two is minimal. Private insurance for services not covered under Medicare is a case in point. As in Britain, there is considerable concern about the development of a two-tier system of health care because of the growth of private insurance for increasingly more health care provision. The debate seems to be more intense in Canada where the pace of government delimitation of services and procedures, on the one hand, and the growth of private insurance to cover these items on the other, is faster (Gordon and Berger, 1996; Dirnfeld, 1996). The two sectors could do much more to coordinate these activities, deciding together and ahead of time what their capacities are to continue past levels of provision or adopt new functions and how each can make exceptions to maintain an adequate level of access and care for more vulnerable social groups. At issue as well is the question of equity, a fundamental principle in the Canadian health care system, and one that is under greater jeopardy in situations where the 'great divide' between public and private sectors is perpetuated.

Canadians have to be particularly wary at this point in time not to rest on the laurels of their success and to remain willing to take note of developments in other countries. Despite their innovations, neither Britain nor the United States are realizing cost savings. Without major system change, Canada is witnessing a dramatic reduction in health care expenditures, from 10.4 per cent of GNP in 1992 to approximately 9.4 per cent at present. In part, this achievement is due to a renewed economic vibrancy in the country. However, real reductions in both public and private health care spending have also occurred. While Britain and the United States ought to be examining the details of Canada's experiments, certain counter-lessons remain relevant.

The case of hospital utilization raises issues about spending patterns that are hidden by the aggregate numbers. Hospital expenditures, which are decreasing in all three countries, have persistently been highest in Canada (OECD, 1995: 33). This situation is paradoxical because Canada has one of the most exemplary methods of controlling hospital expenditures:global budgeting. As it is exercised in Canada, global budgeting is a macro-interventionist tool that ably allows hospitals to make their micro-level decisions about limits; however, operating expenses and capital spending are separated. What is missing is a developed contract mechanism for specifying the role of hospitals in health care delivery. The government in Britain and the private sector in the United States have employed market-based competition to reduce the use and/or total number of hospitals. But when used alone, competition precipitates negative consequences for health care and sets the scene for renewed government regulation. Local authorities in Britain are attempting to widen their vision by building up community care, especially for chronically ill and disabled persons, to offset the changes in hospital care. It is a lesson that Canada has already learned in the nursing home sector, where deinstitutionalization is coupled to some extent by expanded community facilities (Simon *et al.*, 1996). But far more preparation and planning in the use and funding of hospital and community care are needed if unnecessary hospitalization of the elderly is to be avoided. And while cost savings may accrue in hospital budgets, overall social expenditures will need to rise, at least in the short term. The issue is especially pointed in the area of care for the elderly, where the tension between publicly funded hospital care and privately funded nursing home and other forms of community care puts an added strain on 'deinstitutionalized' patients.

In our search for empirical lessons from cross-country comparisons, we must also keep in mind the value of analytical lessons. As Britain and the United States are engaging in increased privatization, the dichotomization between public and private is yielding to a novel relationship in which each sector is attempting to enable the other to perform those functions for which it is best suited. Yet, despite the many reorderings of responsibilities in both countries, the state remains the final authority and protector of the public interest. The road has been rocky to be sure, and not without much trial and error. And the changes in social relations may still exist more in the eyes of the social scientist than in those of the practitioners of health care provision and policy. But old habits are breaking down in these two countries. Privatization in Canada still seems to be embedded in the framework of exclusive public payment for medically necessary services. Canadians can learn from these comparisons the futility of separate spheres, privatization ought not be undertaken without a consistently strong government role. The capacity of government in Canada to forge consensus through negotiations has underpinned past achievements. Extending this process to the new terrain of emerging health care issues remains a fundamental challenge. I have argued here that the future of health care rests not on the initiatives of either the public or the private sector, but on the capacity of both to construct new links to serve public objectives. As a stellar representative of the complexity of public/private mixes, Canada has an important role to play in analytical clarification. But to continue to be a leader in the field of health care, policy-makers and those who contribute to public debate need to stretch their horizons beyond tired categories and outdated agendas. The threshold issue for the 1990s will be the challenge of home and community care for the elderly and disabled. The trade-off associated with downsizing the institutional sector will be the development of a high level home care system.

CONCLUSION

Zelman (1996: 313) suggests that 'policymakers may well wish to define the overriding goal [in health care] as maximizing the positive potential of ... marketplace changes. And they may wish to define the most appropriate strategy as one of allowing and encouraging, as opposed to directing or regulating those changes.' The analysis here suggests that governments in Britain, the United States and, to some extent, Canada are accepting their role in guiding the private sector, but that their strategies are a pragmatic mix of encouragement and direction. A hands-off stance is appropriate when the private sector is meeting its social responsibilities and engaging in self-regulation of abuse. But in countries where the rule of market forces is deeply embedded only strong government prodding, together with active consumer demand, can divert the economic concerns of the private sector toward considerations of quality. Governments in Britain, the United States and Canada have allowed competition among buyers to enter the health care system, but the results have been uneven. Governments are being challenged to fulfil their responsibilities and to ensure access to equitable health care, either through local public, quasi-public, and nonprofit or private actors who are increasingly entering the diverse array of decision-makers and providers. There is much to be learned from how government actors are negotiating agreements for service delivery, brokering liaisons among providers and between providers and recipients, and attempting to coordinate a complex network of care.

It is inaccurate to conclude that changes in health care in Britain, the United States and Canada are becoming similar. Privatization is occurring within the confines of rules for standards of care and protection of principles of equity in access; these rules are set through collaborations between public and private sector actors. However, the substance of these rules and the processes of collaboration remain very different, making each country a hybrid model of a common trend. In investigating the changes underway, I have attempted to identify new forms of social relations among actors. And I have suggested that interactions are coming to be regulated less by former institutionalized patterns of behaviour than by pragmatic responses to situations as they arise. As a result, even within one country, privatization is taking many different forms.

These thoughts carry significance for issues beyond health care. For at stake in the movement toward increased privatization is the future of the welfare state. Privatization is far from an isolated phenomenon; it can be seen in several social policies and programs in the advanced welfare states of Europe, Canada, and the United States, including social security, labour market programs, and welfare reform, to name a few (cf. Feldstein, 1997; Leone, 1997). The force of its appearance, together with ever-sharper cuts in government expenditures, even for such time-honoured programs as those focusing on the elderly, has raised concerns about the demise of the welfare state. It is my position that the emphasis we have put on the word 'state', and the implication that the chief activity of a welfare state revolves around central government expenditure, has clouded the fuller meaning of the term. The welfare state involves a collective commitment to improving individual life chances and social well-being. That commitment, from individuals and social groups, whether acting as taxpayers or citizens, whether immediately or indirectly concerned, has been sorely strained by the intrusion of partisan politics and ideological posturing about the proper roles of the public and private sectors. The collection of official decision-makers who in part constitute the state has tended to represent various fragmented interests more than the common good. A revitalization of state processes is called for and it rests on a realignment of state–society relations. Although the task of realignment is common to all welfare states, the form that realignment takes will be specific, not only to countries but also to social policy fields within countries and even to problems within issue areas. In the field of health, the role of the state is evolving in relation to the role of other social actors, but as long as the state remains the arbiter of last resort we need not forsake our use of the term 'welfare state'.

NOTES

1   See Ruggie (1996: 190–196) for data supporting this discussion.
2   For decades the fate of private beds in public hospitals was tossed back and forth between successive Conservative and Labour governments. It became a highly charged symbolic issue in the struggle over not only financial control of the NHS but also the medical authority of doctors, some of whom wanted to be able to provide preferred treatment to certain patients whether or not they could pay for the privilege of privacy.
3   Trusts must provide basic core and other services, must have a board of directors with demonstrated management skills, and senior professional staff, especially consultants, involved in management; must maintain a working system of medical audits; and must continue to demonstrate financial viability (NHS, 1990: 3).
4   This particular change, as well as the others discussed here, has had a special impact on consultants. In the past, consultants contracted with the NHS through

regional hospital boards and, later, regional health authorities. Salaries and other terms of employment were fairly even among consultants within specialities and regions. They are all now subject to individual negotiations. In addition, from having been accountable basically to their profession, consultants are now explicitly accountable to general managers in their hospitals. At the same time, however, the NHS has granted consultants greater freedom to extend their private practices. Approximately 50 per cent of NHS consultants have full-time contracts that limit their private practice to 10 per cent of their gross income. The remainder undertake unlimited private practice within various agreements to work part-time for the NHS.

5　This is not to say that price is secondary. It appears, for example, in such factors as reduced lengths of stay. But price alone does not dominate purchasing decisions.

6　The capitation payment constitutes a general medical care allowance (from which each GP's income is derived). Each fund holding budget also includes a calculation for typical hospital use, community care services, staff costs, and purchase of equipment.

7　The federal government intended these five required services (in-patient hospitalization, out-patient hospital visits, health clinic visits, lab and X-ray services, and skilled nursing facilities) to constitute the foundations of comprehensive care, expecting states to expand beyond them and provide as full a range of services as they could. Congress intended further legislative amendments to clarify such items as eligibility criteria. Instead, each new measure carried additional administrative and financial burdens, so that the whole added up to less than the sum of its parts.

8　Government reimbursement under the Medicaid program has consistently been below reimbursement for Medicare, although over time the gap has narrowed. By the early 1990s overall Medicaid reimbursement was about 73 per cent of Medicare's, but the range for specific groups of services was from 55 per cent to 78 per cent, and the range among states was 49 per cent in Missouri to 220 per cent in Alaska (below Alaska was Minnesota with 127 per cent) (PPRC, 1995: 352–353).

9　The federal government provides 50 to 80 per cent, depending on per capita income in the states, of state expenditures on Medicaid, as well as additional amounts for administrative costs (PPRC, 1996: 323). Congress regularly discusses switching to a block grant system of funding. While many social programs, including Aid to Families with Dependent Children, have now been folded into a block grant, Medicaid remains cost shared.

10　I use the term 'managed care' here because it has become more generic than health maintenance organization (HMO).

11　Data show that the aggregate number of uninsured persons in the United States continues to rise at the same time. In part this increase is explained by an alarming decline in employer-sponsored plans, at a faster rate than the changes discussed here can accommodate (Holahan *et al.*, 1995).

12　Private providers sometimes welcome regulation. A recent article in the *New York Times* describes a call for more regulation of managed-care plans and 'legally enforceable national standards', made by three HMOs (Kaiser Permanente, HIP Health Insurance Plans, and Group Health Cooperative of Pugent Sound) working in collaboration with two consumer groups (Families USA and the American Association of Retired Persons). Because HMOs 'have failed to convince the public of [their] commitment to quality', the group sees national standards as 'essential to restore confidence in the health care system' (Pear, 1997: A8).

13 These procedures are conducted through the states for the Medicaid program, but directly with HCFA for those managed-care organizations that have enrolled Medicare recipients. The two sets of experiences are enabling HCFA to further enhance its coordinating role.

REFERENCES

Bjorkman, James Warner. 1989. 'Politicizing Medicine and Medicalizing Politics: Physician Power in the United States'. In Giorgio Freddi and James Warner Bjorkman, eds, *Controlling Medical Professionals: The Comparative Politics of Health Governance*, pp. 28–73. Newbury Park, CA: Sage.

Brown, Lawrence D. 1991. 'The National Politics of Oregon's Rationing Plan'. *Health Affairs* 10 (2): 28–51.

Dallek, Geraldine. 1996. 'A Consumer Advocate on Medicaid Managed Care'. *Health Affairs* 15 (3): 174–177.

Dirnfeld, Victor. 1996. 'The Benefits of Privatization'. *Canadian Medical Association Journal* 155: 407–410.

Enthoven, Alan C. 1985. *Reflections on the Management of the National Health Service: An American Looks at Incentives to Efficiency in Health Services Management in the UK*. London: Nuffield Provincial Hospitals Trust.

Etheredge, Lynn, Stanley B. Jones, and Lawrence Lewin. 1996. 'What is Driving Health System Change?' *Health Affairs* 15 (4): 93–104.

Feldstein, Martin. 1997. 'The Case for Privatization'. *Foreign Affairs* 76 (4): 24–38.

Ginsburg, Paul B. and Jeremy D. Pickreign. 1996. 'Tracking Health Care Costs'. *Health Affairs* 15 (3): 140–149.

Gold, Marsha, Michael Sparer and Karyen Chu. 1996. 'Medicaid Managed Care: Lessons from Five States'. *Health Affairs* 15 (3): 153–166.

Gordon, Michael and Philip B. Berger. 1996. 'The Alluring Myth of Private Medicine'. *Canadian Medical Association Journal* 155: 404–407.

Halvorson, George C. 1996. 'An HMO Executive Officer on Medicaid Managed Care'. *Health Affairs* 15 (3): 170–171.

Ham, Chris and Chris Heginbotham. 1991. *Purchasing Together*. London: King's Fund Institute.

Holahan, John, Colin Winterbottom and Shruti Rajan. 1995. 'A Shifting Picture of Health Insurance Coverage'. *Health Affairs* 14 (4): 253–264.

Kamerman, Sheila B. and Alfred J. Kahn, eds 1989. *Privatization and the Welfare State*. Princeton: Princeton University Press.

Kitzhaber, John A. 1996. 'Oregon's Governor on Medicaid Managed Care'. *Health Affairs* 15 (3): 167–169.

Laing and Buisson. 1996. *Laing's Review of Private Health Care*. London: Laing and Buisson.

Leone, Richard C. 1997. 'Stick with Public Pensions'. *Foreign Affairs* 76 (4): 39–53.

Light, Donald W. 1995. The Future of Fundholding. London: Institute of Health Services Management.

Lundqvist, Lennart J. 1988. 'Privatization: Toward a Concept for Comparative Analysis'. *Journal of Public Opinion* 8 (1): 1–19.

Lute, Harold S. 1987. *Health Maintenance Organizations*. New Brunswick, NJ: Transaction Books.

Mark, Tami and Curt Mueller. 1996. 'Access to Care in HMOs and Traditional Insurance Plans'. *Health Affairs* 15 (4): 81–87.

Ministry of Health. 1989. *Working for Patients*. London: HMSO.

NHS, Management Executive. 1990. *Working for Patients: NHS Trusts: A Working Guide*. London: HMSO.

OECD. 1995. *Internal Markets in The Making: Health Systems in Canada, Iceland and the United Kingdom*. Paris: Organization for Economic Cooperation and Development.

Pear, Robert. 1997. '3 Big Plans Join in Call for National Standards'. *New York Times*, 25 September: A28.

PPRC. 1993, 1995, 1996. *Physician Payment Review Commission: Annual Report to Congress*. Washington, DC: Physician Payment Review Commission.

Rowland, Diane and Kristina Hanson. 1996. 'Medicaid: Moving to Managed Care'. *Health Affairs* 15 (3): 150–152.

Ruggie, Mary. 1992. 'The Paradox of Liberal Intervention: Health Policy and the American Welfare State'. *American Journal of Sociology* 97 (4): 919–943.

—— 1996. *Realignments in the Welfare State: Health Policy in the United States, Britain and Sweden*. New York: Columbia University Press.

Simon, Harold J., Barbara L. Brody and Mary Ruggie. 1996. 'Accommodation Through Negotiation: Problem Resolution and Decision Making in the Canadian Long-Term Care System'. *Research in Social Policy* 4: 97–143.

Stevens, Robert and Rosemary Stevens. 1974. *Welfare Medicine in America: A Case Study of Medicaid*. New York: The Free Press.

Zelman, Walter A. 1996. *The Changing Health Care Marketplace: Private Ventures, Public Interests*. San Francisco: Jossey-Bass.

Part III

Decentralization and devolution

New state forms and practices

8   Contrasting visions of decentralization

Louise-Hélène Trottier, François Champagne,
André-Pierre Contandriopoulos, Jean-Louis Denis

Decentralization is a regulatory process, the aim of which is to maintain or establish a balance between national (or provincial) and local levels of organizations. Fundamental social choices lie at the heart of the centralization/ decentralization tension. While centralization encourages national unity through uniformity, decentralization favours diversity by emphasizing local freedoms and the right of local communities to be different. Moreover, the centralization/decentralization process is driven by three different visions of the role of the state: the liberal, the social and the communitarian. The *liberal* vision seeks to minimize the role of the state as much as possible and to expand individual liberties. The *social* vision aims to maximize the role of the state in order to establish mechanisms of collective solidarity. The *community* vision tends to minimize the role of the state while at the same time increasing freedom of choice for local communities.

In the first section of this chapter, we analyse the process of regionalization in the health sector as a mean of regulating the division of power within society and as a mechanism allowing this regional structure to take its place within the state. The second section provides an overview of the evolution of the regionalization of health services in Quebec, concentrating on the most recent reforms. In the third section, we will highlight the role of the actors in the process of emergence, formulation and implementation of public policies. We maintain that at the end of the 1980s, only the community and the liberal visions of the role of the state were able to offer solutions to the management and production problems experienced by the health system in Quebec. One consequence of the present decentralization process is to modify the rules of the game which have prevailed in the health sector over the last twenty years, especially through the frequent use of democratic mechanisms by regional authorities. This is explained by the fact that Quebec opted for a decentralization process that was largely based on the community analysis of the negative effects of state centralism, an analysis which favours the self-management approach and the affirmation of differences among local communities.

DECENTRALIZATION: A POLITICAL ISSUE AND MANAGEMENT TECHNIQUE

The terms 'centralization' and 'decentralization' are often used to inform realities that are very different (Mintzberg, 1979). On the one hand, it allows for the sharing of decision-making powers 'so that individuals who are able to understand the specifics can respond to them'. Power is placed where the knowledge is 'to respond quickly to local conditions', and to stimulate motivation. 'Creative and intelligent people require considerable room to maneuver. The organization can attract and retain such people, and utilize their initiative, only if it gives them considerable power to make decisions' (Mintzberg, 1979: 183).

On the other hand, decentralization is also a political phenomenon (Baguenard, 1985; Laliberty, 1988; Mills *et al.*, 1990; Fomerand, 1994) which aims to establish or maintain the equilibrium between the individual and the collective (Etzioni, 1991). Which of the two entities will prevail? As certain legal experts phrase the question, will it be individual autonomy or the collective responsibility? Or as certain philosophers put it, will it be free choice or moral obligations? Society is in a continuous state of tension between these two forces. One of the principal issues in the political arena is to maintain equilibrium between, on the one side, the right to be different and the expression of multiple preferences and, on the other, the attainment of well-being for the largest number and, consequently, a fair distribution of resources.

In its political dimension, with the establishment of a new division of powers between the centre and the periphery, the current decentralization is creating a new balance between individual liberties and collective responsibilities. Moreover, in its administrative dimension, decentralization allows for the decision-making to be brought closer to where these decisions are to be implemented, triggering faster reaction to local problems, and motivating managers and staff.

The modern centralizing state aims to achieve lasting national development, both politically and economically, by bringing an end to regional disparities, territorial inequities and local injustice. The supporters of a centralized state adhere to a philosophy in which national identity is built through powerful instruments of governance, capable of steering the economic sector, compensating for deficiencies in the private sector and assuring equality, as well as a level of well-being amongst its citizens. The centralizing philosophy leads almost inevitably to the extension of public administrative activity through diverse involvement in social and economic life.

The degree of centralization/decentralization in the management of public services results 'from a dynamic compromise between centripetal forces which push to reinforce unity relative to the State and centrifugal forces which stimulate the flourishing of local diversity' (Baguenard, 1985: 15). Today, globalization of the economy destabilizes the forces which have enabled centralizing states to establish wide-scale public services. According to international lending organizations, public services create a budgetary drag on the gross domestic product (GDP) in the majority of the industrialized countries. These organizations are all currently pressuring countries to adopt the 'better State through less State' approach (Forum national sur la santé/National Health Forum, 1997). This new fiscal imperative is encouraging countries to attempt to streamline the role of the state. It leads to a renegotiation of the division of responsibilities between the state, the private sector and the local or regional authorities.

This new role of the state leads to decentralization. In political terms, it can be analysed in two ways. One can see it as a process of continuity aiming to maintain the centralization state (see Harden, Chapter 11 this volume, for such a Machiavellian ruse). This analysis is based on the notion that elected leaders have little to fear from the delegation of administrative responsibilities to local or regional representatives who reproduce the political system already in existence. Local representatives are likely to resort to the same management methods, the same tools for priority-setting, the same code of ethics and the same dominant ideology based on the representative principle. Seen from this angle, decentralization is unlikely to lead to pluralism in any larger sense of the term (Baguenard, 1985).

Decentralization can also be analysed as a process of breaking with the past to reach a new equilibrium between the centre and the periphery, between responsibilities assumed by the state and those taken on by other sectors of society. Behind this division of responsibilities a fundamental debate is raised between equality and liberty, between obligations and rights.

In political terms, those who support self-management present decentralization as an alternative to the classic opposition between the public sector and the market sector. In their view, decentralization does not weaken democratic will or social solidarity, unlike the market sector. On the contrary, it revitalizes them. Decentralization should allow democracy to rest, not exclusively on the sporadic participation of the citizen-elector and on the lobbying of interest groups, but also on the daily involvement of the citizen in decision-making processes. Theoretically, this integration should allow citizens to act as co-participants in the action of elected representatives, and to refocus concern for management of public services on the betterment of individuals in their everyday lives (Bouvier, 1986; Fomerand, 1994). Moreover, decentralization introduces flexibility in the management of public affairs. It leaves more room for different choices between communities and favours diversity over uniformity.

DECENTRALIZATION: ALSO A MANAGEMENT TECHNIQUE

As a management technique, decentralization refers to a sharing of roles and functions between the state and its subsidiary elements. In this perspective, the state can occupy the largest area and advocate centralism or, on the contrary, it can occupy the smallest area (sovereignty, currency, army) and thus favour decentralization (Fomerand, 1994). Centralization and decentralization are the two opposite poles on the same continuum of administrative management (Mintzberg, 1979; Baguenard, 1985). In fact, for any federation or province, it is necessary to speak of degrees of decentralization since the equilibrium point between these two extremes can be situated anywhere on the continuum.

The premise of administrative efficiency behind centralization rests on the idea that the concentration and reasonable use of expertise, knowledge and skills allow for a lasting, coherent and better-orchestrated national development. A recurrent theme concerning the benefits of governmental centralization of powers and of the extension of public services is a more equitable access to services with the help of government policies, and the mechanisms available to the state to fairly allocate resources among regions (Mills *et al.*, 1990). It is on the basis of such a management philosophy that integrated health systems on the provincial level expanded in Canada. Therefore, to opt for centralization leads to choosing an egalitarian rather than a pluralist type of democracy.

Decentralization is driven by a self-managing approach which permits the elimination of the inflexible and itemized management associated with centralization since it favours autonomous and diversified decision-making. Decentralization thus allows for the resolution of operational problems in potentially different ways from one locality to another, taking into consideration the available resources. The self-management philosophy also holds that decentralization improves the quality of services by making managers, professionals and other staff members more responsible, since it increases the contribution of the talents and skills of each player (Laliberty, 1988). By decentralizing and sharing authority within relatively autonomous decision-making units, one hopes 'to provide comprehensive health care to a large regional community... including a well-defined pattern of referral and supervision' (Mills *et al.*, 1990: 15). Through the participation of the largest number of people in the decision-making process, therefore, one expects that decentralization permits the attainment of greater management efficiency and greater relevance in decision-making, especially with regard to local characteristics and needs

THE REGIONALIZATION OF HEALTH SERVICES IN QUEBEC

Prior to the 1970s, the Quebec provincial government played a passive financial role in the organization of the health care system. It had become clear to the government of Quebec that persistent problems in the health care system demanded a broader role for the state. Regional inequalities in resource allocation, the lack of a universal health insurance plan and managerial inefficiencies prompted the state to exert more control over the health care system (Bozzini, 1993).

In such a context, it is easy to understand that the Commission d'enquête sur la santé et le bien-être social/The Commission of Inquiry Regarding Health and Social Well-Being (Castonguay-Nepveu Commission, 1966–1971) laid the foundations for a public health system that was to be centrally administered, and this Commission has set the broad framework for health care reform since then.

According to this Commission, the democratization and rationalization of services depended among other things on universality of access, comprehensive medical care, complementarity of services, user participation and the regionalization of the decision-making process. The adoption of the Loi sur les services de santé et les services sociaux (The Act reorganizing health and social services) in 1971 laid the present foundations of the integrated network of management and institutions for service delivery. This law created the Regional Health and Social Services Councils (CRSSSs), hospitals (general, specialized and psychiatric) and the local community health service centres (CLSC).

It recommended the creation of twelve health regions. These regions differ not only in terms of their geographic size, but also in terms of the size of the population they serve and the resources at their disposal. Their boards of directors were composed primarily of representatives of health care institutions, with little room for representatives of the local population.[1] The meetings of these boards were held behind closed doors. Apart from the Cree Territory Regional Council, which managed its health and social services institutions directly, the other regional councils have had almost no financial or administrative power. Administration in almost all matters was handled entirely by the Ministry of Health and Social Affairs and the Treasury Board.

In the twenty years following adoption of this law, the Ministry then centrally administered the 900 institutions in the health network and devoted a large portion of its effort to the institutions' budget management and programming but paid relatively little attention to policy planning and the evaluation of services (Turgeon and Anctil, 1994). None the less, new responsibilities were delegated to the regional councils and gradually resulted in transforming them from consultative to management bodies. Thus they have become involved in different sectors including: projects involving buildings and renovations (1975, 1976, 1986); medical staffing plans (1978); service organization – ambulance, emergency, rehabilitation, mental health, admissions, transfers, etc. – (1978, 1981, 1982–1985, 1986); introduction of task forces (1977); development of regional priorities (1978); etc.[2]

This constant delegation of responsibilities enabled the regional councils to assume gradually some part of their administrative role. However, this was done without them having responsibility for determining the financing of the system, the institutions' budget allocations and the structure of their regional network. Nevertheless, the regional councils were not able to fulfil the democratic aspect of their mandate by allowing for the participation of the general public and the community in assuming responsibility for the organization of the health care system.

In 1985, the government felt the need to substantially revise its health delivery organization and structures and created the Commission of Inquiry into Health and Social Services (Rochon Commission) with a broad mandate to focus on all aspects of health care production, including its contribution to the health of the population. This Commission marked a different approach to state intervention in the health care system. Its premise was that a consensus had to be reached among the various stakeholders regarding the problems and challenges facing the health care system, and its task was to secure the support of major stakeholders while protecting the integrity of the system to allow for greater flexibility and change (CESSS, 1988). This led the Commission to adopt a very interactive and consultative process and resulted in major reorientation, including the adoption of a comprehensive health and welfare policy, the further regionalization of the services and the adoption of a population-based approach for the provision of services and the allocation of resources to the regions.

Its Final Report was not well received by politicians, doctors or the general public. Basically, it was criticized on many grounds because it did not pay sufficient attention to long-term care, problems of elective admission delays in acute-care hospitals, the inability to transfer patients to long-term care and the overcrowding in some hospital emergency rooms.

Subsequently, the Ministry of Health and Social Services undertook a vast consultation of all the health and social service regions in Quebec in order to get their input as to whether the solutions proposed by the commission were appropriate and to identify other possible solutions (Bélanger, 1992). Three new reform projects were undertaken.

The first, entitled *Orientations* (MSSS, 1989), called for a major reorganization of the health system and extensive decentralization. It did not succeed because of opposition from the government itself, and in particular from the Treasury Board (Pineault *et al.*, 1993).

The second, entitled *A Citizen-Oriented Reform* (MSSS, 1990), proposed many changes, including the creation of regional boards, the implementation of user fees to reduce the use of hospital emergency rooms, the regional decentralization of budgets allocated for physician remuneration in order to improve the geographical distribution of medical manpower, certification procedures for physicians practising in private offices, patient signature of physician fee statements, and the establishment of a complaints board.

Physicians opposed most of the changes and saw the project as an attempt to subjugate the medical profession to technocratic authority. Confronted with a highly orchestrated public campaign and doctor-led work stoppages, the state made major concessions to the doctors with respect to the regionalization of the overall budget intended for their remuneration and postponed any further decision on major changes to regional boards.

The third reform led to the adoption of Bill 120 on August 28, 1991 with the support of the medical profession that enacted many of the recommendations originally suggested by the Rochon Commission. The statute provided for the decentralization of the management of services, decision-making and budget allocation to regional boards. It rejected the idea of user fees and the service tax principle and established a Regional Medical Commission (CMR),[3] the creation of a referral centre for the certification of executive directors and administrators of regional boards and institutions.

THE STRUCTURE AND RESPONSIBILITIES OF THE REGIONAL BOARDS[4]

The 1991 Statute created eighteen regional boards of health and social services (RRSSS), whose geographic territory, population size and budget (Table 8.1) differ significantly from one region to another. The board of directors of these regional boards have 23–25 members (Table 8.2), of which the largest majority (twenty members) is elected for three years by the regional assemblies. Members of the boards of directors are therefore no longer designated or appointed but rather elected by an electoral body. The composition of the boards of directors is proportionally the same as that of the regional assemblies. These regional assemblies are composed of 70–150 members, depending on the regional population density. These members are chosen from and elected by the members of the institutions' boards of directors (40 per cent), community organizations (20 per cent), social and economic groups (20 per cent), and

Table 8.1 Grants for services per region, 1997–98

	Region	$
1	Bas St-Laurent	287,974,103
2	Saguenay Lac-St-Jean	345,104,686
3	Québec	1,030,347,324
4	Mauricie – Bois-Francs	566,801,089
5	Estrie	368,546,065
6	Montréal-centre	3,266,339,132
7	Outaouais	315,815,990
8	Abitibi-Témiscamingue	205,434,432
9	Côte-Nord	149,542,006
10	Nord-du-québec	23,887,731
11	Gaspésie-Iles-de-la-Madeleine	160,991,599
12	Chaudière-Appalaches	366,797,263
13	Laval	254,386,409
14	Lanaudière	268,462,557
15	Laurentides	341,158,463
16	Montérégie	934,596,902
17	Nunavik	34,722,143
18	Terres-Cries-de-la-Baie-James	29,833,618

elected municipal officials (20 per cent). The regional assemblies are responsible for the election of the members of the boards of directors of the regional boards every three years, the approval of regional priorities and each board's annual activity report.

The regional boards have major administrative responsibilities for the allocation of budgets and grants to institutions, as well as community-based organizations for services in their region. (See Table 8.3 for the divisions of responsibilities between regional boards and the Ministry of Health.)

With regard to the organization of services, the mandate given to the regions allowed them to work towards co-ordinating services among institutions

Table 8.2 Composition of the board of directors of the regional boards

No.	
4	persons from community organizations
4	persons from socioeconomic groups
4	elected officials from municipalities
8	persons from boards of institutions
1–3	coopted person(s) (representing the Faculty of Medicine)
	The Chair of the Medical Commission
	The Executive Director

Table 8.3 Division of responsibilities between regional boards and the Ministry of Health, Canada

Regional boards	*Ministry of Health*
• Ensure public participation and the respect of user's rights	• Coordinate the overall regulation of the system
• Formulate priorities	• Determine the orientations and objectives in health and welfare matters
• Establish regional service organization plans and evaluate the effectiveness of services	• Approve regional priorities and plans for the organization of services
• Allocate the budgets and grants	• Distribute resources among the regions
• Coordinate the special medical activities of physicians	• Prepare policies for the retraining of manpower and negotiate the conditions of remuneration of professionals and staff of the health and social services network
• Implement measures for the protection of public health	• Coordinate the public health program
• Ensure economical and efficient management	• Evaluate the results

and between institutions and the community. They can avoid duplication, review administrative structures, orient decision-making on targeted objectives, and liaise with other sectors such as education, municipalities and justice. Regional boards have been mandated to develop and implement public health programs as well as other health and social services programs.

The boards of directors of the regional boards report to both the regional and provincial levels. At the provincial level, the regional boards must have the Ministry approve the regional organization of services plans and the allocation of budgets to the various service providers in their regions. They must also answer to the Minister, who periodically calls general meetings of the various board chairs and closely monitors the progress of major regional issues. More specifically, the regional boards must go before a social affairs parliamentary commission which represents the provincial legislature once every three years as stipulated in the law.

At the regional level, the boards must hold an annual regional meeting to seek approval for the annual report and regional priorities. They must also hold a public meeting at which they are required to account for their administration. In addition, all board of directors' meetings, that are held on average once a month, are open to the public. Moreover, major operations, such as developing plans to update the health and social services policy, reorganizing the health network, and budget reduction plans, have led the regional boards to work very closely with their communities. While most of these operations fall within a provincial framework, they are very specific as to how they are to be implemented and in the efforts taken to implicate local communities. Thus, the regional boards conduct many consultations and set up various committees as part of a process of regionalization and democratization in order to link all sectors of the community. These consultative processes have been studied in certain boards, notably in the Montreal-Centre Regional Board (Denis *et al.*, 1995).

Under the provisions of the Health Act, the regional boards must fulfil their mandates in consultation with their respective communities: health and social services institutions, community organizations, and organizations and bodies in other sectors such as the municipalities, the courts, the law enforcement agencies, the educational system and environmental groups.

With the 1991 reform, the regional authorities saw their administrative responsibilities and their political autonomy increased, although the latter still remains limited. For example, neither the board nor the regional assembly holds the power of taxation enabling them to inject more financial resources into the regional budget beyond those granted by the provincial government. Furthermore, neither the members of the board nor those of the regional assembly are elected directly by the regional populations. On the other hand, the health regions are more autonomous than they were prior to the reform of 1991 and the decision-making process is now more democratic than it was previously. This is because of the public character of the board of directors; it is the wider range of stakeholders who make up the regional assembly and the board of directors, and the fact that the majority of the members of these two authorities are elected, which has changed their management style towards a more consultative direction.

In fact, the budget cuts and the major reconfiguration of the network which have taken place in the last few years would not have been possible in such a short period of time without the backing of the regional authorities and without these authorities putting into place the mechanisms for a more collective approach to health care organization and administration. Regional boards have gained a lot of experience in restructuring that has enabled them to make important cost savings of some $423 million in 1995/96, $725 million in 1996/97, and $760 million in 1997/98[5] (the costs include reallocation budgets and unindexed expenditures such as collective agreements). Also, under the regional leadership, the province will have diminished the number of boards of directors and general management offices from 900 to approximately 300 to 350 over a period of four to six years.

Decentralization and granting real power to the regions to organize services and allocate budgets have also led to new dynamics between these institutions and local organizations and the regional boards. Local pressure groups have stopped addressing their requests to the Ministry and have zeroed in on a new target; namely, the regional board. Even provincial associations have lost power to the regions and have had to redefine their roles. For example, general practitioners as well as specialists have had to rethink their responsibility for ensuring that the regional population has access to health care services.

There have been important changes between Quebec's health regions. The allocation of budgets to the regions emphasizes the need for the equitable sharing of resources amongst them. Major efforts are now under way to allocate funding on a per capita basis that takes into account factors such as the needs of the population, production costs, and population migration between regions. Obviously, these efforts relate to different issues, including the level of autonomy that should be granted to each region in the development of services; the tertiary and quaternary services that must be grouped together on a supra-regional basis in order to develop expertise, ensure quality, and reduce costs; the right of clients to have access to the professional or health care institution of their choice.

Finally many of these changes have had a marked impact on the organization of medical practice and the remuneration of physicians. Even though the budget for physician remuneration has not yet been decentralized, planners, managers, and physicians themselves are increasingly aware of the budget's importance with respect to the organization of medical services in hospitals and in the community. Now a closer look is being taken at capitation for general practitioners, and the Minister has already announced that the regional budget should include the remuneration of physicians.

THE TWO COMMISSIONS AND DECENTRALIZATION

In spite of the twenty years that separate them, the Rochon Commission made the same choice as the Castonguay-Nepveu Commission (Bergeron, 1990). These two commissions of inquiry both recommended the introduction of strong political and administrative regional organizations. In both inquiries, new social actors took the leadership and the government of Quebec had to redefine the reforms that had been proposed. More importantly technocrats appeared to control the process throughout despite changes of government, quite different policy objectives and a better informed public (Weick, 1969). This phenomenon can certainly be explained in different ways but, as Kingdon (1984) and Lemieux (1994) suggest, it is largely dependent on the place and the influences of the process, formulation and implementation of public policies. According to these authors, the stakeholders do not have equal presence in the different steps in the process of developing public policy which explains why one group is able to dominate despite many conflicting interests at the table.

Take the example of the Rochon Commission. Members of political parties, and especially those in power, dominated the process of identification of the problems then encountered in the health and social services sector which led to the creation of this commission of inquiry. Once the commission of inquiry was established, the members of the political parties were rarely present in the process of formulating solutions. This process was influenced to a greater extent by administrators (technocrats, civil servants, managers, commission members), some intellectuals and representatives of the professions, who were more involved at the management than the clinical levels. During the implementation of the reform, the intellectuals were no longer present in the process, but the administrators, especially the technocrats, remained very influential. They had to deal with new stakeholders such as the medical profession, employee unions, associations of institutions, patient representatives, etc. When the policy was implemented, it was the technocrats, particularly those within the state apparatus, who not only sponsored the whole process but controlled it throughout; that is, from the time the Rochon Commission's report was released, through drafting the White Paper and the negotiations with the physicians, till the drafting of the health and welfare policy (MSSS, 1992).

SOCIAL, LIBERAL, AND COMMUNITY VISIONS OF STATE REFORM

Over the course of the last forty years, Quebec has experienced rapid social change brought about by a declining influence of the Church, the massive entry of women into the workforce, the transformation of the family, and a reduced birth rate. The state was entrusted with a fundamental mission to reduce social inequalities through social, fiscal and industrial policies, facilitate the redistribution of wealth, supply equitable answers to social needs and exercise an indirect control over economic markets in order to increase their stability, efficiency and humaneness. The state thus became a producer of services to fulfil the needs resulting from the recognition of social rights in education, health, labour markets and welfare.

Today in Quebec, as elsewhere, there is a kind of counter-movement against middle class professionals, technocrats, intellectuals from the right but, also, from the public-at-large concerned by the fiscal burden of higher taxes and the growth in Quebec's public sector. The state's presence in the economy is portrayed as a source of rigidity in the goods and services markets and blamed for an increasingly heavy tax burden. New institutional arrangements created by government reform movements in the past are believed to be incapable of producing goods and services in the quantity and quality desired by citizens without going over budget.

Confronted with such allegations of inefficiency in state management practices, there is now a serious debate within Quebec society on what should be the new role and division of power between the individual, the community, the marketplace and the state. It is this fundamental discussion on the restructuring of the division of powers within Quebec society that is at the heart of the current plans for the regionalization of health and social services in Quebec. Not unsurprisingly, it is currently crystallizing around the liberal, social and communitarian vision of the role of the state.

The liberal or neo-liberal vision refers to what Etzioni (1990) calls the classical or neo-classical liberal paradigm in which the individual is perceived as a person who seeks to maximize utility by rationally choosing the best means that would enable the achievement of goals. In the marketplace, these are the individual and rational choices which allow for maximum efficiency and well-being to be generated. For classical or neo-classical liberals, society corresponds to an aggregate of free individuals capable of making rational decisions which allow them to find the best response to their needs and preferences. Applying this logic, any state use of power constrains individual liberties. Thus, as far as is possible, the responsibilities of the state should be limited to the protection of private property, the maintenance of public order and provision of the possibility of entering into contracts.

Historically, liberal thought has taken form, not as a reaction against the state but against the authoritarian power of sovereigns, including the Church and the rigid moral principles on which established power rests. In conservative society, the individual has few liberties. One must conform to the dominant moral values and to the hierarchical authority. In this type of society, the léitmotif is the maintenance of social order and not the preservation of individual liberties: anarchy is perceived as a greater danger than authoritarianism (Etzioni, 1990).

This social vision began to take a shape in the crisis of the 1930s when the malfunctioning of the markets caused considerable losses of employment and income. It then became necessary to find the means to level off cyclical market fluctuations and to provide solutions for the social needs to which these fluctuations gave rise. The social vision refers to what Mishra (1984) calls the arrival of the welfare state supported by Keynesian economic theory and Beveridge's notion of social insurance. With the advent of the welfare state, we moved from a society based on individual choices, equality under the law, civil responsibility and the moral obligation to assist others, to a society of social justice and social rights. From this point on, the state must assume a dual role as regulator of the economy in order to stabilize production and employment and to assure the economic security of its citizens and as a major actor in putting together the resources in order to ensure collective risk coverage (Mishra, 1984).

These new roles which the state must assume call for identification of the 'national community', i.e. the legitimate place from which the collective wealth would be distributed and where the mechanisms for economic security and collective insurance against social risks would be instituted. It is with the arrival of the welfare state and the new roles it assumed that the nation united and centralized and began to take on a concrete and obvious meaning. According to Beveridge and Keynes, the intervention of the state is a positive support to the functioning of the markets since, as a result of this intervention, the markets should become more stable, more harmonious and more productive, while also achieving greater social justice (Mishra, 1984).

The community vision refers to Etzioni's 'I and We' paradigm (1990). This current of thought considers that the best protection from the liberals' excessive individualism or the centrist totalitarianism of the state is the pluralist society constructed on the basis of the liberty of local communities. This vision is opposed to the destruction of the significant social bonds which breed both the market and state centralism (Illich, 1975; Dupuy and Robert, 1976).

Those who adopt the community vision do not subscribe to the liberal philosophy of radical individualism according to which individuals are seen as entirely autonomous agents, detached from the society. For those who embrace the community vision, individuals are members of a collective and one must accept that the individual and the collective each have an equally important moral foundation (Etzioni, 1991). The community paradigm sees the experience of individuals in perpetual tension between, on the one hand, individual desires and preferences and, on the other hand, commitments and moral obligations with regard to the collective. This model affirms that the isolated individual (i.e. the autonomous agent of the liberal theory) is incapable of acting freely. Only those individuals in significant community relations are capable of making sensitive choices of doing justice and of being free (Etzioni, 1990).

According to the community vision, state centralism has had two particularly ill-fated consequences. On the one hand, the centralization of the decision-making process within the state has stimulated the organization of interest groups which, although they have encouraged the expression of the most diverse preferences in the society, have gradually excluded the citizen from the political process. It is their belief that this tendency must be reversed: political decisions can no longer be founded strictly on the interests of the most powerful groups and one can no longer relegate the political role of individuals to their sole participation in electing the government every four years (Godbout, 1987).

On the other hand, state centralism and the mechanisms of solidarity which it has allowed to take form have gradually led to relieving individuals of their responsibilities. In terms of national territory, individuals recognize that they have rights and feel that it is legitimate to claim them, but they acknowledge few duties, obligations, and commitments. According to the community vision, the solution to this shedding of responsibility by individuals depends on a reinvestment in local communities (Etzioni, 1990), which calls for the reconciliation of two apparently contradictory values: solidarity and freedom of choice. To accomplish this, as Godbout (1987) suggests, politics must withdraw from its exclusively state-related domain and establish a social organization in which decisions are made as close as possible to those that are affected by them.

At the end of the 1980s, among the three visions of the state, only the community and liberal visions produced solutions to the problems encountered by the health and social services system in Quebec. The social vision, and its way of looking at the state's role, allowed for the implementation of this system, and the problems it encountered were predictable. In addition, at that time the development of solutions to the problems which the health system was experiencing could only take a form based on either the liberal or the community vision, which favoured changing the role of the state. The liberal vision offered a plan that aimed to reduce considerably the role of the state through deregulation and privatization of the system. Through decentralization of the decision-making process, the community vision proposed a plan aimed both at the reduction of the omnipresence of the state and maintenance of the mechanisms of collective solidarity by resituating them at the local or regional level.

AN ASSESSMENT OF REGIONALIZATION

Health sector reform in the 1990s represents a compromise between the will to maintain the mechanisms of social solidarity that the welfare state established and the will to relax the management of services, to better respond to the diversified needs of the population without increasing the cost of the system.

Fundamentally, there were two major paths to solutions available as a means of making the management and production of health services more flexible and offering a larger choice of responses to the diversified needs of individuals: privatization or decentralization of management and production of services. Put in these terms, privatization should have been the big winner in the process of policy formulation (identification of the problem, formulation of solutions and implementation). But, as we have seen, the liberal philosophy, on which the market is based, is somewhat resistant to the redistribution of collective wealth and to the maintenance of mechanisms of social solidarity. In addition, many health economists are categorical: the privatization of the production of services can only lead to an increase in costs (Evans, 1984; Contandriopoulos *et al.*, 1993; Maynard, 1986; Maynard and Bloor, 1995). The market therefore addresses only part of the problem: that of the increased flexibility and the diversification of management and production. Therefore it is not surprising that neither the Rochon Commission nor the government of Quebec finally opted for this type of solution.

Decentralization of the management of health and social services received bad press in Quebec throughout the 1980s. As we have seen, even if over the years more and more administrative responsibilities were delegated to the regional councils, they did not have popular support but rather had the reputation of being rigid organizations. They did not have a determining control over institutional budgets or over the configuration of the network in their region, and they no longer saw themselves as advocates of the needs of the population and institutions in their region. In such a context, betting on decentralization in order to find a new balance between individual liberties and social responsibilities seemed to come more from the wish to maintain strong bureaucratic controls rather than from a true willingness to increase the plurality of choices in the society. This is, moreover, the analysis that many people made of the situation during the 1990s (Turgeon and Anctil, 1994; Bozzini, 1993). It is possible that this reform may end up being nothing more than a consolidation of a central hierarchical power through the implementation of 'small regional ministries' (Lemieux, 1994: 118).

In our opinion, the choice in favour of decentralization, made by both the Rochon Commission and the government, is nevertheless a promising but complex decision. In order to respond to the dilemma regarding social solidarity, individual liberty and cost control, the option to decentralize necessitates moves which are sometimes contradictory and often at the limit of the possibilities that can theoretically support such an approach.

It is clear that the regionalization of health and social services in Quebec is based largely on the community vision analysis of the negative effects of state centralism. This is true for both aspects of the decentralization process. The administrative aspect is largely based on self-management postulates, and the political aspect attempts to give more weight to the expression of regional freedoms while maintaining mechanisms of collective responsibility.

In its administrative dimension, the decentralization plan draws on self-management postulates in order to make the management and the production of services more flexible and to increase their efficiency. The delegation of administrative powers to regional boards essentially aims to relieve the central power of decisions for which the information it disposes of does not allow a flexible and enlightened management at the provincial level. While creating a strong regional administration which allows the central power to maintain a tight rein on the costs and on general objectives of the system, this plan aims to make all the stakeholders more responsible in order to facilitate the implementation of an integrated network of services at the regional level.

Up until now, this delegation of power seems to have been more fruitful than earlier critics might have suggested. Since the beginning of the 1980s, the government of Quebec has attempted, without much success, particularly as a result of pressure groups, to close some institutions, to merge others, and to reduce the costs of the system. Decentralization has served as a means to reach this goal. By bringing the decision-making to the regional level, decentralization has led to the reorganization of the system. In little more than five years, the regional boards have been successful in restructuring the regional networks for care delivery, in substantially reducing operational costs, and in reducing by approximately one-third the number of institution boards of directors through mergers and closures.

CONCLUSION

For the time being, it is difficult to draw final conclusions regarding this decentralization process. In its political dimension, the decentralization of health and social services has attempted to maintain and revitalize the bonds of solidarity that took form with the welfare state, while reconciling pluralism of choice, without adhering to the radical individualism of the neo-liberals. Therefore, this decentralization plan is seeking to establish new rules of the game so as to allow a different division of powers to take shape among the citizens, the state, the technocrats, the interest groups and the marketplace. As we have seen, the implementation of major social programs (health, education, etc.) and their centralized management has brought about, at least in Quebec, a redistribution of power within society. This power has then moved out of the hands of the local industrial and religious elite, and into those of the technocrats, interest groups and the state (Renaud, 1981). The present plan for regionalization of health services aims at using the region and the collective solidarity that has become part of the social fabric, allowing for both an increase in freedom of choice and the maintenance and revitalization of the mechanisms of redistribution of wealth established by the state over the last forty years.

As Etzioni (1990) implies, the danger associated with such a plan is the return to a conservative society which, through its rigid and hierarchical moral rules, would lead to ossified structures and not to a society constructed on social pluralism. As a result of the implementation of democratic mechanisms, which are able to destabilize the lobbying mechanisms of influential interest groups such as the diverse professional and institutional associations, regionalization has created a place where the interests of elected officials and those of the technocrats converge and have the potential to lead to the emergence of a new alliance between these authorities (Denis *et al.*, 1995). Thus, this decentralization plan seems to be aiming towards a rearrangement of the power relations between the citizens, the state, the marketplace, the managers and the interest groups active in the health and social services sector. The final results are not in, but there is every reason to believe that the reorganization has been set in motion and that the process is irreversible.

NOTES

1   The administrative councils of the CRSSS are composed of twenty-two members, who have a two-year mandate: four are designated by the mayors of the municipalities in the region, two are appointed by the government, three are appointed by the educational institutions in the territory, twelve are appointed by the region's health and social service institutions.

2   1975: evaluation, authorization and reimbursement of requests for repair and renovations in amounts of less than $50,000. 1976: authorization and financing of construction projects, renovations and equipment of less than $1,000,000 (making the CRSSS enter the sensitive area of resource allocation). 1977: creation of the regional administrative commissions, a meeting place for institutions and their CRSSS. 1978: the CRSSS obtain: (1) the power to approve organizational medical resource plans for university-affiliated hospitals, (2) the mandate to develop regional priorities and policy implementation plans concerning rehabilitation, mental health, CLSC services, home-care and home aid services and ambulance transportation. 1980: two pilot projects, in the Eastern Townships and in Saguenay-Lac St-Jean, aimed at making these CRSSSs part of the decision-making process concerning services dispensed in their region. 1981: creation of the emergency coordination centre in the Montreal region; delegation to all CRSSSs of the mandate to rent space and purchase buildings, and participation of the CRSSSs in the 'hospital economic recovery plan'. 1982–1985: modification of the composition of the CRSSS board of directors. The number of members of the administrative council decreases from twenty-two to fifteen. The length of their mandate is increased from two to three years. To ensure better representation from certain groups (councils of doctors, dentists and pharmacists; charitable organizations in the region), the number of representatives from the institutions is decreased from twelve to five (Turgeon and Anctil, 1994); the Ministry also mandates the CRSSSs to manage patient admission and transfer policies, operating norms for the emergency and for the distribution and utilization of beds. 1986: hospitals and nursing homes must have their CRSSSs approve their admission and final discharge criteria, as well as their patient transfer policy. In addition, certain CRSSSs are mandated to develop a plan to reduce overcrowding emergency rooms (CESSS, 1988: 166–168).

3   The Regional Medical Commission is a consultative body which reports to the Board of Directors of its Regional Board and provides advice to it on all matters concerning the organization and distribution of medical services, modes of remuneration and organization of medical practice.

4   This section is in part inspired by a paper presented by Jean-Pierre Duplantie, Executive Director, Eastern Townships Regional Health and Social Services Board,

at the Robarts Centre for Canadian Studies, 'Reorganizing Canadian Health Care: Global Pressures/New Institutional Realities: Quebec's Responses to Regional Processes of Health Care Reform', Toronto, 1 and 2 April 1996.

5   In 1997/98, the budget for the health and social services sector was $12,550.4 billion.

REFERENCES

Baguenard, Jacques. 1985. *La décentralisation*. Deuxième édition refondue, Collection Que sais-je? Paris: PUF.

Bélanger, Jean-Pierre. 1992. 'De la Commission Castonguay à la Commission Rochon . . . Vingt ans d'histoire de l'évolution des services de santé et des services sociaux au Québec', *Service social* 41 (2): 49–70.

Bergeron, Pierre. 1990. 'La Commission Rochon reproduit les solutions de Castonguay-Nepveu', *Recherches sociographiques* 31 (3) : 359–380.

Bouvier, Michel. 1986. *L'État sans politique: tradition et modernité*. Paris : Librairie générale de droit et de jurisprudence.

Bozzini, Luciano. 1993. 'Le nouveau Québec socio-sanitaire: une réforme à petits pas', *Journal d'Économie Médicale* 11 (7–8): 423–444.

CESBES. 1970. 'La santé', Tome II, *Rapport de la Commission d'enquête sur la santé et le bien-être social*. Québec: L'Éditeur Officiel du Québec, Gouvernement du Québec.

CESSS. 1988. *Rapport de la Comission d'enquête sur les services de santé et les services sociaux*. Québec: Les Publications du Québec, Gouvernement du Québec.

Contandriopoulos, André-Pierre, François Champagne, Jean-Louis Denis, Anne Lemay, Stéphanie Ducrot, Marc-André Fournier and Djona Avockssouma. 1993. *Regulatory Mechanisms in the Health Care Systems of Canada and Other Industrialized Countries: Description and Assessment*. Ottawa: Queen's University of Ottawa.

Denis, Jean-Louis, Anne Lemay, André-Pierre Contandriopoulos, Stéphanie Ducrot, Marc-André Fournier and Djona Avocksouma. 1994. 'The Iron Cage Revisited – Technocratic regulation and Cost Control in Health Care System'. In M. Malek (ed.) *Setting Priorities in Health Care*. Brisbane: John Wiley, 275–311.

Denis, Jean-Louis, Ann Langley and André-Pierre Contandriopoulos. 1995. 'La transformation du rôle des instances régionales dans le système de santé au Québec. Le cas de Montréal-Centre', *Revue française d'administration publique* 76 (4): 599–608.

Duplantie, Jean-Pierre. 1996. 'Reorganizing Canadian Health Care: Global Pressures/ New Institutional Realities: Quebec's Responses to Regional Processes of Health Care Reform'. Paper presented at the Robarts Center for Canadian Studies, Toronto, April 1–2.

Dupuy, Jean-Pierre and Jean Robert. 1976. *La trahison de l'opulence*. Paris: PUF.

Etzioni, Amitai. 1990. *The Moral Dimension. Toward a New Economics*. New York: The Free Press.

Etzioni, Amitai. 1991. *A Responsive Society*. San Francisco: Jossey-Bass.

Evans, Robert G. 1984. *The Economics of Canadian Health Care*. Toronto: Butterworth.

Fomerand, Gérard. 1994. *Crise des valeurs et mutation de l'État*. Éditions Loysel.

Forum national sur la santé. 1997. *La santé au Canada: un héritage à faire fructifier*, Volume II. Ottawa: Ministre des travaux publics et gouvernementaux, Gouvernement du Canada.

Godbout, Jacques T. 1987. *La démocratie des usagers*. Montréal: Boréal.

Illich, Ivan D. 1975. *Némésis médicale: l'expropriation de la santé*. Paris: Seuil.

Kingdon, John W. 1984. *Agendas, Alternatives and Public Policies*. New York: Harper-Collins.

Laliberty, Rene. 1988. *Decentralizing Health Care Management. A Manual of Department Heads and Supervisors*. Washington: National Health Publishing.

Lemieux, Vincent. 1994. 'Les politiques publiques et les alliances d'acteurs'. In Vincent Lemieux, Pierre Bergeron, Clermont Bégin, Gérard Bélanger (eds) *Le système de santé au Québec. Organisations, acteurs et enjeux*. Sainte-Foy: Les Presses de l'Université Laval, 107–128.

Maynard, Alan. 1986. 'Public and Private Sector Interactions: An Economic Perspective', *Social Science and Medicine* 22 (11): 1161–1166.

Maynard, Alan and Karen Bloor. 1995. 'Health Care Reform: Informing Difficult Choices', *International Journal of Health Planning and Management* 10: 247–264.

Mills, Anne, Patrick J. Vaughan Duane L. Smith and Geneva Tabidzadeh. 1990. *Health System Decentralization. Concepts, Issues and Country Experience*. Geneva: World Health Organization.

Mintzberg, Henry. 1979. *The Structuring of Organizations*. Englewood Cliffs: Prentice-Hall.

Mishra, Ramesh. 1984. *The Welfare State in Crisis. Social Thought and Social Change*. Brighton: Wheatsheaf Books.

MSSS. 1989. *Orientations. Pour améliorer la santé et le bien-être au Québec*. Québec: Gouvernement du Québec.

MSSS. 1990. *Une réforme axée sur le citoyen: plan d'implantation*. Québec: le Ministre.

MSSS. 1992. *La politique de la santé et du bien-être*. Québec: Gouvernement du Québec.

Pineault, Raynald, Paul A. Lamarche, François Champagne, André-Pierre Contandriopoulos, and Jean-Louis Denis. 1993. 'The Reform of the Quebec Health Care System: Potential for Innovation', *Journal of Public Health Policy* 14 (2): 198–219.

Renaud, Marc. 1981. 'Les réformes québécoises de la santé ou les aventures d'un État "narcissique"'. In Luciano Bozzini, Marc Renaud, Dominique Gaucher, Jaime Llambias-Wolf (eds) *Médecine et société les années 80*. Laval: Les Éditions coopératives Albert Saint-Martin, 513–549.

Turgeon, Jean and Hervé Anctil. 1994. 'Le Ministère et le réseau public'. In Vincent Lemieux, Pierre Bergeron, Clermont Bégin, Gérard Bélanger (eds) *Le système de santé au Québec. Organisations, acteurs et enjeux*. Sainte-Foy: Les Presses de l'Université Laval, 79–106.

Weick, Karl E. 1969. *The Social Psychology of Organizing*. Reading, MA: Addison-Wesley.

9 The evolution of devolution

What does the community want?

Jonathan Lomas

INTRODUCTION

Discussion of devolving powers to the regional level as being a good thing for Canadian health care is not new (Department of National Health and Welfare, 1970). At least two things, however, are new in the 1990s. First, devolution is no longer merely being discussed; it is being implemented in every province except Ontario. Second, and paradoxically, devolution is now largely seen as an instrumental means to achieve other ends, and not as an end in itself.

These changes are arguably the most radical restructuring of medicare since its inception, with far-reaching implications for governments, citizens, physicians, hospitals, and other interest groups (Lomas, 1996). Little, however, has been written about this 'leap in the dark', either in the popular press or in academic journals. Given the concerns over the efficacy of this approach to health policy, it seems even more important to document, monitor, and evaluate progress as these devolved authorities potentially become the governance mechanism for health care within nine of ten provinces (CMA, 1993; Ontario Premier's Council on Health, Well-being and Social Justice, 1994).

This chapter makes a contribution to that process. It begins with a brief overview of the structure of devolution in each province, and highlights that currently only the scope of services controlled by devolved authorities differs substantively across provincial jurisdictions. I then isolate the importance of ongoing negotiation in determining each board's real power and describe the three areas of tension around which negotiation is occurring – provincial government delegation of powers, provider relinquishment of management rights, and the local population's communication of needs and wants. There is also a brief summary of the methodology used for a survey of more than 500 members of 62 devolved authority boards in five provinces (see Box 9.1, p. 174). Finally, the chapter concludes with an assessment of the current performance of the devolved authority reform against provincial governments' objectives of community empowerment, system integration and coordination, and blame avoidance in the face of fiscal retrenchment.

A BRIEF OVERVIEW: A COMPARISON ACROSS PROVINCES

Canada now has 117 devolved authorities in health care (excluding lower tiers in Manitoba and Nova Scotia). The size of population they serve is highly variable, with a range from 7,000 in the Southern Kings region of Prince Edward Island to close to a million in Quebec's or British Columbia's capital regions.

Provinces are, however, at quite different points in their implementation of devolved authority (see Table 9.1). Broadly speaking they can be divided into two groups based on maturity. The five more established ones either started implementation prior to 1994 (Saskatchewan, Quebec, New Brunswick, Prince Edward Island), or implemented so rapidly that tasks being performed by the boards reflect greater maturity (Alberta). The four remaining ones are just emerging from initial implementation (British Columbia, Nova Scotia, Newfoundland, Manitoba). In contrast to the rest of the country, Ontario has signalled its lack of interest in devolving significant authority (Government of Ontario, 1995), being either doomed to or blessed with the role of control group for this experiment in health policy (see Harden, Chapter 11 this volume).

COMPARING THE STRUCTURAL DESIGNS

There are numerous proposed taxonomies to compare and contrast devolved authority structures (Mills *et al.*, 1990). These offer design features for

Table 9.1 Implementation of devolved authority in Canada's provinces, as measured by start of board member appointments

Province	Implementation started
Established boards	
Quebec*	Fall 1991
New Brunswick	Summer 1992
Saskatchewan	Summer 1993
Prince Edward Island	Fall 1993
Alberta	Summer 1994
Immature boards	
Newfoundland	Spring 1994†
Nova Scotia	Winter 1994
British Columbia	Winter 1994
Manitoba	Spring 1996‡

Notes:

* Already had a regional structure; this was the start of reformed regional structures.

† Regional community health boards were established on this date; regional institutional boards were not initiated until Spring 1995.

‡ This is for rural and northern Manitoba only; Winnipeg excluded.

comparative analysis, such as single tier versus two-tier, electoral versus other accountability mechanisms, the degree of decision-making authority, the method of funding, or the scope of services covered. Such comparisons offer a useful starting point, even though they fail to capture the nuances of context that determine the character of devolution in each province.

Unfortunately, most of the variables do not yet appear useful in comparing Canadian jurisdictions. The provinces proposing *two-tier structures*, for instance, have been slow in implementing the second tier, suggesting that this level may never evolve as a significant variable. The *elected versus appointed status* of the devolved boards may become salient in the future because many of the provinces plan to move to elected boards. Currently, however, all except Saskatchewan's thirty District Health Boards are appointed (Driver, 1995).

By contrast, what is striking is that the planned *degree of decision-making authority* is relatively uniform across all the jurisdictions. None have any role in revenue-raising (except the historical local contributions for the capital costs of new construction), but all are responsible for local planning, priority setting, allocating funds, and managing services for greater effectiveness and efficiency, within the constraint of provincially defined broad core services. Many also have some role in delivering services, or at least being the employer of service providers other than physicians. *Board funding* by the province is mostly via a global budget based on historical spending levels for that population, but nearly uniformly at reduced levels. Although many intend to follow Saskatchewan's lead and move eventually to needs-based per capita funding (Birch and Chambers, 1993), this move is being approached cautiously.

Hence, the nine provinces effectively have one-tiered structures, with boards, largely appointed, given broad decision-making authority (constrained, however, by the absence of revenue-raising powers and by provincially determined core services). They are largely funded by reduced global budgets calculated on a basis of historical levels, but with moves towards basing it on explicit population need. This leaves the *scope of services* as the main distinguishing structural characteristic.

This scope varies significantly across the provinces, ranging from hospital care only (e.g. New Brunswick), to broad human services (Prince Edward Island) (Table 9.2). Notably no province, however, has yet included physicians' services or pharmaceuticals as part of the devolved budget. Some have, nevertheless, given their devolved authorities responsibility for human resource planning, including physicians in their jurisdiction.

The differences in major objectives reflect sharply contrasting philosophical beliefs and mandates. New Brunswick, for instance, with a narrow set of goals, included only hospitals and used their aggregation under one board in each region to bring about rationalization of beds and ancillary services. Saskatchewan's changes, for instance, concerned with broad population health as a motivation for reform, were accompanied by a 'wellness model'; in Prince Edward Island there is much discussion of the social determinants of health.

Table 9.2 Breadth of scope under the authority of the devolved boards, by province

Scope	Province
Institutions (hospitals and/or nursing homes)	Newfoundland
Health care (above, plus services such as home care, public health, addiction services)	New Brunswick Nova Scotia Manitoba Saskatchewan Alberta British Columbia
Health and social services (above, plus community support services and social assistance)	Quebec
Human services (above, plus public housing and welfare services)	Prince Edward Island

Note: Physicians' services and pharmaceuticals are outside the scope of devolved authorities in all provinces.

THE INFLUENCE OF ONGOING NEGOTIATION

Ultimately, however, the nature of a devolved authority, including the degree of power it can wield, is less related to its structural characteristics and more determined by the outcomes of the negotiation process that is an integral part of implementing devolution (Putnam, 1993).

Illustrating this is the provincial governments' unwillingness to relinquish financial control over two of the three biggest expenditure areas in health care – physicians and drugs (the third being hospitals). This has resulted in less than optimal circumstances for devolved authorities intent on integrating and coordinating the primary care sector. Commentators in Quebec have noted that the regulatory powers reserved to the provincial government seriously compromise the discretionary power of the Regional Councils (Turgeon, 1993). In Saskatchewan the provincial government has placed a one-way valve on acute care institutional funds, such that district boards only have the discretion to move funds out of but not into that sector.

This raises the importance of distinguishing between the different degrees of devolved power. Mills characterizes three states along a continuum moving towards full devolution:

1 Deconcentration: spatial redistribution of administrative authority to local offices of the central government.

2   Decentralization: transfer to a local authority of some decision-making within a significantly constrained set of centrally determined guidelines and standards.
3   Devolution: transfer to a local authority of significant decision-making with only broad principles determined by central government (Mills *et al.*, 1990).

Where devolved authorities lie on this continuum is heavily influenced by the ongoing negotiating process. This occurs not only between each provincial government and its sub-provincial authorities, but also between each sub-provincial authority and the providers and citizens in its jurisdiction.

The majority of current sub-provincial decision-making in Canada is probably performed within the deconcentration and decentralization states. Most provincial governments are still wary enough of these local/regional governance entities to be nervous about relinquishing full devolutionary powers to them. New Brunswick and Newfoundland, and to a lesser extent Quebec, are particularly constrained in both scope and powers, and are probably best characterized as deconcentration. Alberta, Saskatchewan and Prince Edward Island have perhaps the greatest autonomy and may emerge with truly devolved authority in the coming years. The remaining provinces – Nova Scotia, Manitoba and British Columbia – are currently firmly within the decentralization state, operating within some quite specific centrally determined administrative and fiscal constraints[1].

Finally, even within a province there is variation in the extent to which some devolved authorities are willing or feel mandated locally, either because of their providers or their citizens, to exercise even the powers they have been given (Abelson *et al.*, 1995). This makes it difficult to generalize, not only about inter-but also about intra-provincial variations in power of devolved authorities on the basis of structural descriptions. Structural descriptions fail to tell us how the various tensions inherent to devolution get resolved at the level of each board. Ongoing negotiation is an integral part of the devolution experience.

CENTRALIZING IN ORDER TO DECENTRALIZE: THE INHERENT TENSIONS OF DEVOLVED AUTHORITY

The power of devolved authorities has been created from three sources. The provincial government has given them legitimacy by formally devolving to them powers to plan and allocate provincially derived funds. From the local health care providers and institutions, they have acquired, or they have procured, management rights to reorganize and reform service delivery. From the local or regional population has come their potential credibility and mandate to represent their citizens' needs, wants and preferences.

Thus each devolved authority embodies not only more decentralized formal powers passed down from the provincial government, but also more centralized informal powers garnered up from citizens and individual institutions or providers. For instance, the seventeen regional boards in Alberta replaced more than 200 hospital, health unit, long term care and mental health facility boards. This reflects the sentiments of many of the provincial Royal Commissions and task forces that not only supported the development of new devolved structures but also commented on the historically excessive degree of decentralization in health care which made coordinated management of the system impossible (Hurley *et al.*, 1994).

Individual citizens seeking personal services are now (at least theoretically) less influential than groups of citizens expressing a broad community need. Individual hospitals, now stripped of their autonomous boards and grouped with others under devolved authority, can no longer plan in isolation from the needs of the surrounding system. Physicians and other providers are increasingly hampered in locating where they desire, and instead must comply with human resource plans constructed by the devolved authority. Most of this is done under the name of better managing the health care system. Indeed, the business management literature has underlined this apparent paradoxical need to 'centralize in order to decentralize' (Perrow, 1977).

Each devolved authority is therefore situated at the nexus between its provincial government's expectations, its providers' interests and its citizenry's needs, wants and preferences (Lomas, 1996). Tensions are therefore inevitable.

DEVOLVED AUTHORITIES AND THEIR PROVINCIAL GOVERNMENT

The devolved authorities are acutely aware that the provincial governments that spawned them control both their budgets and the rules under which they operate. To this extent the devolved boards are potentially the locally based central enforcers of provincial government expectations, i.e., deconcentrated arms of their parent body. The move to more objectively determined needs-based funding formulae, such as that in use in Saskatchewan, may afford them some protection from arbitrary fiscal punishment if they deviate from these provincial expectations, but ultimately they are wary about biting the hand that feeds them.

There is also the 'rulebook', often expressed through requirements for delivery of core services. Alberta, Saskatchewan, Nova Scotia, Prince Edward Island and Newfoundland all have such documents either complete or under development. Most core service documents are introduced with quite general wording, affording significant discretion on the part of each devolved authority. To date, however, few devolved authorities have ventured far from traditional allocations of funds. Only time will tell if provincial governments will feel compelled to tighten the wording and reduce the discretion if they observe radical departures from accepted patterns of local resource allocation.

DEVOLVED AUTHORITIES AND PROVIDERS

In setting up the devolved authorities, most of the provinces excluded providers from the boards. This has added to the concern expressed by many providers that to them the reforms look more like centralization than decentralization. They feel excluded from the new channels of advice and influence (Robb, 1995). In response to these concerns, a number of the provinces have taken measures to increase provider involvement. In Alberta and British Columbia, for instance, human resource strategies were negotiated with the health care unions prior to implementation of the reforms. Concern expressed by physicians has been accommodated by such measures as regional medical advisory committees (Alberta), temporary placement of physicians on boards (Prince Edward Island), eligibility to stand as candidates in board elections (Saskatchewan), or formal capturing of their interests as defined constituencies of the board (Quebec).

Nevertheless, most provinces and their devolved boards see health care reform as more likely compromised than facilitated by giving direct decision-making power to providers and their interests, particularly given the reduced budgets that must be accommodated, often with adverse effects on providers. The tension will likely be amplified as the various associations and unions representing provider interests react by reorganizing from their prior provincial or institutional focus to the now more relevant regional or local focus (Lomas, 1996).

DEVOLVED AUTHORITIES AND THEIR CITIZENRY

Perhaps devolved authorities' best protection from either becoming central enforcers on behalf of provincial governments, or being captured on behalf of provider interests, is the extent to which they gain credibility as effective local mirrors for their citizens' needs and preferences. Here the difficulty is in isolating local needs (expressed by well-informed citizens seeking the public interest) from local wants (expressed by narrowly informed citizens seeking satisfaction of self-interest). One of the devolved authorities' biggest challenges will be to gain credibility by discriminating between and differentially valuing these two forms of community expression, while simultaneously maintaining cordial relations with the entire community. Good information will be a necessary, although likely not a sufficient, element in achieving this goal (Hurley *et al.*, 1995; National Health Information Council, 1991).

Nevertheless, the role for the local citizenry in devolved authorities remains unclear. In part this is because of the failure to distinguish between citizen input and citizen governance. Giving input as decisions are made at the local level on local matters – local planning and allocation – is one option. This, however, is not the same as elected local citizenry making the decisions for their locality – community governance. The former implies only community participation through advice and input to experts. The latter implies a more devalued role for experts and a pre-eminent role for the elected local citizens, regardless of their level of knowledge. These two approaches appear, however, to have become inextricably intertwined in Canada's current debates on the governance of devolved authorities. This is despite evidence that most average citizens wish only to be consulted, and both expect and prefer that 'the experts' take responsibility for actually making the decisions (Lomas and Veenstra, 1995).

Hence, in their attempts to negotiate compromise devolved authorities must choose the relative weight they will give to the sometimes competing views of their provincial government, their local providers, and their local citizens. With the provincial government their legitimacy and formal devolved power are at stake. With the providers, their ability to manage the reform process without disgruntled workers is at stake. And with their local citizenry their credibility is at stake.

DEVOLUTION OBJECTIVES: NEW GOVERNORS AND FISCAL RETRENCHMENT

A survey of board members (see Box 9.1 for design and response rates) revealed that devolution of authority for health care did indeed involve many trade-offs between the demands and expectations of government, providers and citizens. This means that the provincial governments' goals of community empowerment, efficiency gains, and contained conflict in the face of expenditure reductions have been variably met depending on how each board has chosen to satisfy its tripartite expectations. Appointed board members are rarely able to represent the interests of their entire community while simultaneously placating providers and satisfying provincial governments. Citizen control, always tenuous in health care (Morone and Marmor, 1981), will only come about if provincial governments discard their ambivalence towards, and health care providers agree to be governed by, local communities.

Provincial governments, however, do not necessarily see citizen control and local health care democracy as an end in itself. Citizen governors are seen as a means to a variety of ends – agents of rationalization, integration, and coordination; or allies in expenditure reduction and the 'taming' of powerful interest groups. The ambivalence of provincial governments is generated by their fear that the local voices of citizens will rise in opposition to government objectives not in support of them, refusing the roles of agent and ally, and derailing provincial governments' ideas of a more effective and efficient health care system.

Most providers, from professionals and unionized workers through to agencies and institutions, have become employees of or dependent upon the decisions of the newly created structures – the centralizing element of decentralization. These providers are expected to relinquish much of their prior

Box 9.1 Survey response rates by province

Province	Boards			Board members		
	No. of boards	*No. participating*	*Response rate (%)*	*No. of members surveyed*	*No. of completed surveys*	*Response rate (%)*
British Columbia	20	14	70.0	205	152	74.0
Alberta	17	12	70.5	172	106	61.5
Saskatchewan	30	27	90.0	314	200	63.5
Nova Scotia	4	4	100	63	34	54.0
P.E.I.	5	5	100	37	22	59.5
Total	76	62	81.5	791	514	65.0

Survey design

The way in which each devolved authority resolves its tensions between provincial government, provider, and citizen expectations, will presumably be influenced most by the dozen or so members of its board. As a first step to evaluate the devolved authority experiment in Canada, the survey was conducted between April and August 1995. Five provinces were selected with the aim of satisfying three selection criteria: (a) the scope of authority for devolved boards in the province had to be at least 'health care' (this excluded Ontario, Newfoundland and New Brunswick), (b) across the five selections there should be a geographic dispersion across the country (we selected three from western and two from eastern Canada), (c) across the five selections there should be a mix of both established and immature boards (we selected three provinces with established boards – Alberta, Saskatchewan, and Prince Edward Island – and two with immature boards – British Columbia and Nova Scotia). For complete results see Lomas *et al.*, (1997a, 1997b).

autonomy and adhere to decisions made in the interests of 'the system'; preservation of private domains is expected to give way to accommodation of public objectives. Not surprisingly, the most vocal opposition to the role of the devolved authorities has come from providers feeling disfranchised from decision domains formerly under their control (Robb, 1995; Russell, 1995). The 'evolution of devolution' (Ontario Premier's Council, 1995) is very much concerned with the balance of power between local citizens, their provincial government, and their health care providers. For some provinces, evidently community empowerment is less important than rationalization and expenditure reduction. In Tuohy's categorization of management tools they have favoured 'hierarchy' over 'collegiality' or 'the market' (Tuohy, 1996).

The 'medicare pact' that accompanied the introduction of national health insurance in Canada – you in government pay the bills and leave us in medicine to practise our profession (Naylor, 1986) – made it difficult for provincial governments to replace collegial management with either hierarchy or the market. The inadequacy of blunt budgetary tools in the hands of provincial governments, the passage of time dimming the recollection of the medicare pact, and the parallel development of information tools and demonstrations of inappropriate care, have all conspired to justify blending hierarchy with collegiality for more aggressive governance of the system. Geographic relocation of some authority has become a way for provincial governments to shed the shackles of their medicare pact history and, under the cloak of devolved authority, adopt a 'command and control' strategy of governance, especially with regard to hospital restructuring (Lomas, 1996).

Finally, one cannot ignore the political context of these structural changes. Provincial governments in Canada have been quick to emulate their federal counterpart and governments in many other countries engaged in global fiscal retrenchment. Devolving authority has been used as a blame avoidance strategy by governments faced with tough choices as service expectations exceed perceived taxation capacity (Pierson, 1994; Rasmussen, 1996; Hoggett, 1996).

Three overarching objectives for devolved authority are therefore swirling around provincial health policy-making, in a variety of mixtures and changing alignments. First is the need to acquire allies, in the form of 'local citizens', for the task of health care restructuring (Hurley *et al.*, 1994). By using community empowerment governments hope to establish an alternative source of legitimate power over dominant and historically prevailing interests. Seventy-two per cent of the board members in our survey felt accountable to all the local citizens, but only 2 per cent felt accountable to local health care providers (Lomas *et al.*, 1997b).

Second is the desire to exact more than blunt budgetary control over health care providers. Local needs assessments, regional budgets, practice guidelines, and business plans are all seen as ways of creating an integrated, effective and efficient system based on widespread use of information for quality clinical care and sound business management. Most of the board members we surveyed declared improved effectiveness and efficiency of the system as their priority objective (Lomas *et al.*, 1997a).

Third is the desire to reduce overall expenditures with a minimum of community complaint, and deflect whatever complaints arise away from the provincial government. Fifty-seven per cent of the surveyed board members believed that this was provincial governments' main motivation for devolving authority (Lomas *et al.*, 1997b). The budgets of most devolved authorities have been constrained or reduced in their first years of operation. Their capacity to absorb further expenditure reductions without community complaint is dependent not only on the size of the cuts but also on such factors as their degree of perceived legitimacy, their progress in creating and rationalizing the delivery system, and their willingness to challenge the provincial government.

In order to evaluate whether devolution 'works' from a provincial government perspective, it must be evaluated against each of these objectives for both its current status and its likely prospects.

CREATING NEW GOVERNORS: COMMUNITY EMPOWERMENT AND ACCOUNTABILITY

One of the many paradoxes of devolved authority is that community empowerment could be fully accomplished as an objective while leaving the health care system unintegrated, uncoordinated, and unrationalized. Community empowerment means only that local citizens feel in control of the decisions that affect delivery of their health care. There is only a presumed and largely unproven link between citizen control and a more cost-effective health care system which delivers the same or higher levels of service with fewer resources. Regional or local control, we are told, will somehow be less susceptible to the overtly political pressure of powerful interests and more likely to engage in rational, evidence-based decision-making. However, why this balance is more attainable at a local or regional than a provincial level is never fully elucidated, nor completely obvious (Lewis, 1997).

In any event, as pointed out above, there may be quite valid reasons why community empowerment is a justifiable goal in and of itself, independent of whether it achieves rationalization of the health care system. Although our survey results suggest that 50 per cent of the members of the devolved authority boards feel constrained by their provincial governments, the appointed board members overwhelmingly feel confident about their decision-making and influential in their role (Lomas et al., 1997b). However, there is no a priori reason to believe that these feelings of empowerment among the appointee board members reflect the feelings of the community members they govern.

For community members to feel empowered they must feel represented by the devolved authority board decision-makers, ascribe legitimacy to them, and at least tolerate if not support the decisions emanating from them. Our data on the backgrounds of board members clearly indicated that current appointees are not socio-demographically representative of the community, which leaves open the question of how well they may represent the views of the community. One-third do view themselves as representing an intra-region geographic or group interest; the other two-thirds mostly see themselves representing and being accountable to all the local citizens. Whether these stated intents and desires of board members actually translate into feelings among local citizens of 'being represented', or whether there is perceived legitimacy of the boards and at least acquiescence to their decisions, cannot be answered generally. It can only be ascertained through jurisdiction-by-jurisdiction assessments. To the extent that these have been done, pessimism appears to dominate optimism (Sullivan and Scattolon, 1995; Bickerton, 1996; Lomas *et al.*, 1997a, 1997b), even with the increased political legitimacy of elected board members (Rasmussen, 1996; O'Neill, 1992).

The function of elections is, however, not only to increase empowerment via legitimacy. It may also be to increase accountability to whomever is the electorate – in theory, the entire community; in practice, those to whom board members feel beholden for election. The 40 per cent of our survey respondents who were willing to stand for election did express a greater tendency than the others to represent specific interests, and if ward-based elections occur they are a natural incentive to represent geographic interests. If hospital workers elect a hospital representative, rural areas a rural representative, social service agencies a social service representative, and so on, then a single accountability to the community may disaggregate into multiple accountabilities to a variety of dominant group and geographic interests. This is precisely the 'management by interest-group' approach that devolved authority was designed to overcome! However, see Trottier *et al.* (Chapter 8 this volume) for how Quebec includes interest groups intentionally in their governance.

As Rasmussen has stated:

> the province provides health care services, but individuals are unlikely to organize to influence the policy process related to health care if they cannot, in some measurable way, privately appropriate the public good … those with material interest in the issues will organize most quickly and most effectively, almost always in defence of the status quo.
>
> (Rasmussen, 1996: 9)

Our own work indicates both that those employed in health care have a greater propensity than average citizens to become involved in local health care decision-making, (Lomas and Veenstra, 1995) and that these average citizens are ready to assign local decision-making to 'health care experts' (Abelson *et al.*, 1995). Compared to appointed board members, elections may, paradoxically, reduce rather than increase the accountability of local boards to the community-at-large and leave community empowerment untouched or even reduced.

A final reason to be sceptical about the ability of devolved authority to empower local communities is the element of centralization that accompanied their creation. In most provinces the local, autonomous boards governing institutions, agencies and services were disbanded and their mandates and powers incorporated into their area's new devolved authority. In Saskatchewan, for instance, 435 such boards were replaced by thirty District Boards. The logic of this in the context of rationalization, integration and coordination of the health care system is fairly obvious. The impact on opportunities for individual citizens to feel they are contributing and participating has been less well recognized. Assuming that each board averaged the same number of members as the replacement District Boards (twelve), 5,220 opportunities for local participation have been replaced with just 360 opportunities. This has presumably 'disempowered' nearly 5,000 citizens. One of the future challenges for devolved authorities is to find ways to harness the energy of these discarded volunteers and recreate the 'social capital' they represent. As Putnam has demonstrated, such social capital is also vital to effective governance by regional authorities (Putnam, 1993; Veenstra and Lomas, 1996). Furthermore, replacing the roles of 435 community boards with thirty District Boards may, by virtue of sheer volume of work, give greater control to staff and a less influential role for even the remaining board members.

CREATING A HEALTH CARE SYSTEM: RATIONALIZATION, COORDINATION AND INTEGRATION

Regardless of the ability of devolved authority to generate community empowerment, it may be able to achieve rationalization of the local or regional health care system by using more finely tuned and community sensitive approaches than are available to a distant provincial government. This is certainly part of provincial governments' theoretical justification for devolving authority (Hurley *et al.*, 1994), and explains the assignment of resource allocation power to the boards.

Our survey indicated that three-quarters or more of board members were actively using resource allocation and the other governance tools provided to them such as need assessments, priority-setting, effectiveness and efficiency measures, and data. Indeed, two-thirds felt they had enough information to make good decisions, although this information appears to be dominated by cost and utilization data rather than documentation of benefits or citizen preferences (Lomas *et al.*, 1997a).

Central to the creation of a health care system is the ability of the devolved authorities to use these governance tools to rationalize, integrate and coordinate across previously autonomous and sometimes competing services. Such rationalization can occur vertically – between institutional and community-based services – and horizontally – across either institutional or community-based services (Leatt *et al.*, 1996). In two provinces – New Brunswick and Newfoundland – the scope of the boards has been limited to institutional services, making anything other than horizontal integration of institutions difficult to achieve (although Newfoundland did establish separate boards for community services).

However, even in the remaining provinces, devolved authorities have tended to focus on institutions, partly because they are the largest identifiable component of their budgets, but also because of two significant omissions from their resource allocation power – physician and pharmaceutical budgets. These latter two items are the lion's share of primary care resources, and it is hard for any board to embark seriously on horizontal integration of community-based services (or even vertical integration between them and institutional services) in the absence of budgetary control. As Evans and Tuohy have noted, governance of a sector without budgetary authority is akin to 'pushing on a string' (Tuohy and Evans, 1984).

In provinces with two-tier structures of Regional and Community Boards – British Columbia (initially), Manitoba and Nova Scotia (still) – inherent confusion over relative roles and responsibilities also hampers rationalization efforts, especially for community-based services. As budgetary authority is usually given to the regional level, where institutional issues predominate, hospital integration inevitably dominates concerns about rationalization. Reducing duplication across and gaps between community service agencies, physicians' offices, home care programs and so on may involve fewer dollars, but is probably more challenging in the long run given the sheer number and diversity of delivery units. This task will depend to a greater extent than does hospital rationalization on local community knowledge and sensitivity. The as-yet unanswered question is whether the task can be achieved by Community Boards with minimal budgetary authority and far less information than is available for the hospital sector. Conversely, in provinces with only Regional Boards – Alberta, Quebec and New Brunswick – the unanswered question is whether they will have enough resources and the local knowledge successfully to rationalize the primary care and support services within multiple communities under their jurisdiction.

The main opposition to these changes in the status quo is likely to be from the various provider groups and agencies whose operations are being disrupted. Provider groups have successfully mobilized opposition to a number of attempts at rationalization, even forcing the members of one devolved authority to resign and pass the task back to the provincial Minister of Health (Wightman, 1995) – not all boards are willing to absorb the displaced blame.

Rebuffed rationalizations, however, tend to gain far more coverage than do those occasions when successful rationalization occurs, and are concentrated in those jurisdictions continuing to rely primarily on collegial management by local professionals. Those jurisdictions exploiting the capacity to blend hierarchical and collegial governance have been more willing to weather the community outcry and persist with rationalization 'over the heads' of protesting providers and, sometimes, local citizens. There is clearly a tension between a devolved authority's exercise of its hierarchical governance authority and its ability to maintain provider morale and retain local legitimacy as a voice of the community. It is perhaps for this reason that some provincial governments used their hierarchical authority to disband hospital boards and close or downsize hospitals before initiating the devolved authorities (e.g. New Brunswick and Saskatchewan).

Once again it is difficult to generalize across all devolved authorities, but most have been able to sustain provincially generated horizontal integration of some institutional services or achieve their own such integration. Horizontal integration of community services and vertical integration between community services and institutions are less commonplace. This is both because of the structural handicaps inherent in the current design of devolved authorities and their need to listen to local voices that are relatively easily mobilized in opposition by threatened agencies and providers. In this context the adoption by devolved boards of a primary objective of community empowerment may come into direct conflict with their objective of achieving a more effective and efficient health care system. Unless professionals, agencies and institutions adopt more system-oriented thinking, and focus less on the preservation of their particular 'silo', provincial governments and devolved authorities will rely increasingly on hierarchical governance in order to mandate a real health care system.

REDUCING EXPENDITURES: BLAME AVOIDANCE AND CONFLICT CONTAINMENT

Provincial governments did not need to devolve authority in order to reduce expenditures on health care. Devolved authorities are, however, a convenient way to shift blame and place a buffer between themselves and community discontent with the consequences of fiscal retrenchment. The same tactic has been used by national governments downloading to local government (Pierson, 1994). The fact that over half the board members we surveyed recognized this motivation is a testament to their realism; that only a quarter felt that it interfered with their ability to make long-term plans is a testament to their optimism. Despite this optimism, their success in containing or overcoming any discontent will strongly influence their ability to move forward on health care system rationalization and/or citizen empowerment.

Whether planned or not, many provinces have handicapped the devolved authorities out of the starting blocks by coupling their creation with major expenditure reduction plans. In Alberta, for instance, Regional Boards were expected to come up with business plans premised on more than 5 per cent annual reductions in their budgets within 90 days of their appointment (Church, 1996). This made clear that the preoccupying task was expenditure reduction.

The Alberta experience demonstrates the danger for provincial governments of over-reliance on devolved authorities as the sponges for local discontent. If the budget is perceived to be squeezed too hard, as was the case for some regions in Alberta, then the devolved authorities can turn on the provincial government, adding their authority and legitimacy to the claims of underfunding (Mitchell, 1995). As more provinces move to elected boards, the devolved authorities' legitimacy as potential lobbyists for under-funding may be increased.

It was this consideration that had some provinces contemplating, although none implemented, revenue-raising powers for the devolved authorities (Rasmussen, 1996). This places the fiscal accountability back in the local jurisdiction. It also, as the federal government is discovering with regard to national standards for social programs, reduces the legitimacy of the provincial government in determining the outcomes of heath care system restructuring – less proportionate funding, less clout (Deber, 1996). Interestingly, only 1 per cent of the board members we surveyed desired any revenue-raising powers for their boards.

The role of the boards in containing the conflict from provincial expenditure reductions can only be pushed as long as the board members feel there is 'slack' in the system that can be taken up with effectiveness and efficiency measures, thus leaving quality of and access to care unaffected. Once board members no longer believe this they are likely to leave local discontent uncontained, if not fan its flames.

More than half the board members we surveyed indicated that improving effectiveness and efficiency should be the primary objective of devolved authorities. Unattended local discontent and conflict make it difficult to achieve such improvements. Hence, as long as board members remain convinced that there are efficiencies to be achieved, both their objective and the provincial governments' desires for containment of conflict will be compatible. Most provincial governments are, therefore, engaged in a careful political calculation to stay just inside the 'squeal' threshold as they tighten down on expenditures. One of the new signs of when they have exceeded it is when devolved authorities join with and orchestrate the local discontent. In other words, devolved authorities can be either a facilitator of or a brake on expenditure reductions, depending on the 'slack' they perceive to be left in the system.

CONCLUSIONS

Let us re-visit the question of whether devolved authority 'works'. First, and perhaps most importantly, it is difficult to generalize about the performance of 117 devolved authorities in nine provinces. Each devolved authority arrives at its own resolution of the inherent conflict it faces between its provincial government's expectations, providers' interests and citizens' perceived needs and wants. The chosen path of resolution will tip the balance more in favour of community empowerment, system rationalization or expenditure reduction, but not likely in favour of all three because, as described above, there are elements of mutual incompatibility among these objectives.

Initial assessment, however, suggests that most devolved authorities favour system rationalization as a primary objective and can claim some success at horizontal integration of institutions. They are tolerating the expenditure reduction requirements imposed upon them, but are exchanging the role of provincial government ally for aggressive lobbyist against under-funding once such reductions exceed thresholds of acceptability. Finally, they are trying hard to represent, although not necessarily empower, their communities.

Future progress on integration and coordination of the system beyond rationalization of institutional care will be difficult if they are not given a broader scope of budgetary authority, including at least physicians and pharmaceuticals and perhaps some social and other human services such as those included in Quebec's and Prince Edward Island's reforms. Even with this expanded scope, devolved authorities may still struggle to make reality from the widespread rhetoric about the importance of the broader determinants of health, especially given their need to maintain morale among their existing dominant providers as they absorb expenditure reductions.

The future of citizen governance and empowerment is intimately tied to the issue of elected boards. The current appointed boards appear to be well-intentioned in representing and being accountable to the entire community. Whether with elections this will break down into representation of and accountability to specific interest groups will depend on whether electoral turnout is large and representative enough to affirm community-wide interests. The average 35 per cent turnouts in Saskatchewan's direct elections of fall 1995 (substantially less in the urban areas) do not bode well; as Evans and Tuohy note, 'A mandate drawn from substantially less than 35 per cent of the voting population does not constitute a very effective political resource in dealing with cohesively organized provider groups' (Tuohy and Evans, 1984: 106).

These unknowns point up the importance of undertaking evaluations of the impact of devolving authority on at least the above objectives, as well as on other objectives unique to particular provinces. The only jurisdiction undertaking such an evaluation is Prince Edward Island, where the System Evaluation Project is a partnership between the province and Health Canada designed to generate national policy learning and provincial mid-course corrections on devolved authority for health (Chaulk et al., 1996). Ontario will offer an interesting natural experiment, acting as a contrasting option that is more engaged in centralizing authority over the health care system than devolving it.

Whether or not devolved authority for health care turns out to have been a good or bad overall policy for Canada's provinces remains to be seen. There are now 117 instead of ten provincial opportunities for cross-jurisdictional learning. What this diversity holds requires much close scrutiny in the future.

ACKNOWLEDGEMENTS

The survey reported in this chapter was funded by the former Premier's Council of Ontario, the Health Gain program of Glaxo-Wellcome Canada, and by provision of some staffing by the UK's National Health Service Trainee Program. The survey would not have been possible without the hard work, organizational skills and analytic abilities of John Woods and Gerry Veenstra. The Centre for Health Economics and Policy Analysis receives partial funding from the Ontario Ministry of Health. This chapter is a reworking of earlier work published in the *Canadian Medical Association Journal*, reproduced here with permission.

NOTE

1   Of course, as noted earlier, we have little evaluative information that would help judge which state is preferable for achieving which policy objectives. There are, for instance, many analysts who express concern about equity across a fully devolved system (O'Neill, 1992; Pierson, 1994).

REFERENCES

Abelson, J., J., Lomas, J., Eyles, S., Birch, and G. Veenstra, 1995. Does the community want devolved authority? Results of deliberative polling in Ontario. *Canadian Medical Association Journal* 153: 403–412.

Bickerton, J. 1996. Health care reform in Nova Scotia: redesigning democracy? Paper presented to Annual Meeting of Canadian Political Science Association, St. Catharine's, Ontario, 2–4 June.

Birch, S. and S. Chambers, 1993. To each according to their needs: a community-based approach to resource allocation in health care. *Canadian Medical Association Journal* 149: 607–612.

Canadian Medical Association (CMA). 1993. *The Language of Health System Reform: Report of the Working Group on Regionalization and Decentralization.* Ottawa: Canadian Medical Association.

Chaulk, P., J., Lomas, J., Eyles, J., Ross-Keizer, J., Macdonald, and D. Gallant, 1996. Linking evaluation with health policy development and implementation: the PEI system evaluation project. Paper presented at Annual Meeting of the Canadian Public Health Association, Vancouver, BC, 3–5 July.

Church, J. 1996. Health reform in Alberta: a cautionary tale. Paper presented at Annual Meeting of Canadian Political Science Association, St. Catharine's, Ontario, 2–4 June.

Deber, R. 1996. National standards in health care. *Policy Options*, June: 43–45.

Department of National Health and Welfare. 1970. *Report of the Task Force on the Cost of Health Services in Canada.* Ottawa: Ministry of Supply and Services, p. 19.

Driver, D. 1995. Doctor turnout high in Sask. health board vote. *Medical Post*, 14 November, p. 53.

Government of Ontario. 1995. *Bill 26, The Savings and Restructuring Act.* Toronto: Queen's Printer (December).

Hoggett, P. 1996. New modes of control in public service. *Public Administration* 74: 9–32.

Hurley, J., J., Lomas, and V. Bhatia, 1994. When tinkering is not enough: provincial reform to manage health care resources. *Canadian Public Administration* 37: 490–514.

Hurley, J., S., Birch, and J. Eyles, 1995. Information, efficiency and decentralization within health care systems. *Social Science & Medicine* 41: 3–11.

Leatt, P., G., Pink, and C. D. Naylor, 1996. Integrated delivery systems: has their time come in Canada? *Canadian Medical Association Journal* 154: 803–809.

Lewis, S. 1997. *Regionalization and Devolution: Transforming Health, Reshaping Politics?* Health Services Utilization and Research Commission Working Paper, Saskatoon, Saskatchewan.

Lomas, J. 1996. Devolved authorities in Canada: the new site of health care system conflict? In *How Many Roads? Regionalization and Decentralization in Health Care*, J. Dorland and S. M. Davis (eds). Kingston, Ontario: Queen's University School of Policy Studies.

Lomas, J., and G. Veenstra, 1995. If you build it who will come? Governments, consultation and biased publics. *Policy Options* 16 (9): 37–40.

Lomas, J., G., Veenstra, and J. Woods, 1997a. Devolving authority for health care in Canada's provinces: 2. Backgrounds, resources and activities of board members. *Canadian Medical Association Journal* (Educ.), 156 (4): 513–20.

Lomas, J., G., Veenstra, and J. Woods, 1997b. Devolving authority for health care in Canada's provinces: 3. Motivations, attitudes and approaches of board members. *Canadian Medical Association Journal* (Educ.) 156 (5): 669–76.

Mills, A., J. P., Vaughan, D., Smith, and I. Tabibzadeh, 1990. *Health System Decentralization: Concepts, Issues and Country Experiences*. Geneva: World Health Organization.

Mitchell, A. 1995. Alberta backs down on cuts as wildcat strikes hit hospitals. *Globe and Mail* Nov. 23: 4.

Morone, J., and T. Marmor, 1981. Representing consumer interests: the case of American health planning. In *Citizens and Health Care: Participation and Planning for Social Change*, B. Checkoway (ed.). New York: Pergamon Press.

National Health Information Council. 1991. Community Health Information Systems Working Group. *Description of Federal Databases and Surveys*. Ottawa.

Naylor, C. D. 1986. *Private Practice, Public Payment*. Montreal: McGill-Queen's University Press.

O'Neill, M. 1992. Community participation in Quebec's health system: a strategy to curtail community empowerment. *International Journal of Health Services* 22: 287–301.

Ontario Premier's Council. 1995. *Challenging Assumptions: Restructuring Health Systems Across Canada. Devolution or Dog's Breakfast?* Toronto: Project Team on Health Reform, Ontario Premier's Council.

Ontario Premier's Council on Health, Well-being and Social Justice. 1994. *A Framework for Evaluating Devolution*. Toronto: Task Force on Devolution, Ontario Premier's Council on Health, Well-being and Social Justice.

Perrow, C. 1977. The bureaucratic paradox: the efficient organization centralizes in order to decentralize. *Organizational Dynamics* 5 (Spring): 3–14.

Pierson, P. 1994. *Dismantling the Welfare State: Reagan, Thatcher and the Politics of Retrenchment*. Cambridge: Cambridge University Press.

Putnam, R. 1993. *Making Democracy Work*. Princeton: Princeton University Press.

Rasmussen, K. 1996. Institutional change and policy outcomes. District Health Boards in Saskatchewan. Paper presented to Annual Meeting of the Canadian Political Science Association, St. Catharine's, Ontario, June 2–4.

Robb, N. 1995. Some physicians remain sceptical as metamorphosis of health care continues in PEI. *Canadian Medical Association Journal* 153: 1155–1159.

Sullivan, M. and Y. Scattolon, 1995. Health policy planning: a look at consumer involvement in Nova Scotia. *Canadian Journal of Public Health* 86: 319–322.

Tuohy, C. 1996. Health reform, health policy – towards 2000. Canada in the comparative perspective. Paper presented at the 'Four Country Conference', Montebello, Quebec, 16–18 May.

Tuohy, C. and R. Evans, 1984. Pushing on a string: the decentralization of health planning in Ontario. In *The Costs of Federalism*, R. Golembiewski, A. Wildavsky (eds). New Brunswick, NJ: Transaction Books.

Turgeon, J. 1993. Second debut for the third level: health and social services regions in Quebec. Paper presented at Centre for Health Economics and Policy Analysis's 6th Annual Health Policy Conference, Hamilton, May.

Veenstra, G. and J. Lomas, 1996. Home is where the governing is: social capital and regional health governance. McMaster University Centre for Health Economics and Policy Analysis Working Paper C96-1, June.

Wightman, R. 1995. Health board tenders resignation. *The Guardian* (Prince Edward Island), Nov. 1: 5.

10 Fiscal austerity through decentralization

John Church and Tom Noseworthy

During the 1990s, the Province of Alberta has undergone unprecedented change in the public sector. Significant downsizing of administrative structures at the provincial level, and regionalization of governance and service delivery at the local level, has characterized this. In the case of health care, the government of Alberta embarked on a plan to reduce expenditures by 19 per cent over a three-year period, as part of a commitment to eliminate a $3.4 billion annual deficit. The elimination of the deficit was to be achieved entirely on the expenditure side, without an increase in taxes. In what followed as a response to this fiscal imperative, the health care sector was restructured through the elimination of most existing local boards and the creation of seventeen regional health authorities with responsibility for most health care services, and two provincial boards.

On the surface, these changes resemble similar actions taken by other provinces. What differentiates Alberta from other provinces is the approach to and extent of the reforms. With the exception of Ontario, no province chose to cut expenditures in health care as deeply or as quickly as Alberta. This gives Alberta the dubious honour of being one of the richest Canadian provinces, 'while providing the lowest level of provincial public services' (MacMillan, 1996: 14).

The organization and reform of the public health sector in Alberta reflects a marked tendency for a *laissez-faire*, pluralist approach to policy development, with responsibility for the formulation and implementation of health care policy being dispersed across a variety of governmental and non-governmental agencies. Limited public debate is a part of this tradition. In addition, the provincial government has chosen not to regulate the private side of the health care market. The result of this inaction has been the *ad hoc* development of a variety of private clinics (MRI, opthalmological and abortion) to serve at the margins of the public system. A combination of legislative and policy changes, a shrinking public market, a preference for private market solutions, and carefully orchestrated public debate have created a climate in which private providers with strong political affiliations to the current government benefit.

In the areas of social and health policy, the government has exhibited a marked preference for a residual[1] or a *laissez-faire* approach to the market.

This is well illustrated in health care by the stated preference of the Alberta government for a private market solution to health care when the federal government was investigating the establishment of national medical care insurance, the fight against the elimination of extra-billing by physicians, and, most recently, the protection of private clinics that were violating the Canada Health Act (Taylor, 1986; Barr, 1974).

Underlying this ideological preference has been a pluralist approach to the administration of the health care system. This is illustrated by the reluctance of the government to consolidate the majority of health services, which were not consolidated under a single organizational entity, Alberta Health, until 1988 (Alberta Health, 1996: 10). In addition, the views of public servants in the health care sector indicate a fairly strict adherence to the theoretical separation of administration from policy making. This dominant bureaucratic culture and the dispersal of authority have led ultimately to a weak state presence in the Alberta health care sector (Boase, 1994).

With these historical undercurrents in mind, we now turn to a closer examination of the recent health care reforms in the province.

HEALTH CARE WITHIN A GOVERNMENT REFORM CONTEXT

Health care reform in Alberta has taken place within a larger context of government-wide reforms. The major themes shaping these reforms have included deficit and debt reduction; downsizing and restructuring to create a 'smaller' and 'more responsive' public sector; and deregulation and privatization. Despite this, the Klein Government did not invent the general direction for health care reform. Instead, it was the result of a combination of a provincial health policy review process initiated during the late 1980s and a general sense of the need for health reform that had been a central topic in federal–provincial policy circles for at least a decade (Plain, 1995; Angus, 1994; Philippon and Wasylyshyn, 1996).

The general direction that reform would take was outlined in the report of the Premier's Commission on Future Health Care (1989), which recommended, among other things, the creation of nine autonomous administrative regions accountable through Regional Health Authorities (Premier's Commission, 1989). The report called for a 'serious redistribution' of 'planning and power' away from Alberta Health to local communities, individuals and newly created provincial entities known as Regional Health Authorities. However, the political timing would not be right until after the election of a new party leader and a provincial election. In the lead-up to the 1992 election, the Conservatives stressed the urgent need to address a mounting provincial debt and continuing annual deficits. An extensive public consultation process, dubbed 'provincial roundtables', was undertaken to convince Albertans of the new political agenda (Lisac, 1995). Despite the limited nature of the public debate that was generated by the consultation process, the Conservatives were successful in pushing the fiscal austerity agenda and won the provincial election handily.

Having legitimated the political agenda, the government announced its Three-Year Business Plan for the Ministry of Health. This Plan disclosed expenditure reductions of $740 million, from $4.2 billion in 1992/93 to $3.4 million in 1996/97. The major thrust of the cuts was directed at the acute care sector, where hospital beds were targeted for reduction from 4.5 beds/1,000 to 2.4 beds/1,000. At this time, bed utilization was particularly high. For instance, Edmonton had 1,089 bed-days/1,000 at a time when some other provinces operated in the range of 550–650 bed-days/1,000.

Once the fiscal targets were established at the provincial level, government introduced Bill C-20, the Regional Health Authorities Act, for the disestablishment of 200 local hospital, public health and continuing care boards, and the creation of seventeen regional health authorities (RHAs) and two provincial health authorities, each with appointed boards of governance and management infrastructures. This involved both the divestiture of programs and services previously planned or provided by the province, such as home care and communicable disease control, and consolidation of existing acute care, home and continuing care, and public health under the new organizational structures. Mental Health is being phased into the responsibilities of RHAs, while the Provincial Cancer Board has remained as a separate quaternary entity. Notable for their exclusion from the regional umbrella of service delivery responsibilities were ambulance services, which continue to be the responsibilities of municipalities; physicians' services, which continue to be delivered by physicians as independent fee-for-service contractors with the province; and services provided by non-hospital pharmacists.

For the purposes of this chapter 'privatization of health services refers to reduced levels of public provision, subsidy, or regulation of either preventive or curative health services'. This definition might involve, 'reductions in government regulation (allowing more providers into the health care market), subsidy (increasing monthly co-insurance payments, out-of-pocket charges, or the cost of medical vouchers), or provision (substituting private providers for public ones)' (Scarpaci, 1989: 5–6).

The commitment of the government to private market solutions in health care is well illustrated by the protracted battle that took place with the federal government over the issue of facility fees. In short, the provincial government allowed a small number of private clinics, including the Gimbel Eye clinics, to bill the provincial health insurance plan for services, while at the same time levying direct user charges at the point of service. From the perspective of the federal government, this clearly contravened the Canada Health Act and justified financial penalties. After a year of failed efforts to negotiate a compromise, the federal government began in November 1995 to impose fines of $422,000 per month. As the months ensued and the financial penalties began to mount, a compromise was reached. The province agreed to cover the cost of both the service fee and the user charges, until the RHAs could negotiate agreements with the individual service providers. By doing so, in essence the province allowed further expansion in service delivery and capacity, but only on the private side of the market. The result is that Alberta now has both private and public providers of opthalmological services being publicly funded by regional health authorities. The difference is that the private providers are actually being paid more for providing the same service.

The preference of the government for private market solutions has been reinforced through the legislative framework. For example, section 15 of the Regional Health Authorities Act allows either the Minister or the RHAs to contract out the delivery of services. Section 5 requires, among other things, that the region ensures reasonable access to health services. Thus, as long as the region ensures access, it can contract with a private individual or corporation for the provision of the service. It is these provisions that have allowed RHAs to enter into arrangements with private contractors for the delivery of laboratory and ophthalmology services. In addition, section 22 allows the Minister to make regulations so that the regions can charge fees for those services provided that are not covered by the provincial health insurance plan. Marriott (1994: 41) has suggested that the wording of the legislation 'will allow for the creation of a two-tier health care system in so far as it allows and requires the participation of private industry in order to be successful'. This is consistent with other recent provincial legislation allowing provincial departments to pursue similar arrangements.

A poignant example of where this legislative framework is leading can be found in a recent proposal by a private health care corporation to provide private hospital services within a regional health authority. Health Resource Group (HRG), a private health care company, announced plans to open what constitutes a private hospital facility in Calgary. If fully realized the facility would provide a range of in-patient and out-patient surgical procedures to a variety of potential clients, including Workmen's Compensation Board patients, Native Band Councils, regional health authorities, provincial, territorial and federal governments, out-of-country patients, and other third party insurers. HRG has freely admitted that the reduced capacity of the public health system in Calgary has created a viable market opportunity. Principals in HRG include the former Chief Operating Officer of the Calgary Regional Health Authority, a former Dean of the Faculty of Medicine at the University of Calgary and former Deputy Minister of Health, the Chief of Orthopaedic Surgery at the Foothills Hospital in Calgary, and the spouse of a current Conservative MLA. At the time of writing, the Alberta College of Physicians and Surgeons has blocked the in-hospital aspects of the proposal, and called for a broader public debate on the implications of the HRG initiative for the nature of the health care system (Health Resource Group, 1997a, 1997b, 1997c; Arnold, 1997a, 1997b; Chambers and Arnold, 1997; Dolik, 1997; Pederson, 1997).

PROVINCIAL HEALTH CARE EXPENDITURE AND REVENUE PATTERNS

One of the goals of health care reform has been to reduce overall public health care expenditures by 15 per cent. As Table 10.1 indicates, public health care expenditures between 1993 and 1997 have actually decreased by approximately 19 per cent or 1.9 per cent of the provincial gross domestic product. During the same time period, total private expenditures on health care increased by approximately 28 per cent and remained relatively stable as a percentage of the gross domestic product. A clear trend, then, in health care expenditure patterns since health care reform began, is a shift from public to private expenditures on health care.

A significant proportion of this shift may be explained by increased health care premiums. As Table 10.1 indicates, in 1995/96 health care premiums represented approximately 17 per cent of Ministry of Health expenses, a 4.7 per cent increase as a portion of Ministry expenses since 1992. This increasing shift to out-of-pocket payment is consistent with the stated intention of the government to increase premiums. One of the four goals of the Alberta Health business plan was to increase financial contributions from Albertans, based on ability to pay. The 1995–1998, and the 1996–1999 plans indicated that revenue from premiums would increase from 11 per cent of health care expenditures to 20 per cent. If the target of 20 per cent is realized, this will translate to an increase in revenues from premiums over 1992/93 of approximately 50 per cent.

Table 10.1 Alberta: health care expenditure and revenue patterns, 1993–1997

	1993	1994	1995	1996*	1997*	Total
Total annual %						
Public	−2.1	−7.2	−6.2	−1.3	−1.8	−18.6
Private	4.8	7.7	5.1	5.4	5.1	28.1
Per capita annual % change						
Public	−2.7	−6.5	−7	−1.2	−1.9	−19.3
Private	2	6.6	3.7	4	3.8	20.1
% of GDP						
Public	6.5	5.7	5.3	5.2	n/a	−1.9
Private	2.1	2	2.1	2.2		0
Health care premium revenue as % of Ministry of Health Expenses						
Public	11.1	14.2	16.7	15.8	n/a	4.7

Sources: Health Canada, *National Health Expenditures in Canada*, June 1997; Canadian Institute of Health Information, *Alberta Health Expenditures*, 1997; Alberta Health, *Annual Report 1995–1996*; Alberta Health, *Annual Report 1996–1997*.

Note:
* Numbers are forecasts only.

Table 10.2 Regional health authority expenditures, 1995–96

	% of pro-forma² Total 1996	% of pro-forma Total 1995	% change from 1995
Facility based in-patient services	22.4	24.0	−11.8
Facility based emergency	6.5	5.8	4.4
Facility based continuing care services	15.2	14.9	−3.9
Community and home based	5.8	4.8	14.7
Diagnostic and therapeutic	18.3	18.7	−7.8
Promotion, prevention and protection services	2.4	2.1	9.4
Research and education	2.4	2.6	−12.2
Support services	15.6	16.6	−11.3
Administration	6.5	7.3	−16.1

Source: Alberta Health, *Annual Report* 1995–1996.

Where health care premiums were once used to subsidize expenditures on physicians' service, they are now being used to subsidize all medically necessary services covered by the provincial health insurance plan. 'It is estimated the funds generated under this new policy will cover almost 95 per cent of the total medical services payments made to physicians' (Plain, 1995: 12). When this occurs, the ability of the government to transfer the administration of payments to physicians to the private sector will be greatly enhanced.

A number of other services, such as excuse slips and telephone consults now carry a direct charge, whereas previously they occurred out of good will. Furthermore, increased premiums and co-payments for extended health benefits provided through private insurance have also occurred, along with decreasing levels of care provided by plans (Plain, 1995).

Table 10.2 indicates a discernible trend in the regional health authority expenditures away from institutional care and toward out-patient, community-based, and prevention and promotion services. Additional cost shifting is occurring as pre-operative and early-discharge patients, and/or their families or employers, must now pay for drugs and other hospital supplies that used to be covered through in-patient care. Community care for chronically, terminally and mentally ill is on the increase, and a good deal of the burden for providing it has shifted, particularly to women in the home or those who take time off work. The extent of this shift is currently unknown. Although not clearly indicated in Table 10.2, physicians have experienced cutbacks totalling approximately 10 per cent over the past four years (CIHI, 1997).

SOCIAL IMPACTS OF SPENDING REDUCTIONS

Alberta's health care workforce has not fared well either. According to Statistics Canada data, the total number of employees in the hospital, non-institutional, and laboratory categories declined by 14,667 (based on annual averages) between 1992 and the Spring of 1997 (Statistics Canada, 1997).[3] Over this period, there was a 43 per cent reduction in registered nurses, a 42 per cent reduction in licensed practical nurses, and a 33 per cent reduction in medical laboratory technologists (Alberta, 1991; Alberta Health, 1996). At the provincial level alone, the downsizing has involved the elimination of 482 FTEs, or 25 per cent, including the shift of mental health services to other organizations. The government has targeted to eliminate a total of 1,295 FTEs from the Department of Health or a 68 per cent reduction from 1992. How the Department can maintain a leadership role with such a diminished level of staffing is highly questionable.

A recent analysis of Alberta's economy suggests that the growth of government during the Lougheed years led to a large public sector, compared to other provinces. The authors noted that in the order of 15,000 jobs could be eliminated in order to bring the public sector into line with other provinces, although such a policy was not necessarily desirable. Given that government has eliminated this number of jobs in health care alone, it could well be argued that their efforts to downsize the public sector exceeded what was necessary (Dickerson and Flanagan, 1995).

The downsizing that has taken place in the acute care sector has involved to varying degrees significant bumping, and de-skilling, especially of nursing staff. One of the results of this has been that many senior nurses have been shifted into specialized areas for which they have not received adequate training, while many junior nurses with such training are unemployed. Another, as yet undocumented, result of the uncoordinated and rapid reduction of the labour force has been reduced good will and increased stress on front-line workers. What the long-term impact and cost of these changes will be is currently unknown. However, the Region ten Medical Staff of the Capital Health Authority noted in a recent report,

> there are insufficient numbers of adequately trained individuals to monitor patients' progress, change bed clothing, assist with ADL's, perform dressing changes, turn patients, supervise intravenous therapy, and provide suitable post-operative or convalescent nursing care. Nurses are also so rushed that they cannot document their activities adequately. This means that physicians are inadequately informed of their patients' progress.
>
> (Capital Health Authority, 1996: 17–18)

Although anecdotal in nature, this assessment must hold some level of validity, given the subsequent announcement by government that it will fund the regions to hire 1,000 additional nurses and other front-line staff.

While downsizing of the labour force has been occurring, government has also re-examined professional roles and scope of practice. In July 1994, the Ministers of Labour and Health established the Health Workforce Rebalancing Committee to address identified health workforce issues. An initial discussion paper placed a heavy emphasis on the professional regulatory system and scope of practice in health care. The regulatory model proposed in the discussion paper called for existing regulatory bodies to be accountable to a single public Health Professions Board, for the consolidation of existing regulatory legislation, and for an Interprofessional Committee with representation from all professions. A series of 'public consultations'[4] was held in late 1994. This was followed by consultation with professional regulatory bodies. The major response of the health professions to the proposed model was that it appeared to undermine the principles of professional self-governance. A second discussion paper was released in July of 1995. To date, government has taken very little substantive action on the recommendations of the Committee.

ENHANCED ACCOUNTABILITY?

One of the basic tenets of health reform has been shifting responsibility and authority to communities for health care decision-making, and making health care decision-makers more accountable to the communities they serve. Underlying this thrust in health care reform is the widely held perception that governments and health care professionals have become unresponsive and unaccountable to citizens for public expenditures. The proposed solution is to make decision-making more participatory and democratic, based on the assumption that local government is more responsive and accountable and thus more democratic than provincial governments. A second underlying assumption is that consumers are sovereign in the marketplace, and thus best qualified to make health care decisions. Both of these assumptions have serious flaws, especially in their application to health care policy (Church and Barker, 1998). As has been well outlined in the existing academic literature on citizen participation in health care, the mechanism chosen in Alberta to enhance accountability to local communities – regional boards of governance – has not led to enhanced accountability in other jurisdictions, even where such boards have been elected.

Given that the provincial government appoints the current boards, there is no direct accountability link to local communities. In fact, many of the appointees were former hospital board members friendly to the government, an accommodation of hospital governance in the regional authorities. The indirect link to communities remains, as in the past, through the accountability of the Minister of Health to the Provincial Legislative Assembly, which is itself considered by some analysts to be a weak form of accountability. Attempts on the part of government throughout the reform process to deny this accountability link, and the tendency of political incumbents with substantial majorities to tightly control the legislative assembly, indicate that this linkage is perhaps even weaker than the previous ministerial accountability relationship. How accountable is the Minister of Health, if the Provincial Legislature only has one session per year? This reflects the current reality if Alberta.

While regional governance structures have been put in place, their autonomy from the provincial government and their accountability to the communities they serve remains questionable. At best, the current arrangement does little more than enlarge the political buffer for the provincial government (Church, 1986). Even when the RHAs move to elect two-thirds of their members in 1998, past experience in other jurisdictions suggests that accountability to local communities may remain limited. If anything, direct election will reinforce the existing power structure and lead to a power struggle between the province and the regions. In the spring of 1997, the government announced that it would delay the election of a regional health authority board for several more years.

At the provincial level, the *ad hoc* creation of a large number of committees and the lack of clear mandates has made clear lines of accountability difficult to discern. Since the launch of health care reform, the province has established sixteen new committees or advisory boards populated by Conservative MLAs and non-elected individuals. Of these committees, twelve are linked to health care reform. For example, the Health Planning Secretariat was created to develop a strategy for implementation of health care reform. The Committee was also used to investigate claims by the Capital Health Authority that it was underfunded. A Provincial Health Council was formed to monitor health care reform and report directly to the Minister.

Each time a serious concern has arisen, yet another advisory body, committee or council has been appointed. While delegating significant responsibility to these extra-departmental entities, the Ministry of Health was, nonetheless, engaged in an ongoing process of restructuring, downsizing, divestiture and outsourcing. Clearly, the tradition of administrative pluralism and reliance on agencies outside of line departments for policy advice has continued during the health care reform process.

Until recently, even the Minister of Health has had difficulty in explaining the lines of accountability of provincial committees external to Alberta Health, but intimately involved in health care reform (Alberta, Legislative Assembly, 1995). As the provincial landscape has become increasing pluralist in nature, Alberta Health, the line agency responsible for health policy, has been incrementally divested of responsibilities. Some of the decisions about divestiture, such as decentralizing communicable disease control – clearly a provincial function – appear counter-intuitive to a population-based approach to service delivery.

The business plan in health accompanying the recent reform was supposed to provide a framework within which the regions could operate over a three-year period. It has been revised on a number of occasions as a result of *ad hoc* political responses to public pressure. The RHAs have suggested that the Plan provides, on the one hand, insufficient guidance for management, and on the other, excessive requirements for reporting to Alberta Health on programs and expenditures (Provincial Health Council, 1996). A prime example of this is the Capital Health Authority, which has been subjected to four major audits in the past 18 months, during which time the RHA has maintained that it is underfunded. In the corresponding period, Capital Health has rebudgeted no fewer than eight times in an attempt to maintain operations in the face of government cuts.

Nor has the Regional Health Authorities Act offered much help in clarifying accountability relationships. In short, the legislation is worded in such a way that the degree of authority that RHAs have when exercising their responsibilities is unclear. The Minister of Health maintains the authority to replace regional boards with appointed administrators and to prescribe regulations for the management of the authorities (Marriott, 1994: 36) Clearly, the province is grappling with the dilemma of balancing how much authority it retains with how much it relinquishes to the regional level. After repeated criticism from the Provincial Health Council and the provincial auditor, the government released two reports in an attempt to clarify accountability relationships (Alberta Health, 1997a; Alberta Health, 1997b). Both of these documents are an important first step in defining the current accountability relationships in the system. Interestingly, the government notes that the medical profession is largely unaccountable for the expenditure of public funds in health care under the current accountability arrangements.

DOES SIZE MATTER?

One of the alleged benefits of moving to a regional delivery system is to eliminate duplication and overlap, and realize economies of scale and perhaps scope. A unified administrative structure, it is argued, enhances the ability to shift funds across service delivery sectors and instils a sense of system-wide thinking among planners and providers of health services (Hollander, 1994). Several issues are pertinent here.

Realizing economies of scale requires determining the optimal size for the most efficient delivery of services. The current reforms assume that economies of scale can be realized through the management and provision of most services by larger units within geographically defined boundaries. The underlying logic is that outputs of a particular service can be maintained or enhanced while inputs are decreased. However, the evidence about economies of scale is mixed and incomplete. As Bish and Ostrom have noted:

> economies of scale vary among the different services supplied in the public sector. Some services are more efficiently produced by larger jurisdictions; others are more efficiently produced by smaller units.
>
> (Bish and Ostrom, 1973: 78)

In other words, size may be a function of the characteristics of particular services, not the other way around. Although research on this issue is limited, the implication is that 'soft services' such as policing and social services, which tend to be labour intensive, are not likely to realize economies of scale when provided by larger regional units. Research on the integration of hospital services in the United States does not consistently support the economies of scale argument, although it does suggest that some services and procedures can realize economies of scale (Shortell, 1988; Finkler, 1981). Studies have also suggested that costs may actually increase along with measures aimed at quality improvement (Howard and Alidina, 1987). Furthermore, it remains debatable as to whether home care and acute care services should cover the same geographic area.

While acknowledging that regionalization has the potential to eliminate duplication and overlap in administration and service provision, there has to be a balance given that some level of duplication in health care service delivery is desirable because of the essential nature of many of the services provided. Notwithstanding this argument, it has not been clearly demonstrated in Alberta's move to regionalization that elimination of duplication and overlap has been achieved. As noted in the Annual Report of the Provincial Health Council, 'unfortunately, there is still much evidence of fragmentation and duplicated energy' (Provincial Health Council, 1996).

The question of size in general involves the issue of whether the regions, as geographically defined units, possess populations of sufficient size to integrate service delivery fully. Experience in other jurisdictions suggests that in the case of Alberta, only Calgary and Edmonton with populations of approximately 700,000 each are large enough to realize economies and thus support full service delivery, regional programs.

Another issue of particular relevance is creating regions that are geographically large enough to be self-contained; that is, to prevent the transfer of costs from one region to another through cross-boundary patient traffic or deliberate exporting of costs (Tuohy and Evans, 1986). One solution is to create very large regions based on historical trade and health care utilization patterns. Undoubtedly, this crossed the minds of the authors of the report of the Premier's Commission when they recommended creating nine health regions for the province. The stated criteria for determining regional boundaries included these technical considerations. However, in the ensuing political debate over which communities were to be grouped and, more importantly, whose hospital or health unit was to be closed, technical arguments were discarded and replaced by political calculus. In the end, census population was chosen over service population as the basis of the boundary calculations. This resulted in several interesting anomalies arising from differences between service and census populations. For instance, none of the existing hospitals adjacent to metropolitan Edmonton were included, adding to the approximate 30 per cent referred-in service population, which was clearly a substantial addition to the census population. This is compared with a referred-in population in Calgary of approximately 18 per cent. This fact alone, regardless of differences in demographic and socio-economic characteristics of the two cities, has caused considerable debate and discontent between Edmonton and Calgary when focusing on budget allocations between them. Most recently, it has been a major consideration in the negative budget variance faced by Edmonton's Capital Health Authority.

Another anomaly in the regional designations has been the variance in size of the census populations. This varied from 16,551 to 795,750 people, with obvious implications for the range of services available and travel between regions to access them. Not unexpectedly, approximately one-quarter of the regions, as constituted, provided hospital care for less than 60 per cent of the people who resided within their regions (Plain, 1995). Since regionalization has taken place, a number of communities bordering on the Capital Health Region have been, or will be, included within the boundaries of the larger region. A recent review of the regional boundaries concluded that 'significant boundary alignment problems exist' between the two largest regions (Calgary and Edmonton) and the Peace Health Authority, and the surrounding regions which export large numbers of patients to these three regions (Plain, 1997).

The externalities issue raises one additional matter. To be truly efficient, global budgeting will require some means for regions to charge-back services provided to residents from other regions. Unless patients are limited to receiving basic health services within a limited geographic area, charge-back arrangements could potentially apply to all health services. This implies a potential increase in transaction costs unless this is built into the budget prospectively. As indicated earlier, this is part of the explanation for the Capital Health Authority having a chronic budgetary problem.

A final issue to consider is the failure of regional budgets in Alberta to include physicians' services or drug costs. Given that these two areas represent major cost drivers in the health care system, control over regional health care expenditures will remain difficult for regions without control over these budgets. It is not surprising, however, that government chose not to engage the two most powerful interest groups in open conflict, given the breadth of the task with which they were already faced. The same can be said about the decision not to include ambulance services, which appear to be a natural choice for regional delivery, given the current incomplete, patchwork approach. A strong counter-argument to these potential inclusions in regional budgets, however, rests with the perspective that this method of governance, management and service integration should first be shown to be capable of improving efficiency and effectiveness.

A funding formula based on population characteristics and identified needs is the preferred reform option in most Canadian jurisdictions, including Alberta. However, the development of the funding formula in Alberta has been in progress for the past two years, mired at the provincial level by the political implications for rural constituencies. Although a funding formula has been released, it still fails to guarantee that RHAs will recover the full costs of treating patients from outside of their boundaries (Plain, 1997). Even if the boundaries are technically efficient and the methodological problems associated with population-based funding are resolved, how many regions will

actively seek or be able to improve the health status of their regional populations if the funding approach calls for allocating fewer resources to healthier
populations?

QUALITY SURVEILLANCE

A key element to successfully shifting the system to a focus on regions is the
ability to measure the health status of the population and in turn to link this to
decisions about the allocation of resources in health care in particular, and other
areas of public expenditure in general. So far, the province has not done well at
the development of measurement tools. The province and the regions have
been attempting to come to agreement on a common set of population health
indicators and performance measures for the past two years. While the first
version of the Alberta Health business plan contained a number of population
health indicators and performance measures, most were listed as being under
development, and were therefore not operational at the outset of reform.
Subsequent revised plans are emerging for a comprehensive, provincial health
information system, thereby offering Alberta a chance to catch up to many
other provinces. The success of these plans will depend on dealing with the
thorny political issue of the protection of privacy.

No assessment of current health care reforms in Alberta would be complete
without some consideration of the impact of such radical change on the quality

Table 10.3 Alberta health care quality indicators 1994/95 and 1995/96[5]

Quality indicators	Year	Excellent	Good	Fair	Poor difficult
Overall rating	1994/95	17.7	47.1	23.6	11.6
	1995/96	11.3	48	30.2	10.5
	% Change	−36.16	1.91	27.97	−9.48
Overall quality	1994/95	21.4	56.9	18.4	3.4
	1995/96	18.1	60.9	16.3	4.7
	% Change	−15.42	7.03	−11.41	38.24
Overall availability	1994/95	24	49.5	19.7	6.8
	1995/96	19.7	55.5	18.7	6.1
	% Change	−17.92	12.12	−5.08	−10.29
Overall quality of	1994/95	39.3	47.6	10.8	2.4
personal care	1995/96	33.9	51.9	11.3	2.9
	% Change	−13.74	9.03	4.63	20.83
Ease of access		Very easy	Easy	A bit difficult	Very difficult
	1994/95	29.2	50.6	17.2	3
	1995/96	23.2	52.6	20.6	3.6
	% Change	−20.55	3.95	19.77	20.0

Source: Alberta Health, *Annual Report*, 1995–1996.

of care. While the government stressed the need to reduce expenditures in health, it also made a commitment to ensure that quality of care did not suffer. Table 10.3 suggests that the indicators chosen by the government to represent quality from the perspective of the average Albertan indicate a perception among the public that the quality of the health care system has diminished between 1994/95 and 1995/96 as a result of health care reforms.

The regions have been monitoring quality using some administrative and clinical indicators, but this information is not currently publicly reported. Interestingly enough, Capital Health was including administrative and clinical indicators in its quarterly reports to the public until it received negative publicity for some bad numbers. Clearly, a fuller assessment of the impact of the reforms on quality is in order.

CONCLUSIONS

During the past two years, the Province of Alberta has undertaken one of the most comprehensive reforms of its public health care system since the introduction of universal medical insurance in the late 1960s. The nature of these reforms has included a significant downsizing of the acute care sector and an overall expenditure reduction of approximately 19 per cent over four years. This has not occurred in isolation, but has been part of a larger government strategy to eliminate the deficit and debt, and reduce the size and role of the public sector. Given the history of the province, we should not be surprised that the current government would adopt an agenda of fiscal conservatism.

In health care policy, government has demonstrated a preference for the dispersal of responsibility among a variety of provincial and regional agencies, and a preference for private market involvement in the delivery of health care services. Serious concerns have been raised about the accountability and integrity of the publicly funded system in the face of this increasing dispersal of responsibility and (possibly) authority for the provision of health care services. To ensure that quality is maintained in such an environment, clear lines of accountability will be essential, as will good and consistent information for decision-makers. Alberta has not yet adequately addressed either of these key issues, and there is some indication that quality of care has been adversely affected by the changes.

At the current time, regional health authorities are empowered to contract with private providers, if these arrangements do not involve the provision of medical necessary services. However, the lack of clarity on the definition of these services has allowed a variety of new arrangements to emerge between regional health authorities and private providers to supplement the diminished capacity of the publicly funded system. The extent of this emerging market appears limited because of the provisions of the Canada Health Act and the willingness of the federal government to enforce these provisions. However, the failure of the federal government to establish the boundaries of the public system clearly may in the future allow for an increasing role for the private sector in the provision of publicly funded services.

For example, Alberta is now moving to define 'core services' in health care. In essence, the government is attempting to establish a list of services that are funded by provincial health insurance and which regional health authorities will be required to provide. While this list will provide Alberta Health with a powerful regulatory instrument for ensuring some uniformity in service delivery across the regions, it may also in the future provide a means of further limiting the scope of services funded by provincial health insurance. This list may over time vary significantly from other provinces and may be at odds with the federal government interpretation of what constitutes essential. To a certain extent the range of publicly funded services is already being limited through deinsurance of individual procedures. This is creating new opportunities for private insurers providing supplemental health coverage. If other provinces follow Alberta's lead, a further balkanization of health care in Canada could occur.

Another powerful policy tool is insurance premiums. The province has stated unequivocally that it intends to increase the levels of premiums to the point where they will effectively pay for medical services. This is already well underway and could lead to the privatization of the administration of these premiums and payments to physicians.

Finally, the proposed introduction of some sort of arrangements whereby groups of physicians will hold budgets for a defined group of patients and act as purchasers of services on their patients' behalf has further implications for privatization. Given that private corporations are now entering or seeking to enter into contractual arrangements with regional health authorities, what will prevent similar arrangements being made with physician groups if they become, in effect, purchasers of services as is now the case with regions? Clearly, the possibility of expanding the private market that these policy developments may hold has not been lost on private providers such as the Health Resources Group.

On the matter of deficit and expenditure reduction and downsizing of government, the province has been successful: it has eliminated the deficit and reduced overall expenditures in health care by approximately 19 per cent; and it has concentrated decision-making responsibility in the hands of a smaller number of regional boards. Expenditures on acute care services are still predominant as is, some might argue, the underlying organizational and professional culture. However, a marked reduction in acute care has been matched by a noticeable, if unequal, increase in expenditures on community-based and out-patient services.

With two successive years of budget surpluses and a thriving economy, the government has announced that it will 'reinvest' nearly as much money in the system over the next three years as it took out over the past three years. This money will likely be reinvested in all service areas, with continuing emphasis being placed on non-acute services. Whether these services are delivered publicly or privately will remain a matter of significant debate in Alberta for some time to come.

NOTES

1   As defined by Guest (1991), 'residual' refers to a view of social security commonly held in Canada until the 1940s that sees family and the private market as the first line of defence against substantial financial loss and loss of health.
2   According to Alberta Health, as a means to enhancing comparability of information, pro-forma information was used because it 'reflects the impact of programs transferred from Alberta Health in the 1995/1996 year as though these programs had been operated by the Health Authorities since April 1, 1994'.
3   This does not include homes for personal and nursing care.
4   Only 18 per cent of those who spoke at the public consultations were classified as consumers.
5   The way in which this information is reported in the 1996/97 *Annual Report* does not make the information readily comparable with previous years.

REFERENCES

Alberta. *Submission to the Royal Commission on Health Services*, 1962.

Alberta. (1989). *An Agenda for Action*. Report of the Advisory Committee on the Utilization of Medical Services.

Alberta. (1991). *Partners in Health: the Government of Alberta's Official Response to the Premier's Commission on Future Health Care for Albertans*, p. 39.

Alberta Health. (1991). *A History of the Health System in Alberta*. Research and Planning Division.

Alberta. Health and Social Services Disciplines Committee. (1991). *Inventory of Health and Social Services Personnel, 1991*.

Alberta. Health Planning Secretariat. (1993). *Starting Points: Recommendations for Creating A More Accountable and Affordable Health System*.

Alberta. Health Workforce Rebalancing Committee. (1995). Discussion Paper II.

Alberta Health. (1996). Action on Health to Ensure Access, Quality and Stability (news release), 25 November.

Alberta Health, *Annual Report*, 1994–1995.

Alberta Health, *Annual Report*, 1995–1996.

Alberta Health. (1996). *Inventory of Health Workforce in Alberta, 1995*.

Alberta Health. *Annual Report*, 1996–1997.

Alberta Health. (1997a). *Accountability: An Action on Health Initiative*, June.

Alberta Health. (1997b). *A Report on Corporate Governance of Regional Health Authorities*, June.

Alberta. Legislative Assembly. *Hansard*. 3 Session, 23 Legislature, 17 October 1995, p. 1945.

Alberta. Legislative Assembly. Sessional Paper No. 1079/95. 3 Session, 23 Legislature.

Alberta. Premier's Commission on Future Health Care for Albertans (1989). *The Rainbow Report: Our Vision for Health*. Final Report.

Auditor-General of Alberta. (1996). *Annual Report of the Auditor-General of Alberta, 1995–96*. 15 September, p. 115.

Angus, Douglas. (1994). *Health Care Reform: Revisiting the Review of Significant Health Care Commissions and Task Forces*. Ottawa: Canadian Nurses Association.

Arnold, Tom. (1997a). Health Chief Gets Warning, *Edmonton Journal*, 15 May, p. A-3.

Arnold, Tom. (1997b). Tory MLA Unaware Her Husband Chair of Firm Opening Private Calgary Hospital, *Edmonton Journal*, 16 May, p. A-7.

Barr, John J. (1974). *The Dynasty: Rise and Fall of the Social Credit in Alberta*. Toronto: McClelland and Stewart.

Bish, Robert L. and Vincent Ostrom. (1973). *Understanding Urban Government*. Washington, DC: American Enterprise Institute for Public Policy Research.

Boase, Joan. (1994). *Shifting Sands: Government–Group Relationships in the Health Care Sector*. Montreal: McGill-Queen's University Press.

Canadian Institute for Health Information (CIHI). *Alberta Health Expenditures*. (1997).

Capital Health Authority. (1996). *Report of the Critical Assessment Committee Region Ten Medical Staff*. 22 October.

Chambers, Allan and Tom Arnold. (1997). Feds Won't Let Calgary Private Hospital Open, *Edmonton Journal*, 16 May, p. A-1.

Church, John. (1986). District Health Councils: The Local Advisory Body and Health Care Policy in Ontario. Unpublished Master's Thesis, University of Waterloo, Waterloo, Ontario.

Church, John and Paul Barker. (1998). Regionalization of Health Services in Canada: A Critical Perspective. *International Journal of Health Services*.

C. M. MacDonald and Associates. (1997). Towards a Core Health Services Framework for Alberta (Consultants' Report).

Dickerson, Mark O. and Greg L. Flanagan. The Unique Fiscal Situation of Alberta: Can Alberta's Deficit Reduction Model Be Exported. Paper presented at the Annual Meeting of the Canadian Political Science Association, Montreal, May 1995.

Dolik, Helen. (1997). Hospital Care in Comfort. *Edmonton Journal*, 17 May, p. B8.

Edmonton Social Planning Council. (1996). *Two Paycheques Away: Social Policy and Hunger in Edmonton*.

Finkler, S. A. (1981). Cost effectiveness of regionalization – further results for heart surgery. *Health Services Research* 16: 325–333.

Guest, Dennis. (1991). *The Emergence of Social Security in Canada*. 2nd edition. Vancouver: University of British Columbia Press.

Health Resource Group Inc. (1997a). *Business Plan*. March.

Health Resource Group Inc. (1997b). *A Plan for the Organization and Delivery of Complimentary Services in Canada* (April).

Health Resource Group Inc. (1997c). *A Plan for the Organization and Delivery of Complimentary Services in Canada* (May).

Hollander, Marcus J. (1994). *The Costs and Cost-effectiveness of Continuing Care Services in Canada*. Queen's University of Ottawa Economics Projects, Working Paper No. 94-06. Ottawa: University of Ottawa.

Howard, J. W. and S. Alidina (1987). Multihospital Systems: Increased Costs . . . and Quality. *Dimensions* 64 (2): 20–24.

Laxer, Gordon and Trevor Harrison. (1996). *The Trojan Horse: Alberta and the Future of Canada*. Montreal: Black Rose Press.

Lisac, Marc. (1995). *The Klein Revolution*. Edmonton: NeWest Press.

MacMillan, Melville L. (1996). *Leading the Way or Missing the Mark? The Klein Government's Fiscal Plan*. Information Bulletin No. 37. University of Alberta: Western Centre for Economic Research.

Marriott, Gillian D. (1994). The Regional Health Authorities Act and the Privatization of Health Care in Alberta. *Health Law Review* 3: 35–45.

Pederson, Rick. (1997). Private Clinic Loses Bid for Overnight Care, *Edmonton Journal*, 6 December, p. A-1.

Philippon, Donald J. and Sheila A. Wasylyshyn (1996). Health Care Reform in Alberta. *Canadian Public Administration* 39: 70–84.

Plain, Richard H. M. (1995). *The Role Played by Health Reform in the Re-inventing of Government Within Alberta*. Ottawa: Health Canada.

Plain, Richard H. M. (1997). Working Together: The Reform of Regional Health Authority Boundaries Within Alberta. A report presented to the MLA Committee on the Review of Health Region Boundaries, August.

Provincial Health Council of Alberta. (1996). *Health Checkup*.

Regional Health Authorities Act. C. R-9.07, 1994.

Sheldon, T. A, G. D. Smith, and G. Bevan, (1993). Weighting in the Dark: Resource Allocation in the NHS. *British Medical Journal* 306: 835–839.

Shortell, Stephen. (1988). The Evolution of Hospital Systems: Unfulfilled Promises and Self-Fulfilling Prophesies. *Medical Care Review* 45: 177–214.

Statistics Canada. (1997). *Employment, Earnings and Hours*, April. Breakdown of Major Group 86, health and social service industries, groups 861, 863 and 868.

Taras, David and Allan Tupper. (1994). Politics and Deficits: Alberta's Challenge to the Canadian Political Agenda, in Douglas M. Brown and Janet Hiebert (eds), *State of the Federation 1994*. Kingston: Queen's University, 61–83.

Taylor, Malcolm G. (1986). *Health Insurance and Canadian Public Policy: The Server Decisions that Created the Canadian Health Care System*. Montreal: McGill-Queen's University Press.

Tuohy, Carolyn J. and Robert G. Evans (1986). Pushing on a String: The Decentralization of Health Planning in Ontario, in R. T. Gotembiewski and A. Wildavsky (eds), *The Costs of Federalism*, Transaction Books: New Brunswick, NJ, 89–115.

11 The rhetoric of community control in a neo-liberal era

Joel Davison Harden

When the history books are written about Ontario's medicare system in the 1990s, they will certainly note how fiscal pressures both captivated policy-makers and dramatically changed the lives of citizens. Since the Conservatives assumed power in 1995, over 1.5 billion dollars has been restructured within Ontario's medicare system.[1] But while the scope of this restructuring is dramatic, it is only part of a major re-orientation of the fiscal structure of the province. The Conservatives have embarked upon a 'common sense revolution' that has systematically sought to shrink the size of the state and 'marketize' its remaining elements. This agenda has meant drastic change in the medicare sector, numerous hospitals have either closed or merged with others, staff has been pared, District Health Councils have been pushed into compliance, and specialized programs (such as the home oxygen service for lung patients) have been cut.[2] To state the case succinctly, fiscal restraint policies have not only changed the present face of Ontario politics, they have, perhaps irreparably, changed the character of Ontario's medicare system.

The socio-political climate of neo-liberalism has certainly made the most dramatic and obvious impact on Ontario's medicare system in the 1990s, but the issue of greater local control has also emerged as a significant theme for health care activists. Juxtaposed to each other, the rise of neo-liberal politics and the prominence of debates concerning local control strategies is puzzling indeed. How does one understand the emergence of these two opposing trends?

In my view, the answer lies in the evolution of the discourse in which the demand for local control in Ontario's medicare system has taken place. It is a situation where political elites preach the merits of local control and integration, but in practice resort to fiscal centralism to ensure a reform agenda that offloads the consequences of cutbacks to local communities. What is decentralized currently in Ontario is not any degree of power or autonomy in the financing, administration, or delivery of health services, but something very different. The most ironic fact about this reform process is that, regardless of the government's endorsement of small government, an activist and centralist state has been the decisive agent forcing reform in Ontario.

To get some perspective on this argument, it is necessary to outline the history behind the debate over local control in Ontario's medicare system, and two case studies will be provided to illustrate more concretely what is meant here by decentralization in neo-liberal terms.

LOCAL CONTROL AND MEDICARE: SASKATCHEWAN'S 'FAUSTIAN BARGAIN'

To understand fully the structural forces and fiscal pressures that have contributed to the shift in the management of Ontario's health services in the 1990s, one must begin by analysing the 'Faustian bargain' involved in the Commenwealth Cooperative Federation's medical reform agenda. The 'Saskatchewan experiment' left a key element of the province's health system untouched; namely, the ability of the College of Physicians and Surgeons to function (hereafter referred to as 'the College') as a 'private government' responsible for the regulation and reimbursement of doctors' services. This initial strategy of elite accommodation has created serious structural problems for the future democratic administration of health services. Douglas himself, with regret, acknowledged that:

> when we began to plan Medicare, we pointed out that it would be in two phases. The first phase would be to remove the financial barrier between those giving the service and those receiving it. The second phase would be to reorganize and revamp the delivery system – and of course, that's the big item. It's the big thing we haven't done yet.[3]

From the beginning of its dealings with the Commenwealth Cooperative Federation (CCF), the College – and for that matter, the Canadian Medical Association – was clear in its opposition to any experiments in citizen control in the delivery of health services, and fought bitterly to ensure that the fee-for-service system remained as the province's payment scheme for physicians.[4] The Swift Current project, an early CCF initiative for greater local control, went forward initially with the College's consent; but it was condemned ten years later, and even this experiment preserved the fee-for-service system.[5] In this political climate, the CCF chose to implement its health system in two phases: they would address the issue of accessibility to quality medical care first, and deal with the delivery of health services afterwards. While one could argue that such a priority sequence was unavoidable, even necessary, to ensure that medicare was at least accessible to all residents of Saskatchewan, it had the effect of further entrenching the power of medical elites. As the CCF's example became the model for the rest of Canada, this public payment/private priority model of medicare system became institutionalized and to this day has yet to be changed in its fundamental parameters.

THE HISTORY OF LOCAL CONTROL IN ONTARIO'S MEDICARE SYSTEM

The CCF's 'compromise', however, did not draw closure to the question of decentralization and local control in Canada's medicare systems.[6] The initial Hall Commission's Report in 1964 recommended regionalized health systems as a 'desired objective', and the report of the Federal Task Force on the Costs of Health Care in 1969 also endorsed a regionalized system as a means to reduce costs and enhance the efficiency and coordination of medical care.[7]

Discussion of local control in Ontario's health care system began in earnest with the 1974 *Report of the Health Planning Task Force*, headed by Dr Fraser Mustard. This Report was the first support for the creation of District Health Councils (DHCs) in hopes of providing more 'community input' to the Ministry of Health in its decisions.[8] In 1973 the province was divided up into 'health regions', and DHCs were established by an Order-in-Council. The DHCs, however, were mandated to fulfil only an advisory role to the Ministry of Health in a deconcentrated scenario; the 'control from above' that characterized Ontario's medicare system did not allow for much democratic administration in the Task Force's Report. The Report supported the province's legal role to control funding in a centralized system, given the enormity of the costs involved and the need for accountability, which the Task Force felt could only be achieved with a centralized model.[9]

In terms of giving communities greater control and input over decisions regarding medical care, these worthwhile early efforts were indeed short of the mark. No important (fiscal) decision-making power was shifting from the province to DHCs, so the role for the latter was simply to provide information to guide the Ministry. The introduction of DHCs in no way challenged the power of the medical establishment in Ontario. None the less, it is interesting to note that despite the relatively benign presence DHCs brought to Ontario's medicare system, the Ontario Hospital Association (OHA) still loudly opposed their creation.[10]

The emergence and experience of Community Health Centres (CHCs) was another important event in the history of local control that occurred at this time. In contrast to regular health clinics and hospitals, CHCs incorporated a multi-disciplinary approach in practitioners, paid its practitioners by salary, and encouraged the participation of patients by maintaining a board of directors run largely by community members. The first clinic of this type, interestingly enough, was created in Sault St. Marie in 1963 by the local steelworkers union before the Pearson government introduced the Medicare Act in 1966. The centre was structured on a pre-payment scheme initially, but later developed a system of capitation payments for its practitioners which was funded by the Ontario Health Insurance Plan (OHIP).[11] Organized medicine reacted predictably: the Sault St. Marie Medical Society warned the union that doctors would refuse to participate and staged vigorous media campaigns against the Centre, while the CMA distributed a shrill pamphlet to patients in 1961 which cautioned that the centre 'could endanger the welfare of a community' and would abrogate the 'best practice of medicine' as well as 'the democratic rights of free people'.[12] As York describes, the doctors who opted to work at the Centre were socially and professionally ostracized by their colleagues, and were frequent recipients of mental and physical abuse. These attacks did chase many doctors away, but ultimately the Centre endured; today the Centre services the health needs of 50,000 people in the Sault – over half the city's population.[13]

The inspiration for Community Health Centres was aided by the success of the Sault experience, but CHCs received their first formal endorsement with the release of the 1972 *Report on the Community Health Centre Project* to the Conference of Health Ministers (commonly referred as the 'Hastings Report', after its chair, Dr John Hastings). The Hastings Report threw its complete support behind the notion of CHCs and endorsed their integration into the health system through global or block budgets from the province. It even went on to state that other alternatives to the fee-for-service system should be pursued more rigorously.[14] The reaction to the Hastings Report was disappointing. It elicited much discussion but little action from the provinces, except Quebec, where a province-wide system of local community health centres is now in place (CLSCs). In Ontario one of the key factors that inhibited the proliferation of the CHCs was the OMA, who felt threatened by the CHCs' challenge to the fee-for-service payment scheme. In 1975, they convinced Tory Health Minster Frank Miller to freeze the development of CHCs. While CHCs did incur a larger start-up cost than regular clinics, over time their payment system saved money by reducing the amount of reliance patients had on turnstile, fee-for-service medical care. The freeze on the CHCs was eventually lifted by Tory Health Minister Larry Grossman in 1982, but not before enduring ten years of arrested growth and suspicion. At the moment, about fifty CHCs exist in Ontario, they are all community administered and structured on the basis of local needs These CHCs continue to reimburse their practitioners by salary, and are generally designed to meet the medical needs of under-served, low-income areas. The success of the CHCs can certainly be regarded as a victory for the model of local 'democratic administration' in the delivery of health services.

The other major event in the history of local control in Ontario that occurred during the late-1970s to early 1980s was the conflict over the issue of extra-billing that led to the 1986 doctors' strike. Tuohy notes that a 'Medicare in Crisis' coalition began to form in Ontario (largely Toronto-based) in the wake of the extra-billing dispute; its membership contained a wide spectrum of labour, social service, church-related, nursing and consumer groups.[15] In a brief presented to the Ontario Cabinet in 1979, the coalition argued that greater local control over medical care would encourage a more holistic approach, and address many of the inadequacies of Ontario's medicare system which the debate over extra-billing had highlighted. The coalition was succinct in its belief that residents of communities should have input into the programming and budget allocation of their local health services, stating that 'the people know better than any government the needs of their own community'.[16] This coalition was a vocal element of the campaign against extra-billing 'from below' (i.e. outside the medicare system) coupled with a small segment of doctors who opposed the OMA's defence of extra-billing and rejection of decentralized delivery systems. This group would eventually have a significant impact on the public's negative reaction to the 1986 doctors' strike.[17]

The success of the debate over local control was also evident in the 1987 report of the Ontario Health Review Panel. The report discussed the 26 DHCs in existence at the time, noting their lack of authority and confinement to an advisory role.[18] The panel suggested that a Premier's Council on Health Strategy be created and that it should include diverse representation. The goal of the proposed Council would be to investigate a more comprehensive health strategy that would capitalize more on the knowledge of DHCs, giving them a greater role. The Review Panel itself felt that DHCs were the most progressive conduit for reform. They asked that 'DHC's be designated the local agencies responsible to take the lead in the health goals process'.[19] In the history of local control debate in Ontario, this recommendation was the first written indication of an interest in the Ontario government to shift more power to the regional level. However, given the strong presence of doctors on DHCs, it is noteworthy to recognize that this decentralization was still occurring within a profoundly elitist framework.[20]

On the heels of the Review Panel's suggestions was the report of the 1989 interim Premier's Council Integration and Coordination Committee to David Peterson's Liberal government. It was at this point that the issue of local control in Ontario moved beyond advocating mere deconcentration or delegation from Queen's Park to regional bodies and local governments, and began to evaluate devolution of fiscal and managerial decision-making authority as a viable alternative for health care reform. On the positive side, the report argued that devolution would help diminish the individual lobbying efforts of government officials by powerful interests outside Queen's Park and closer to the regions themselves. A drawback the report cited about devolution was that some regions and communities may have fewer skilled people and resources properly to administer a large health care envelope. Ultimately, three recommendations were made: first, that a thorough review for establishing regional authorities be looked at; second, that the Ontario government develop an equitable funding formula for regional authorities that would be sensitive to health needs and regional factors; and, last, that the Ontario government develop pilot projects and evaluate them.[21]

Following these recommendations was the 1991 final report of the Integration and Coordination Committee of the Premier's Council under Bob Rae's NDP government. Rather than the 1989 report, which only discussed the pros and cons of devolution, the 1991 report came out as a strong advocate. In fact, the Integration and Coordination Committee argued that the responsibilities for the planning and delivery of health care and social services as well should be devolved from the provincial to the local level.[22] In support of its position, the Integration and Coordination Committee argued that devolution would create increased opportunity for public input and participation, make services more coordinated and responsive to those who use them, and make costs more efficient and predictable.

But beyond these arguments, the key message the Integration and Coordination Committee put forth was that tinkering reforms with Ontario's health care system would not suffice. In advocating devolution, they argued for a complete overhaul of the 'control from above' system, ultimately in the hopes of making Queen's Park more aware and accountable to the different health care needs of Ontario's communities. As they explained:

> it would be inadequate simply to re-arrange the elements of a system which is responsive enough to individual and community needs. We propose instead a realignment of responsibility for the planning and delivery of services so that, first, an array of services can be designed in each community to meet the specific needs of the people living there and, second, so that services can respond better to the needs of community members, particularly those vulnerable minorities whose perspectives have not been sufficiently included in decision-making.[23]

Although the Integration and Coordination Committee recognized that there would be growing pains with devolving responsibility for the administration of health services to local agencies, it argued that these costs would be far outweighed by a more efficient and accountable system. The best way to maximize health care dollars, they argued, was to 'empower' local and regional boards who hold the greatest insight about what their needs are.[24] Devolution was seen as not merely a means to ensure cost effectiveness, more importantly it was a genuine attempt to ensure greater accountability through democratic reform. Still, it is noteworthy though that devolution, while portrayed as 'revolutionary change' in the Rae government's reports, in no way challenged doctors' monopolistic power.

In the same year, the report of the Southwestern Ontario Comprehensive Health System Planning Commission (chaired by Earl Orser, and referred to as the Orser Report) also endorsed the devolution of provincial powers in health care decisions.[25] The Orser Commission was established by the Minister of Health in 1990 to develop a ten-year strategic plan for health services in London and the Southwestern region. The Orser Commission carried out an 'extensive review' of the Southwestern region in consulting widely with various groups, taking note of socio-demographic trends and mortality patterns.

In its recommendations, the Orser Report advocated some degree of devolution through the creation of a regional board of governance.[26] The board would be simultaneously accountable to the Minister of Health and the people of the

Southwestern region, and responsible for long-term planning, allocating operating funds, approving capital expenditures, managing human resources, and supporting the coordination of the education of health professionals. It is important to note, however, that the Orser Report felt that members of the Board should be appointed (presumably by the Minister of Health), and accountable to the Minister of Health and the people of the region. The Orser Report did not contain the radical proposals for community administration which the 'Medicare in Crisis Coalition' had offered, and opted instead to follow the elitist tradition of appointment which organized medicine had long favoured over more democratized alternatives. After two decades of debate over local control, the Orser Commission had demonstrated the limitations for democratic reform in Ontario's medicare system under neo-liberalism: health experts were prepared to advocate for the devolution of important decision-making powers to regional bodies, but any notion of 'community administration' in these structures was not possible.

Even more revealing, however, is the fact that no Ontario government has acted on these recommendations. The Ontario government has changed hands twice since, with the social democratic NDP government between 1990–1995 and, more recently, the conservative government assuming power in June of 1995. Despite the power of organized medicine to deter the policy progress of local control inniatives, the publication of the numerous government documents on the subject suggested that finally action on this matter was imminent.

MEDICARE AND DECENTRALIZATION IN NEO-LIBERAL ONTARIO

During both recent governments, 'community care' and 'local input' became frequent catchphrases that have appeared in their respective health agendas. In each case, however, while the language of local control has remained in the rhetoric of speeches and policy papers, the essential demand for democratization in medicare decision-making processes had not been met and the meaning purposefully distorted. Above all, the factor which deterred the success of the Orser Report – and, for that matter, the entire local control movement – was the pronounced arrival of neo-liberal ideas that had come to dominate Ontario politics.

In 1992, with the NDP gaining office in Ontario, discussion of devolution re-emerged with greater force. The Resource Management Committee (RMC) of the Premier's Council made devolution a key priority for the Rae government, and established a Task Force on devolution. The responsibilities of the Task Force would be to 'provide concrete advice to the government on policy decisions based on an evaluation of actual experiences'.[27] After reviewing findings from previous studies, and efforts at devolution in other areas, the Task Force worked to gather enough information on the advisability of a widespread provincial policy of devolution of health and social services.[28]

The first goal the Task Force pursued was to develop a plan for 3–5 devolution pilot projects in Ontario. The plan included various preparation stages, which outlined the goals in devolution and the scope of the project altogether.[29] Once the workplan was developed, the Task Force then proceeded to draft official letters to both the Ministries of Health and Social Services to ask for explicit agreement and support for 'the implementation of a limited number of carefully controlled and evaluated demonstration models of devolved decision making'.[30] Unfortunately, as the Task Force explained,

> The Ministry of Community and Social Services was clear in its early decision that it would not be able to participate in implementing pilot models at that time. The Ministry of Health, however, initially supported collaboration on a study involving the evaluation of devolution projects confined to health and excluding social services. But, by Spring 1993, the Ministry of Health indicated that it would only be in a position to support the Task Force's work if it were 'viewed within the context of the existing health reform agenda.' The then-Deputy Minister of Health, in a letter to the Chair of the Task Force, recommended that the Task Force 'consider evaluating projects already underway in the Ministry which demonstrate elements of devolution of authority' citing examples such as, the Northern Diabetes Network, the Comprehensive Health Organization (CHO) project, and the enhanced role of District Health Councils (DHC's).[31]

Because they felt that such a study would 'restrict the debate on devolution', the Task Force did not follow the Ministry of Health's recommendation. They argued that concentrating on particular programs within a Ministry would not yield the same benefits as a large-scale initiative, where a significant amount of power had been devolved from the province to either the region or local government.[32]

In attempting to answer why devolution became a lower priority, the Task Force pointed to a number of possible reasons. Among them were the high degree of political and bureaucratic opposition they had received in response to the concept of devolution, Ontario's prior negative experience with devolution in the case of regional school boards, and internal senior government changes in personnel (including those working closely with the Task Force).[33]

Beyond the above factors, the Task Force gave its most pointed response to this question: 'about six months into its work, it became clear to the Task Force that the fiscal and political concerns of the government (and subsequent program reforms underway) would prohibit the key ministries from participating in the implementation of actual pilot projects in the province'.[34] In short, it was the 1989–92 Canadian economic recession – the worst in Ontario's history since the Great Depression of the 1930s – which hindered the progress of the Task Force's work.

Having been denied the opportunity to test devolution as a strategy for making Ontario's medicare system more accountable and efficient, the Task

Force decided to concentrate its efforts on developing a framework that would help the evaluation of devolution in the future. In June, 1994, they presented three recommendations to the government, the most notable being the call for the creation of more pilot projects involving devolution in Ontario. These recommendations obtained the endorsement of the Premier's Council of the Rae government, and action was expected in the fall of 1994.

However much they liked the idea of devolution, the government continued to present the argument of 'unfortunate necessity' concerning austerity measures. Due to circumstances beyond their control, the neo-liberal economic priorities of deficit management had to take precedence over previously stated commitments to devolution in the financing and administration of health and social services. The RMC argued that this precarious climate had been caused by 'the impact of industrial restructuring, driven by new global trading patterns and new technologies'.[35] In the end, the NDP's endorsement of devolution as a means of medicare health reform was quashed under the overriding desire to fight the debt/deficit. Administrative innovation would be sacrificed to fiscal orthodoxy and the strengthening of the central agencies of expenditure and management control.

FISCAL CUTS AND A HEAVY DOSE OF CENTRALISM: ENTER THE HARRIS TORIES

Since assuming office in June, 1995, the Harris Tories have shelved local control strategies while retaining the 'community input' rhetoric, and moved quickly to introduce a neo-liberal, 'quasi-market' round of restructuring. The Tories have favoured market-oriented 'benchmark standards' to gauge their restructuring agenda, but have also endeavoured to create a rigidly centralist model for health care decision-making. By late 1997, the Health Services Restructuring Commission (HSRC) was cutting a swathe through Ontario's health delivery system, despite a prior commitment made by Mike Harris in the Tories' election campaign to not 'cut hospitals'. Towards the end of reducing government expenditures, the HSRC has been given sweeping powers to close and merge hospitals across Ontario, and is charged with cutting 1.3 billion dollars from the hospital budget in two years.[36] The HSRC obtained these sweeping powers from Bill 26 (The Savings and Restructuring Act) which passed January 31, 1996. Bill 26 was an omnibus piece of legislation affecting more than forty pieces of provincial legislation, especially in the Treasury, Health, and Municipal Affairs Ministries.[37]

In defence of this dramatic move, Premier Mike Harris evoked the New Right stance that 'this legislation was required to undo the disastrous damage of the last 10 years that has left us with an overburgeoning bureaucracy and $10 billion a year in deficits'.[38] The dominant trend in the Harris government's reform agenda was quickly to consolidate centralized control over fiscal restructuring while decentralizing the responsibility for, and consequences of, imposing austerity programs. In practice, this has offloaded the responsibility of making fiscal cuts to municipal governments, who – like many hospitals – have been forced to amalgamate into regional bodies and face dramatic cuts in their provincial transfer payments.[39] In spite of the twenty-year history of the debate over local control and the devolution in health and social services, the Tory approach to date has been to push for more centralized control in deciding the financing and delivery of health services. By giving vast powers to the HSRC to implement far-reaching reforms without legislative debate, the Tories have also insulated themselves from direct attack.

District Health Councils have remained involved, but only in helping to decide which hospitals to close, how many workers to lay-off, and what services to cut. The 'marketization' slant of this agenda has been clear. While the Harris government's 'mission statement' states that 'the government of Ontario is committed to the Taxpayer in everything it does', in practice they have been more committed to their oft-repeated agenda to 'run the province's business like a business'.[40]

Two case studies of recent hospital restructuring help to focus attention on the kind of decentralization that is occurring in neo-liberal Ontario. First, the emergence of Total Quality Management (TQM) in the administration of health services and, second, the Ottawa-Carleton DHCs recent conflict with the Harris government over the latter's restructuring agenda. Each illustrates how neo-liberal ideas have fostered a model of decentralization where fiscal controls and political power are centralized within the state, while local bodies are saddled with the responsibility of helping to install austerity programs.

CASE STUDY ONE: TOTAL QUALITY MANAGEMENT AS 'QUASI-MARKET' REFORM AND WORKER CONTROL IN HEALTH SERVICES

In Ontario's recent round of neo-liberal restructuring, no other organizational strategy has met with as much approval in the medical establishment as that of Total Quality Management (TQM). Given that fiscal pressures have dictated the agenda for Canadian governments in the 1990s, it is not surprising that TQM, an organizational strategy endorsed by many profitable firms, would be well received. In 1994, the Ontario Premier's Council on Health Strategy proudly promoted TQM strategies, stating that the 'health care sector can learn a great deal from modern management science – and particularly from the Japanese and American experiences in the total quality management of individuals and organizations'.[41]

Phillip Hassen, President of St Joseph's Health Care Centre in London (Ontario), has been one of the most enthusiastic supporters of TQM for Ontario's health care system. According to Hassen, TQM programs have the capacity to maximize 'human skills, creativity and resourcefulness, customer satisfaction, employee involvement, effective and efficient use of resources, continuous improvement of all processes large or small, and the consistent achievement of high standards of service and equality'.[42] This is an impressive list of claims. But how does TQM go about achieving them? As Pat and Hugh Armstrong explain, the central concept which TQM revolves around is continuous quality improvement:

> This comes from focussing on processes rather than outcomes and from responding to consumer needs. Each process is to be improved by autonomous employees working in teams, committed to improving both the product and the process because they have pride in their work and have adopted a new philosophy. Training, education, and self-improvement will replace inspection, monitoring, slogans, exhortations, and targets, as workers learn to focus on zero defects and innovation, and as everybody works together to accomplish the transformation. Fear will be driven out of the work relationship, providing a firm basis for a new approach.[43]

According to TQM advocates, this system is one where 'everybody wins': administrators win by fostering a more efficient and cooperative environment, workers win more respect and autonomy from their superiors, patients win by receiving better quality care, and taxpayers win by getting more for their money. The United States was the first place where TQM strategies were applied to hospitals and health delivery, and it was not long until Canadian health administrators followed their example. As John Price explains, by 1994 major health facilities such as St Joseph's Health Centre in London, and Metro Toronto hospitals including Women's College, Doctors, Mount Sinai, Sunnybrook Health Science Centre, and St Michael's had initiated TQM programs.[44]

A TQM-like approach, therefore, has been central to the Harris government in their restructuring of Ontario's medicare system. While the Rae government expressed interest in TQM, even funded some TQM initiatives, the Tories have set rigid benchmarks and 'performance indicators' for the delivery of health services on their own.[45] With the extended powers granted through Bill 26, the Health Ministry has written it will 'shift its emphasis from transferring funding to hospitals to becoming system manager, policy-maker and facilitator for integrating hospital and community services'.[46] To date, the Tories have taken this very posture, one not far removed from the 'managed care' scenarios designed by private insurers in the United States. The recent example of the Harris government illustrates the embedded neo-liberal reality that exists beneath the declared commitments of TQM strategies. Despite any rhetoric to the contrary, TQM has not involved workers but subjected them to the centralized control of medical elites, who, in turn, restructure medicare systems to respond to fiscal pressures. As Price explains, time and again in the TQM literature it is stressed that *management alone* must lead the quality movement, not in any partnership with hospital workers or community members. Consequently, this leads Price to conclude that TQM programs come 'prepackaged with a fixed agenda. In a number of cases, TQM programs bypass the unions entirely and try to create divisions between workers and the union by recruiting volunteers to sit on committees that are often dealing with collective bargaining issues'.[47] At St Joseph's in London, Ontario, the union only has a substantial voice on the Quality of Work Life committee, not the Quality Council which makes all important decisions regarding budget, personnel, and tasks relating to the TQM program. Membership in the latter is restricted to the CEO, the five vice-presidents, the chairperson of the Medical Advisory Committee, and the director of TQM.[48]

The experience of St Joseph's illustrates that the 'autonomy' which TQM supposedly gives to workers is circumscribed by the centralized power of medical elites. Workers are endowed with as much autonomy as they wish, provided they follow the TQM guidelines set by management. As Pat and Hugh Armstrong explain, it is management which is really granted autonomy under TQM, and, contrary to the rhetoric, workers' fear of management remains the foundation of the workplace. They argue:

> in other words, [TQM] is top-down rather than bottom-up autonomy. Management is still very much in charge, although some middle managers are supposed to develop innovative ways to eliminate their own jobs as workplace hierarchies are flattened. Workers are to improve processes so fewer people are required to do the work. Under such circumstances, it is difficult to drive out fear.[49]

The history of TQM in Ontario's hospitals has shown that the strategy has not only entrenched the Taylorist hierarchies that already exist in health care delivery, but has accentuated them by giving administrators an excuse to pare down staff to meet the demands of fiscal retrenchment coming from Queen's Park.[50] Exasperated hospital workers and unions have been furious about insistent reminders by management 'to use bed linens wisely', and the notion that teamwork and cooperation were nonexistent prior to the introduction of TQM. Workers have been observed by 'TQM-watch' teams led by management to ensure they were moving swiftly between tasks, scolded upon failing to meet 'performance standards' but rarely praised when they did, and compelled to adopt the vision of patients as 'customers of health services'.[51] This spread of market language is a key component of the shift to 'quasi-market' reforms in Ontario's medicare system, and it has helped to mask the real objectives in striving for 'continuous innovation', 'worker empowerment', and 'quality improvement'. TQM has not resulted in 'worker empowerment', but in worker control as a means to meet the demands of government cutbacks. TQM proposes a decentralized organizational form, but in fact merges with centralized fiscal controls and purely formal local control.

CASE STUDY TWO: THE OTTAWA-CARLETON DISTRICT
HEALTH COUNCIL AND THE HARRIS GOVERNMENT

The recent conflict between the Harris government and the Ottawa-Carleton District Health Council is another good example of the way in which decentralization strategies have been designed to meet the demands of fiscal pressures. At a meeting of the Ottawa-Carleton District Health Council on October 16, 1995, Health Ministry officials floored those in attendance by announcing that its own 'management team' would take over the DHC's hospital reconfiguration project.[52] Many were outraged by the action, arguing it was heavy-handed and fuelled by ideological motivations. Dr Pierre Soucie, Chair of the Ottawa-Carleton DHC, expressed his fear that the larger hospitals had lobbied the Tories to avoid closure, and that the public was the real loser in the event having not been consulted on the radical move.

The very next day however saw a curious shift in strategy from Queen's Park. The Health Minister claimed that he had no intention of assuming control of the Ottawa-Carleton DHC's task force on cutting hospital costs. The Minister stated that the Ministry officials had acted without his knowledge or consent, and that the whole episode was a 'misunderstanding of what this government's policy is'.[53] He went on to add that the 'District Health Councils are the ears, eyes and conscience of the local community. We want them to conduct the hospital restructuring studies and in no way do we want to interfere with those studies.'[54] Wilson explained that the role of the Ministry was to provide 'technical support' and 'encouragement' for DHCs undergoing restructuring reviews, but nothing beyond that.

Despite these pronouncements, on 21 December 1995, the Tories produced a series of administrative delays that stalled the progress of the Ottawa-Carleton DHC for a number of weeks.[55] The move was regarded by the DHC as an indication of the Harris government's disapproval at the scope of the suggested reforms that were being considered. DHC Chair Pierre Soucie remarked that likely the proposed changes were not 'creative enough' for the Tories, that the government was looking for proposals with deeper cuts and more recommendations for providing health care outside hospitals. True to form, the Tories applied centralized pressure to 'encourage' drastic reform, but also decentralized the responsibility for making the politically dangerous decisions about the content of the restructuring plans. France Gelinas, a senior planning consultant with the health ministry, would only comment that 'we have a government that has a very aggressive agenda for reform', and that the Tories needed time to review and comment on the Ottawa-Carleton DHC's proposals as they developed.[56] Still, this position was a far cry from the Minister's previous non-interventionist position, a position now regarded as completely fictitious. Even though the province was not to get involved until February when the DHC released their report, it was clear at this point that they would interrupt the restructuring process if the content of the DHC's plan was not along lines they approved of.

On 8 February 1996, the Harris government pursued more drastic measures by dumping five of the DHC members.[57] The five in question – all appointments under the previous Rae administration – were not re-appointed by the Tories, a move seen by many as an attempt by the government to stack the DHC with people agreeable to their agenda. A spokesperson for Wilson stated that it is technically the 'Minister's prerogative' to decide membership on the council, and denied that any political motive was involved. Ottawa Regional Councillor Alex Munter, also a council member, was of a decidedly different opinion. Munter argued that 'this government has been unable to bully the DHC into being as aggressive about cuts as the government wants it to be', and that 'what this appears to be is a case of cleaning house, removing people who are not prepared to aggressively cut hospital budgets'.[58] But while the Tories were successful in restructuring the DHC, it came with a political cost. The next day, when the DHC decided to extend its deadline on hospital plans to 7 May 1996, angry Council members publicly lambasted the Harris government for its actions while more than 30,000 people swamped the DHC with phone calls, letters, and petitions. This resilience clearly informed the DHC's final report on 29 May 1996, which recommended that no hospitals should be closed.[59] While the merging of the Ottawa Civic and General hospitals' administrations was narrowly approved, and the Tories forced the region to cut $100 million from its $600 million budget, its initial proposals were far less aggressive than those in other Ontario communities facing the same funding cuts.[60]

This case – like the experience of TQM in Ontario – is an excellent example of the trend noted in this chapter as decentralization in neo-liberal terms. In practising rigid fiscal centralism and cutting one-sixth of the Ottawa-Carleton DHC's budget, the Harris Tories forced a situation where politically dangerous decisions about the nature of cuts to health services would be made by agents outside Queen's Park. When this strategy encountered some resistance from DHC members, the Tories' 'control from above' posture went a step further. The DHC experienced administrative delays, its very membership was altered, and Ministry officials were sent to 'encourage' a more drastic approach. These actions are not indicative of the pure market strategy that wishes to replace the state with unfettered 'market forces'. Rather, inasmuch as the Harris government's 'quasi-market' approach offers anything new, it is an ideological and not an organizational innovation in right-wing theorizing.

OBSERVATIONS AND CONCLUSIONS

A sobering fact must be acknowledged in light of this discussion: in Ontario's medicare system, efforts to promote local control have, to date, foundered due to an inability to articulate a meaningful alternative to the political force of neo-liberalism. The political elite in Ontario, even the social democratic NDP, have entrenched the ideology of 'unfortunate necessity' around austerity measures. The Rae (Social Democratic) and Harris (Conservative) administrations have embraced the neo-liberal agenda of deficit reduction through deep cuts in social spending – one passively and fitfully and the other openly and forcefully – and have tilted Ontario politics to the political right. Many Ontarians now firmly believe that radical restructuring to the post-war welfare state system is imperative under the pressure of towering federal and provincial debt loads.

It is crucial, however, not to view these events in a historical vacuum. The aggressive restructuring agenda of the Harris government, while appearing to many Ontarians as a historical anomaly or a necessity today, is a symptom and not the cause of the crisis before Ontario's medicare system. The fiscal pressures that have frustrated the alternative of local control in Ontario stem from the structural contradictions of capitalism at the end of this century. These are the larger links between national health systems in crisis and the pressures emerging from the demands on internationalized capital. This is why the political economy approach cited earlier is crucial to understanding the phenomenon of decentralization in neo-liberal terms in Ontario's medicare system. Only such an analysis allows one to make the broader links between local control and the instabilities of the international financial system.

The case studies of TQM and the Harris government's conflict with the Ottawa-Carleton DHC demonstrate the extent to which fiscal restraint measures have fostered an environment to support a discourse of Ontario's 'statist/ social engineering' medicare system.

If the phenomenon of decentralization in neo-liberal terms is systemic and not confined to any one parliamentary alternative, it follows that the most appropriate avenue of resistance today is community activism and organization which names and challenges the demands of global capitalism and its representation in neo-liberal fiscal pressures. One should not romanticize the case of the Ottawa-Carleton DHC's conflict against the agenda of the government, or point to it as a panacea for communities facing neo-liberal fiscal pressures. The fact that the government (via the HSRC) has recently forced the Ottawa-Carleton DHC (and others) into making unpopular decisions such as hospital closures illustrates that the traditional modes of parliamentary resistance (i.e. letters, petitions, and civil demonstrations to parliament) will not stop the implementation of neo-liberal reforms in Ontario.[61] On the other hand, the potential of creative, extra-parliamentary activism should not be underestimated as a means to spark larger mobilizations against medicare restructuring begun from the demands of global capital. The recent 'Days of Action' in Ontario cities put on by labour unions and community groups has provoked critical debate about the Harris government's reform agenda, and demonstrated that the ideology behind neo-liberal restructuring may not have a permanent hold on Ontarians.

Many Canadians in today's precarious social conditions know from first-hand experience that the current arrangements of market and state are far beyond democratic control, and are in dire need of substantial reform. To date, however, it has been the political Right in Canada which has responded to these anxieties with market-based populism. As health services in Ontario continue to deteriorate, a new vision of medicare reform must be articulated that emphasizes democratic administration as its central vision. This vision must attest that local control in health services is not devolution as the Orser Report defined with appointed officials, and that centralized standards concerning Ontarians' right to quality health services are a necessity. This vision must be voiced from the community level, hopefully finding its way through to larger mobilizations of protest.

If patients, health care workers and activists are truly concerned with promoting local control in the financing and delivery of health services, they must attempt to democratize the state through extra-parliamentary pressure. While it may be a tall order, they must adopt a structural analysis to complement their immediate experience and begin to link their specific struggles to a broader 'democracy movement' challenging neo-liberalism in Ontario's medicare system and elsewhere. Most importantly, however, it is time to begin to develop a genuinely transformative political project as part of this oppositional struggle. For advocates of local control, this will require a way of thinking about health that does not end when governments retreat from medicare cuts, only to make up the shortfall in deeper cuts to social assistance, employment standards, and environmental protection laws.

NOTES

1   The Ontario Federation of Labour (OFL) (1996), p. 2. It is also noteworthy here to emphasize a point which the Harris government has made repeatedly regarding their restructuring plans for Ontario's medicare system. Altogether, the Tories have not cut back on the amount of money the province puts into the medicare system; in fact, they have increased the health budget by 300 million to 17.4 billion dollars. What the Harris government has done however is to make dramatic cuts to important areas of the medicare system (the 16 per cent across-the-board cut of all Ontario hospitals being the most notable of these), cut numerous preventive care programs in favour of allopathic arrangements, and work tirelessly to centralize all levers of control into their hands. The restructuring afoot in the medicare system, as Mike Harris himself has stated, is a key part of a larger strategy to introduce 'a complete reorganization of government' quickly (*Ottawa Citizen*, 20 December 1996, p. A4). It is this reorientation and its consequences which are the objects of critique in this chapter.

2   OFL (1996), p. 4.

3   Tommy Douglas in Decter (1994), p. 14.

4   Taylor (1987), pp. 251–268.

5   Ibid., pp. 245–247.

6   As Taylor (1987) explains, the issue of greater local control did not disappear in Saskatchewan after the alternative of the Swift Current model was defeated by public referenda. Although local control remained a 'suppressed alternative' in Saskatchewan in a broader scale, one of the most frustrating factors for the College during and after the passage of universal medical insurance were immigrating doctors

(predominantly British) who kept the few rural community clinics alive and empowered local residents by educating them on how to prevent illness (pp. 325–326).

7 Ibid., p. 9.

8 Ibid., p. 2.

9 Ibid., p. 5.

10 CMA (1993), p. 84.

11 Taylor (1987), p. 484. See Lomas (1982) for a complete history of the Sault Ste. Marie Steelworkers Community Health Centre.

12 York (1987), p. 102.

13 Ibid., p. 102.

14 Taylor (1987), p. 484.

15 Tuohy (1992), pp. 148–149.

16 What the coalition meant by a 'holistic approach' to medical care was medical care that responded to the health needs of 'the whole individual as he or she lives' (ibid., 148). In describing how this would work in practice, the coalition explained that 'teams of medical, dental and social service workers would provide those services dictated by the particular characteristics of the surrounding community or neighbourhood' (ibid., 149).

17 Ibid., p. 130, and York (1987), pp. 20–22, 30–33.

18 CMA (1993), p. 86.

19 Ibid., p. 87.

20 Fulton (1993), pp. 18–19. Rachlis and Kushner (1994) also explain that, altogether, doctors are responsible for close to 80 per cent of all medical decision-making in Canada (p. 174).

21 Government of Ontario (1991).

22 Ibid., p. 2.

23 Ibid., p. 3.

24 Ibid., p. 5.

25 CMA (1993), p. 91.

26 In its entirety, the model proposed by the Orser Report is quite complex. While the Regional Board would have overall responsibility for overseeing the system, underneath it would be six Area Health Management Boards and one Regional Health Sciences Management Board. The Area Boards would have responsibilities similar to DHCs today, and would be filled by Area residents by appointment (presumably by the Minister) (CMA, 1993, p. 92).

27 Government of Ontario (1994b, p. 3).

28 Ibid., p. 5.

29 More specifically, the workplan included 'the establishment of broad principles for devolution; the development of a detailed process (including criteria) for selecting communities to participate in the projects; and, a series of guidelines for evaluating the project's outcomes' (ibid., p. 6).

30 Ibid., p. 7.

31 Ibid., pp. 7–8.

32 Ibid., p. 8.

33 Ibid. It is unclear whom the Task Force was receiving information from to buttress their conclusion that Ontario had undergone a 'negative experience' in the case of school boards. Indeed, this claim was made without any reference to information detailing why devolved decision-making in Ontario's school boards had been ineffective.

34 Ibid., p. i.
35 Ibid., p. 8.
36 *The Toronto Star*, 7 July 1996, p. A1.
37 Ibid.
38 *The Toronto Sun*, 30 January 1996, p. A4.
39 *The Ottawa Citizen*, 20 December 1996, p. C1. Ron Eade of *The Citizen* reports that in the Ottawa-Carleton area alone, the Tories are cutting grants by 40 per cent for 1997. The cuts to Ottawa-Carleton, he explains, are part of a larger objective to 'save money by squeezing cities, towns and townships, who may have no option but to amalgamate or consolidate services as they try to cope with the shortfall' (p. C1). Altogether, the Harris Tories have reduced transfer payments to all Ontario municipalities by 47 per cent, giving 735.8 million in 1997 as opposed to the Rae government's allotment of 1.4 billion in 1995.
40 Government of Ontario (1996), p. 3.
41 Armstrong and Armstrong (1996), p. 122.
42 Hassen in Price (1994), p. 15.
43 Armstrong and Armstrong (1996), pp. 122–123.
44 Price (1994), p. 15.
45 Price (1994), p. 16, reports that the NDP gave $400,000 to help hospital administrators communicate through an Ontario TQM network.
46 Government of Ontario (1996), p. 9.
47 Price (1994), p. 18.
48 Some examples are illustrated Marshall (1995). Marshall's piece is written from the example of Toronto's Sunnybrook Hospital's attempt to move towards a model of 'patient focused' and 'quality' care. The beginning of the piece notes that 'senior management' could no longer find ways to trim around the edges of the budget each year to satisfy the millions that need to be cut, so *they* saw the necessity of the project (p. 32). Once the reworking of the tasks was completed, 'prototype schedules were prepared by the *patient care managers* in the four pilot units and employees were made aware of changes to their work scheduling that would be necessary to undertake the new role' (p. 34). Marshall explains that employees were *allowed* the option of declining to participate in the study 'if schedules or *perceived learning abilities* prevented them from taking on the new role' (p. 34).
49 Armstrong and Armstrong (1996), p. 123.
50 Ibid., 123–130, 209–211, and Price (1994), pp. 17–18. Another important point which deserves brief mention is the fact that lay-offs in the health care sector have predominantly feminized consequences. On the one hand, the Armstrongs (1996) explain that nine out of ten health care workers are women, and on the other, that patients who are victims of early discharge are usually shouldered by informal care at home by women (this trend is called deinstitutionalization), (pp. 212–216).
51 Armstrong *et al.* (1996), pp. 14, 18, 26.
52 *The Ottawa Citizen*, 17 October 1995, pp. A1–A2.
53 *The Ottawa Citizen*, 18 October 1995, p. A1.
54 Ibid., p. A1.
55 *The Ottawa Citizen*, 22 December 1995, p. A1.
56 Ibid., p. A1.
57 *The Ottawa Citizen*, 8 February 1996, p. B1.
58 Ibid.
59 *The Ottawa Citizen*, 30 May 1996, p. A1.

60 Ibid. Metro Toronto's DHC has expressed the willingness to close 11 of its 44 hospitals, Thunder Bay (as previously mentioned) has already closed three of five, and Windsor's DHC has advocated closing one of its four.
61 *The Toronto Star*, 8 March 1997, pp. A1, A4, A5.

REFERENCES

Armstrong, P. and H. Armstrong. 1996. *Wasting Away: The Undermining of Canadian Health Care*. Toronto: Oxford University Press.

Armstrong, P., H. Armstrong, J. Choiniere, E. Mykhalovskiy and J. P. White. 1996. *The Promise and the Price: New Work Organizations in Ontario Hospitals*. North York: York University Centre for Health Studies, April.

Canadian Medical Association (CMA). 1993. *The Language of Health Reform*. Ottawa: CMA Press.

Decter, M. 1994. *Healing Medicare: Managing System Change the Canadian Way*. Toronto: McGilligan Books.

Fulton, J. 1993. *Canada's Health System: Bordering on the Possible*. Toronto: Faulkner and Gray.

Government of Ontario. 1991. Integration and Coordination Committee of the Premier's Council. *Local Decision-Making in Health and Social Services*. Toronto: Queen's Printer.

Government of Ontario. 1994a. Premier's Council on Health, Well-Being and Social Justice. *A Framework for Devolution*. Toronto: Queen's Printer.

Government of Ontario. 1994b. Premier's Council on Health, Well-Being and Social Justice. *Devolution of Health and Social Services in Ontario: Refocusing the Debate*. Toronto: Queen's Printer.

Government of Ontario. 1996. Management Board of Cabinet. *Doing Better for Less*. Toronto: Queen's Printer.

Lomas, J. 1982. *First and Foremost*. Toronto: University of Toronto Press.

Marshall, K. 1995. 'Multiskilling – Re-engineering the Work Process', *Health Management Forum* 8 (2).

Ontario Federation of Labour, 1996. *Fight Back Facts*. Toronto: Ontario Federation of Labour.

Price, J. 1994. 'Total Quality Management Threatens Medicare', *Canadian Dimension* (Jan.–Feb.).

Rachlis, M. and C. Kushner. 1994. *Strong Medicine: How to Save Canada's Health Care System*. Toronto: HarperCollins.

Taylor, M. 1987. *Health Insurance in Canada: The Seven Decisions That Created the Canadian Health Insurance System and Their Outcomes*. Kingston: McGill-Queen's University Press.

Tuohy, C. 1992. *Policy and Politics in Canada: Institutionalized Ambivalence*. Philadelphia: Temple University Press.

York, G. 1987. *The High Price of Health: A Patient's Guide to the Hazards of Medical Politics*. Toronto: Lorimer.

Part IV

The political economy of health reform in Canada

12 Downsizing, passive privatization and fiscal arrangements

Carl Sonnen and Mike McCracken

The importance of health care in the economy is one of the principal features of Canadian public policy. The widespread and sustained effort by successive federal governments to contain the growth of health care expenditures has been a difficult exercise that has produced widespread changes to Canada's health care system. Yet the fact remains that an increasing allocation of the economy's spending to health care over the past generation has predictably generated an increasing use of the economy's resources to delivery of this demand (see Table 12.1). Among the industrial countries, Canada has been regarded as allocating relatively high proportions of its resources to health care, following behind the United States, which uses the largest proportion of all countries.

This rush to make the system more "efficient" has many 'macro' as well as 'micro' consequences on Canada's health system. This chapter is concentrated on exploring the pressures that are reshaping Canada's health system and the degree to which government policy is capable of responding to them. The question to be addressed is whether a downsized system will force a re-examination of the principles of the Canadian Health Act, including the introduction of privatization. Should that eventuality come to pass, Canada's health system would be ill-prepared to cope with such radical changes to the existing health care system. The chapter concludes with an examination of federal–provincial arrangements. Whether other national

Table 12.1 Health demand and supply indicators

	1972	1977	1984	1991	1996
Demand (% of GDP at market prices)					
Total expenditures[1]	7.2	7.0	8.0	9.2	8.4
Public and private service outlays	6.4	6.3	7.2	8.1	7.2
Personal drugs and insurance	0.8	0.7	0.8	1.1	1.2
Production, direct health care services (% of GDP at factor cost)					
Total	5.3	5.3	6.1	7.0	6.6
Employment (% of total-economy employment)	6.3	6.9	7.8	8.5	8.8

policy instruments can provide a stable and satisfactory basis for health reform remains to be seen.

THE GROWTH OF HEALTH DEMANDS

Although growth has been continuous over the past generation this is no longer the case. Further 'downsizing' will continue through 1998. Given this, we will see that projected total real resources available to the hospital system in 1998 will be 9 per cent less than in 1991. Fewer people will be working in the health sector (employment is expected to be reduced from a base of 485,000 by about 28,000 person years). Per-patient real resources available to the hospital system will have been reduced to 80 per cent of their 1991 levels by 1998. Also, other measures are being employed to exercise financial restraint. So governments, who finance three-quarters of the production system will judge that the restructuring (including hospital downsizing) will have produced a new, 'efficient', equilibrium between production of services and desirable health outcomes. Notwithstanding these downward pressures, it is projected that total real resources allocated to health care should change little over the period 1992–98.

Household as well as government expenditures are key factors that determine overall growth of health demands (see Table 12.2). Prominent in this record of the last fifteen years is the recent sharp increase in the proportion of

Table 12.2 Distribution of health demands (% of total health spending)

	1981 (%)	1984 (%)	1991 (%)	1996 (%)
Total affecting service delivery	89.8	89.5	88.4	85.5
Public sector	70.0	68.7	69.2	65.7
Medicare	17.6	17.5	19.8	17.6
Hospital system	40.1	39.9	39.2	38.0
Public workers	12.3	11.3	10.2	10.1
Personal	19.7	20.8	19.2	19.9
Households	17.3	18.1	16.5	17.0
Medical and dental	3.1	3.6	3.2	3.2
Hospital care	4.0	3.5	3.9	3.8
Special care facilities	6.1	6.7	4.8	5.3
Other health care	4.1	4.3	4.6	4.7
Non-profit (unions, assns)	2.4	2.6	2.7	2.8
Memo: personal health				
Drugs and sundries	8.4	9.0	9.8	11.7
Other (e.g. insurance)	1.8	1.5	1.8	2.7
Personal sector from above	19.7	20.8	19.2	19.9
Total personal sector health	30.0	31.3	30.8	34.3
Total health	100.0	100.0	100.0	100.0

total health demand accounted for by household spending for pharmaceuticals and private insurance, and declines in the shares of Medicare and hospital spending. There are no pronounced trends in the split between public and private demands that affect health service producers. The public share has remained largely unchanged, including recent years. A steady erosion in direct spending of provincial and municipal governments for delivery of support to the disabled, nursing homes, and other social services has been offset by a rise in the amount allocated to Medicare. It is noteworthy that of personal-sector spending affecting health services, about one-sixth occurs through unions, benevolent associations and other non-profit arrangements. Thus, advocates of 'voluntarism' should recognize that, while 'free' time of households may help to remove the burden of financing health care, institutions are also involved. They constitute a significant source of demand (financing almost $2 billion in 1996), and their spending is sensitive to their own financial circumstances.

Is this an increase in 'real' demand, or does it reflect changing prices among the several sources of demand? Table 12.3 reports changes in real (after-inflation) spending. The periods selected represent respectively (1) a strong general economic recovery from the recession of 1981/82, (2) the first two years of a recession at the opening of this decade, and (3) the muted economic recovery since that time.

Table 12.3 Spending affecting health system output ($1986, millions)

	Average annual growth		
	1983–89	*1990–91*	*1992–96*
Total affecting service delivery	3.5	3.4	−0.8
Public sector	3.6	4.1	−1.1
Medicare	5.2	7.0	−0.8
Hospital system	3.3	2.9	−1.5
Public workers	1.7	2.5	−0.4
Personal	3.2	1.2	0.3
Households	3.0	0.8	0.2
Medical and dental	3.6	2.2	−0.2
Hospital care	3.9	3.5	−0.9
Special care facilities	1.3	−4.3	1.1
Other health care	3.9	3.3	0.5
Non-profit (unions, assns)	4.3	3.8	0.8
Memo: personal health			
Drugs and sundries	5.2	−0.3	4.6
Other (e.g. insurance)	9.3	−4.2	4.5
Personal sector from above	3.2	1.2	0.3
Total personal sector health	4.1	0.4	2.0
Total health	3.7	2.9	−0.2

As Table 12.3 indicates, a relatively strong expansion of real demand was sustained through 1991. For the opening years of the 1990s, this reflects the continued strong growth of public-sector spending. The sensitivity of personal consumption to declining disposable income of households in 1990/91 is reflected in reduced spending for some health-related items (support for the elderly and disabled, and net spending for private insurance), but overall, personal spending growth only slowed.

Results for the years since 1991 reflect what may be fundamental changes to health care financing and service delivery. Although most heavily concentrated in the hospital sector, the last five years are marked by a widespread reduction in public spending that provides real resources to health care. And, despite generalized economic recovery, spending by households has stagnated, or, where growth has occurred, has been concentrated in spending for drugs and insurance, which are largely outside of publicly insured services. Such increases have been modest by historical comparison. Note that this indicates little 'shifting' of the demand for hospital and physician services from public to private financing has occurred to this point.

Two of the principal reasons for this record are indicated in Table 12.4. Comparison of changes in consumer spending in Table 12.3 with household income changes in Table 12.4 will clearly indicate that such spending is income sensitive. In recent years, both the muted nature of the general economic recovery and its unusually weak ability to generate employment have been reflected in poor household income growth.

Note that over the past fifteen years, an increasing proportion of consumer spending has been allocated to health care. From 4.0 per cent of total spending in 1981, we estimate it has reached 4.8 per cent in 1996. That additional proportion (0.8 per centage points) is equivalent to an additional $3.8 billion in spending this year.

For public-sector spending, provincial fiscal initiatives are key. Although reduced transfers from the federal to provincial governments (recently further downsized with the introduction of the Canada Health and Social Transfer Act) are also important, the provincial governments are for all intents and purposes the relevant fiscal authority in the health system. They alone fund the Medicare system, they provide the preponderant share of financing that is used to operate the hospital system, and typically, they are the source for about one-half of municipal government financing, where delivery of some important social-service agencies is concentrated.[2]

Table 12.4 reports an otherwise well-known story that the run-up of provincial government deficits early in the 1990s has generated a quick rise in their debt. With one or two exceptions, reducing annual deficits has become the main priority of provincial governments. In 1996, the primary balance (the balance less interest payments) will be in surplus reflecting this priority. This has been accomplished by reducing transfers to hospitals and spending for Medicare. Provincial spending allocated to health care has been reduced to 24.5 per cent of total program spending from its peak of 25.5 per cent in 1991. Put

Table 12.4 Health-related demand drivers, income, national accounts basis

	Average annual growth		
	1983–89	*1990–91*	*1992–96*
Households			
Disposable income ($86)	2.9	−0.7	0.9
Per household	0.7	−2.7	−0.8
Provincial financial responsibilities (% of GDP)			
Provincial, local, hospitals			
Surplus/deficit	(a) −0.7	−1.3	−1.0
Debt	(a) 7.8	10.3	18.4
Primary surplus/deficit	(a) −0.8	−1.0	−0.6
Provincial			
Surplus/deficit	(a) −0.7	−1.5	−1.7
Debt	(a) 3.9	7.0	15.3
Primary surplus/deficit	(a) −1.3	−1.4	−1.2
Municipal			
Surplus/deficit	(a) 0.0	0.1	0.4
Debt	(a) 3.8	3.2	3.1
Primary surplus/deficit	(a) 0.4	0.4	0.7
Hospitals			
Surplus/deficit	(a) 0.0	0.1	0.4
Debt	(a) 0.1	0.1	0.0
Primary surplus/deficit	(a) 0.1	0.0	0.0

Note: (a) Indicates average.

in dollar terms, the one percentage point reduction in health care restraint has provided about $1.4 billion more to debt reduction than any other spending restraint in that year.

Measured changes in demand for health care also reflect price movements, which are reported in Table 12.5. Although there were exceptions, changes to the public and private costs of health care systematically outpaced the general growth of consumer and other prices in the 1980s. As Table 12.5 indicates, that pattern has continued into the 1990s where spending levels have been affected by changed buying practices in provincial and private formularies, the introduction of the Goods and Service Tax,[3] and the margins of pharmacists.

COSTS OF HEALTH CARE AND THE 'SUPPLY SIDE'

The costs of operating private and public health services including capital depreciation in 1996 amounted to about $57 billion. As Table 12.6 reports, most of this was required to compensate paid labour, or among physician proprietors, to provide unincorporated income. As is indicated by returns to

Table 12.5 Prices by spending category (implicit deflators, 1986 = 1)

	Average annual growth		
	1983–89	*1990–91*	*1992–96*
Total affecting service delivery	4.8	4.4	1.8
Public sector	4.6	4.4	1.7
Medicare	5.1	2.3	0.1
Hospital system	4.5	5.1	2.5
Public workers	4.0	6.3	1.7
Households	5.7	4.4	2.1
Medical and dental	7.1	−0.3	2.0
Hospital care	4.9	6.7	2.1
Special care facilities	5.2	5.6	2.4
Other health care	6.1	4.9	1.8
Non-profit (unions, assns)	5.5	5.2	1.4
Memo: personal health			
Drugs and sundries	6.6	4.7	0.8
Other (e.g. insurance)	6.4	4.8	6.6
Personal sector from above	5.7	4.5	2.0
Total personal sector health	6.0	4.6	1.9
Total health	5.0	4.4	1.8
GDP deflator	3.9	3.0	1.1
General consumer deflator	4.3	4.6	1.3

Table 12.6 Allocation of health-service costs, 1996 (% of total)

Purchases from other industries	21
Labour compensation	75
Paid labour	60
Unincorporated income	15
Returns to corporations and public sector depreciation	4

corporations and public-sector depreciation, payments to support financing of real fixed capital are required, and purchases from other industries are significant at about $12 billion in 1996.

It is assumed that the restructuring of the health care system will continue into 1998, regardless of general economic conditions. From the standpoint of the provincial health ministries that directly fund health care, several options are available to cut costs:

- reduce labour costs by layoffs, use of lower skilled and contingent workers and outsourcing;
- cost-effective purchasing which has the least effect on patient outcomes;
- replace labour inputs with information-automation technology;

- shift the demand for services and costs from hospitals to non-traditional sources of health care such as accommodation to households or social service agencies;
- move activity from institution-based care to clinics, or community- and home-based care.

It is not clear which options governments may favour since they may choose among these various cost cutting techniques. Among the factors which limit the governments' choice of constraint measures is the growth of compensation and input costs. If physicians' wages go up, something else must go down.

Table 12.7 reveals that managers of the health services system will have approximately the same amount of resources in 1998 to directly manage as

Table 12.7 Health system real input indicators

	Average annual rates of growth					
	Low		*Base*		*High*	
	1992– 98	*1999– 2005*	*1992– 98*	*1999– 2005*	*1992– 98*	*1999– 2005*
GDP at factor cost ($86 m)						
Total	0.3	1.7	0.3	2.3	0.3	3.0
Hospitals	−1.2	1.7	−1.3	2.2	−1.4	2.7
Physicians and institutions	1.5	1.7	1.4	2.4	1.4	3.2
By type of production						
Public	0.0	1.5	0.0	1.9	0.0	2.3
Business/private	1.1	2.1	0.9	3.2	0.7	4.3
Labour, employment (000s per year)						
Total	1.4	1.6	1.4	2.1	1.4	2.6
Hospitals	−0.5	1.8	−0.5	2.2	−0.6	2.7
Physicians and institutions	3.0	1.4	3.0	1.9	3.1	2.5
By type of production						
Public	0.8	1.5	0.9	1.8	0.9	2.2
Business/private	3.7	1.9	3.5	2.9	3.4	4.0
Population, weighted for care						
Hospitals	1.9	1.6	1.9	1.8	1.9	1.9
Physicians	1.6	1.4	1.6	1.6	1.6	1.9
Inputs of Goods and Services ($86 m)						
Total	−0.9	2.0	−0.6	3.1	−0.3	4.1
Hospitals	−1.7	2.0	−1.1	3.0	−0.4	3.9
Physicians and institutions	0.0	2.0	−0.1	3.1	−0.1	4.2
By type of production						
Public	−1.8	1.8	−1.2	2.8	−0.5	3.7
Business/private	0.3	2.1	0.2	3.3	0.0	4.6

were available in 1991. Significantly, their use of purchased materials and services will be smaller.[4] It is estimated that by 1998 per-patient reductions in real inputs to private and public health services combined will have amounted to 7.5–10 per cent. Much of this is being concentrated in the hospital system, where the absolute level of resources available is being reduced. Per-patient, real resources for operating hospitals in 1998 are likely to be as much as 25 per cent smaller than in 1991. Caution should be taken in interpreting the relatively rapid 3.5 per cent average growth of private sector employment over 1992–98 as unambiguous evidence of a shift to private delivery. Since employment growth in preceding periods was much higher (5+ per cent per year in the years 1982–91), it should be kept in mind that the per-patient load on personnel in this sector has been growing quickly. On balance, Canada's health delivery has been pared back not only with respect to employment but there have also been a large number of bed closures, shortened lengths-of-stay and other anecdotal evidence suggesting that this is heavily concentrated so far in 'non-medical' materials – food and accommodation supplies, energy for heating, inputs to administration, etc.

Obviously, some of this "accommodation" (e.g., food, space to rest) is being supplied from other sources (or, people would otherwise be literally "on the street"). This suggests that part of the burden is being downloaded on to households. And some element of such cuts would also fall on businesses providing operating supplies, repair construction, and some elements of medical supply. In addition, capital budgets are being cut. Real spending for construction and/or renovation of health-system structures has been reduced by more than 10 per cent since 1990. In contrast, spending for equipment has continued to expand at a relatively fast pace. Whether this indicates that special efforts are being made to use automation and advanced medical devices as substitutes for labour and other inputs, or represents a longer-term effect of changing medical and administrative procedures, is unclear. For employees and managers in both the private and public systems, per-patient transformations of the data suggest longer queues, and more stress for employees and in relations between service providers and patients.[5]

Finally, the years after 1998 indicate that the future of Canada's health care spending needs is dependent on the general economic outlook for the economy. In a low-growth environment, few new resources are likely to be available. With one-third of Canada's aggregate economic demand now tied directly through our exports to the US, a recession in that country could be a trigger to a much worse scenario.

COMPENSATION

Table 12.8 reports the extent to which compensation in health services is above or below averages for the economy as a whole, and how those have changed over the past fifteen years. In this measure of payment, unincorporated income is

Table 12.8 Labour income per employee, including unincorporated
(% + or − relative to total economy average)

	1981	1989	1991	1996
Government and social service sector	15.2	13.4	18.2	15.7
Health and social services	3.1	8.2	9.8	6.3
Business	98.3	83.5	90.6	82.2
Physicians, Institutional	102.0	85.4	93.5	84.4
Private portion of hospital	17.3	17.9	6.2	2.8
Nonbusiness	−15.2	−10.1	−9.4	−15.2
Hospitals	−5.1	−1.6	3.9	2.4
Institutional care	−33.0	−23.5	−28.1	−36.9
Government administrative services	21.6	24.3	31.3	35.7
Education	21.0	8.4	15.2	10.6

included to reflect the large weight it plays in compensating physicians and other professionals in private practice. It should be recognized, however, that at least some element of this represents a return to capital to finance investment in office structures and equipment. It is also important to note that the wide variations in compensation in the health care industries reflect the extent to which workers are trained and credentialled, the varying degrees of market power between suppliers and those who finance spending, and, possibly, how changing "social" values play a role in these distinctions. Has, for example, gender-equity legislation and/or the role of organized labour played a role in reducing the gap between average compensation of those in the hospital system and the average compensation in the economy, or compared to those operating in the private physician and institutional sector?

We do not have sufficient information in our analytical framework to isolate these influences, but some "large" conclusions can be reasonably deduced from this record. Changes in relative compensation in health services between 1991 and 1996 indicate that restraints on compensation are being used to cut costs. This is widespread across all sectors of delivery. These restraints in private delivery are part of a longer record. Whether physicians in private practice *per se* have had their relative compensation reduced cannot be determined from this evidence, but an almost 20 percentile swing in relative compensation for their industry suggests this is probable. An erosion in unincorporated income per non-salaried worker in this industry relative to other industries, and a rise in industry relative wages and salaries per paid worker, either indicate a shift in the form of compensation for physicians or, as likely, some erosion in their relative compensation.

The relative compensation in the private physician sector is significant when compared to a number of other industry sectors. In 1981, compensation in this sector was exceeded only by that in the upstream oil and gas industry − testament to the insensitivity of health care spending to immediate market swings. Average compensation in the public sector that delivers institutional care services remains significantly below the levels of the rest of the economy. Some attribute this to the nature of the services delivered (e.g. assistance and care of the disabled by birth, emotional disturbance, abuse, or addiction). Compensation is above that of only a few other industries – agriculture, fishing, retail trade, personal services, and food and accommodation.

From the standpoint of encouraging persons to train for and enter the health care service industries, the record of compensation erosion for the industries that are heavily weighted to highly trained professions suggests some risks for the future. On the one hand, compensation in the private sector remains relatively high, and performance-based measures of adequacy have suggested to some that an 'over supply' still exists. A long erosion in compensation is underway, and has brought compensation standards to levels where comparison to industries with 'lower' skills requirements is obvious.[6]

HEALTH SERVICE'S REAL CAPITAL

To operate health services requires real capital (Table 12.9). Annual spending averaged $1.9 billion over 1989–95, of which $1.2 billion was for the construction of new, or major renovation of existing, structures. The balance was spending for machinery and equipment, most of it for specialized medical devices and information technology equipment.[7] In 1996, it is estimated that

Table 12.9 Health services capital

		Average annual growth		
		75–82	83–91	92–96
Health-weighted population		2.1	1.8	1.8
Capital stock ($86 m)				
Total		4.2	4.5	3.4
Structures		3.9	3.3	1.9
Machinery and equipment		7.0	13.4	9.7
Investment effort (% of GDP, $C)	(a)	6.2	5.7	4.2
Sector employment (000s)		4.0	3.2	1.6
Capital–labour ratio		0.1	1.2	1.8
Structures		−0.1	0.1	0.3
Machinery and equipment		0.1	1.2	1.8
Investment deflators				
Structures		7.9	2.6	1.1
Machinery and equipment		4.5	−3.6	−6.6
Memo: GDP deflator		8.9	3.7	1.1
Total factor productivity		−0.7	−0.2	−1.8

Note: (a) Indicates average.

total spending was reduced to $1.8 billion, with this reduction split evenly between spending for new structures and equipment.

The foregoing paints a national picture of modest adjustment to real resources from the administrators' point of view and significant cuts from the patients' perspective, prospects of employment in the public system, and the compensation of all employees regardless of whether they are in the public or private system. Some significant additions to the burden of care may also have been shifted to households, but a major shift to privatization of financing or delivering health care overstates events so far. Does a provincial perspective alter this?

OVERVIEW OF PROVINCIAL HEALTH PRODUCTION

Nationally, a little less than two-thirds of health care services are produced by public sector organizations – public hospitals, provincial and municipal government social service agencies, public nursing homes, etc. The balance of health care (although heavily funded by public Medicare programs) is "privately" produced.[8]

As Table 12.10 indicates, for Canada as a whole, there is a slowly emerging trend towards relatively more private delivery. As the discussion on national trends indicated, this reflects the downsizing of the public hospital system, and relatively slow growth of provincial and municipal government social service delivery organizations. There are significant variations from the national norm and trends among the provinces, however. Generally, "poorer" provinces are more heavily reliant on publicly managed delivery systems. Ontario stands out as the province with a comparatively large proportion of private delivery.

In looking forward, for the country as a whole, it is assumed that the trend towards an increasing proportion of private delivery will continue. There are no clear indications that this will be widespread among the provinces, however. A shift towards relatively more private delivery is apparent in several provinces, and is particularly evident in Nova Scotia and Ontario.[9] In others, public delivery appears to have increased. What do changes in service delivery look like from the patients' point of view? Keeping in mind that population is a poor and generally understated measure of patient number increases, Table 12.11 reveals that rapid reductions in per-patient real inputs to service delivery are also widespread across the provinces. The possible single exception is in the Territories, where federal spending to meet a commitment to improving standards of living for aboriginal peoples has a relatively strong influence. Recent announcements about fiscal actions in Quebec and Ontario suggest stronger reductions in those provinces than are reported in the table.

In sum, all these cutbacks result in a complex picture indicating a number of long-term trends. First, reductions in health spending inputs are a national phenomenon. A presumption that the Canada Health Act will force provinces to move in "lock step" is also unwarranted. In fact, while the Canada Health Act

Table 12.10 Provincial health care output relative to population, and public/private distribution

	1981	1991	1998
Per cent of Canada's total health production			
Newfoundland	1.7	1.7	1.5
Prince Edward Island	0.4	0.4	0.4
Nova Scotia	3.2	3.2	3.1
Brunswick	2.1	2.2	2.0
Quebec	25.6	23.1	23.2
Ontario	39.0	39.8	40.7
Manitoba	4.2	3.9	3.8
Saskatchewan	3.6	3.5	3.2
Alberta	8.6	9.9	9.1
British Columbia	11.4	11.9	12.6
Territories	0.2	0.3	0.3
Population			
Newfoundland	2.3	2.1	1.9
Prince Edward Island	0.5	0.5	0.5
Nova Scotia	3.4	3.3	3.1
New Brunswick	2.8	2.7	2.5
Quebec	26.4	25.2	24.7
Ontario	35.5	37.2	37.5
Manitoba	4.2	4.0	3.8
Saskatchewan	3.9	3.6	3.4
Alberta	9.3	9.3	9.4
Territories	0.3	0.3	0.3
Public as % of Canada's total production, and for each Province			
Canada	66.7	65.9	63.4
Newfoundland	78.5	77.7	79.0
Prince Edward Island	.74.7	73.2	74.6
Nova Scotia	68.2	71.9	66.3
New Brunswick	73.4	74.2	75.3
Quebec	66.9	69.1	67.8
Ontario	65.5	60.9	56.8
Manitoba	66.9	71.6	69.3
Saskatchewan	75.1	76.3	77.5
Alberta	67.8	68.8	66.6
British Columbia	62.9	63.7	64.0
Territories	62.8	62.8	62.8

guarantees health care for everyone (by a public single payer) it does not specify the mix of public and private delivery vehicles. What is striking is the extent of variation among the provinces' health care delivered through "private" or "public" delivery systems. There is also diversity among the provinces in the

Table 12.11 Provincial health system output and employment ($86 per capita)

	Average annual rates of growth	
	1982–91	*1992–98*
Total health production		
Newfoundland	3.3	−1.5
Prince Edward Island	2.8	−1.0
Nova Scotia	2.5	−0.4
New Brunswick	3.4	−1.4
Quebec	1.4	−0.4
Ontario	1.7	−0.5
Manitoba	1.8	−0.8
Saskatchewan	2.5	−1.0
Alberta	3.5	−2.0
British Columbia	1.9	−1.0
Territories	3.3	0.2

mix between organized hospital and disability, social service, and other agencies. Through the 1980s, Nova Scotia, Quebec, and Manitoba shifted from private to public production, and indeed steadily reduced per capita private production over those years. In contrast, this was a decade when Ontario's private production was expanding relatively rapidly, with modest, per capita reductions in public production. The 1990s are yet a different story.

FEDERAL ACTION: WHAT'S NEXT?

In the 1995 Budget, the federal government dashed provincial hopes for a return to some joint basis for funding social programs by announcing a new Canada Health and Social Transfer (CHST) as a replacement for the earlier federal social transfers known as EPF (Established Programs Financing) and CAP (Canada Assistance Plan). This new transfer involved further major cut-backs in cash transfers to the provinces and the maintenance of the imbalances that resulted from capping the previous transfers. In the 1996 Budget, and with a close call in Quebec on the referendum, the federal government announced their own rules for the allocation of payments among the provinces, and committed to a minimum cash payment of $11 billion from fiscal year 1998/99 through 2002/03. This 'iron-clad' guarantee is viewed by the federal government as a major positive move: 'This is the first budget to take action to increase the rate of growth in these transfers since the era of restraint began in the mid-1980s' (*Finance*, 1996: 57).

Presumably the federal government was not considering the 'actions' taken by previous governments which resulted in a major recession and a substantial increase in CAP payments, at least to some provinces. In turn, the choices of higher unemployment and increased inequality are also choices about health, even though this dimension is rarely featured in government reports (Sullivan, 1998). In a recent UK paper, Richard Wilkinson claims, "the distribution of income is the single most important determinant of levels of health in the developed world" (Wilkinson, 1993: 35).

Finally, in the course of the 1997 federal election campaign, an announcement was made that CHST would be increased starting in 1998/99 by $700 million, with subsequent increases to about $1,400 million, This essentially raises the CHST cash floor to $12.5 billion, beginning in 1998/99 (Liberal Party of Canada, 1997: 58).

TRANSFER IMPLICATIONS FOR PROVINCES

Over the next several years provinces face substantial reductions in cash transfers from the federal government. Permanent drops of about $3 billion in 1996/97 and another $3 billion in 1997/98 will reduce cash transfers (for health, education, and social assistance) from about $18.5 billion in 1995/96 to $12.5 billion in two years. In essence, the provinces are now responsible for 100 per cent of any growth in health and education whether attributable to inflation or increased demographic pressures or upgrading of services. For social assistance, even the relatively poorer provinces no longer face a 50–50 sharing regime. All social assistance funding increases are the responsibility of the provincial government.

Of course there is one advantage for the province. Any savings that materialize in social assistance, health, or education will accrue entirely to the provincial government. This provides a major incentive to "pare down" the social systems wherever possible. Nevertheless, the major cutbacks of transfers to the provinces will ensure that the provinces remain under the "fiscal gun", with tax increases, expenditure cuts, and "down-loading" on to municipalities and 'privatization' of functions to be expected in many areas. And that is the good news! By contrast, the bad news is that in the next recession, the fiscal hit will occur on the provinces much more so than the federal government. The "automatic stabilizers" of the past have been severely weakened, and provinces are much more likely to be forced to cut their expenditures or raise taxes during the recession, steps which will ensure that the recession is deeper and longer than is necessary.

SUGGESTED PRINCIPLES FOR FEDERAL–PROVINCIAL PROGRAMS

The CHST is a federal program, without any meaningful provincial input and with the continuing threat of unilateral change by the federal government, without notice. This "right" has been confirmed by the federal courts in the context of the provincial challenge to the "cap" on CAP in 1991. Although there is no immediate indication of any willingness of the federal government to modify this autocratic, paternal stance, what follows are some thoughts about what might be a more desirable system for all parties – federal and provincial governments and the clients of these social programs. From this perspective, the proposed principles are consistent with a federation and the notion of subsidiarity. The federal government has a better capacity to raise revenue in a less distorting and more efficient way than the provincial governments. As well, it has a leadership role to promote standards and to promote rapid transmission of new ideas and productivity improvements. At the same time, provinces (or their agents – local governments, universities and hospitals) have some advantages in the delivery of services to people.

The question is whether some national (federal and provincial) arrangement can evolve which is more stable and satisfactory to all of those involved. With the increasing talk of pharmacare and a national homecare program, everyone will be discussing new arrangements. It is to that end that the following federal/provincial financing principles are offered for consideration. There are ten in all:

Talk cash: Only the federal government continues to use 'tax points' and cash in describing its programs. This makes the numbers look bigger, and is a reminder to the provinces that it gave them tax room when it modified the shared-cost programs in the early 1970s. Although the EPF system was a blend of tax points and cash, with a base level indexed to GDP and population growth, the CAP was a shared cost program of cash transfers only. If the federal government intends to be directly involved in the health, education, and social assistance areas in the future it is necessary and desirable for them to make a meaningful commitment in the form of a cash amount each year, according to a defined arrangement.

Long-term commitment: The agreement between the federal and provincial governments should be on a multi-year basis, of at least five years, with a provision that it continues unless renegotiated after prior notice of several years by either party.

Minimum level: The federal government should commit to a minimum cash transfer. If instead the federal government wishes to retain the ability to alter the amount at any time, without prior notice, then it would be better if the federal government did not waste people's time with consultation, etc.

Reasonable distribution formula: With the issue of cash distribution, then any needs-based formula becomes a variant of equalization with better-off provinces giving up cash for the benefit of other provinces. Alternatively, if an equal per capita cash transfer is used, then the better-off provinces will receive the same amount of cash and the only redistribution program among provinces will be equalization. Indeed, this is what would have happened under the 1995 federal proposals around 2007–2010, when EPF cash transfers went to zero. The 1996 Budget indicates its intention to move towards an equal cash amount per capita, but at a pace that will still maintain a significant regional redistribution element.

National standards for access: In return for the creation of a stable, predictable, and fair cash transfer system, the provinces should agree to establish a set of national access standards that they will adhere to as a minimum. These standards might also include some specific elements that would be of interest to all provinces and could assist Canadian citizens, regardless of where they live. Examples might include:

- Full access to the health system for a Canadian living in any province.
- Full access to the health system for a Canadian visiting any province.
- Equal treatment of health costs incurred abroad, regardless of province of residence.
- Opportunity to apply for entry to any educational institution in Canada, with admittance ensuring equal tuition cost regardless of province of residence.
- Ability for any Canadian to receive social assistance in any province, if otherwise qualified in that province. Such assistance to be available without residency requirements.

National standards for performance: Although more controversial, it may be useful if there are at least some minimum standards for performance in relation to health. These might include:

- Maximum waiting times for health care services (i.e. six weeks for hip or knee replacement).
- Target mortality rates for various conditions and procedures (i.e. hysterectomy, cholecystectomy).
- Minimum nutritional levels for children living in poverty (as per Health Canada's Nutrition Guide).

Such measures could be part of a broader set of goals and objectives for social indicators, as is done in Oregon (Oregon Progress Board, 1995). One key aspect would be to ensure that progress is being made over time and across regions.

Cyclical instability: Since cyclical shocks and contracyclical actions are a federal responsibility, it is not appropriate for the transfers to the provinces or to persons to be reduced in a downturn. Indeed, it is more sensible to be increasing them as part of a stabilization effort, if the federal government chooses to do so. Social assistance, which is particularly cyclically sensitive, might be better treated with some additional funding mechanism that promotes planning for cyclical instability, such as an earmarked fund for handling cyclical increases.

Indexing to population: Since provincial population growth rates may be faster or slower than national rates, it is desirable that formulas used in the allocation of any transfers reflect this reality in some form.

Indexing to real growth: Since more real growth usually enhances the capacity of a province to deal with economic demands more easily, indexing to real growth should not be part of the formula. If GDP falls nationally, or for a region, then again this should not affect the transfers, except for contracyclical considerations.

Indexing to inflation: Inflation is not something over which the provinces have much control. Given the federal responsibility for its management, it is appropriate for the transfer to be indexed in some way for inflation. If a general measure is not desired, then there could be agreement on a way for defining an indexing factor.

COMPLIANCE ISSUES

If one or more provinces will not comply with the national standards, then the issues of penalties and processes to bring about compliance are real challenges. As well, conflicts may arise between two provinces, particularly if there are movements of people from one province to another for purposes of receiving health care, education, or social assistance. Of course, provinces may also have major differences with the federal government, particularly if 'iron-clad' agreements change in future federal budgets. Furthermore, the design of compliance 'incentives' depends on the nature of the 'agreement' between the federal government and the provinces. If the program remains a federal one, with no real role for the provinces except to graciously accept the money and comply, then the current system of the threat of withholding cash is likely to be the default enforcement mechanism. Finally, if another form of agreement were to evolve, then issues of compliance would be dealt with as part of the design of that new arrangement.

WHAT ABOUT THE CURRENT FEDERAL CHST PROGRAM?

How does the current CHST match the criteria above? The current federal program has limited indexing to both real growth and inflation (GDP less 1 per cent after a transitional period). There is no cyclical component. Provinces will have to handle any increased demand for rising social assistance from their own resources or by spreading their weaker revenue among more recipients in a recession. The major problem is that any federal government can unilaterally change the program without notice and for whatever purpose it may wish to achieve. Such an action is not unthinkable, since federal governments have been cutting major social transfers for many years.

Although the CHST is now a federal program, it is 'thinkable' that a 'national' program might be more appropriate for social areas. In our mind, a 'national' program is one in which the federal and provincial governments cooperate, with at least an equal voice between the federal government and some majority of the provinces. Changes in transfers would then be jointly discussed and a result of joint deliberations. The rationale for such programs is that there are large social externalities associated with good social policy, with delegation of total responsibility to more geographically specific levels likely to result in substantial under-investment in social capital.

One or all of the social programs could be designated as a federal program, either by constitutional amendment or by delegation from the provinces to the federal government. With Unemployment Insurance a federal program, there might be some logic to putting social assistance at the same level. Universities could be viewed as an area that has expanded in a way not anticipated by the founding fathers who designated education as a provincial responsibility. With increased emphasis on healthiness over the life-cycle it could be argued that the federal government should undertake such a long-term program as health care for all of its citizens. Perhaps the strongest argument for the joint consideration of all of the social programs is the many linkages between them and their interdependence with labour market outcomes and income distribution.

PROVINCIAL PROGRAMS

At the other extreme, provinces could deliver all of the social programs, including those currently linked to the labour market such as Unemployment Insurance (renamed "Employment Insurance"), training, native programs, or old age (veterans' pensions, OAS (Old Age Supplement)/GIS (Guaranteed Income Supplement). Furthermore, on the assumption of a federal state, then delivery of services as close to the need (subsidiarity), with national planning of the system, research, standards setting, and funding is likely to be most appropriate and efficient. (By "national" is meant federal plus provincial plus local delivery entities.) By contrast, what if coordination can't be achieved? One can wring one's hands, but it helps to recognize that it is not the end of the world. Indeed, inefficiencies may be acceptable if the local community is able to express its voice and more readily accept the taxes, queues, and other aspects of such programs.

Some would simply counsel giving up on state-mandated delivery of health, social services, or education with a strong belief that the market will deliver the appropriate level of services most efficiently. To move to such a system will require some transition, perhaps with privatization of existing facilities and a substitution of private insurance for public funding. Although it would be useful to report that such a move would lead to substantially fewer resources being needed, the US example for health care is not reassuring.

CONCLUSION: THE NEXT TEN YEARS

As Canada emerges from its recent fiscal straitjacket, the debate will begin on how to most effectively use the improved fiscal room that emerges from lower real interest rates, large cutbacks in services, and some return of economic performance towards more normal levels. Of course the "plans" may be dashed by the economy being thrown back into another recession, either because of an external shock (e.g. US interest rate hike, OPEC price shock) or domestic policies (e.g. Bank of Canada moves, Quebec separation completed).

With the recent report of the National Forum on Health (NFH, 1997) discussion has begun on new areas for federal and provincial governments to improve the national health system. In the Liberal Party "Red Book II" (Liberal Party of Canada, 1997: 71) health care received substantial emphasis.

In these areas an opportunity exists for the development of a truly national approach, with full participation of both the federal and provincial governments, along with the health community. Only time will tell if such an approach becomes a reality. It is critical that individual Canadians play an important role. First they need to insist that federal and provincial governments stop playing games and start cooperating on a regular basis. Then, citizens need to insist on the regular publication of real objectives for health, education, and social assistance, along with measured progress against these objectives. And if these objectives are not met, then they must vote for a change in government.

NOTES

1 Estimates for spending vary modestly from accounts reported in *National Health Expenditures (NHE)*. Estimates in Table 1 for 1994 sum to $66 billion. This amount excludes federal direct spending reported for 1994 as ($2.5 billion for current spending), Workers Compensation Board spending of $0.6 billion, and spending for capital by both the public and private sectors equivalent to $2 billion. Included in our estimates, but not in the *NHE*, is spending of $1.6 billion by households for medical insurance. Data from this chapter derive from the system of national accounts in 1994/95 and all prior years. The forecasting from 1995 forward is based on Informetrica's usual modelling work. Some variance from National Health Expenditures is to be expected, given some differences in data sources.

2 Private financing of hospitals, which includes spending and contributions of households and business, appears to be growing in importance, however. From about 11 per cent of total financing through until 1994, it is estimated that revenues from hospital sales of goods and services rose to almost 12.5 per cent in 1996, or $3.2 billion.

3 The GST does not apply to drugs. More generally, readers should note that current reviews of Bill C-91 may, among other outcomes, help to disentangle the several influences that are now acting on drug price increases.

4 A growing population indicates an increase in the number of patients. Although we do not measure effects directly, economic and social conditions over the past half decade suggest that the population-indicated change in patient numbers is probably an understated estimate. Finally, more recent data describing results in 1996 suggests stronger downsizing than we had earlier estimated for the year, and

recent provincial announcements indicate somewhat stronger restraint for 1997 and 1998 than initially thought. Restoration of funds to health care in Alberta are offset by recent announcements of stronger reductions in Ontario and indications of the same for Quebec.

5   A partial view of effects on queues and waiting times is available. See *Patients Waiting Longer for Medical Treatment* at http://fraserinstitute.ca/news/html#top, an abstract of *Waiting Your Turn* (6th edn), August 1996.

6   This at least suggests some constraints to cost cutters of altering forms of payment – moving physicians to a salaried basis. At a minimum, it does imply that 'serious' attention to the "facts" will be required. Further, one can easily infer from the discussion above that the "facts" are part of a complicated context in which occupational and institutional responsibilities are changing.

7   These spending flows understate the demand for major supplying industries. Three-quarters to four-fifths of the investment spending that is reported can be accounted for by the public hospital system. Since this system accounts for less than one-half of total health service delivery, this either suggests the other public and private elements of health care are under-capitalized, are not properly accounted for in the data, or that these elements of service delivery purchase capital services from other industries.

8   In this sense, the private producer refers to the delivery, not the financing.

9   Some care should be taken in interpreting Ontario's relatively large private system as a measure of capacity to deliver health services to the province's patient population. Included as producers in the sector will be headquarters of national standards, business and professional association, and advocacy organizations. These play a national, rather than provincial, role.

REFERENCES

Department of Finance. 1996. *Budget Plan*. Canada. 6 March.

Department of Finance. 1997. *Budget Plan*. Canada. 18 February.

Liberal Party of Canada. 1997. *Securing Our Future Together* (also referred to as Red Book II). Ottawa, April.

National Forum on Health. 1997. *Canada Health Action: Building on the Legacy*. Supply and Services Canada. Ottawa.

Oregon Progress Board. 1995. *Oregon Benchmarks*, Salem.

Sullivan T. 1998. Commentary on health care expenditures, social spending and health status. In: *National Forum on Health. Canada health action: building on the legacy*. Volume 4. *Striking a Balance: health care systems in Canada and elsewhere*. Sainte-Foy, Quebec: Mulitmodes, 346–364.

Wilkinson, Richard. 1993. Health, redistribution and growth (Andrew Glyn and David Miliband, eds), *Paying for Inequality*, London: IPPR/Rivers Oram Press.

13 Squeezing the balloon

The fallacy of demand modification

Gail Donner

Health care reform has become the 'buzzword' of the 1990s and recommendations for change are being proposed by consumers, providers and policy-makers alike. Health care reform is a complex concept, involving both structural and operational revisions to the system, and in its ideal form represents a change in the fundamental relationships among the stakeholders within the system. Although cost effectiveness is one, and only one, piece of reform, it has been the driver of most if not all of the changes proposed or implemented in jurisdictions in much of the industrialized world. Debt and deficit preoccupation has undoubtedly caused this determination to control health care costs which in Ontario, for example, represent roughly one-third of the provincial budget. The bulk of the activity in Canada and in North America has been focused on controlling costs through managing the supply side of the picture and in that way decreasing utilization. Thus, there is considerable attention directed at numbers and mix of providers, decreasing the numbers of hospitals and measuring the outcomes of various clinical interventions. As yet, the evidence is inconclusive as to the size of the effect that can be expected from this approach to controlling costs. What is clear, however, is that the public values Medicare in Canada and is wary and often angry at the prospect of its close-to-home services being reduced and even eliminated. The inability of policy-makers to balance public anger with reduction in costs has led them to consider demand management strategies directed to controlling and reducing the demand for services.

DEFINING THE ISSUES

The central feature of demand management is that its focus is on consumers and their health care and health seeking behaviours. It has been defined as the 'use of decision and self-management support systems to enable and encourage its consumers to make appropriate use of medical care' (Vickery and Lynch, 1995). Its goal is thus to direct consumers to the right health behaviours rather than simply discourage the wrong behaviours (Partridge, 1996). While the primary focus of demand management is on the *appropriate* use of services, obviously demand management can also be a tool used to decrease demand and thus decrease costs of all services, regardless of their appropriateness. That is why it is particularly appealing to policy-makers at this time. While it may have as its primary goal the appropriate use of the appropriate service in the appropriate place by the appropriate provider, the obvious risk is that the actual objective is to use demand management simply as a tool to reduce costs rather than as a strategy toward real reform: improving the health of populations. This has certainly been the case in the US where a variety of demand management strategies have been implemented to decrease utilization of expensive services and thereby decrease costs. In the US, demand management has become an increasingly significant part of managed care (Bell, 1996; Montrose, 1995; Vickery and Lynch, 1995). The strategies used include computerized health risk appraisals, patient education centres, nurse-telephone diagnosis and triage, and home health telemonitoring. These strategies are only beginning to appear in Canada in any significant way.

The reality of the 1990s is that provincial and federal finance ministers have driven health care policy through their cutbacks. These budgetary cuts have barely responded to the question of efficient allocation of health care resources. This chapter will argue that the current strategies for dealing with utilization do not by themselves adequately address the need for health reform. To accomplish *real* health reform, significant structural reform is required. Structural reform in this context takes place within an overall funding health care allocation (or budget) and involves shifting available health care resources (or supply) in the direction of providing the most efficient health care outcomes. In other words, structural change is very much evidence-based and operates within the given funding levels. Specifically, this chapter will address the question: How (if at all) can managing demand affect the utilization of services and what are the associated difficulties with the demand management approach?

It further describes the current pressures on the Canadian system and their relationship to the supply of and demand for services, the role education, as one aspect of demand management, has played in altering consumer and provider behaviours, and concludes with reflections on and recommendations for what will be required to create the necessary momentum for sustainable health care reform.

The central proposition of this chapter is that demand management alone cannot, nor should, be the only instrument to affect the appropriate allocation of health care resources. It argues that both demand and supply policy developments are needed, and that they should complement each other rather than work in opposition.

Let us be clear what we mean by demand management within the context of the health care sector. Unlike the typical private sector activity governed by market forces and fluctuating prices, both the supply and (indirectly) the demand for health care delivery are shaped very much by the public sector. At the national level, delivery and utilization are influenced by the Canada Health Act and the five principles of Medicare. Health care is a provincial legislative priority, and its delivery continues to be primarily influenced by provincial governments' priorities and budget constraints.

The supply side of the health care delivery picture, then, is very much determined by government policies and funding priorities, structural changes and new health care delivery technologies. The demand side, in contrast, is also determined by individuals seeking health care (demographic pressures such as the ageing population), but also by the system of supply. But supply and demand are not truly separate, other than in a very simple and misleading conceptual sense. It is well known that an increase in the supply of physicians will trigger an apparent increase in consumer demand, and hence an increase in utilization.

WHAT IS HEALTH CARE REFORM? AND WHAT IT IS NOT!

The two major and interdependent issues shaping the health care system in Canada today are fiscal pressures and health care reform. The fiscal pressures are clear and hard to avoid – the deficit, the debt, and health spending. Health care reform is less clear. Health care in Canada until the late 1980s was characterized by growth – in numbers and varieties of providers, in hospitals, in technology and in consumer knowledge and demand. But alongside that growth was also the remaining issue to be resolved from the introduction of Medicare in the 1960s – the development of system reforms to match the hospital and physician changes that were central to the introduction of a national health care plan.

Modern health care reform has its modern origin in the Lalonde Report (Lalonde, 1975), and in the many reports and commissions since then. A number of provincial commissions and federal policy papers, as well as World Health Organization activities (Evans, 1987; Gallant, 1989; Gouvernement du Quebec, 1990; Hyndman, 1989; McKelvey, 1989; Murray, 1990; National Forum on Health, 1997; Organization for Economic Cooperation and Development, 1990; Podborski, 1989; Spasoff, 1987; World Health Organization, 1984), pointed to the need for reform and outlined the basic requirements to enable the system to continue to be the 'jewel in the crown' of Canadian society.

Simply put, modern health care reform is marked by the change in public policy:

- from health care policy to healthy public policy;
- from equality of access to medical care to achieving equity of access to health;
- from health as an absence of disease to health as a resource for living;
- from a focus on treatment and cure to a focus on health promotion and disease prevention;
- from a provider driven to a consumer driven system;
- from institution-based care to community-based care;
- from centralized to decentralized decision-making and regionalization;
- from a series of independent institutions to a system of horizontally and vertically integrated delivery systems;

- from utilization driven to needs-based health services; and
- from expert opinion to evidence based practice.

In the 1990s the debt – the increasing deficit along with increasing unemployment and the seeming unwillingness of the voter to tolerate increased government spending – led to a sense of urgency about getting on with the job of introducing health care reform in Canada. As we approach the next millennium, we are faced with the competing interests between the need to focus on reform for the long term and the urgency of controlling costs in the short term, and thus, along with reform initiatives, have come a number of strategies at both the meso and macro levels that are directed at controlling spending. Table 13.1 describes how Canadians spend their dollars on health and health care. It is interesting to note that hospital and physician services account for over 55 per cent of public expenditures. Private spending has been growing faster than public spending, but public spending on drugs has been growing more rapidly than private spending. Although there has been greater growth in private expenditures in hospitals, this spending has been in the areas of upgraded accommodation and revenue from added services rather than from those deemed 'medically necessary' (National Forum on Health, 1997).

Some of the changes being proposed will lead to 'true' reform; however, most of them are directed towards the resolution of short-term problems. Some short-term strategies, hospital restructuring and re-engineering, mergers and closures have led to a downsizing of the numbers of beds in the system, a shortage of community based services and to increasing unemployment or underemployment among hospital workers. Reform is, in theory, a compre-

Table 13.1 Breakdown of health expenditures by financial source, 1975–1994

	1975			1994			Avg. annual compounded growth, 1975–94	
	Public $ million	Private $ million	Ratio $ million	Public $ million	Private $ million	Ratio	Public (%)	Private (%)
Hospitals	5,196	316	94:6	24,206	2,793	90:10	8.4	12.2
Other institutions	796	328	71:29	4,952	2,138	70:30	10.1	10.4
Physicians	1,813	27	99:1	10,222	100	99:1	9.5	7.1
Other professionals	135	766	15:85	847	5,346	14:86	10.1	10.8
Drugs	158	916	15:85	2,929	6,250	32:68	16.6	10.6
Other	1,264	540	70:30	8,905	3,773	70:30	10.8	10.8
Total	9,361	2,893	76:24	52,061	20,401	72:28	9.5	10.8

Source: National Health Expenditure in Canada, 1975–94.

Note: Numbers may not add up due to rounding.

hensive look at what kind of a system we want, along with a reasoned strategy to get there. Much of the activity in the 1990s has been only in part about that vision. The problem is that policy-makers wish to have the benefits of both reform and cost containment at the same time and that is probably impossible, at least in the short term. Much of the reform requires the redistribution of resources – both money and people. When those resources are redistributed solely to fight the deficit, change results but not necessarily health care reform.

UTILIZATION MANAGEMENT AND HEALTH CARE REFORM

The supply of health services in Canada have in the most part been determined by hospitals and physicians. The health care system in Canada is illness-based and physician-centred and the very existence of these services has been a major contributor to increased demand. The Canada Health Act itself was developed with a focus on hospital-based and 'medically necessary' services and did not anticipate that many services would be provided to ambulatory patients in the community rather than to hospitalized patients. The recently released report of the National Forum on Health (1997) states that the existing 'gap' in insured services, specifically the provision of drugs and home care, must be addressed if Medicare is to continue to be a vital part of Canadian public policy.

However, if the public were educated to develop healthy behaviours, to avoid using the system when it is not 'medically necessary', can we ensure that costs would be controlled? The short answer is a very qualified 'perhaps'. The consumer is only one of the players in the health care delivery game. Providers, i.e. health care professionals, the pharmaceutical industry and health care institutions are the other and significantly more powerful players. Education directed towards both consumer and providers as a form of modifying demand will have some effect on utilization; however, we cannot accomplish the goals of both reducing costs and improving and ensuring population health without significant structural reform.

EDUCATION: FOR WHOM AND FOR WHAT?

There are many examples in the health promotion and health services utilization literature that document the difficulties and lack of success in altering behaviour through education alone. Those activities include using education to alter consumer health behaviours (for example, smoking), as well as to alter use of services, as in the case of emergency room use. Those educational activities also occur with providers – for example, using physician education to alter their clinical behaviours and thus indirectly influence service utilization.

The Metropolitan Toronto District Health Council Hospital Restructuring Report (1995) summarized emergency room usage in Toronto as follows: 'Emergency services are an important component of the services provided by the acute care hospital system. More than 35 per cent of all admissions to hospitals are through emergency rooms (ERs) and public concern about access to acute care hospital services often focuses on quick access to an ER' (p. 60). The Report goes on to state that in a review of 1992 data from six hospitals, 1 per cent of Emergency room visits could be considered emergency, 21 per cent urgent and 78 per cent deferable. Other studies of Toronto teaching hospitals have identified that only 2.5 per cent of visits could be categorized as emergencies. These data are probably reflective of most Emergency room statistics across the country. There is other research that identifies the socio-demographic characteristics of frequent users, and the reasons people use ERs rather than primary care physicians is also well researched.

We know the size of the problem and the why of the problem; what we haven't been able to do is muster the political will to solve the problem. The question posed in the title of this chapter implies that the source of the problem is, at least in part, the consumer. Gill (1994) suggests that some types of non-urgent care, e.g. pap smear and immunization accessibility, may be more important than continuity for improving health outcomes. A recent Institute for Clinical Evaluative Sciences (ICES) study by Brown and Goel (1996) described a project in Ontario that used public education about caring for the common cold as a method to decrease visits to physicians.

THE LONDON PILOT

The pilot project was commissioned by the Ontario Ministry of Health to 'promote self-care and thereby reduce the number of visits to physicians' (Brown and Goel, 1996: 835). The project was one of the requirements of an agreement between the Ontario Medical Association and the Ministry of Health. Educating the public about how to treat the common cold as a method of reducing office visits is a more palatable method for decreasing utilization than strategies such as user fees and privatization, thus the project seemed a reasonable one.

The project was conducted in a representative Ontario city with a population of about 300,000 people. The intervention was the delivery of a pamphlet of self-care to each household in the city. The pamphlet was developed and assessed by consumer and provider focus groups and the campaign was announced in the local press, on radio and through special community events. Billings of physicians in the city for the two months after the campaign were compared with billings of physicians during the two months before the start of the campaign and during the same periods two years earlier. Physicians elsewhere in Ontario were the control group. Ontario Health Insurance Plan payments data were used for the study. Regrettably, evaluation of the campaign was not planned until after the project had been designed and implemented. Thus the researchers were not involved in constructing the project. Another significant limitation in the study was that the cold season arrived much earlier in the study period than it had two years earlier, thus billings differed in the two periods. Although there was a small reduction in visit billings attached to colds and flu compared to the rest of Ontario, there were a number of study limitations that made the results less than conclusive. The data themselves prevented comprehensive statistical analyses and made it impossible for the investigators to calculate population-based rates or differences in age and sex of populations. As well, physicians' variation in diagnostic coding presented another difficulty. It is clear that some of the problems in the study could have been avoided if the evaluation had been part of the original study design. 'Ideally, a community trial would have been desirable for assessing this intervention' (Brown and Goel, 1996: 838). The authors of the study suggest strategies supported by the literature that could be used to strengthen public education programs. These strategies include using endorsements through personal explanation and telephone advice by groups familiar to the public. They also point out the importance of physician support for education campaigns. Physicians must believe that these strategies are in the best interest of good medical care.

This study is of interest for a number of reasons. It identifies not only the need for research in the effects of public education but also advises as to the design of such research. It also implies the need for education of both consumers and providers. While educating consumers may modify demand, providers also must be educated as to the variety of strategies that exist that could be used to supplement (or even replace) medical care in order to decrease costs. There are other system complications. It may be that in a fee-for-service system, a decrease in physician visits that results in a decrease in physician incomes would not be a strategy physicians would warmly embrace. In Canada with its essentially fixed cap system, attempts to alter demand result in substitutions rather than cost reductions. The challenge is to ensure that the substitutions do not result in less effective care, but rather that they allow demand to be met within the existing cost framework – that is, that although the balloon is being squeezed it does not break, only its shape is altered.

Smith and McNamara (1988) studied the use of paediatric ERs for weekday emergencies to understand the factors that motivate people to use ERs rather than paediatricians' offices. Their findings demonstrate that a substantial proportion of the children seen for minor illnesses have either no paediatric provider or have limited access to that provider. For those who did have providers, economic factors, parental knowledge, provider/parent communication, and transportation were reasons cited for use of the ER. These and other studies do identify a number (albeit a small number) of methods that could work to change consumer behaviour. These methods would involve better teaching as part of the provider/consumer relationship, massive public education relating to alternatives and their effectiveness, to say nothing of significant incentives and disincentives within the system itself. Although the study was conducted in the US, where access is a problem for many, the lessons learned are similar to those reflected in the Goel and Brown study.

PATIENT AND PUBLIC EDUCATION

Just as with supply management strategies, there is little conclusive and comprehensive evidence as to the cost reductions achieved by these strategies. That being said, there are of course other reasons that education should be pursued as part of health care reform rather than purely as part of cost reduction. The most important reason is that increasing public education has a potential empowering effect on consumers and could increase their participation in strengthening the effectiveness and appropriateness of their care. Empowerment means giving people both the opportunity and capability to participate in decisions that affect programming, policy and physical environments. Participation in community governance structures and institutions is an effective mechanism through which individuals and communities may gain greater control over their life conditions. (Spassof, 1987).

As patient satisfaction has become an important variable in measuring outcomes of care, so might it be a measure of the value of involving consumers in their care. Public education may also affect the decision-making capacity of consumers – both in terms of quality and frequency – and the influence on consumer decision-making and outcomes is another area to be pursued. Participation by consumers on boards and committees, education of young people related to health-promoting behaviours and easier access to information are all parts of an empowerment strategy. It is clear that the system has primarily been using 'downstream endeavors' (McKinlay, 1979), i.e. short-term individual-based interventions, and that they must be replaced by 'upstream activities that . . . focus on modifying economic, political, and environmental factors that have been shown to be the precursors of poor health throughout the world' (Butterfield, 1990: 2). The provision of incentives to keep people well, the integration of housing, transportation, environmental and fiscal policies as part of healthy public policy and a system reorientation towards what constitutes health policy would constitute a beginning to real reform at a system level. Unless policy-makers are willing to ask themselves, 'What would the impact of this policy be on the health of Canadians', at every policy decision, we will be continuing to try to rescue people at the bottom of the river rather than preventing them from getting into the water upstream. It is not individual members of society who are causing the escalating costs and the focus on illness and treatment, it is the reluctance of those in power to make the necessary changes to the way we 'do business' in delivering health services.

IN SEARCH OF THE MAGIC BULLET

Trying to use education to alter physician clinical behaviour (and thus indirectly utilization of services) seems to be equally difficult. A recent review of over a hundred trials of intervention to alter physician practice (Oxman, *et al.*, 1995: 1427) concludes that 'There are no "magic bullets" for improving the quality of health care.' They did find that there were interventions available that if used in appropriate combination could lead to better care. Some of the interventions improved provider performance; health outcomes were improved to a lesser degree. Again, there were many limitations in the studies they reviewed and in their own analysis. Of course that begs the question, why, when we pay lip service to the importance of 'knowing' and evidence-based practice, do we have so little good research to assist us? The difficulty of conducting this kind of research and the lack of available research when we need it may be part of the impetus to look to the consumer as the source of the problem of utilization. The more recent focus on determining practice guide-lines, providing health organization/hospital report cards is a significant and hopeful beginning to address the supply and demand side of the issue.

What all of this tells us is that there is little real knowledge and evidence about how education changes behaviour except that it is more complex than it might at first seem. More research in this area is absolutely essential, and here a cautionary note seems indicated. There is presently a determined effort to provide more and better research to guide clinical practice. Through the Institute of Clinical Evaluative Sciences (ICES), or other initiatives, researchers are able to let providers know what makes a difference so that they can take this evidence and alter their behaviour. Two things seem to be happening with that body of research. First, it is being made available to physicians, those in practice and those in training, to guide them in their practice. Second, it is being used by policy-makers to guide policy. Changing behaviour in the interests of contributing to population health and to healthy public policy is more complex than taking clinical outcomes research and applying it like a band-aid to an open wound. What is needed is concurrent broad policy research to ensure that the infrastructure exists to sustain these changes.

The particular outcome of a particular intervention may be known, but the understanding of its effects on the rest of the system may not have been adequately known or addressed. For example, the dramatic decrease in length of stay has created a problem with drug utilization in that in-patient drugs are covered through the Canada Health Act as part of the *medically necessary* care; however, once a patient is discharged the consumer (or the private drug plans where they exist) picks up those costs. Thus, we are at great risk of ignoring its relevance if we see cost control as a method of health care reform.

COST CONTROL IS NOT HEALTH CARE REFORM

The simple answer to the question of 'Can modifying demand affect utilization and thus reduce costs?' is probably, 'to some extent'. However, that is not the most important question, nor is it the answer to real reform in a capped global budget where it is likely to result in 'squeezing the balloon' and reducing the use of some services to some people while increasing services to others. The more important question may be, 'How must the health system be structured in order to maximize population health in a cost-effective manner?' The answer in a fixed cap system lies in substitution towards more cost-effective services while not jeopardizing the health status of the population. The goal must be changed from one that focuses on decreasing costs and utilization to achieving the twin objectives of improving the health of populations and moving from changing health care to implementing healthy public policy. This can only be accomplished if substantial structural reform to the system is undertaken before (or at least concurrently with) cost reduction strategies – whether on the supply side, the demand side, or both. Without this more substantive change, we will continually be fighting the supply and demand issues and continually looking for ways to control costs rather than ensure a healthy population. Again, some of the examples of education at the individual consumer, individual provider and system levels can guide the thinking here.

Some might argue that setting spending targets is a very effective way in which to manage the system; however, unless there is a vision and well articulated consensus on what constitutes health and health care in Canada, financial targets too easily become the dartboard at which critics take aim. The focus of attention should be on the kind of system we want and then the costs can be determined.

Smoking cessation programs, television ads, tough talks with authority figures (teachers, physicians, etc.) have done little to alter the health behaviour of individuals. Young people are smoking, middle aged people are smoking and old people are smoking and everyone knows that smoking is bad. What we do know, however, is that there are policy changes that can influence health behaviours. The increase in sales taxes on tobacco products did change behaviour, limited access to tobacco does limit adolescents smoking behaviours, brown wrappers, no advertising, the list goes on. If we make it harder to do a thing, people don't do it as easily. That is the real demand and supply reality – in health care and health practices as well as in other arenas.

Talking to and at people about their inappropriate use of emergency rooms will do nothing to change their behaviour, but providing alternatives will. Access to care, close enough to home, within the system, and with less 'hassle' than emergency rooms and equal outcomes in terms of customer satisfaction and good health are all important reform objectives. The Metropolitan Toronto District Health Council report process revealed that people who go to ERs go there because they 'need' to go there to get care, because they have no other place to get that care. Thus, when determining the size of the system, and the number of ERs, access for the same number of people in the post-restructuring system as in the current system had to be ensured. The simple fact is that there is currently no system in place that provides care in a comprehensive, accessible and publicly funded responsible way to replace the ERs in Toronto (and in other jurisdictions as well).

THE PATH TO REFORM

The development of integrated delivery system with a system of primary care at its centre, the more appropriate use of the variety of providers, and a change in physician remuneration as principal components of that system is a requirement for a truly *reformed* system (Decter, 1994; Health Services Restructuring Commission, 1997; Hospital Management Research Unit, 1996; Leatt *et al.*, 1996; Rachlis and Kushner, 1994) For primarily historical reasons (how Medicare was introduced, the focus on hospital and physicians and the limitations of legislation among others) the health care delivery system is focused primarily on the delivery of acute care in hospitals, with primary care being delivered mainly through independent physician entrepreneurs. The system is open ended, the incentive is to see and treat patients and the 'piece-work' nature of the work encourages attention to illness – by both the provider and the patient – rather than a focus on maintaining health, keeping out of hospital and even taking responsibility for one's own health. It is through a significant restructuring of primary care that we will achieve some of the individual behavioural changes as well as the broader reforms required.

It is clear that there is no comprehensive health human resource planning framework in Canada or in any of the provinces. What attention there has been to this important area has centred on physician requirements. The time for a comprehensive needs-based planning approach to health human resources has come (Turner *et al.*, 1993). Health human resource planning that determines local, provincial and national levels, and the need for the services of the range of health care providers is another key part of the structural reform required, based on an assessment of the health of the population and the project need for services.

As long as the centre of the health care delivery system is hospitals, public demand for and utilization of expensive and illness-focused care will continue. The current system of health/illness care has been the most influential *educator* of the public. Until the focus of the health care delivery system is changed, it is unlikely that the public's behaviour will change. As long as the incentives for utilization on both the consumer side (ERs instead of Community Health Centres for example) and physicians (fee for service instead of salary) favour the expensive and illness focused behaviours, we will not alter utilization. In fact, we will create an even more frustrated consumer, provider and policy-maker.

THREE PIECES OF THE PUZZLE

The solution rests on three key pieces: integrated delivery systems, substitution of non-physician providers and changes in physician remuneration practices.

Integrated delivery systems have been best described as 'a network of organizations that provides or arranges to provide a coordinated continuum of services to a defined population and is willing to be held clinically and fiscally accountable for the outcomes and the health status of the populations served' (Shortell *et al.*, 1993: 447). Integrated delivery systems (IDS) are characterized by both functional integration (coordinated support functions) and clinical integration (coordinated patient care functions). In an integrated delivery system of care, populations (usually in geographically defined regions) are provided with care, from prevention through to palliation, in a coordinated and integrated manner with accountability back to the community. Whether or not Canadian jurisdictions adopt the integrated delivery system model as it is currently being proposed, clearly, the objectives of IDS help guide the reform agenda. Without coordinated human resource planning as a part of integrated delivery systems, however, it will not be possible to achieve the objectives of healthier populations and greater fiscal accountability. Achieving these object-ives will demand considerable political will, since it is unlikely to be accom-plished without the risk of physician 'unemployment'. As long as hospitals and public dependence on hospitals and physicians remain at the centre of the system, reform cannot be achieved; instead merely cost containment and control will continue.

Coordinated health human resource planning means rationalizing of provi-ders and substitutions both 'up' and 'down' the hierarchy. The second compon-ent of structural reform is the substitution in the use of non-physician providers as part of the transformation from a loose arrangement of indepen-dent providers to a system of primary care. Without this substitution, the balloon will surely burst. Research both in Canada and in other jurisdictions has provided enough evidence related to positive outcomes in areas of quality of care, patient satisfaction and effectiveness to warrant the introduction of Nurse Practitioners in Canada (Mitchell et al., 1993) to substitute for physi-cians in a number of areas, beginning with under-serviced areas. The recent proclamation of legislation in Ontario (and earlier similar legislation in Alberta) to expand the independent acts which Nurse Practitioners may per-form will enable these providers to work collaboratively with physicians and to substitute for physicians in primary care (Ministry of Health, 30 April 1997). Midwives are also gradually being introduced across the country. We can expect to see a wider range of providers delivering care in the future. Research that evaluates the influence of those providers on client outcomes, both in terms of health and attitude towards non-physician providers, as well as their impact on costs, must become a priority.

The third requirement for real reform is the replacement of the current physician fee-for-service system to a capitation system for primary care physi-cians and further consideration of the most appropriate payment mechanisms for specialists and sub-specialists (Hospital Management Research Unit, 1996). While at this point there is no conclusive evidence of the cost savings from this system, it has been the opinion of leaders and scholars in the field that it is the major change required to refocus the system on health needs rather than mere service volume. As long as there is a group of providers who are permitted to act as entrepreneurs in a publicly funded and capped system, the distortion in the redistribution of both dollars and services will continue to be a serious problem.

These changes are obviously very difficult ones. They are, however, the necessary requirements for true health reform. While the fiscal demands necessitate immediate attention to controlling and reducing costs of health care, those objectives will not necessarily be achieved without costs to the public's health unless the reform initiatives are also implemented. Without structural reform, without attention to the needs of the population and the role healthy public policy plays in health, health care delivery in Canada will continue to be dominated by 'brand of the month' solutions. Providers will continually be blamed for their ineffective practices and and the consumer will continue to be identified as the perpetrator, rather than the victim of unnecessary or inappropriate use of the system.

Structural reform is the key to improving Canada's health care system. Structural reform requires changes both on the demand side (squeeze the balloon) and the supply side (expand the balloon, change the inputs). The fact that supply and demand are so interrelated and that public sector finances affect both supply and demand, makes the task difficult and challenging – but not impossible! The goal of structural reform in health care delivery is certainly achievable.

NOTE

1   For a thorough review of reports and commissions on the subject, see Mhatre, and Deber (1992). From equal access to health care to equitable access to health, see 'A review of Canadian provincial health commissions and reports', *International Journal of Health Services* 22 (4): 645–668. The reports from the National Forum on Health also provide overview material.

REFERENCES

Bell, William H. 1996. Telephone-based demand management: What you need to know now. *Health Care Strategic Management*, February: 6–8.

Brown, E. M. and V. Goel 1996. Reducing demand for physician visits through public education: A look at the pilot cold-and-flu campaign in London, Ontario. *Canadian Medical Association Journal*, 154 (6): 835–840.

Butterfield, Patricia G. 1990. Thinking upstream: Nurturing a conceptual understanding of the societal context of health behavior. *Advances in Nursing Science* 12 (2): 1–8.

Decter, M. B. 1994. *Healing Medicare: Managing health system change the Canadian way.* Toronto: McGilligan Books.

Evans, J. R. (chair). 1987. *Toward a shared direction for health in Ontario: report of the Ontario health review panel.* Toronto: Ontario Ministry of Health.

Gallant, J. C. (chair). 1989. *The report of the Nova Scotia Royal Commission on Health Care: toward a new strategy.* Nova Scotia.

Gill, J. M. 1994. Non-urgent use of the emergency department: Appropriate or not? *Annals of Emergency Medicine* 24 (5): 953–957.

258   *G. Donner*

Gouvernment du Quebec. 1990. *A reform centred on the citizen*. Quebec City: Ministry of Health and Social Services.

Health Services Restructuring Commission. 1997. *A vision of Ontario's health services system*. Toronto: HSRC.

Hospital Management Research Unit. 1996. *Integrated delivery systems: providing a continuum of health care. A working paper*. Toronto: HMRU.

Hyndman, L. (chair). 1991. *The rainbow report: our vision for health*. Vols I–III. Edmonton, Alberta: Premier's Commission on Further Health Care for Albertans.

Lalonde, M. 1975. *A new perspective on the health of Canadians*. Ottawa: Information Canada.

Leatt, P., G. H. Pink, and C. D. Naylor, 1996. Integrated delivery systems: Has their time come in Canada? *Canadian Medical Association Journal* 154 (6): 803–809.

McKelvey, E. N. (chair). 1989. *Report of the Commission on Selected Health Care Programs*. New Brunswick.

McKinlay, J. B. 1979. A case for refocusing upstream: the political economy of illness. In E. G. Jaco (ed.) *Patients, physicians, and illness*. 3rd edition. New York: Free Press, 9–25.

Metropolitan District Health Council. 1995. *Directions for change: Toward a coordinated hospital system for Metro Toronto*. Toronto.

Mhaitre, S. L. and R. B. Deber, 1992. From equal access to health care to equitable access to health: a review of Canadian provicial health commissions and reports. *International Journal of Health Services* 22 (4): 645–668.

Mitchell, A., J., Pinelli, C. Patterson, and D. Southwell, 1993. *Utilization of nurse practitioners in Ontario*. Discussion paper prepared for the Ontario Ministry of Health. Hamilton, Ontario: Quality of Nursing Worklife Research Unit, Working Paper 93–4.

Montrose, G. 1995. Demand management may help stem costs. *Health Management Technology*, 16 (2): 18–21.

Murray, R. G. (chair). 1990. *Future directions for health care in Saskatchewan*. Regina: Saskatchewan Commission on Directions in Health Care.

National Forum on Health. 1997. *Canada health action: building on the legacy*. Ottawa: National Forum on Health.

Organization for Economic Cooperation and Development. 1990. *Health care systems in transition: the search for efficiency*. Paris: OECD.

Oxman, A. D., M. A., Thomson, D. A. Davis, and B. Haynes, 1995. No magic bullets: A systematic review of 102 trials of interventions to improve professional practice. *Canadian Medical Association Journal* 153 (10): 1423–1431.

Partridge, P. 1996. Demand management moving to forefront. *Health Care Strategic Management*, April: 14–16.

Podborski, S. 1987. *Health promotion matters in Ontario: Report of the Minister's Advisory Group on health promotion*. Toronto: Ministry of Health of Ontario.

Rachlis, M. and C. Kushner, 1994. *Strong medicine*. Toronto: HarperCollins.

Shortell, S. *et al.*, 1993. Creating organized delivery systems: The barriers and facilitators. *Hospital and Health Services Administration*, Winter: 447–466.

Smith, R. D. and McNamara, J. J. 1988. Why not your pediatrician's office? A study of weekday pediatric emergency department use for minor illness care in a community hospital. *Pediatric Emergency Care* 4 (2): 107–111.

Spassof, R. (chair). 1987. *Health for all Ontario: report of the panel on health goals for Ontario*. Toronto: Ontario Ministry of Health.

Turner, L. A., T. Ostbye, and L. L. Pederson, 1993. Workforce planning in the 90s. Part I: Efficiency, economy and political will – the need for a new approach. *Management FORUM* 6 (1): 34–40.

Vickery, D. M. and W. D. Lynch, 1995. Demand management: Enabling patients to use medical care appropriately. *Journal of Occupational and Environmental Medicine* 37 (5): 551–557.

World Health Organization. 1984. *Health promotion: a discussion document on the concept and principles*. Copenhagen: WHO Regional Office for Europe.

14 The rage for reform

Sense and nonsense in health policy[1]

Ted Marmor

The perspectives of foreign commentators on the issues and public choices of another nation are much more problematic than the usual citation of the brilliant (but rare) example. For every de Tocqueville there is some number of superficial commentators whose observations are best ignored. Even the truly useful reflections can be annoying if presented with unvarnished certitude. The sensible posture of the cross-national commentator, then, would appear to be restrained certitude.

My certitudes, such as they are, fall into three categories. The first can be described as preventive – Canadian protection against what Robert Evans more than once described as 'intellectual acid rain'.[2] Commentary about Canadian health care and those of the United States come – sometimes profusely – from media and professional channels south of the border and through that channel enter Canadian health politics. The second argument is that the increased cross-national diffusion of health care commentary extends far beyond North America and calls for different kinds of interpretation, learning, and protection. The analysts of health care are awash in flows of information – from similar societies, very different societies, and made-up societies. There is no escaping some influence from these sources, thus raising the question of what form of international commentary would be useful in the Canadian context. The third set of reactions have to do with the particular features of this book's focus on recent developments in Canadian health debate and policy.

FACT AND FICTION IN THE US DEBATE OVER HEALTH CARE REFORM: SHOULD CANADIANS CARE?

There was during 1993–94, as few Canadians will have failed to note, a momentous and contentious public debate about health reform in the United States. President Clinton ran for his office partly on the promise of 'comprehensive' health reform; he made a number of major, widely noticed addresses on the subject; and the failure of his proposal in the fall of 1994 stimulated an industry of blaming. The whole period was marked by a media circus of speculation, half-baked commentary and downright mythmaking – some of it about Canadian Medicare.[3]

Canadians might well regard this excited US debate – and the aftermath of blame and substantial private sector change in American medicine – as irrelevant. After all, the fate of Canadian Medicare in the early 1990s – amidst the worst recession in years – provided more than enough to worry about. Federal and provincial elections continue to raise the spectre of user charges, an issue that, like a zombie, refuses to die. A number of provinces had royal commissions in the late 1980s and early 1990s to review Canada's federal/provincial form of universal health insurance. What is more, since 1994, US attention has not centred on the merits or demerits of Canada's Medicare, but rather on the enormous changes taking place in the financing and delivery of medical care in the wake of President Clinton's failed reform. So there might appear to be a case for judicious ignoring of commentary from the United States.

None the less, for Canadians to ignore American health care debates would be a mistake, a serious one. In recent years, and particularly between 1989 and 1992, Canadian public health insurance again figured prominently in American health care debates. But the truth about Canadian Medicare could not possibly have been extracted from the mix of myths and misleading interpretations that special interest groups regularly disseminated and to which the media – especially television – gave considerable expression.[4] The problem is that the truth about any major program is complicated. Moreover, the US health care and insurance pressure groups have little interest in the truth, and the media is not capable of conveying complexity. The result has been (and still is) constant US distortion of Canada's experience with public health insurance.

But, so what, you might ask? Why should Canadians worry about US distortion of their experience? The reasons that are compelling are many. First, the media market is North American and the US media reaches most Canadian homes. That means US commentary on health care is far more prevalent in Canada than Canadian commentary is in the United States. And, as a result, when mythmakers claim Canada's Medicare is as expensive as the United States' 'non-system', the myth attacks the faith of Canadians that they have found a decent balance among cost, quality, and access to health care. That is precisely what the Health Insurance Association of America claimed during the early 1990s, mounting a vigorous campaign to tell the world that Canada had not found an answer to medical inflation.

The second myth concerns the connection regularly made between 'price controls' and the rationing of medical care. Canadians will have heard plenty already from many sources of traditional economic thought that price controls always lead to rationing and that simply must be bad policy. President Clinton, for one, repeated this claim when he decided against such controls on the drug industry in his Health Security bill. But the problem is that some health care interests in Canada – and not only the drug industry – will use this language of micro-economic theology to attack Medicare's economic controls. The repetition of stories about Canadian waiting lists – already a feature of Canadian journalism – have ready amplifiers south of the border. And one of the main amplifiers in recent years was the President of the United States, a source of citation in the television and print media that surely reached the majority of Canadian homes. (This is not to suggest that reaching Canadian homes is equivalent to persuasion. Rather, as with all marketing, repetition of a message has an impact quite independently of its truth value.)

Third, there is the persistent mythmaking – magnified in the wake of the 1994 US elections – about the certain failure of 'government regulation'. Nations cannot sensibly regulate professionals, firms, unions – indeed anything – according to Republican propagandists south of the border. Clinton's new Democrats, bent on 'reinventing government', have regularly employed the same government-bashing that Ronald Reagan made popular, that many Canadian politicians have used in recent years, and that Newt Gingrich has turned into a secular sermon. If a nation cannot regulate health care sensibly it must rely on the fabled market to control costs and distribute access – right? Wrong! – but that will not stop the endless claims of ineffective and inefficient government regulation from ideological zealots of the market.

Related is the more general argument that one of the worst problems of modern life is the complexity of public bureaucracies and that Canada's Medicare and the US's program by the same name are good illustrations. In fact, Canadian Medicare is by any comparative standard straightforward – for patients, for doctors, for hospitals, and for regulators. But one would not know that from the most widely disseminated publicized US commentary on government medicine – what used to be known as 'socialized medicine'. Younger Americans – without experience of the national Medicare program for the aged and disabled and no knowledge at all of Canadian Medicare – are the target audience. And the rich coffers of American pressure groups – the health insurers, the American Medical Association, the National Association of Manufacturers – have provided ample funds to repeat this message. As a result, no Canadian discussion of Medicare's future will be fully free of this cant. Put another way, Canadians should beware of government-bashing south of the border on health care matters in addition to the similar claims at home.

Finally, there is the more insidious effects of insistence, regularly expressed in US health policy debates, that the quality of medical care is the key to improving a nation's health. Any limit on technology, any restraint on drug firm profits, any fee schedule for doctors – all will supposedly ruin the quality of the US's health care. Those willing to challenge that presumption are hard pressed to gain access to the media. As Canada continuously struggles to control its health care budgets – whether amidst recession or growth – it will have to face up to the lessons of cross-national experience with methods of improving the health of populations.

As Japan learned in the post-war period while becoming the healthiest population in the world, medical care (and its quality) is significant, but not the most important factor. At the end of the twentieth century, fewer Japanese babies die and their older citizens live longer than those of any other country. Yet Japanese medical care does not provide the explanation for that extraordinary development over the past fifty years. Economic growth, a seemingly fair distribution of income, social stability and a host of other factors are far more important. No North American would marvel at Japanese medical care (though it is widely available). But all of us should marvel at Japan's climb to the top of the league tables in measures of healthiness. No Canadian will learn such lessons from the United States.[5]

There are other myths that cross the Canadian border regularly, including more recently the notion that the management skills of for-profit firms would right Medicare's troubles. But the most important point to this outsider is truly simple: Medicare is Canada's post-war public miracle. It is an example of success in bringing access to decent care to most of the population and at a price that, while comparatively high, is 40 per cent less than the US pays per capita for its very uneven system. The necessary consequence of Canada's structure of finance and expenditure – paying for medical care from a single provincial budget where other competitors for public dollars help restrain the voracious appetite of modern medicine for funds – is controversy about how much to spend, on what, and for whom. If the world were just, there would be an effluent tax on nonsense spread over the airwaves. Or, as, to rephrase Robert Evans again, much of American health care commentary is like 'intellectual acid rain', polluting those on whom it falls.

AN INTERNATIONAL PERSPECTIVE: BENEFITS AND CAUTIONS

Canadian health policy discussions might also benefit substantially from more cross-national discussion – whether parallel portraits of Canada and comparable industrial democracies, presentations of the place of Canada in broader worldwide studies, or simply the observations about Canadian Medicare from the reasonably well-informed outsider. Why this conclusion, one might well ask, in light of the sceptical views just presented about commentary from the United States. My answer is this. After reviewing many of the provincial reports on Medicare over the past five years, I am convinced that the diagnosis of Medicare as troubled and threatened is quite distorted. I am almost certain of the former contention (Medicare as troubled) and only slightly less so about the latter (Medicare as threatened). The distortions of much US commentary is undeniable and is worth protecting against. But the more outside experts examined Canadian Medicare, the more their commentary would bolster the program's principles, practices, and backers.[6] It is worth noting that, for most of its history, Medicare has been an enormous source of pride for Canadians, hardly needing outsiders to bolster its place in Canadian national life. But the twin impact of economic misery and constitutional strife in recent years has been severe; fearfulness appears more widespread than pride or confidence in Canadian institutions of any sort.

There is an additional irony in my making this argument. In other contexts I have written about the contemporary danger of cross-national miscommunication concerning health care systems. Let me first explain what danger I have in mind so as to set the full context for my appeal for incorporating more cross-national comparisons into contemporary Medicare debates.

No analyst of health care, as Rudolf Klein rightly noted in discussing cross-national comparisons in health care, can escape the 'bombardment of information about what is happening in other countries'. Yet there is an extraordinary imbalance between the speed and magnitude of the information flows and the capacity to learn useful lessons from them. Indeed, the speed of communication *about* developments abroad actually has reduced the likelihood of reliable cross-national learning.[7] Why might that be so and what does that suggest about more promising forms of international intellectual exchange?

The political setting: health reforms everywhere on the public agenda

There is little doubt about the salience of health policy[8] on the public agenda of most industrial democracies. Canada's form of universal health insurance, while a model of achievement for many observers and the destination of many policy travellers in search of illumination, has been and is the object of provincial and national government hand wringing. The United States, as noted above, has been an obvious recent example of medical care worries rising to the top of the public agenda. For most of 1994, only the legal troubles of O.J. Simpson could dominate health reform for the attention of the media, with the ubiquitous CNN ensuring that the world would know something about both topics.[9] (And since then, the growth of chains of hospitals, the expansion of nationwide firms calling themselves health maintenance organizations, and contentious disputes about health insurance coverage have replaced 'health reform' in the media's agenda.)

In Holland, vigorous disputes about policy change are on-going and the degree of interest is, at least in the United States, unprecedented in its level if not comprehension. One could obviously go on with examples of health policy controversies in Germany (burdened by the fiscal pressures of unification), in Great Britain (competing with the scandals in the Major government), in Sweden (with fiscal and unemployment pressures of enormous force), and so on.

The politics of cross-national claims: timing, use and misuse

The puzzle is not whether there is such widespread interest in health policy, but why now, indeed why throughout the 1990s. And why has international evidence (arguments, claims, caricatures) seemed more prominent in this round of 'reform' than, say, during the fiscal strains of the 1970s or the tribulations of the 1980s? What can be usefully said not only about the substance of the experience of different nations, but about the political processes of introducing and acting upon policy change? Let me raise these issues directly.

Why Now?

There is a simple answer to this question that one hopes is not simple minded. Health policy came everywhere to the forefront of public agendas for one or more of the following reasons. First, the financing of personal medical care has everywhere become a major financial component of the budgets[10] of welfare states and, when fiscal strain arises – especially from prolonged recession, policy scrutiny (not simply incremental budgeting) – is the predictable result. Second, mature welfare states, as Rudolf Klein argued in the late 1980s,[11] under almost all circumstances come to have less capacity for bold fiscal expansion into new areas. This means managing existing programs (in new ways perhaps, but in changing economic circumstances) necessarily assumes a larger share of the public agenda. Third, there is what might be termed the wearing out (perhaps wearing down) of the post-war consensus about the welfare state – the effects of more than two decades of fretfulness about the affordability, desirability, and governability of the welfare state.[12] All of these forces have been at work in Canada. Little of the discussion in this volume emphasizes – or even notes – that truth.

Begun in earnest during the 1973–74 oil shock, sustained by stagflation, and bolstered by electoral victories (or advance) of parties opposed to welfare state expansion, critics assumed a bolder posture and mass publics came increasingly to hear challenges to programs that had for decades seemed sacrosanct.[13] From Mulroney to Thatcher, from New Zealand to The Netherlands, the message of necessary change was heard. Accordingly, when economic strain reappeared, the inner rim of programmatic protection – not interest group commitment, but social faith – was weaker and the incentives to explore transformative but not fiscally burdensome options became relatively stronger. That helps to explain the international pattern of welfare state review – including health policy – since the mid-1980s. And it is reflected in the fearful tone of so much writing about contemporary social policy, health policy included.

Even accepting this contention, there still remains the question of why there has been such increased attention in these reviews to other national experiences. (The turning to American experience – especially fashionable ideas about managing health institutions – is particularly puzzling. After all, as laggards on coverage and cost control, the United States might have tried to learn relevant lessons from others, but did not. What the US's experience can offer as a model remains a mystery.)

Consider the following interpretation of increased cross-national commentary in health care, one that arises from my own experience just noted. Times of policy change sharply increase the demand for new ideas – or at least new means to old ends. Just as many have turned to Canada's example of universal health insurance, so Canadian, German, Dutch, and other intellectual entrepreneurs turned internationally in recent years. One sees why in the interests reported and expectations cited by participants in international conferences. Conferees are typically interested in getting better policy answers to the problems they face at home: how, for example, to find a balance between 'solidarity and subsidiarity', how to maintain a 'high quality health system in times of economic stress', even an optimistic interest in 'what are the optimum relations between patients, insurers, providers, and the government'.[14] Understood as simply wanting to stretch one's mind – to explore what's possible conceptually, or what others have managed to achieve – this is unexceptionable. Understood as the pursuit of the best model, absent further exploration of the political, social, and economic context required for implementation, this is wishful thinking.

Many international conferees see the opportunity for an informational version of this intellectual mind-stretching: quests for exchange of 'policy information' of various sorts without commitment to policy importation, 'exchanging views with kindred spirits', and explicit calls for stimulation (as with the hope for 'specific initiatives (from other countries) to generate thoughts about [for example] Canada's system'). All of this is the learning anthropologists have long extolled – understanding the range of possibility and seeing one's own circumstances more clearly by contrast.

But what about drawing policy lessons from such exercises? What are the rules of defensible conduct here? The truth is that, whatever the appearances, most domestic policy debates in most countries are (and will remain) parochial affairs. They address national problems, they emphasize historical and contemporary national developments in the particular domain (pensions, medical finance, transportation), and embody conflicting visions of what policies the particular country should adopt. Only rarely are the experiences of other nations – and the lessons they embody – seriously investigated and thoughtfully considered. (Japan is the exception that supports the rule.)

When cross-national experiences are employed in parochial struggles, their use is typically that of policy warfare, not policy understanding and careful lesson-drawing. And, one must add, there are fewer knowledgeable critics at home of ideas about 'solutions' abroad, a further inducement to the casual invocation of cross-national 'lessons'. (In the world of American medical debate, the misuse of British and Canadian experience surely illustrates this point. The National Health Service was from the late 1940s to the late 1970s the spectre of what 'government medicine' and 'rationing' could mean. In recent years, myth-making about Canada has dominated the distortion league tables in North America.[15])

The reasons are almost too obvious to cite. Policy-makers are busy with day-to-day pressures. Practical concerns incline them, if they take the time for comparative inquiry, to pay more attention to what appears to work, not academic reasons for what is and is not transferable and why. Policy debaters – whether politicians, policy analysts or interest group figures – are in struggles, not seminars. Like lawyers, they seek victory, not illumination. For that purpose, compelling stories, whether well-substantiated or not, are more useful than careful conclusions. Interest groups, as their label suggests, have material and symbolic stakes in policy outcomes, not reputations for intellectual precision to protect.[16] None of these considerations are new – or surprising. But the increased flow of cross-national claims in health policy generates new reasons to reconsider the meaning and constraints of cross-national policy learning. It means as well that one must simultaneously applaud sensible cross-national work while remaining on the lookout for hype and hyperbole passing across borders.

There is, in addition, a sharp distinction between learning about and learning from cross-national experience. If the point of comparison is to draw instrumental lessons (learning from), there is no difference in the intellectual requirements between substantive and procedural lesson-drawing. The argument, elaborated elsewhere, is this. There are two possible bases for drawing strong policy lessons from the experience of others. First, there are the lessons that can be learned from quite similar collectivities. If conditions are broadly comparable – economically, politically, culturally – one can be reasonably confident that a particular policy is possible, that it might well be implementable, and that, roughly speaking, the results in country A are likely to be the consequences in one's own country. In short, policy transplantability and structural similarity are closely linked. (The Nordic nations, to the outsider, appear to provide many instances of this process.)

With this form of learning, however, comes constraints. The most promising, appealing compelling policy 'answers' to a national problem may, for instance, lie elsewhere – in a very different sort of society. What is to be done then? Perhaps nothing, necessarily. Understanding that to be the case is the beginning and the end of that exercise. This, of course, is another way of saying that learning about other national experiences is not the same as learning from them.

There is, however, one other form of lesson-drawing that is rare, but powerful. Some describe this as generalizing from the widest variety of cases – the very opposite of a 'similar system' design. If a policy generalization holds over many divergent cases, some powerful factor is at work, something policy-makers and administrators ignore at their (and their constituents' peril). The logic is straightforward: if Q follows from policy Z in countries A to T, why should nation Z believe its experience will be different? Just as the most similar design narrows the range of findings, so too does the most different design narrow the likely number of such generalizations. But in the latter instance the narrowing is not of countries, but the likelihood there will be a large number of such transplantable generalizations. One example might be that the costs of implementing new policies are always much larger than those estimated by their advocates. Another might be that wholesale transformation of the ways doctors are paid – a familiar yearning of health policy analysts – is almost never a practical option. If accepted, this lesson has practical importance for payment policy debates. More relevant to this volume is that Canada's mode of cost control – countervailing the pressures of medical inflation with monopsonistic power – is an instance of a more general pattern in the OECD world. American claims about cost control through competition is speculative; the monopsonist model is not.

More particularly, Canadian health debates

The Canadianocentric orientation is not wrong in itself. But it does seem important at this period of Canadian political struggle to have a comparative perspective.

That perspective would, for example, bolster François Beland's contention that 'Canada's current health system can meet the challenges it faces.' International commentary would, in addition, highlight the United States as the leading victim of medical inflation. It would show that Canada has controlled costs relatively well. The expression 'relatively well' requires, of course, a comparative reference. The OECD monitoring of health care costs would place Canada, in 1996, as the fourth most expensive system. The current gap between Canada and the United States is huge (about 9 per cent of Canadian GNP as against about 14 per cent of US GNP) when compared with the clustering of Canada, France, Germany, Sweden, and other Western European nations in the 8–10 per cent range. The point is not that Canada's health care is cheap, but that its system for managing costs is workable and the availability of other panaceas is blinkered thinking.

There is another striking example in current Canadian discussions where an international perspective would be clearly helpful. There is disagreement between the demographic warnings about Canada's ageing society and the argument, made forcefully by Bob Evans and his colleagues at the University of British Columbia, that aging *per se* accounts for little of the cost control pressure Canada has faced so far and will face in the decades ahead. Increases in patterns of utilization have been the engines of Canadian expenditure Evans *et al.* documented – rightly in my estimation. But note that neither party to the dispute has emphasized the obvious cross-national point. Germany and Sweden were already 'as old' in 1980 as North America will become by the year 2000.[17] This, in itself, suggests that treating demography as financial destiny is fundamentally misplaced. If Germany and the Nordic countries were dramatically different from Canada – in wealth, social expectations for medical care and the care of the old, or modes of political representation – that would provide good grounds for ignoring this comparison and the perspective it provides. But Canada is not that peculiar and the loss of perspective is unwarranted.[18]

EPILOGUE

This chapter has commented on a number of themes and drawn most of its documentation from developments in the 1985–95 decade. Writing in late 1997, one wants to close by considering briefly whether more recent events have challenged any of the major arguments.

As for media commentary from the United States, there has been a sharp fall-off in attention to Canadian Medicare. Universal health insurance has been off the public agenda since 1994 and the subsequent policy disputes are much narrower – issues like insurance law reform, the disputes over Medicare and Medicaid, and the regulatory squabbles over, for example, how many days in the hospital an insured woman can stay after giving birth. These disputes do not *seem* to call for much discussion of Canadian experience. But that conclusion is misleading, drawn by paying too much attention to what the national media in the United States regard as relevant. If, one looks instead at the professional literature about the finance and delivery of health care, the picture is quite different. American firms – especially national firms offering 'health plans' to American businesses and unions – are very interested in expanding their market to Canada. In some cases, the exports have to do with information systems and associated purchases. In others, what is to be sold are services – managerial, consulting, insurance for what Canadian Medicare does not cover. The expansionist impulse, combined with the flows of information, will mean ideas south of the border will continue to travel north, but not necessarily by the same routes of television and the magazine weeklies.

Moreover, the startling development in the 1990s from this standpoint is the explicit importation by Canadian politicians of American ideological stances. Premier Harris is perhaps the most striking illustration, invoking Newt Gingrichian images just as Gingrich's Contract with America was heading his party to a massive Presidential defeat in 1996. But echoes of anti-welfare state sentiment from south of the border – earlier apparent in Alberta – now amplifies Canadian expressions of earlier years.

Most striking of all is the spread north of what one might call the rhetoric of medical managerialism, a rhetoric that powerfully and misleadingly combines the marketing jargon of modern management schools with the lingo of advertising. The jargon of the former and the hyperbole of the latter have made reasoned thought about North American health care increasingly difficult.

Consider, for example, the spreading use of persuasive definitions in health policy circles – the incantation of 'integrated delivery systems' as the label for what to do, the appeal to 'managed care' when what that means remains completely opaque, for the substitution of innovation in monikers for what used to be a world of modest names for medical institutions. The older pattern was to label organizations by their location (a Vancouver General), by type of patient (a children's hospital), or by an icon that had to do with a profession (like the nursing cap). Now, terms like PacifiCare come into use, with the associations of beach, pacification, and caring all rolled into one. Both the non-rational associative mode of advertising and the numbing banality of managerial abstractions are threats to coherent thought – about health care, or anything else for that matter.

Canada, to the extent both global and North American carriers of such innovation penetrate the border, will need protection from the worst of these developments. For many years, the hallowed place of Medicare in the Canadian public household was protection enough. That, however, no longer seems clearly to be the case. As a result, Canadian health policy and politics could well use a larger amount of sophisticated and critical cross-national commentary.

NOTES

1   This chapter was originally prepared for a conference held at the Robarts Centre for Canadian Studies in April of 1996. It then reflected an earlier article prepared for the special issue of the *Canadian Journal on Aging*, Vol. 4, No. 2, 1995, edited by François Beland and Evelyn Shapiro. At these stages, various commentators gave helpful suggestions, especially François Beland, Daniel Drache, and Terry Sullivan, and I have tried to incorporate some of them in this version (revised in September of 1997).

2   In more than twenty years of affiliation with Evans' I have often heard this expression. It surely has found its way into Evans's prolific writings but no sensible purpose would be served by searching for that particular expression.

3   For extensive discussion of the debate – and its myths – see The Health Care Study Group, 'Understanding the Choices in Health Care Reform', *Journal of Health Politics, Policy and Law*, Vol. 19, No. 3, Fall 1994, pp. 499–541, and T. R. Marmor and J. Oberlander, 'A Citizen's Guide to the Healthcare Reform Debate', *Yale Journal on Regulation*, Vol. 11, No. 2, Summer 1994, pp. 495–506.

4   This is the theme of my essay, 'Patterns of Fact and Fiction in Use of the Canadian Experience', in T. R. Marmor, *Understanding Health Care Reform* (New Haven: Yale University Press, 1994), Ch. 12, pp. 177–194. Originally published in the *American Journal of Canadian Studies*, Vol. 23, No. 1, Spring 1993, pp. 47–64.

5   For further elabouration of this argument, see 'Japan – A Sobering Lesson', in *Understanding Health Care Reform*, op. cit., pp. 195–201. This essay originally appeared in the *Health Management Quarterly*, Vol. 14, No. 3, 1992, pp. 10–14.

6   This is not to claim that Medicare is problem-free. No program is. Rather it is to argue that, compared with most of the health care financing arrangements in industrial democracies, Canada's performance would be judged quite admirable. I have made this argument in many settings; my point here is that I would not be distinctive if the supply of cross-national investigators of Medicare was substantially increased. And, finally, it is my contention that the debate within Canada would be affected by more international adulation in this sector, especially at this moment of fiscal and constitutional history.

7   This sceptical argument is advanced, with Anglo-American examples from medical care and welfare, in T. R. Marmor and W. Plowden, 'Rhetoric and Reality in the Intellectual Jet Stream: The Export to Britain from America of Questionable

Ideas', *Journal of Health Politics, Policy and Law*, Vol. 16, No. 4, 1991, pp. 807–812. On the other hand, there is very rapid communication of scientific findings and claims, with journals and meetings regarded as the proper sites for evaluation. As of yet, there is no journal in the political economy of medical care that has enough authority, audience, or acuteness to play the evaluative role assumed, in my admittedly limited experience, by *The New England Journal of Medicine, Lancet, BMJ*, or *JAMA*.

8 Readers may be puzzled by my reluctance in this note to treat 'reform' as the object of commentary. This paragraph's parade of substitutes – health policy, concerns, worries, etc. – reflects discomfort with the marketing connotations of the 'reform' expression. That there are pressures for change is obvious and understanding them is part of our gathering's point, but reforming can obviously be a benefit, a burden, or beside the point.

9 For a mostly serious discussion of the media treatment of both subjects see my 'A Summer of Discontent: Press Coverage of Murder and Medical Care Reform', *Journal of Health Politics, Policy and Law*, Vol. 20, No. 2, Summer 1995, pp. 495–501.

10 Technically, this is not strictly true of course, as is evident in the sickness fund financing of care in Germany, The Netherlands, and elsewhere. But, since mandatory contributions are close cousins of 'taxes', budget officials must obviously treat these outlays as constraints on direct tax increases. Moreover, the precise level of acceptable cost increases is a regulatory issue of great controversiality.

11 See R. Klein and M. O'Higgins, 'Defusing the Crisis of the Welfare State: A New Interpretation', in T. R. Marmor and J. L. Mashaw, eds, *Social Security: Beyond the Rhetoric of Crisis*, (Princeton, NJ: Princeton University Press, 1988), esp. pp. 219–224.

12 The bulk of this ideological struggle took place, of course, within national borders, free from the spread of 'foreign' ideas. To the extent similar arguments arose cross-nationally, as Kieke Okma has noted, mostly that represented 'parallel development'. But, there are striking contemporary examples of the explicit international transfer and highlighting of welfare state commentary. Some of this takes place through think-tank networks; some takes place through media campaigns on behalf of particular figures; and, of course, some takes place through academic exchanges and official meetings. Charles Murray – the controversial author of *Losing Ground* (1984) and co-author of *The Bell Curve* (1994) – illustrates all three of these phenomena, as our British conferees can attest. The medium of transfer seems to have changed in the post-war period. Where the Beveridge Report would have been known to social policy elites very broadly, however much they used it, the modern form seems to be the long newspaper or magazine article and the media interview.

13 This is the argument developed in T. R. Marmor, J. L. Mashaw, and P. L. Harvey, *America's Misunderstood Welfare State: Persistent Myths, Continuing Realities* (New York: Basic Books, 1992), esp. ch. 3. The wider scholarly literature on the subject is the focus of a review essay, 'Understanding the Welfare State: Crisis, Critics, and Countercritics,' *Critical Review*, Vol. 7, No. 4, 1993, pp. 461–477.

14 These examples are all drawn from the expectations of participants in a Four Country Conference on Health Care Policies and Health Care Reform, held in Holland, 23–25 February 1995. Sponsored by the Dutch Ministry of Health, the conferees whose statements are cited were from Canada, the United States,

Germany and, of course, The Netherlands. This group has continued to meet annually – in Canada in 1996 and in Germany in 1997. The enthusiasm for finding cross-national answers to policy problems at home persists.

15 For an elaboration of this point, see my 'Patterns of Fact and Fiction in the Use of the Canadian Experience', op. cit., ch. 12. A particularly careful and extensive treatment of the North American experience is the review article by R. G. Evans, M. L. Barer, and C. Hertzman, 'The 20-Year Experiment: Accounting for, Explaining, and Evaluating Health Care Cost Containment in Canada and the United States', *Annual Review of Public Health* Vol. 12, 1991, pp. 481–518.

16 The political fight over the Clinton health plan vividly illustrates these generalizations. The number of interest groups with a stake in the Clinton plan's fate – given the nearly one trillion dollar medical economy – was enormous; there were more than 8,000 *registered* lobbyists alone in Washington and thousands more trying to influence the outcome under some other label. The estimates of expenditures on the battle are in the hundreds of millions; one trade association, The Pharmaceutical Manufacturer's Association, spent $7 million on 'public relations' by 1993. The most noted effort was that of the Health Insurance Association of America, the group representing the smaller insurers who produced their infamous Harry and Louise ads months after the President. Washington is awash in interest group activities, but its meaning is far from clear.

17 Derived from Table 1.A.2, 'Population structure in selected OECD countries', OECD, Social Policy Studies, No. 19, *Caring for Frail Elderly People: Policies in Evolution* (Paris, 1996), p. 23.

18 For an attempt to provide precisely that perspective, see *Economic Security and Intergenerational Justice: A Look at North America*, edited by T. R. Marmor, T. M. Smeeding, and V. L. Greene (Washington: The Urban Institute Press, 1994), especially ch. 1. On the other hand, there are international organizations on both sides of this argument. The OECD has published a series of studies that question the presumption that ageing populations represent some dire threat to the affordability of major welfare state programs like universal health insurance or retirement pensions. The World Bank, by contrast, emphasizes the coming of an old age 'crisis', mirroring the language popularized by Wall Street figures like Peter Peterson and groups like the Concord Coalition. See, the World Bank policy research report, *Averting the Old Age Crisis: Policies to Protect the Old and Promote Growth* (New York: Oxford University Press, 1994).

Part V
On the frontier of reform

15 One million decisions at the micro-level

Patient choice

Raisa Deber and Natasha Sharpe

Although health reform may occur at a macro systems level, in the final analysis its impact is felt in a myriad of interactions among individual patients and providers. Medical costs are the summation of millions of individual decisions – to perform or not perform tests, to prescribe or not prescribe drugs, to operate, to admit to hospital, or to watch and wait. Who should make these decisions accordingly becomes a potent policy issue. Should it be the provider, who has the expertise, but whose income is also affected? Should it be the patient or 'consumer'? Or should such judgements be left to the payer (whether government, or third-party insurer)? Perhaps they should be made by 'the community', possibly as represented by institutional or regional boards?

Answers to these questions are complex. One may justify a societal role in making macro allocation decisions about how many resources would be allocated to health care. It is more difficult to justify micro-management of such inherently personal decisions as the medical treatment an individual should receive. This chapter focuses primarily at the micro level, and in particular on the issue of whether it is feasible to establish a genuine partnership between patients and their providers. However, it will make some links – albeit tentative ones – to the implications for establishing a health care system in which clinical judgments can be made largely independent of provider remuneration, while controlling overall health care expenditures.

Our opening question is whether, and how, people want to participate in health care decisions. We accordingly review some conceptual issues involved in analysing participation and choices at macro and micro levels. We then present some data from a series of studies we are conducting on the roles patients wish to play in making treatment decisions about their own care, and the impact of one particular approach – the interactive videodisc Shared Decision-making Program, or SDP, in helping them do so (Kasper *et al.*, 1992).

ASPECTS OF PARTICIPATION: CITIZENS

As Charles and DeMaio have noted, it is important to distinguish between two aspects of public participation (Charles and DeMaio, 1993). The first aspect involves participation as citizens in a democratic society – participation which is generally directed at macro levels of decisions. For example, the public may be involved – either directly or indirectly – in helping to decide the magnitude and distribution of resources to be allocated to health care, or the mix of public and private responsibilities desired in a particular society.

Despite its appeal, it is far from clear the extent to which such participation can be justified. At first glance, citizen participation appears democratic and empowering. A participative culture might breed better citizens; more input may also lead to decisions which better reflect community desires and priorities. In practice, however, the participating public often represents a highly skewed segment of the population. As political science has long recognized, people vary considerably in their interest in participating (Verba and Nie, 1972). Time and resources are limited, and most of us have to pick our spots. For that reason, what are termed 'concentrated' interests – to whom the issues are usually crucial – are known to be far more likely to become involved than the 'diffuse' interests of the general public (Pross, 1992). It is accordingly not surprising that most attempts to seek public participation tend to attract highly unrepresentative groups with a considerable interest in the outcomes of deliberations. As one example, participation theory would predict that discussions of how to manage a hospital will energize those who work in the hospital or those who seek a lot of care there, but are less likely to engage the average citizen who may save a bit in taxes, or would have access to a different service mix in the event that they become ill. Indeed, these theoretical predictions were confirmed by Abelson *et al.*, who have shown that the general public in Ontario shows little interest in being involved in deciding how to allocate health care resources (Abelson *et al.*, 1995). A policy problem arises; is it appropriate for this skewed sample to decide how others should be treated? For example, was it appropriate for an affluent and educated segment of the Oregon public to decide what treatments could be received by welfare patients, particularly when those decisions would not apply to the citizens making the 'tough choices' (Brown, 1991)?

ASPECTS OF PARTICIPATION: PATIENTS

The second aspect of participation occurs at the micro level – participation as a patient, or recipient of care. We note at the outset our own preference for referring to such care recipients as 'patients', rather than the more fashionable terms of 'customers', 'clients', or 'consumers' (Deber, 1995). The terms 'customer' and 'consumer' carry with them the implication of using economic goods or commodities, whereas the term 'patient' conveys an implication of illness and the need for health care services. However, it must be recognized that acceptance of a market viewpoint markedly simplifies the question of patient roles to that of customer, deciding which services to 'demand'. For that reason, it may be worth a brief detour to examine the reasons why we believe

that market approaches do not work well when considering 'medically necessary' services (Deber, Narine *et al.*, 1996).

The issue of the limits to markets is a profoundly ideological one. The
United States, for example, is characterized by a strong belief in the primacy of
markets; its health economists generally assume that people will 'overconsume'
'free' services, and that market mechanisms (e.g. prices) are needed to encourage wise consumption. Particularly in the US, the idea that patients are merely
consumers is becoming increasingly accepted, with the corollary that those
receiving care should pay for it. For example, one US physician advocated
forcing patients into becoming their own utilization reviewers so that they
'would truly become consumers of medical care' (Wright, 1993). In contrast,
such Canadian health economists as Robert G. Evans stress that people rarely
wish to purchase medical services *per se*; rather, they wish to obtain health, and
rarely know the 'production function' which translates medical services into
health gains (Evans, 1984). One key factor distinguishing medical markets
from 'normal' markets is precisely the issue of need.

Market commodities are distributed on the basis of supply and demand.
Price operates as the link. If there is excess supply, prices should fall until
enough new demand is created to restore market equilibrium. If there is excess
demand, prices should rise until enough people are priced out of the market.
Providing services on the basis of need violates both of these assumptions. One
handy way of making the distinction is the following 'thought experiment'.
Suppose you are offered a free dinner at your favourite restaurant at a mutually
convenient time. Would you accept? Most people would. Now, in contrast,
suppose you are offered free open heart surgery at your favourite hospital.
Would you accept? The response 'only if I needed it' violates the assumptions
inherent in normal markets; charitable impulses may wish to ensure that no
one starves, but it is not an issue whether someone 'needs' the free dinner.
Although public policy is not concerned if I purchase an 'unnecessary' pair of
shoes, performing unneeded surgery would not only be considered unprofes-
sional, but indeed unethical. As a second thought experiment, consider
whether an individual who presents to a hospital emergency room with a
ruptured appendix and an empty wallet should be turned away. If we answer
that someone should ensure that no one is denied 'needed' services for financial
reasons, we also reveal our unwillingness to allow people to be priced out of the
market. The manner in which such services are paid for can vary – jurisdictions
may handle this through charity, *pro bono* work by professionals, government
plans for the indigent, or universal coverage – but most consider it unacceptable to turn away sick people when treatment which may help them is
available. But this double-edged role of need – not wishing to provide services
which are not needed, nor to deny services which are – means that market
mechanisms cannot be used as the way of allocating services at the micro level.
What kind of market can exist if no one can be priced out of it (Deber, 1993)?

Acceptance of the view that health services should be supplied only on the
basis of need has a number of implications, which are still being worked

through (Birch and Abelson, 1993; Birch and Eyles, 1993; Eyles *et al.*, 1991). For example, 'needs-based' planning fits well with an emphasis on requiring better evidence of effectiveness. (Goel *et al.*, 1996; Laupacis *et al.*, 1992; Naylor, 1995; Naylor *et al.*, 1994).

However, it is less clear how this viewpoint will be reconciled with a greater emphasis on consumerism. In our view, there is an inherent contradiction between the trend towards making decisions on the basis of patient needs, and another recent trend towards a consumerist model, in which the patient makes all significant decisions and limits the physician's role to that of an agent. The increased stress on patient autonomy in North America implies that people are far less likely to follow doctors' orders blindly. The paternalistic 'don't worry about it' viewpoint is no longer considered acceptable in North American medical ethics (Veatch, 1991). Autonomy has become the catchphrase that symbolizes the moral and legal right of the patient to make his or her own decisions, regardless of how beneficent the physician's intentions may be. The operationalization of respect for patient autonomy lies in the doctrine of informed consent, which is the keystone for the contemporary practice of medicine. Our review of the empirical literature clearly suggests that most people want to be informed (Davison *et al.*, 1995; Deber, 1994a, 1994b; Degner and Sloan, 1992; Hack *et al.*, 1994; Sutherland *et al.*, 1989). However, the extent to which they wish to be involved is more problematic. In a counter-reaction to autonomy-based approaches, others have argued that the conception of the patient–physician relationship as a contract where the physician is obligated to give information so that the patient may make an informed choice is impossible in a relationship where one of the parties is vulnerable, ill, and frightened. Indeed, our review also noted a literature which at first glance appears to suggest that people do not want to take responsibility for making decisions about their own care (Deber, 1994a, 1994b).

DECISION-MAKING V. PROBLEM-SOLVING

Previous work done with Andrea Baumann, Allan Detsky, Jane Irvine, Nancy Kraetschmer, and John Trachtenberg suggests that things are not that simple. To understand what role people wish to play in decision-making, one must first clarify what is meant by a decision. We hypothesized that the existing studies had not distinguished between two elements of choice. What we term 'problem-solving' (PS) tasks have one right answer, and often require expert information. For such tasks, preferences are irrelevant. It does not matter whether we would prefer that a lump be benign and not malignant, as our desires cannot affect the diagnosis. Neither can our preferences affect the available treatment options, their risks and benefits, or the statistical like-lihood that particular outcomes will be achieved. In contrast, the category of tasks we term 'decision-making' (DM) indeed incorporate preferences; defining what alternatives are available does not tell us which one we should select.

DM tasks accordingly require both prior problem-solving, and the incorporation of personal preferences (Deber and Baumann, 1992).

Such a distinction between the two elements of medical choice provides a solution to the inconsistency between what providers were finding in practice and what was being cited as ethical conduct in the bioethics literature. The physician–patient relationship must be sensitive to what has been called the 'fact of illness' (Pellegrino, 1978). The disadvantage in terms of knowledge and expertise that the patient has can be almost insurmountable; given the time constraints of some illnesses it is implausible to suggest that the patient can be the physician's equal in this mode. None the less, given appropriate information, people may well wish to help decide what treatments they wish to receive.

To investigate this hypothesis, we studied people scheduled for an angiogram at a Toronto, Ontario teaching hospital. We asked them to complete a questionnaire which included questions on preferred decision-making role, information needs, coping style, as well as demographic information. The instrument we call the Problem-Solving Decision-Making (PSDM) scale consisted of three brief vignettes. What we term the *morbidity* vignette read: 'Suppose you often experience a burning sensation when you go to the bathroom. You usually have to push to begin to urinate and sometimes dribbling occurs after urination'; the *mortality* vignette read: 'Suppose you had mild chest pain for three days and decided that you should visit your doctor about this'; and the *quality of life* vignette read: 'Suppose you and your partner have been trying for pregnancy, but have been unsuccessful for more than a year.' (The item, but not the labels, were used in the questionnaire.) For each vignette, the PSDM asked 'who should decide' about a series of six tasks, written to encompass both problem-solving and decision-making activities. To enhance comparability with previous studies, response categories used the same five-point scale employed by Ende (Ende *et al.* 1989): '1 = the doctor alone'; '2 = mostly the doctor'; '3 = both equally'; '4 = mostly me'; and '5 = me alone'. We refer to the four problem-solving tasks on the PSDM as:

1 *Diagnosis:* 'Who should determine (diagnose) what the likely causes of your symptoms are?'
2 *Treatment options:* 'Who should determine what the treatment options are?'
3 *Risks/benefits:* 'Who should determine what the risks and benefits for each treatment option are?'
4 *Probabilities:* 'Who should determine how likely each of these risks and benefits are to happen?'

We refer to the two decision-making tasks as:

1 *Utilities:* Given the risks and benefits of these possible treatments, who should decide how acceptable those risks and benefits are for you?'

2   *What is done:* 'Given all the information about risks and benefits of the possible treatments, who should decide which treatment option should be selected?'

Again, the wording, but not the labels, appeared on the questionnaire.

The PSDM scale was validated in a number of ways, including factor analysis, reliability testing, and test–retest using a separate sample of nursing students (Kraetschmer, 1994). We had responses from 300 patients (response rate, 72 per cent). Their mean age was 59 (range 24–82); 75 per cent were male.

A series of statistical analyses (including paired t-tests for differences of means) indicated that patients overwhelmingly wished the PS tasks to be performed by or shared with the doctor (98.4 per cent of the twelve PS scores were between 1 and 3), but wanted to be involved in decision-making (78 per cent of the six DM scores were between 3 and 5); all paired t-tests comparing DM v. PS scores were significant at $p = 0.0001$ (Deber, Kraetschmer and Irvine, 1996). These results indicate that patients are indeed willing to hand over control of problem-solving tasks, but that many wish to retain a role in treatment decision-making.

We are currently involved in a series of studies which examine different patient populations to see whether they have similar views. To date, we have seen similar patterns among nursing students, men with benign prostatic hyperplasia, people with low back pain, cardiac patients viewing an educational videodisc, and women attending an educational session on menopause. The scores most people give to problem-solving tasks almost always fall between 1 and 3 – although there is some variation in the extent to which they wish to hand over control to physicians (score of 1) or wish to share responsibility (score of 3). However, we are not finding a ground swell of individuals – even those who are quite knowledgeable and independent – who wish to assume control over problem-solving tasks (scores of 4 or 5). In contrast, a sizeable proportion do wish control over decision-making. We hope to determine what characteristics are associated with these differing desires to participate, but feel confident in concluding that most people, under the right situations, do wish to take at least some responsibility for making treatment decisions, if they have the necessary information to do so.

Acceptance of this viewpoint suggests that health professionals have two primary roles in encouraging patient participation; performing the problem-solving and presenting such information in a way to ease decision-making; and working with patients (including giving emotional support) to assist them in making decisions. At the micro level, therefore, there would seem to be scope for a genuine partnership, particularly if reimbursement incentives were altered to ensure that clinical judgments were independent of remuneration. The question of how one can find the time to inform patients in a busy clinical practice, however, remains.

THE SHARED DECISION-MAKING PROGRAM

We therefore became involved in a series of studies to examine an innovative educational technology, the Shared Decision-Making (SDP) project directed by John Wennberg and his colleagues in the Foundation for Informed Medical Decision-Making (FIMDM) (Barry *et al.*, 1995; Barry *et al.*, 1988; Deber and Kraetschmer, 1995; Deber *et al.*, 1994; Fowler *et al.*, 1988; Trachtenberg *et al.*, 1993; Wagner *et al.*, 1995; Wennberg, 1990; Wennberg *et al.*, 1988). This innovative educational technology was based on medical outcomes research, and attempted to provide personalized, unbiased information about treatment alternatives. The information is incorporated into an interactive videodisc, and attempted to provide 'vicarious experience' by including video segments in which patients described their experiences. Videodiscs were produced for such conditions as benign prostatic hyperplasia (BPH), low back pain, hypertension, breast cancer, and stable angina. Our studies concentrated on the BPH decision. BPH is a 'nuisance' condition which affects most ageing men, giving rise to a variety of urological symptoms of varying severity. At the time of the study, there were two major contending treatments – a watch-and-wait strategy, or surgery (usually a transurethral resection of the prostate or TURP). Barry's decision analysis had shown that the amount of utility patients received from TURP depends on the utility they ascribed to being in various health states (Barry and Fowler, 1994; Barry *et al.*, 1988). Surgery was preferred for those who found that the symptoms of prostatism negatively influenced their quality of life; for other patients, the potential complications of the procedure were seen as worse than living with their current symptoms. The choice of optimal therapy was thus emphatically what we term a decision-making problem, which would depend upon the patient's preferences. Prior analysis, such as that contained in the SDP videodisc program, could inform the patient of the available choices, provide the necessary probabilities, and indicate which utilities must be assessed. The next step, informed decision-making, would assist the patient in using this information to participate in making the actual treatment choice.

Although funding agencies did suggest that this clinical situation is not politically correct, since the study only included men, BPH did have a number of advantages in examining whether the shared decision-making ideal could be operationalized. Most importantly, our theoretical distinction between problem-solving and decision-making would make a clinical difference, since no treatment alternative was 'dominant'. Performing the problem-solving would therefore not dictate a treatment protocol for most men with this condition; indeed, the American Urological Association (AUA) had issued a clinical guideline suggesting that treatment protocols should depend upon patient preferences (Barry *et al.*, 1992).

We accordingly implemented use of the Benign Prostatic Hyperplasia Shared Decision-Making Program (SDP) in nine Canadian sites. The study was largely funded by the Ontario Ministry of Health, with supplementary

Table 15.1 Breakdown of respondents by site

Site	Director	Number	%
Victoria (Victoria General)	G. Bruce Piercy, MD	262	36.7
Toronto (Toronto Hospital)	J. Trachtenberg, MD	186	26.1
Winnipeg (Health Sciences Center)	E. W. Ramsey, MD	69	9.7
Halifax (Nova Scotia Prostate Center)	R. Norman, MD	53	7.4
Vancouver (Vancouver General)	L. Goldenberg, MD	53	7.4
Oakville (Men's Health Clinic)	R. Casey, MD	35	4.9
Kingston (Kingston General)	J. C. Nickel, MD	24	3.4
Montreal (Royal Victoria)	M. Elhilali, MD	19	2.7
Montreal (St. Luc's)	J. P. Perreault, MD	12	1.7
Total		713	100.0

funding from the Canadian Prostate Health Council (CPHC). We closed patient recruitment as of 30 April 1995, having accrued 713 patients. All patients completed a pre-test questionnaire before viewing the videodisc, and a post-viewing questionnaire after seeing it. We also conducted a mailed one-year follow-up study. Table 15.1 shows the break down of respondents by site.

The SDP automatically classifies patients according to the older version of the American Urological Association (AUA) symptom score. Of the 630 with complete information, 31.5 per cent were classified as having mild symptoms, 47 per cent in the moderate category and 21.6 per cent as having severe symptoms.

Across all sites, 16.4 per cent of patients were under 55 years of age, 32 per cent were between 55–64 years, 40.3 per cent were between 65–74 years, and 11.2 per cent were 75 years or older. Median age was 63.5; 83.6 per cent were married. This group of patients tends to have a fairly high level of education: 8.6 per cent had elementary school or less, 37.6 per cent had some or completed high school, while 53.7 per cent had at least some, completed or advanced university education.

The patients expressed high satisfaction with the length, amount of information, and the clarity – although this leaves some scope for improvement: 81.9 per cent rated the amount of information as about right, and another 7.9 per cent said they would have liked more information; in terms of program length, 85 per cent thought it was about right, with 12.8 per cent rating the program as slightly 'too long'; clarity seemed high, with 62.3 per cent saying that 'everything' was clear, and another 35.5 per cent that 'most things' were clear. They also thought it was balanced and fair, albeit with a slight pro-surgical bias, and were very positive about other patients seeing it before making treatment decisions. Overall, 72.1 per cent of patients thought the program was completely balanced, with the perceived bias coming in both directions (19.8 per cent feeling it favoured surgery, and 8.1 per cent feeling it favoured non-surgical alternatives). In response to the question, 'In general, how do you feel about patients seeing a presentation like this before deciding whether or not to have prostate surgery?', 71.4 per cent chose 'very positive' as their response, and another 21.5 per cent chose 'generally positive', 6.9 per cent neutral, and only 0.1 per cent (one patient) being even slightly negative.

Next, we asked some very holistic questions about perceived knowledge, using a scale from 1 = little to 5 = very knowledgeable, pre- and post-viewing. We asked how knowledgeable they felt about each of: 'your prostate condition', 'the treatment options available for your prostate condition', 'the risks and benefits for each of these treatment options', 'your present symptoms', and 'your treatment preference'.

We examined the 'before' and 'after' scores on a number of items asking for patient perceptions of their knowledge about a number of areas (we did not give patients a formal test). As shown in Table 15.2, the change in subjective knowledge on all five items was both statistically significant (at $p < 0.0001$) and sizeable (over 1 point on the five-point scale). Viewing the material significantly improved patients' subjective knowledge. A sense of the magnitude of the improvement can also be seen by examining the extreme values. For example, 25.4 per cent had felt poorly informed about 'your prostate condition'; this decreased to 1.8 per cent after viewing the SDP. Similarly, 35.8 per cent had felt poorly informed about treatment options; this decreased to 1.1 per cent after viewing the SDP, whereas those feeling very knowledgeable increased from 3.8 per cent to 21.7 per cent. Those claiming little knowledge about the risks and benefits decreased from 46.6 per cent to 0.5 per cent, of 'your present symptoms' from 26.9 per cent to 2 per cent, and of 'your treatment preference' from 44.4 per cent to 1.5 per cent. The bottom line question was whether people felt able to make a decision – in that connection, those feeling 'very knowledgeable' about 'your treatment preference' increased from 3.8 per cent to 21.1 per cent, with another 44.7 per cent scoring themselves at 4 on the five-point scale. These improvements indeed suggest that the SDP is an effective mechanism for improving patient knowledge.

But does it change choice? In response to a question about how the videodisc program influenced their treatment decision, 10.4 per cent responded 'a great deal', 27.1 per cent 'quite a lot', 36.1 per cent 'a moderate amount', 21.1 per cent 'not much', and 5.3 per cent 'not at all'.

Table 15.3 contrasts pre- and post-treatment preferences. We find that viewing the material has an effect on patient choice in less than one-third of the respondents to date. Not surprisingly, the effect is most pronounced for

Table 15.2 Changes in perceived knowledge

Change in (post-viewing–pre-viewing):	N	Mean	Std Dev.	t	Sig(t)
Knowledge of your prostate condition	651	1.09	1.14	24.33	0
Knowledge of treatment options	651	1.51	1.23	31.45	0
Knowledge of risks and benefits	654	1.78	1.17	38.77	0
Knowledge of your present symptoms	654	1.12	1.22	23.5	0
Knowledge of your treatment preference	654	1.65	1.24	34.06	0

Table 15.3 Changes in treatment preference (pre-test v. post-test)

Pre-test preferences	Post-test preferences					
	Surgery definite	Surgery probable	No pref./not sure	Non-surgery probable	Non-surgery definite	Total
Surgery definite	12	3	0	0	0	15
Surgery probable	10	29	2	4	0	45
No pref./not sure	6	42	69	62	25	204
Non-surgery probable	2	11	20	127	58	218
Non-surgery definite	1	3	8	48	128	188
Total	31	88	99	241	211	670

those who were initially undecided. As the entries in bold indicate, of 60 definitely or probably leaning towards surgery before viewing the SDP, 54 still preferred it in the post-viewing test (90 per cent); similarly 361 of 406 (89 per cent) continued to lean towards non-surgical alternatives. However, only 69 of the 204 remained unsure (34 per cent). This data suggests that strong preferences are less likely to change, although the intensity may vary, and that any changes which do occur appear more likely to move to 'undecided' rather than switch among alternatives. It was notable that of this preliminary group of patients, few who were strongly determined to have surgery or to have non-surgical therapy changed their view as a result of viewing the program. These results provide additional confidence that the SDP for BPH provides unbiased information, since choices appear as likely to switch towards as away from surgery. Our findings accordingly cast some doubt upon the frequent justification of informed choice on the grounds that it will save money by reducing procedures. It is possible that the physicians with whom we are working tended to be more conservative, and performed fewer questionable surgeries in the first place. However, it must be recognized that informed patients may result in increased or reduced rates of selecting procedures; the justification for patient education must lie on grounds of appropriateness, since there is no certainty that costs will be reduced.

This satisfaction with viewing the SDP persisted at one-year follow up. A series of questions were asked, all rated on a five-point Likert scale (usually between 'strongly agree' and 'strongly disagree', with a 'neither agree nor disagree' neutral point). When asked how they feel now about having seen the video, over 88 per cent gave positive responses, and less than 3 per cent negative ones. Over 90 per cent agreed that they were better informed after having seen the video, and 86.6 per cent agreed that they were more satisfied with their decision-making.

A common argument made by physicians is that such elaborate patient education is not needed since they, themselves, do it. Our physicians represent a very select group who do, indeed, devote a lot of time to patient education.

However, patients emphatically do not agree that the SDP is redundant. On the question 'the video is redundant – my physician gave me all the necessary information', 21.5 per cent strongly disagreed, 53.1 per cent disagreed, 16.9 per cent took the middle road of 'neither agree nor disagree', 6.7 per cent agreed, and 1.8 per cent strongly agreed.

An interesting issue, which we are currently exploring in other research, is the impact of shared decision-making on medical practice and the doctor–patient relationship. A few clues arise from the follow-up data. These patients were satisfied with their role; 88.6 per cent found their role 'just right'. Similarly, 88.6 per cent felt that the role their physician took was 'just right.' These patients liked the medical care they received (88.9 per cent indicated satisfaction and only 3.3 per cent any degree of dissatisfaction). Most interesting, 58.5 per cent agreed that they trusted their doctor more because of seeing the video.

The SDP itself is unlikely to play a major role in patient education. Although the intervention itself was both successful and liked by patients (Deber and Kraetschmer, 1995; Deber *et al.*, 1994), it was not simple to integrate into busy and fairly underfunded clinics. The amount of staff time required was not high, but it was necessary to have a trained person available on site to help patients begin and end the module, use the mouse, and on occasion to provide clarification of the video. Indeed, some of our most enthusiastic sites had to discontinue using the videodisc for their patients when local budget cuts removed their supporting nursing staff. Neither was it simple for FIMDM to keep the videodisc clinically up to date. As practice patterns changed, the information provided became outmoded, and all sites eventually stopped using it. A 'Cadillac' educational product such as the SDM may be necessary for conditions for which the best clinical information varies considerably for patient sub-groups; however, most conditions can probably be dealt with through less complex mechanisms. In future, as multimedia becomes less expensive, one can envision an array of educational material on CD, videotape, audiotape, booklet, and even through the Internet.

Our results have several important implications for relationships between providers and recipients of care. First, although almost no one wishes to take control over problem solving tasks, many do wish to be involved in decision-making if they have the necessary information. A partnership implies compromises on both parts. This approach does not mean that patients have all of their demands met, particularly if the problem-solving implies that certain treatments would not be seen as appropriate. However, it does imply that providers should not expect to 'usurp patient prerogatives' (Kassirer, 1983) and take over decision-making tasks.

Second, there are a number of technologies which can assist in providing such information, which can vary considerably in sophistication and expense.

Third, genuinely shared decision-making need not threaten doctor–patient relationships; it may indeed strengthen them. Distinguishing between problem-solving and decision-making is intuitively more satisfactory to providers, who may be frustrated by ethical principles which demand that their patients make 'autonomous' decisions at the same time the real-life patients ask for their providers' advice. It also provides a solution for patients who desire to be informed and participate in medical decisions about their care without being overwhelmed by arcane details about technical aspects of possible treatments.

TRANSFERRING MICRO PARTNERSHIPS TO MACRO POLICY-MAKING

Partnerships between patients and providers in turn imply some obligation to ensure that clinical judgments are at least somewhat isolated from financial implications. After all, how much can patients trust a recommendation for or against surgery if the provider's income depends upon what decision is made? In the BPH case, a remuneration system which would pay the doctor far more for surgery than for educating and monitoring sets up perverse incentives; it forces ethical doctors to go counter to their economic interest, and provides little incentive for informing patients and respecting their wishes. Similarly, payment mechanisms giving bonuses to physicians if they under-use services may provide perverse incentives in the opposite direction. In either case, remuneration systems can place providers in a conflict of interest. As some providers have noted, physicians have an ethical responsibility to act as an advocate for their patients, a responsibility which can be blurred if they are also expected to act as the agent for controlling the costs to third-party payers (MacKay, 1993). Many physicians in the United States are dismayed by the ethical difficulties posed by cost containment under managed care, and the implications for eroding trust between patient and provider. Some are seeking – with minimal success to date – to create systems where physicians are uninfluenced by questions of economic interests (Nash, 1994; Relman, 1993). Although this is far beyond the scope of this chapter, partnership issues may thus provide a compelling reason for moving away from fee-for-service, as well as for avoiding certain types of incentives in physician reimbursement systems.

Because resources are not unlimited, a difficult balancing act becomes necessary. Decisions should not be made by providers in place of the patient; however, neither can they be made by an individual patient (or individual provider) in isolation from the rest of society.

In other work we have proposed what we call the Global Four Screen Model as a possible way of making resource allocation decisions (Deber *et al.*, 1993. Deber, Narine *et al.*, 1996). The model begins at a 'micro' (individual) level, considering whether to pay for a particular intervention for a particular individual, although it can then be aggregated to the meso (organization) and macro (health system) levels. Decisions about coverage are made as a function of four 'screens', arranged hierarchically, such that only those interventions passing an earlier screen need be considered at the next stage. The first two screens are evidence-based. Screen 1 (Effectiveness) examines whether the given intervention works. Screen 2 (Appropriateness) incorporates information about the risks and benefits to particular individuals, and is therefore individualized to a particular person in a particular setting. The model does not presume that 'proven ineffective' is the same as 'not proven effective'; since so much of medical practice has not yet been evaluated, a rigid approach to evidence would reject most interventions, including many which are likely to be of considerable benefit' (Deber, 1992). Instead, such interventions would receive a 'conditional pass', contingent upon incorporating evaluation such that future decisions can be made on better evidence (Canadian Medical Association, 1994).

The third and fourth screens are based on values. People would not be offered choices unless those options had passed the first two screens; however, at Screen 3 (Informed Choice), a patient–provider partnership would determine whether an individual patient wanted that particular intervention. This screen recognizes that many clinical decisions are what are termed 'toss ups', and suggests that patient values and preferences should accordingly play an important role in making choices.

The model contends that items which do not pass the first three screens should not be paid for by anyone – if something is ineffective, inappropriate, or not wanted, it is difficult to justify why it should be provided at all. The key dilemmas thus arise at Screen 4 (Public Provision). Given that something might benefit an individual, should a third party payer pay for it? Deber *et al.* (1993) proposed that such decisions should include at least the following three criteria: research, cost minimization, and social values.

Research. Data should be collected to 'feed back' information about the conditional passes at Screens 1 and 2, such that future decisions can be more solidly grounded in evidence.

Cost minimization. The item should be the most effective way of achieving a desired goal (which is not the same as being the most cost-effective; no assumptions are made by this model about whether the particular benefit is worth purchasing). For example, exercise may be beneficial to health, but if there are many inexpensive ways of exercising, health club fees need not be publicly financed. Similarly, providers should be encouraged to deliver care as efficiently as possible (which might include major restructuring of the system of care).

Social values. The model proposed asking the following question: 'If an individual would like to receive an intervention which is likely to benefit him/her, but cannot afford it, do we as a society find it acceptable that the intervention is withheld from that person?' We proposed that a 'no' answer should imply that we find the procedure 'medically necessary' for that individual. As the literature suggested, single source financing is preferable under such circumstances, and hence public financing is appropriate for reasons of cost control and avoidance of risk selection. However, if we do find it acceptable to deny care, there is no justification for inclusion of such procedures in the publicly financed plan.

This approach differs from the current coverage under the Canada Health Act, in that it enables coverage to be tailored (using Screens 2 and 3) rather than requiring the sorts of 'all or nothing' decisions inherent in fee schedules. That in turn implies that significant changes would have to be made in other parts of the health care system. Although incompatible with fee schedules, the Global Four Screen Model could be used by planners, with budgets set at the macro level, to make meso level allocation decisions by determining how many of each procedure is likely to be 'needed' for a defined population; indeed, the global budget could be computed using a 'bottom up' process on this basis. In other words, rather than list which procedures would be covered, the global budget would be based upon epidemiological predictions that, for a given population, there should be approximately X hip replacements, Y cases of diabetes, Z with treatable high blood pressure, and so on which would have passed the four screens. However, providers and patients would then determine the precise allocations within the organization and make individual clinical decisions. The approach should be a flexible one; new therapies could be substituted and reallocations performed as long as the total budget was respected and expected outcomes attained. For example, an extra hip replacement might be performed if resources could be diverted from other lower-priority services. To maintain accountability, the funder would have enforceable performance expectations, and appeal mechanisms would be in place for patients dissatisfied with allocation decisions. However, the organization would have the flexibility to redeploy resources within those expectations.

Squaring circles is never easy; reconciling individual decisions with societal constraints is also unlikely to be simple. In the final analysis, we believe that there are enough resources to ensure that individuals can receive high quality timely care for genuine needs, particularly if system incentives encourage this. Recognition that micro decisions are unlikely to be standardized or routine in turn implies a need to listen to the wants and needs of individuals as patients needing care, while providing them with the information they need to make genuinely shared decisions.

ACKNOWLEDGEMENTS

We would like to thank NHRDP, SSHRC, the Ontario Ministry of Health, Canadian Prostate Health Council, and the Prostate Centre, Toronto Hospital, who funded various aspects of this program of research. We would also like to thank Eleanor Ross, Nancy Kraetschmer, Dr John Trachtenberg, Dr A. Detsky, Dr A. Baumann, Dr I. Lieberman, Ann Pendleton, the Foundation for Informed Medical Decision Making, and the doctors, nurses, and patients without whom this research would not have been possible. This chapter was based on a presentation given to the conference Globalization, State Choices, and Citizens' Participation in Canadian Health Care, Robarts Centre for Canadian Studies, York University, April 1–2, 1996.

REFERENCES

Abelson, J., J., Lomas, J., Eyles, S. Birch, and G. Veenstra, 1995. Does the community want devolved authority? Results of deliberative polling in Ontario. *Canadian Medical Association Journal* 153: 403–412.

Barry, M. J. and F. J., Jr. Fowler, 1994. The methodology for evaluating the subjective outcomes of treatment for benign prostatic hyperplasia. *Advances in Urology* 6: 83–99.

Barry, M. J., A. G., Jr., Mulley, F. J., Jr. Fowler, and J. W. Wennberg, 1988. Watchful waiting vs immediate transurethral resection for symptomatic prostatism. *Journal of the American Medical Association* 259: 3010–3017.

Barry, M. J., F. J., Jr. Fowler, and M. P. O'Leary, 1992. The American Urological Association symptom index for benign prostatic hyperplasia. *Journal of Urology* 148: 1549–1557.

Barry, M. J., F. J., Jr., Fowler, A. G., Jr., Mulley, J. V. Henderson, and J. E. Wennberg, 1995. Patient reactions to a program designed to facilitate patient participation in treatment decisions for Benign Prostatic Hyperplasia. *Medical Care* 33: 771–782.

Birch, S. and J. Abelson, 1993. Is reasonable access what we want? Implications of, and challenges to, current Canadian policy on equity in health care. *International Journal of Health Services* 23: 629–653.

Birch, S. and J. Eyles, 1993. Needs-based planning of health care: a critical appraisal of the literature. *Canadian Journal of Public Health* 84: 112–117.

Brown, L. D. 1991. The national politics of Oregon's rationing plan. *Health Affairs* 10: 28–51.

Canadian Medical Association. 1994. *Core and Comprehensive Health Care Services: A Framework for Decision-Making*. Ottawa: Canadian Medical Association.

Charles, C. A. and S. DeMaio, 1993. Lay participation in health care decision making: a conceptual framework. *Journal of Health Politics, Policy and Law* 18: 881–904.

Davison, B. J., L. F. Degner, and T. R. Morgan, 1995. Information and decision-making preferences of men with prostate cancer. *Oncology Nursing Forum* 22: 1401–1408.

Deber, R. B. 1992. Translating technology assessment into policy: conceptual issues and tough choices. *International Journal of Technology Assessment in Health Care* 8: 131–137.

Deber, R. B. 1993. Canadian medicare: can it work in the United States? Will it survive in Canada? *American Journal of Law and Medicine* 19: 75–93.

Deber, R. B. 1994a. The patient–physician partnership: changing roles, and the desire for information. *Canadian Medical Association Journal* 151: 171–176.

Deber, R. B. 1994b. The patient–physician partnership: decision making, problem solving, and the desire to participate. *Canadian Medical Association Journal* 151: 423–427.

Deber, R. B. 1995. From Paternalism to Consumerism. Centre for Health Economics and Policy Analysis 8th Annual Policy Conference, 'Jurisdictional Roles in Health Policy: Who's on First and What's Up Next?', 18–19 May, Toronto, Conference Summary Report, pp. 13–14.

Deber, R. B. and A. O. Baumann, 1992. Clinical reasoning in medicine and nursing: decision making versus problem solving. *Teaching and Learning in Medicine* 4: 140–146.

Deber, R. B. and N. Kraetschmer, 1995. How does shared decision making affect patient attitudes: trust and satisfaction after one-year follow-up (abstract). *Medical Decision Making* 15: 427.

Deber, R. B., E. Ross, and M. Catz, 1993. *Comprehensiveness in Health Care*. Ottawa: HEAL, The Health Action Lobby.

Deber, R. B., N. Kraetschmer, and J. Trachtenberg, 1994. Shared decision making: how does one measure success? (abstract). *Medical Decision Making* 14: 429.

Deber, R. B., N. Kraetschmer, and J. Irvine, 1996. What role do patients wish to play in treatment decision making? *Archives of Internal Medicine* 156: 1414–1420.

Deber, R. B., L., Narine, P., Baranek, N., Hilfer, K. M., Duvalco, R., Zlotnik-Shaul, G. Pink, and A. P. Williams, 1996. The Public–Private Mix in Health Care. In National Forum on Health, *Striking a Balance: Health Care Systems in Canada and Elsewhere. Canada Health Action: Building on the Legacy*. Vol. 4. Sainte-Foy, Quebec: Editions MultiModes.

Degner, L. F. and J. A. Sloan, 1992. Decision making during serious illness: what role do patients really want to play? *Journal of Clinical Epidemiology* 45: 941–949.

Ende, J., L., Kazis, A. B. Ash, and M. A. Moskowitz, 1989. Measuring patients' desire for autonomy: decision making and information-seeking preferences among medical patients. *Journal of General Internal Medicine* 4: 23–30.

Evans, R. G. 1984. *Strained Mercy: The Economics of Canadian Health Care*. Toronto: Butterworths and Co.

Eyles, J., S., Birch, S., Chambers, J. Hurley, and B. Hutchison, 1991. A needs-based methodology for allocating health care resources in Ontario, Canada: development and an application. *Social Science and Medicine* 33: 489–500.

Fowler, F. J., Jr., J. E., Wennberg, R. P., Timothy, M. J., Barry, A. G., Jr. Mulley, and D. Hanley, 1988. Symptom status and quality of life after prostatectomy. *Journal of the American Medical Association* 259: 3018–3022.

Goel, V., J. I., Williams, G. M., Anderson, P., Blackstien-Hirsch, C. Fooks, and C. D. Naylor, (eds). 1996. *Patterns of Health Care in Ontario: The ICES Practice Atlas* (2nd ed). Ottawa: Canadian Medical Association.

Hack, T. F., L. F. Degner, and D. G. Dyck, 1994. Relationship between preferences for decisional control and illness information among women with breast cancer: a quantitative and qualitative analysis. *Social Science and Medicine* 39: 279–289.

Kasper, J. F., A. G., Jr. Mulley, and J. E. Wennberg, 1992. Developing shared decision-making programs to improve the quality of health care. *Quality Review Bulletin* 18: 183–190.

Kassirer, J. P. 1983. Adding insult to injury: usurping patients' prerogatives. *New England Journal of Medicine* 308: 898–901.

Kraetschmer, N. 1994. Preferences of patients undergoing angiogram for participation in treatment decisions: coping style and the problem solving–decision making scale. M.Sc. thesis, Graduate Department of Community Health, University of Toronto.

Laupacis, A., D. H., Feeny, A. S. Detsky, and P. X. Tugwell, 1992. How attractive does a new technology have to be to warrant adoption and utilization? Tentative guidelines for using clinical and economic evaluations. *Canadian Medical Association Journal* 146: 473–481.

MacKay, D. N. 1993. Letter to the Editor. *New England Journal of Medicine* 329: 385.

Nash, I. S. 1994. Letter to the Editor. *New England Journal of Medicine* 330: 1011.

Naylor, C. D. 1995. Grey zones of clinical practice: some limits to evidence-based medicine. *Lancet* 345: 840–842.

Naylor, C. D., G. M. Anderson, and V. Goel, (eds). 1994. *Patterns of Health Care in Ontario: The ICES Practice Atlas* (Vol. 1). Ottawa: Canadian Medical Association.

Pellegrino, E. D. 1978. Medical economics and morality: the conflict of canons. *Hospital Progress* 59: 50–55.

Pross, A. P. 1992. *Group Politics and Public Policy* (2nd edn). Toronto: Oxford University Press.

Relman, A. S. 1993. Medical practice under the Clinton reforms: avoiding domination by business. *New England Journal of Medicine* 329: 1574–1576.

Sutherland, H. J., H. A., Llewellyn-Thomas, G. A., Lockwood, D. L. Tritchler, and J. E. Till, 1989. Cancer patients: their desire for information and participation in treatment decisions. *Journal of the Royal Society of Medicine* 82: 260–263.

Trachtenberg, J., N., Kraetschmer, K. Monrose, and R. B. Deber, 1993. Focus on the prostate: benign prostatic hypertrophy interactive videodisc project. *Contemporary Urology* 4: 13–14.

Veatch, R. M. 1991. *The Patient–Physician Relation: The Patient as Partner, Part 2.* Bloomington: Indiana University Press.

Verba, S. and N. H. Nie, 1972. *Participation in America: Political Democracy and Social Equality.* New York: Harper and Row.

Wagner, E. H., P., Barrett, M. J., Barry, W. Barlow, and F. J., Jr. Fowler, 1995. The effect of a shared decisionmaking program on rates of surgery for Benign Prostatic Hyperplasia: pilot results. *Medical Care* 33: 765–770.

Wennberg, J. E. 1990. On the status of the prostate disease assessment team. *Health Services Research* 25: 709–716.

Wennberg, J. E., A. G., Jr., Mulley, D., Hanley, R. P., Timothy, F. J., Jr., Fowler, N. P., Roos, M. J., Barry, K., McPherson, E. R., Greenberg, D., Soule, T. A., Bubolz, E. S., Fisher, and D. J. Malenka, 1988. An assessment of prostatectomy for benign urinary tract obstruction: geographic variations and the evaluation of medical care outcomes. *Journal of the American Medical Association* 259: 3027–3030.

Wright, J. D. 1993. Letter to the Editor. *New England Journal of Medicine* 329: 885–886.

16 Controlling pharmaceutical expenditures in Canada

Joel Lexchin

INTRODUCTION: GROWTH IN PHARMACEUTICAL EXPENDITURES

Dramatic cost increases are driving the push to control pharmaceutical expenditures. Drug costs in Canada have been rising more rapidly than other health care expenditures. Lost in the frenzied debate over how to control drug costs is the question of whether an increase in the percentage of the health care budget going to drugs represents cost-effective use of the money available. It may be that spending more money on drugs produces proportionately greater savings in areas like hospital expenditures. This question cannot be answered without knowledge of how appropriately physicians are prescribing them and measurement of outcomes from different forms of therapy (e.g., hospitalization versus pharmacotherapy). So far, this type of information is distinctly lacking in the Canadian context.

This chapter will first look at reasons for the growth in spending, including the federal role in determining drug prices, and then at interventions, in both the public and private sectors, to control this growth. Next, I will look at some possible future changes in the organization of health care and the implications for cost control in pharmaceuticals. Finally, as part of the conclusion, I will offer some tentative suggestions of my own for dealing with this issue.

REASONS FOR THE GROWTH

Forty-eight million drug claims made between 1989 and 1994 were obtained from four large private drug-plan administrators: Blue Cross of Atlantic Canada, Commission de la Construction du Quebec, Green Shield Canada and Shared Health Network Services (Brogan Consulting Inc., 1995). Altogether there was a total rise in drug plan costs of just over $200 million: 41.7 per cent of that was accounted for by a change in the number of beneficiaries, but excluding this factor the three largest contributors to the observed changes were pharmacy fees, increased utilization (the number of

Table 16.1 Pharmaceutical expenditure in Canada, 1975–1996

Year	Public sector*	Private sector† ($000,000)	Total	% public expenditure	% total health expenditure
1975	329.4	775.9	1105.3	29.8	9.0
1976	403.7	835.9	1239.6	32.6	8.8
1977	462.7	894.2	1356.9	34.1	8.8
1978	542.4	933.9	1476.3	36.7	8.6
1979	627.4	1040.4	1667.8	37.6	8.6
1980	731.2	1148.6	1879.8	38.9	8.4
1981	876.0	1459.0	2335.0	37.5	8.8
1982	1051.4	1621.3	2672.7	39.3	8.6
1983	1224.3	1740.3	2964.6	41.3	8.7
1984	1394.0	1876.5	3270.5	42.6	8.9
1985	1620.8	2105.9	3726.7	43.5	9.3
1986	1881.3	2443.9	4325.2	43.5	9.9
1987	2106.7	2664.1	4770.8	44.1	10.1
1988	2379.5	2982.4	5361.9	44.4	10.5
1989	2714.6	3342.2	6056.8	44.8	10.8
1990	3079.2	3687.2	6766.4	45.5	11.1
1991	3456.6	4049.6	7506.2	46.0	11.3
1992	3760.8	4466.3	8227.1	45.7	11.7
1993	3874.9	4732.5	8607.4	45.0	12.0
1994	3906.1	4985.0	8891.1	43.9	12.2
1995	3964.3	5260.4	9224.7	43.0	12.4
1996	3859.8	5570.8	9430.6	40.9	12.5

Source: Dingwall (1997).

Notes:

* Includes spending on prescription and over-the-counter drugs by federal and provincial governments, workers' compensation, hospitals and other institutions and public health departments.
† Includes spending on prescription and over-the-counter drugs by individuals and private insurance plans. Spending on 'personal health supplies' has been removed from the totals.

claims per beneficiary and the number of medication units per claim) and new (since 1990) drugs at 28.6 per cent, 25.5 per cent and 19 per cent, respectively.

Aside from pharmacy fees, the cost drivers in both the public and private plans were the same: an increased number of beneficiaries, increased utilization and increased drug costs. Pharmacy fees in the private sector are rising as pharmacists attempt to compensate for restrictions on their fees in provincially funded drug programs. The prominence of new drugs as a cause for cost increases is reflected in Ontario data gathered by Green Shield (1994), a not-for-profit corporation offering prepaid health insurance plans. Over half of the rise in prescription costs in the private sector in that province was due to the introduction of new drugs, specifically new (since 1987) patented medications.

Table 16.2 Increases in prescription prices, 1987–1993*

	Cost per prescription ($)		
	New patented drugs	Existing patented drugs	Unpatented drugs
1987	—	23.79	10.38
1988	29.96	25.68	11.67
1989	32.45	28.17	12.59
1990	41.45	30.13	13.46
1991	45.90	31.63	14.26
1992	53.60	34.48	15.81
1993	56.07	35.75	16.16
Average annual increase 1987/88–1993	13.4%	7.0%	7.6%

Source: Green Shield Canada (1994).

Note:

* Includes manufacturer and wholesale distribution costs; excludes dispensing fee.

Prices for prescriptions containing new patented medications rose at a rate of 13.4 per cent per annum since 1988 compared to 7.6 per cent for prices for prescriptions using non-patented drugs (Table 16.2). Despite the premium being charged for these new drugs, in many cases there is no evidence that they are any safer or more effective than existing drug therapies (Lexchin, 1992).

Significantly, the federal government is a minor player when it comes to paying for drugs, but its actions and policies play a significant role in determining drug prices and in increasing or limiting the options available to provinces and private payers.

As a result of the legislation which first restricted and then abolished compulsory licensing for prescription drugs (Bills C-22 and C-91) the Patented Medicine Prices Review Board was created. The mandate of the PMPRB was to monitor the introductory price of new patented medications and to keep the price of all patented drugs from rising faster than the rate of inflation as measured by the Consumer Price Index.

In order to determine if the introductory price for a new drug is appropriate, one of the criteria that the PMPRB uses is the price of the same product in seven other countries: France, Germany, Italy, Sweden, Switzerland, United Kingdom and the United States. By the end of 1994, Canadian prices for the top 200 selling patented drugs were below the median international prices approximately 57 per cent of the time and Canadian prices were the highest for less than 8 per cent of the products (Patented Medicine Prices Review Board, 1996b).

Comparing Canadian prices to those in the seven selected countries might not give an accurate picture about how the cost of drugs in Canada compares to those in the majority of industrialized countries. Purchasing power parities (PPPs) are the rates of currency conversion that equalize the purchasing power of different currencies. When PPPs are used to compare pharmaceutical prices in the seven reference countries that the PMPRB uses to those in all 24 industrialized countries in the Organization for Economic Co-operation and Development it turns out that prices are 6–7 per cent higher in the PMPRB's reference group of countries (Organization for Economic Co-operation and Development, 1996).

A recent report from the PMPRB claims that over the period 1988 to 1995 federal regulation of patented drug prices has saved the Canadian health care system between $2.9 billion and $4.2 billion (Patented Medicine Prices Review Board, 1997). But over the time that the PMPRB has been operating provincial governments have also been taking their own independent initiatives to limit drug prices.

One way of separating out the effects of the PMPRB and the provinces is to look at what happened to the prices for non-patented medications. The PMPRB only regulates the prices for patented drugs, while provincial controls should have affected patented and non-patented products equally. The PMPRB study makes this comparison by constructing a non-patented medicine price index (NPMPI) and comparing the annual change in this index to the index for patented medications (the PMPI). According to the PMPRB, the NPMPI went up at a rate of 4.25 per cent annually between 1988 and 1995 while the PMPI only went up at 1.63 per cent annually over the same period. The difference, 2.62 per cent per year, is attributed to the effects of the PMPRB regulations and this translates into total savings of $3.68 billion. The validity of the PMPRB's conclusion rests on the methodology it used to construct its NPMPI. A report commissioned by the Federal/Provincial/Territorial Pharmaceutical Policy Committee used a different approach and calculated a NPMPI with an annual change of only 0.7 per cent between 1989 and 1994; a lower rate of growth than the index for patented medications (Brogan Consulting Inc. *et al.*, 1995). If the prices of non-patented drugs are rising slower than those of patented drugs then any savings should be attributed to the actions of the provinces and not the PMPRB.

The conflicting results about the rate of rise of prices for non-patented drugs also raises the question about whether extending the PMPRB's mandate to include this group of medications would have any impact on overall drug prices.

Between 1969 and 1991 Canada had a system of compulsory licensing for pharmaceuticals. In essence, a compulsory licence is a permit which effectively negates a patent. Compulsory licensing allowed generic versions of the more successful drugs to appear on the Canadian market within 4–5 years after the original brand-name drug was marketed. Bill C-22 passed in 1987 granted brand-name manufacturers a 7–10 year window before a compulsory licence could be awarded, and Bill C-91 passed in 1993, but made retroactive to December 1991, abolished compulsory licensing completely.

The first generic competitor in the Canadian market typically enters at a price discount of about 25–30 per cent compared to the original product; when there are four or five generic competitors there is a difference of 50–60 per cent between the brand-name product and the least expensive generic version (Lexchin, 1993). According to figures in the Commission of Inquiry on the Pharmaceutical Industry (1985), in 1982 generic competition had, at a minimum, resulted in estimated savings to the Canadian public of $211 million, or, in other words, in the absence of generic competition Canada's drug bill would have increased from $1.53 billion to almost $1.74 billion.

It is difficult to reach any firm conclusions about how the abolition of compulsory licensing has affected drug expenditures. A report produced for the Canadian Drug Manufacturers Association, the organization representing Canadian owned generic companies, estimated that the cumulative costs of Bill C-91 from 1993 to 2000 would be $1.7 billion and by 2010 the cumulative costs from 1993 would be $4 billion (Schondelmeyer, 1993).

Using the figure of a 12 per cent saving from compulsory licensing reported by the Commission of Inquiry on the Pharmaceutical Industry and applying it to 1988–1995 sales of patented medications (Patented Medicine Prices Review Board, 1997) means that the abolition of compulsory licensing may have increased total drug costs by $2.30–$2.43 billion over the seven-year period. These lost savings may or may not have been offset by price regulation by the PMPRB.

STRATEGIES FOR LIMITING COSTS IN THE PUBLIC SECTOR

It should be remembered that the large majority of public spending comes from provincial drug plans (Table 16.3) and therefore this section will only deal with cost containment measures that have been undertaken by provincial governments. Although provincial plans cover only about 19 per cent of the population they account for about 41 per cent of prescription dollar spending because of the demographics of plan coverage, i.e. the fact that all provinces and territories provide coverage for some or all people aged 65 and over. (Sixty-two per cent of Canadians have private drug coverage, 19 per cent provincial

Table 16.3 Breakdown of public spending on pharmaceuticals, 1996*

	Provincial governments	Federal government	Workers' compensation	Hospitals and other institutions	Public health departments
Dollars (000,000)	2755.9	159.1	40.8	790.6	82.6
Percentage of total	72.0	4.2	1.1	20.6	2.2

Source: Dingwall (1997).

Notes:

* Includes prescription and over-the-counter drugs. Numbers do not add to 100 due to rounding.

drug plan coverage, 7 per cent public and private coverage and 12 per cent are without any drug coverage (Dingwall, 1997).) Nearly all provinces already attempt to control costs by encouraging the dispensing of generic drugs, by either mandating the dispensing of the lowest cost generic equivalent or else by limiting payments to pharmacists to the price of the least expensive generic equivalent (Anderson, 1990). This is an acceptable strategy now, but with the limitations placed on the availability of generics due to the abolition of compulsory licensing the importance of generic substitution as a cost control measure may diminish.

In controlling drug costs the governments have utilized one or more of a variety of options: formulary restrictions, cost-shifting, better formulary management, reference-based pricing and restricting price changes for drugs on formularies. To some extent these categories are artificial in that initiatives may have more than one effect, e.g. de-listing over-the-counter medications is a form of formulary restriction, but if the patient continues to use the medication it also constitutes cost shifting. In a similar vein, some of these measures, such as cost shifting, may also affect utilization.

FORMULARY RESTRICTIONS

All the provinces use restrictive formularies to limit the drugs that their various programs cover, with the rationale being that these restrictions help to contain costs. Anis (1994) argues that it is not formularies *per se* that keep drug costs down but rather the level of generic substitution and that this factor is not tied to the use of a formulary.

The brand-name pharmaceutical industry also often calls the whole concept of formularies into question. Besides the obvious economic interests involved, the industry claims that although formularies may decrease drug costs they increase costs elsewhere in the system and result in overall higher health care costs. In the absence of any Canadian studies on this topic, opponents of formularies usually rely on work looking at what happens when US states switch from an open Medicaid formulary (i.e. paying for any drug prescribed) to a restricted formulary or go in the reverse direction. (Medicaid pays for medical costs for the poor.) One significant weakness of these studies is their failure to consider how rational the restrictive formularies are. A poorly constructed formulary that leaves off important medications may be expected to result in increased overall costs. One study of formularies in 52 large American hospitals affiliated to medical schools found that 50 per cent of the formularies contained over 20 per cent or more pharmaceutical products which not only failed to meet the desired medical objective but were judged as marginally effective by five independent indices (Rucker, 1981) Furthermore, in addition to formulary restrictions Medicaid also places limits on other things such as the number or frequency of physician visits, limits which do not exist under Medicare in Canada.

While the question of whether or not formularies *per se* result in overall savings is still being debated, nevertheless provinces have taken a variety of steps to restrict their formularies: by de-listing products; by tightening up the conditions for listing drugs; and by restricting the use of some medications.

As part of its plan to control costs the Ontario government de-listed most long-acting prescription medications and most OTC drugs in the early 1990s. Whether or not this tactic led to any savings is a matter of conjecture as the government did not try to analyse the effects of de-listing. A survey of physicians in the Kingston area indicated that doctors usually substituted listed medications for de-listed ones (Godwin *et al.*, 1996).

The Republic of Ireland removed many of the same drugs as Ontario did from its reimbursed list. A preliminary analysis of those changes found that there was an increased prescribing of medicines with a higher ingredient cost, suggesting that any cost savings would have been negligible (Ferrando *et al.*, 1987). Further evidence that a simple policy of de-listing drugs will not produce any substantial savings comes from an assessment of the impact of de-listing of twelve categories of drugs of questionable efficacy from the New Jersey Medicaid formulary. Although withdrawn drugs accounted for 7 per cent of prescriptions in the base year, there was no measurable reduction in overall drug use or expenditures after the elimination of the target drugs. Furthermore, although the drugs were of questionable therapeutic benefit the overall quality of prescribing did not measurably improve as both desirable and undesirable therapeutic substitutions were observed (Soumerai *et al.*, 1990).

Ontario has followed a similar policy of placing restrictions on some categories of costly and potentially misused mediations. However, the ability of these measures to control use, and costs, depends on how well the system is managed. The Ontario Auditor-General (Office of the Provincial Auditor, 1996) looked into the auditing of the Limited Use category for his 1996 report. Based on a review of this class of drugs dispensed between January and June 1995, he found that expenditures for limited use drugs totalled $38 million; 13 per cent of claims had 'other' as a reason for the product being prescribed and an additional 21 per cent ($6.6 million) of the claims had a reason for use that did not apply for the drug dispensed. (The Ministry has now eliminated the 'other' category.)

Ontario and British Columbia now require a pharmacoeconomic assessment of drugs before they will be considered for formulary listing. The rationale here is that drugs should not only be safe and effective before they are listed, but also cost-effective compared to alternative therapies. The idea is not necessarily to limit drug costs, but to maximize the use of resources. Coyle and Drummond (1993) reviewed 85 evaluations published between 1986 and 1991 and concluded that they were potentially useful for decision-making, but many had methodological weaknesses and it was difficult to establish whether there was a methodological bias relating to the sponsorship of the studies.[1]

Finally, provincial payers are refusing to list new, often expensive, drugs. From 1990 to early 1995, provinces turned down 14–52 per cent of new products coming from multinational companies (Anon., 1995a). The Pharmaceutical Manufacturers Association of Canada (PMAC) is particularly concerned about this. The PMAC President is quoted as saying that 'Because these new drugs are often more cost-effective than existing therapies, they have the potential of saving the health care system money in the long run' (quoted in Anon., 1995a: 2) The accuracy of this statement is in some doubt as the Patented Medicine Prices Review Board has classified only 8 per cent of the drugs marketed from January 1991 to December 1995 as either 'break-through' medications or substantial improvements over existing therapies (Patented Medicine Prices Review Board, 1996a). When it comes to influencing prescribing, the effects of a policy of denying formulary listing may be similar to those of de-listing products: sometimes a less appropriate drug will be used in place of the one that is not available and sometimes a more appropriate drug will be used.

In summary, as of yet, there is no convincing evidence that provincial formulary restrictions have led to any significant overall cost savings.

COST SHIFTING

In 1996, Ontario became the final province to impose a system of copayments and deductibles on beneficiaries of its drug program. The objective here is to shift costs from the public payer to the individual receiving the drug therapy. Ontario is hoping to save $225 million per year; in British Columbia, after a copayment was put on pharmacists' dispensing fees, the amount the provincial government spent on this aspect of drug costs dropped from $28 million in 1986/87 to about $6 million in 1988/89 (Anderson *et al.*, 1993). So clearly cost shifting can save money, but the question is, do people subjected to user fees or deductibles forgo the purchase of necessary drugs and how does that affect their health? Harris and coworkers (1990) looked at the effects of a copayment on the use of 'essential' and 'discretionary' drugs in a health maintenance organization. The utilization of both types of medication decreased, but the decreases were larger for discretionary medications. Lexchin (1996) analysed direct out-of-pocket spending on pharmaceuticals by low and high income groups in Canada between 1964 and 1990. Even after the introduction of provincial drug plans, per capita spending by individuals in the low income group was seven times that of the high income group as a percentage of total family expenditure.

There is some Canadian evidence to support the contention that user fees will deter people from getting prescriptions filled. Nova Scotia imposed a $3 copayment on all seniors (age 65+), except for those in nursing homes and homes for the aged, on 1 June, 1990. Preliminary data showed a decline in the total number of people using the Pharmacare Plan, as well as a decline in the number of prescriptions filled for people not exempt from the copayment (Research & Statistics, Maritime Medical Care Incorporated, 1991).[2]

While Nova Scotia did not investigate the health effects of a decline in drug use other work has demonstrated adverse health outcomes for the poor when financial barriers were erected. Soumerai and colleagues (1991, 1994) took advantage of a 'natural' experiment to study what happened when the state of New Hampshire imposed a cap of three prescriptions per month on recipients of its Medicaid program. During the 11-month period that the cap was on, patients who regularly took three or more medications prior to the cap were much more likely to be admitted to a nursing home, and once admitted, in general, they did not return to the community (Soumerai *et al.*, 1991). In a population of psychiatric patients, the cap resulted in immediate reductions in the use of antipsychotic drugs, antidepressants, lithium and anxiolytic and hypnotic drugs. It also caused coincident increases of one to two visits per patient per month to community mental health centres and sharp increases in the use of emergency mental health services. The estimated average increase in mental health care costs per patient during the cap exceeded the savings in drug costs to Medicaid by a factor of 17 (Soumerai *et al.*, 1994).

It seems reasonably clear that for the poor and elderly cost shifting will lead to less appropriate use of medications and quite possibly an overall increase in costs to the health care system, offsetting any savings in drug costs.

BETTER FORMULARY MANAGEMENT

On-line health networks are a reality now in almost all provinces. These have been introduced by provinces in an attempt to better manage their drug programs. Typically, they link pharmacists and provide them with a variety of information when a prescription is presented. The Pharmanet computer network in British Columbia provides complete drug profiles, drug use review, adverse interaction checking and on-line, real-time adjudication. Saskatchewan's system has a warning system alerting pharmacists when a patient requests the same drug within a seven-day period. Through a retrospective drug utilization review (DUR) via the computerized network in New Brunswick physicians are notified when quantity limits for individual patients have been exceeded, and physicians have to justify continuation of the prescription (Fishman and McLaughlin, 1995).

The hope is that these prospective and retrospective DURs will lead to better quality prescribing and cost savings. To date there have not been any published evaluations of the effectiveness of these networks. Similar systems have been implemented by American states in their Medicaid programs. Soumerai and Lipton (1995) have recently reviewed the state of the art there and the following analysis comes from their paper. Claims that DUR is cost-effective because it reduces the incidence of drug-related illness and hospitalization tend to be inflated and based on unpublished, poorly controlled or biased studies. The efficacy of computer-based DUR rests on the assumption that greater adherence to the many published criteria regarding drug interactions, excessive dosages and other potential drug-therapy problems will reduce the incidence of serious adverse effects. Unfortunately, there is little evidence to support this assumption since most screening material in use lacks validation. Limitations inherent in the current technology and databases mean that DURs focus on overuse of medications ignoring problems of underuse of effective drug therapy (e.g. in hypertension or depression). Denial of refills of medication because the patient requests the refill too early may signal possible fraud or abuse, but other explanations are possible.

REFERENCE-BASED PRICING

In reference-based pricing systems a reimbursement price is set for a therapeutic category of drugs and patients are required to pay any difference between the cost of the product prescribed and the reference price. Therapeutic categories are selected where expert advice indicates that all the available medications are equally effective and have similar safety profiles. In these cases the most cost-effective form of prescribing is to use the reference product.

So far only British Columbia has introduced reference-based pricing starting with three drug categories: nonsteroidal anti-inflammatory agents (used for arthritis), nitrates (used for cardiac problems) and H2 blockers (e.g. ranitidine or Zantac) plus omeprazole (used primarily for ulcer therapy). According to figures from the British Columbia Ministry of Health from October 1995, when the program started, until August 1996 there were total drug savings of $21 million (Hudson, 1996).[3]

Other jurisdictions such as Denmark, Germany, The Netherlands, New Zealand and Sweden have also introduced reference-based pricing. A review of the European experience claims that the system has largely been a failure. According to Zammit-Lucia and Dasgupta (1995) there have been transient decreases in the price component of pharmaceuticals following the start of reference-based pricing, but overall expenditures have not moderated. The explanation offered is that other factors such as the volume of drugs prescribed and prescribing structure (switching from older to newer medications) are the main cost drivers. However, in the British Columbia case this scenario falls down as prescribing structure is exactly what reference-based pricing is influencing. Just as drug companies use promotion to shift prescribing patterns to newer, more expensive drugs, in British Columbia the aim is to shift prescribing to less expensive, but equally safe and effective products.

The multinational pharmaceutical industry, led by PMAC, has been very vocal in its denunciation of the British Columbia initiative and has publicized its opposition through an extensive advertising campaign and also challenged the program in court.[4] PMAC charges that the reference product is usually an older therapy which has been largely superseded by newer products which offer better efficacy and/or side effect profiles for many patients, with the likely effect that overall health costs will rise and thus offset any drug savings (Anon.,

1995c). However, aside from some anecdotal evidence PMAC has not produced any concrete data to back up its claims.

In the early 1990s Quebec sought to apply the PMPRB guidelines for price increases to non-patented medications listed on the Quebec formulary. In 1992–93, the Ontario Ministry established a guideline of 2 per cent for drug price increases, with the threat of de-listing products with increases greater than that. The following year (1994) Ontario imposed a price freeze on formulary drugs. Crude measures like these will obviously limit public expenditures on pharmaceuticals. Changes in prescribing habits and overall health costs may occur if products are de-listed, but otherwise this type of initiative is unlikely to have any other effect.

As Table 16.1 shows, overall public spending dropped from 1995 to 1996 and this is reflected in a decline in drug expenditures by provincial drug plans from $2.86 billion in 1995 to $2.76 billion the following year. The PMPRB may have played a role in effecting some of this decline, but it seems reasonable to assume that collectively the measures undertaken by provincial governments have also been a factor. A lack of data makes it impossible to determine the role of the different provincial initiatives. Even more importantly, there is a lack of information to show if prescribing behaviour and overall health costs have been changed by cost control measures in the drug sector.

STRATEGIES FOR LIMITING COSTS IN THE PRIVATE SECTOR

The private insured sector accounts for about 44 per cent of the Canadian prescription drug dollar volume, slightly more than the public sector. Drugs are by far the largest health expenditure item for the private sector representing just over 30 per cent of its health care spending. Until recently there was no attempt to control costs in private drug plans. Even now, with benefits packages as high as 7 per cent of an employee's total compensation package (Fishman and McLaughlin, 1995) and with companies identifying rising drug costs as the number one cost driver in increasing the cost of health benefits, only a minority of companies are taking any action. The most common strategy used in controlling drug costs, introducing generic substitution at the point of purchase, had been undertaken by less than 16 per cent of 401 companies surveyed by the Conference Board of Canada (Taylor, 1996). Even fewer companies were using other methods such as formularies, caps on dispensing fees, and mail order pharmacies. Only five companies had purchased the services of a pharmaceutical drug adjudicator (PDA), the Canadian equivalent of pharmaceutical benefits managers (PBMs), and another thirty-three were considering doing so. Despite this low uptake it is likely that these organizations will assume an increasingly prominent role as insurers opt to get out of managing pharmacy benefits themselves. A number of factors are fuelling this movement toward PDAs: strong pressure on costs (and premiums) due to an older workforce, increased disability benefits, cost-shifting by provincial governments and a higher rate of utilization of the health-care system; development of flexible plans that offer a wide range of options and premiums; a rapid evolution in pharmacy computer networks that will open up the market for the electronic pay-direct plans that PDAs operate.

PDAs provide the following services for insurance companies: adjudication of claims made against the plan; regular information and reports to the insurer and/or employer regarding drug usage and plan performance; billing of the third party payer (insurer) on a regular basis for claims made; assistance with the administration and management of the formulary; and interface with pharmacies for adjudication and reimbursement (Anon., 1995b). As the description of their role implies PDAs are attempting to control costs through a variety of measures, some similar to those employed in the public sector (Fishman and McLaughlin,, 1995).

Formularies are being developed, usually adapted from provincial plan formularies, but with provisions to cover working populations. Some PDAs, like the Canadian subsidiary of FoxMeyer Corporation, are electronically linking pharmacies, like in the provincial plans, and engaging in drug utilization review to check for multiple doctoring, multiple pharmacy visits and prescriptions being filled too soon or too late (McLaren, 1995). Electronic networks are also being used to adjudicate a submitted claim in real-time so that both the provider and the plan member are informed of eligibility and payment terms at the time of dispensing. Some plans are utilizing the so-called 'mail order pharmacy services' in order to reduce dispensing fees, as increases in these figure much more prominently in the private sector plans than in the public sector. FoxMeyer and others such as Liberty Mutual (formerly Ontario Blue Cross) are trying to establish preferred provider networks: having pharmacies sign contracts promising low dispensing fees in return for the promise of prescription volumes coming from employee groups with preferred provider incentives built into their drug plans.

Despite all this activity there is little or no published data to evaluate the effectiveness of any of these measures. FoxMeyer claims that its electronic drug use monitoring programs reduce employers' drug benefit costs by as much as 25 per cent. According to a spokesperson for FoxMeyer, 40 per cent of the 25 per cent is from drug utilization management (McLaren, 1995). Leaving aside any independent verification of these claims, whether or not these savings translate into more appropriate prescribing and system wide savings is unclear. An American survey of the nine largest PBMs and benefits managers at eight large employers concluded that until PBMs develop the ability to track long-term outcomes and costs of disease they will lack the ability to definitively show the effect of their programs (Schulman *et al.*, 1996).

The use of mail order pharmacy may also not be cost-effective. Although these operations offer dispensing fees of about $5 compared to $10–$15 in community pharmacies, they also dispense drugs in larger volumes which results in more wastage; this wastage may offset any savings gained through the lower dispensing fees. Research is also lacking in areas such as patient satisfaction and indicators of quality of care (Kirking *et al.*, 1990).

One trend that is starting is the takeover of PDAs by pharmaceutical companies. In May 1995, Eli Lilly bought Rx Plus, the country's second-largest PDA, which manages health benefits for about 1,200 corporate clients employing some 500,000 people (Anon., 1995b). The merger raises a serious concern about conflict of interest: that the PDA would reflect the interests of the pharmaceutical owner rather than those of competitors and patients. The vice-president of marketing and business development for Rx Plus counters that 'we can't push any company's drugs, whether it's Lilly's or somebody else's to the detriment of our customers, because that'll be uncovered very quickly, and it will hurt our ability to be competitive in the claims processing market' (quoted in McLaren, 1995).

However, the experience in the United States strongly suggests that the main motivation behind the purchase of PDAs is market expansion for the drugs produced by the pharmaceutical company doing the acquisition. In 1993, Merck, then the world's largest pharmaceutical company, bought Medco Containment Services, the United States' largest mail order prescription house and one of the three largest PBMs. The next year, a Medco senior vice-president was quoted as saying that Medco has given Merck information that helped Merck develop competitive bids for Medco business (Anon., 1994a). A report from the General Accounting Office (GAO), released in November 1995, revealed that since the Merck–Medco merger Medco's formularies substantially increased their representation of Merck drugs. The GAO also found that Medco removed some competitors' products that competed with those of its parent pharmaceutical company (Schulman *et al.*, 1996).

In 1994, the American parent of Lilly acquired PCS Health Systems, that country's largest manager of drug benefit programs. There, as in Canada, Lilly downplayed the potential to increase volume sales of its products by manipulating the PCS formulary. At the same time, the chairman of Lilly, addressing his company's purchase of PCS, stated that 'this [purchase] will help sell even more Prozac' (quoted in Schulman *et al.*, 1996). Lilly's assurances that it would not meddle with the PCS formulary were not sufficient for the Federal Trade Commission, which imposed a number of restrictions on its relationship with PCS (Gibaldi, 1995).[5]

THE FUTURE FOR PHARMACEUTICAL COST CONTAINMENT

The move to roster patients in the primary care sector is gaining momentum. Under this scheme patients would be registered with a general practitioner and receive their care, and access to speciality services, through her or him. Rostering opens up a new avenue for controlling pharmaceutical costs. Once you know who a general practitioner's patients are, then you can estimate how much drug therapy those patients will require and the cost of that therapy. Essentially, that is what has happened in the United Kingdom with 'fundholding' practices. These practices are given a budget that includes the projected cost of pharmacotherapy as well as the cost of speciality and subspeciality consultations. Fundholding practices are given an incentive to restrain their prescribing budget since they can retain any savings for investment in other approved areas of service development. Work in the UK shows that these incentives can produce changes in prescribing costs in a relatively short period of time (Wilson *et al.*, 1995). At the same time, research has only focused on the costs of prescribing, not on its quality or cost-effectiveness. Improvements in cost containment must be shown not to come on the back of a deterioration in quality.

There are other unresolved issues in devolving drug budgets to primary care. Drug budgets are usually set based on the age and sex distribution of patients in a practice. This method can lead to GPs 'cream skimming' or setting up barriers to discourage people with chronic, costly problems such as AIDS, from registering with their practices. Therefore, a method needs to be developed to incorporate a measure of 'need' into the calculations for drug budgets. GPs may also be tempted to refer people to hospitals early and to try to prevent early discharge, since while patients are hospitalized drug costs come from the hospital's budget not the GP's.

More importantly, there is growing recognition that in order to better manage the Canadian health care system there has to be greater integration of all the various actors involved. The idea is to find a model that provides efficient, integrated care in a way that balances quality, accessibility and cost control. One proposal that is gaining increasing attention is something called an integrated delivery system (IDS). An IDS is a network of health care organizations that would provide or arrange to provide, a coordinated continuum of services to a defined population and would be held clinically and fiscally accountable for the health status of that population (Leatt *et al.*, 1996).

Financing of an IDS would be on a capitation model, i.e., for each enrolled client the provincial ministry of health would provide a fixed prospective payment that would vary depending on the patient's age, sex and some measure of morbidity. These payments would cover all of the publicly funded health care services that the population requires during the year, including drugs and devices, visits to primary care practitioners, services provided by IDS-managed institutions and agencies and IDS-affiliated professionals (Leatt *et al.*, 1996).

If the IDS model is adopted in Canada it opens the way for the introduction of 'disease management'. Disease management is a way of controlling more than just drug costs; in its broadest definition it 'is a process which encompasses all aspects of healthcare from prevention and education, through diagnosis and integrated primary and secondary treatment to aftercare and monitoring, and finally to further education' (Hall, 1995). In the United

States pharmaceutical companies have been in the forefront of the movement to disease management for a number of reasons:

- an increasing awareness that profitability in pharmaceuticals will probably never again reach the levels of previous decades and that new opportunities must be sought;
- a recognition that traditional research and development is yielding diminishing returns as most of the 'easy' diseases have been addressed;
- an appreciation that those who pay for health care are increasingly looking at total costs of treatment, not just the pharmaceutical costs (Hall, 1995).

About a dozen companies are aiming to put together packages of pharmaceuticals, other treatment elements (e.g., diagnostics, delivery systems) and services (e.g., outcomes analysis, protocol development) for chronic major problems such as Alzheimer's, asthma, depression, epilepsy and ulcers (Anders, 1995).

Here in Canada pharmaceutical companies are also beginning the process. Marion Merrell Dow (now Hoechst Marion Roussell) purchased Clinidata, a medical information systems company (Anon., 1994b), and Merck has established a PATIENT HEALTH MANAGEMENT™ program (Anon., 1996b).

While the concept of disease management is attractive, some of the assumptions on which it is based may be flawed. For example, in promoting disease management, pharmaceutical companies often make the argument that better compliance with a drug regimen will result in fewer downstream costs such as doctors' visits, tests and hospitalizations. While superficially appealing this argument is erroneous. For instance, many widely accepted drug regimens are based on the original Health Protection Branch approval studies or on existing practice patterns which are not necessarily optimal (Harris, 1996); often the clinical significance of poor compliance has never been adequately documented and therefore measures to improve compliance may not have positive health outcomes.

As in the case of pharmaceutical company ownership of PBMs/PDAs, their involvement with disease management raises serious questions. In the US, some big health plans balk at letting drug companies deal directly with their members because of doubts that the companies can be objective about patients' best interests. As one medical director bluntly put it 'They're going to push their drug, no matter what they say about wanting to lower overall costs.' Doctors are worried that the sponsor of a disease management program may be reluctant to let patients switch to a competitor's product, while benefits managers may not want to turn over confidential patient information to an outside company (Anders, 1995).

Finally, there is a serious concern in Canada about the erosion of the publicly funded medical system. In 1975, the public sector accounted for over 76 cents of every health dollar spent; by 1994 this was down to under 72 cents (Policy and Consultation Branch, Health Canada, 1996). Integrated delivery systems have the potential to open up a still larger part of the health system to private for-profit corporations, further weakening the role of the public sector. In some IDS models these corporations will be allowed to bid for the right to provide services, including disease management. Private sector funding generally means greater overall costs because of larger administrative expenses (Himmelstein *et al.*, 1994) and more difficulty in health care planning because of a larger number of independent payers. Greater private funding is also associated with the development of a two-tier medical system, something that has been substantially abolished with the advent of Medicare.

CONCLUSION

Drug costs are the most rapidly escalating part of overall health care expenditures in both the public and private sectors. In the absence of any data to show that putting more money into drugs is cost effective, public and private payers will continue to try and control drug costs. One of the main factors contributing to the increase in cost is the introduction of new, more expensive, but not necessarily more effective, drugs. This phenomenon is not something new, but when compulsory licensing was in place lower cost generic equivalents were often quickly available to offer price competition. Since the passage of Bill C-91 this is no longer the case. Instead, the PMPRB is suppose to control the introductory price of new products, but there are serious questions about how well it is doing its job.

Both public and private payers have developed programs to control costs. While some of these methods have lowered direct costs to payers there is considerable doubt as to whether they have done anything to improve the appropriateness of prescribing and to contain overall health care costs. Furthermore, with the exception of pharmacoeconomic studies and reference-based pricing, none of these programs deal with the question of the high cost of new drugs and the jury is still out as to how effective both of these measures will be.

Both the private and public sectors seem to be interested in adapting American programs for Canada: pharmaceutical drug adjudicators and managed care. In each case, in the United States, the pharmaceutical industry is heavily involved and this raises serious concerns about conflicts of interest and increasing private control over the Canadian health care system. Furthermore, neither of these programs seems to have been particularly successful in reining in drug costs south of the border. From 1988 to 1995, the factory gate price for pharmaceuticals in the US increased at 5.3 per cent annually compared to 3.1 per cent here in Canada (Patented Medicine Prices Review Board, 1997).

The key to controlling drug expenditures is twofold: regulating the introductory prices of new medications and ensuring cost-effective prescribing.

Deciding on the appropriate price for a new drug cannot simply be done by comparing the Canadian price with that in seven other countries as the PMPRB current does. Even expanding the number of comparitor countries may not be adequate as companies are increasingly adopting a relatively uniform international price for their new drugs. The PMPRB does not have either the mandate or the resources to seek out and analyse these costs.

Cost-effective prescribing is a complex problem that involves more than just conducting pharmacoeconomic studies. At a minimum, this move would involve an undertaking to fund proven methods of improving physician prescribing, consumer education, the development of databases to monitor drug prescribing and use, and the development and dissemination of objective sources of information about medications (Lexchin, 1997). One model of how such a system might operate exists in the Australian Pharmaceutical Health and Rational Use of Medicines Working Party (PHARM) which was formed by the federal Department of Health in 1991. PHARM is a cross-sectoral group representing consumers, industry, government and health professionals, with skills in areas including health education and promotion, research, behavioural science, specialist and general practice, community ownership and participation, nursing and pharmacy. Its approach is based on the current understanding of medicines and good clinical practice, and on relevant ethical principles and consumer rights (Murray, 1995).

To date, amidst much rhetoric and counter claims, neither public nor private payers have shown either the political will or the commitment of resources that will make it possible to control introductory prices and encourage cost-effective prescribing.

NOTES

1 Admittedly, Coyle and Drummond's conclusions were reached in the relatively early days of pharmacoeconomics and the quality may have improved since then. However, Evans (1995) questions the whole idea of pharmacoeconomics. According to him, many methodologic problems in this area, such as 'What is the value of a human life?', may be unresolvable since they represent different theories of how economies function, or conflicting ideological prejudices as to how they should function. At this point, the jury is still out as to whether or not pharmacoeconomics is going to produce more effective use of resources.

2 These figures were adjusted for prescription size so the decline in the number of prescriptions being filled cannot be explained by an increase in the number of units dispensed.

3 In early 1997, British Columbia added two classes of drugs used to control blood pressure to the list of products covered under reference-based pricing.

4 The industry lost the court challenge in the British Columbia Supreme Court (Anon., 1996a). To date only British Columbia has been prepared to weather the industry storm of reference-based pricing, with other provinces watching with interest.

5   It is ironic that while the drug companies complain about the restrictive formularies run by Canadian provinces, they are prepared to operate restrictive formularies when they take over PBMs/PDAs.

REFERENCES

Anders, G. 1995. Drug makers help manage patient care. *Wall Street Journal*, 17 May, p. B1.

Anderson, G. M., K. J., Kerluke, I. R., Pulcins, C., Hertzman, M. L. Barer, 1993. Trends and determinants of prescription drug expenditures in the elderly: data from the British Columbia Pharmacare Program. *Inquiry* 30: 199–207.

Anderson, L. J. 1990. *Provincial and territorial drug reimbursement programs: descriptive summary.* Ottawa: Drugs Directorate, Health Protection Branch, Health and Welfare Canada.

Anis, A. H. 1994. Substitution laws, insurance coverage, and generic drug use. *Med Care* 32: 240–256.

Anon. 1994a. Repercussions of Lilly/FTC pact. Scrip No. 1972, 4 Nov., p. 7.

Anon. 1994b. Canadian managed-care move for MMD. Scrip No. 1980, 2 Dec., p. 13.

Anon. 1995a. Dramatic changes in 1994 pharmaceutical sales reflect increasing problem of access to new medicines. *PMAC News*, March, pp. 1–3.

Anon. 1995b. Eli Lilly buys Canadian claims processor. Scrip No. 2026, 19 May, p. 9.

Anon. 1995c. PMAC launches campaign against reference-based pricing. *PMAC News*, September, pp. 1–2.

Anon. 1996a. Reference pricing to stay in Canada. Scrip No. 2138, 18 June, p. 14.

Anon. 1996b. Recipe for better health. Best Health Management: A Merck Frosst Seminar on Managing Health Care for a Better Tomorrow.

Brogan Consulting Inc. 1995. Facts on escalating drug plan costs. *Group Healthcare Management* 3 (11): 1–27.

Brogan Consulting Inc., W. N. Palmer & Associates. 1995. Review of prescription non-patented drug prices in Canada using public and private drug plan data 1989–1994. Submitted to Federal/Provincial/Territorial Pharmaceutical Policy Committee.

Commission of Inquiry on the Pharmaceutical Industry. 1985. *Report*. Ottawa: Supply and Services Canada.

Coyle, D., and M. Drummond, 1993. Does expenditure on pharmaceuticals give good value for money?: current evidence and policy implications. *Health Policy* 26: 55–75.

Dingwall, D. C. 1997. Drug costs in Canada. Submitted to the House of Commons Standing Committee on Industry for the review of the Patent Act Amendment Act, 1992.

Evans, R. G. 1995. Manufacturing consensus, marketing truth: guidelines for economic evaluation. *Ann Intern Med* 123: 59–60.

Ferrando, C., M. C., Henman, O. I. Corrigan, 1987. Impact of a nationwide limited prescribing list: preliminary findings. *Drug Intell Clin Pharm* 21: 653–658.

Fishman, R. and D. McLaughlin, 1995. *PharmaFocus Canada 1999: looking forward with confidence.* Pharma Strategy Group, IMS International.

Gibaldi, M. 1995. Vertical integration: the drug industry and prescription benefits managers. *Pharmacotherapy* 15: 265–271.

Godwin, M., J., Chapman, D., Mowat, W., Racz, J., McBride, J. Tang, 1996. Delisting of drugs in Ontario: how attitudes and prescribing strategies of family physicians in the Kingston area changed. *Can Fam Physician* 42: 1309–1316.

Green Shield Canada. 1994. *A report on drug costs.* Toronto.

Hall, M. 1995. Disease management—what role for the industry in Europe? *Scrip Magazine*, June, pp. 29–32.

Harris, B. L., A. Stergachis, and L. D. Reid, 1990. The effect of drug co-payments on utilization and cost of pharmaceuticals in a health maintenance organization. *Med Care* 28: 907–917.

Harris, J. M., Jr. 1996. Disease management: new wine in new bottles? *Ann Intern Med* 124: 838–842.

Himmelstein, D. U. and S. Woolhandler, 1994. *The national health program book: a source guide for advocates.* Monroe, ME: Common Courage Press.

Hudson, R. 1996. Reference based pricing in British Columbia's Pharmacare Program. Presented at First National Conference on Cost Effective Drug Therapy, Toronto, 27 November .

Kirking, D. M., F. J. Ascione, and J. W. Richards, 1990. Choices in prescription-drug benefit programs: mail versus community pharmacy services. *Milbank Quarterly* 68: 29–51.

Leatt, P., G. H. Pink, and C. D. Naylor, 1996. Integrated delivery systems: has their time come in Canada? *Can Med Assoc J* 154: 803–809.

Lexchin, J. 1992. Prescribing and drug costs in the province of Ontario. *Int J Health Serv* 22: 471–487.

Lexchin, J. 1993. The effect of generic competition on the price of prescription drugs in the Province of Ontario. *Can Med Assoc J* 148: 35–38.

Lexchin, J. 1996. Income class and pharmaceutical expenditure in Canada: 1964–1990. *Can J Public Health* 87: 46–50.

Lexchin, J. 1997. After compulsory licensing: coming issues in Canadian pharmaceutical policy and politics. *Health Policy* 40: 69–80.

McLaren, S. 1995. Managed care: a wealth of options. *Can Pharm J* 128 (10): 34–39.

Murray, M. 1995. Australian national drug policies: facilitating or fragmenting health? *Development Dialogue*, No. 1: 149–192.

Office of the Provincial Auditor. 1996. *1996 annual report: accounting, accountability, value for money.* Toronto: Queen's Printer for Ontario.

Organization for Economic Co-operation and Development. 1996. *Purchasing power parities and real expenditures: GK results, volume II, 1993.* Paris: OECD.

Patented Medicine Prices Review Board. 1996a. *Eighth annual report for the year ended December 31, 1995.* Ottawa: Supply and Services Canada.

Patented Medicine Prices Review Board. 1996b. *The top 200 selling patented drug products in Canada (1994).* Ottawa: Patented Medicine Prices Review Board, Publication No. S-9607.

Patented Medicine Prices Review Board. 1997. *The impact of federal regulation of patented drug prices.* Ottawa: Patented Medicine Prices Review Board, PMPRB Study Series S-9708.

Policy and Consultation Branch, Health Canada. 1996. *National health expenditures in Canada, 1975–1994.* Ottawa: Supply and Services Canada.

Research & Statistics, Maritime Medical Care Incorporated. 1991. *The effects of co-payment on utilization of the MSI seniors pharmacare plan.*

Rucker, T. D. 1981. Effective formulary development—which direction? *Topics in Hosp Pharm Manage* 1: 29–45.

Schondelmeyer, S. W. 1993. *The cost of Bill C-91: an economic impact analysis of the elimination of compulsory licensing of pharmaceuticals in Canada.* Canadian Drug Manufacturers Association.

Schulman, K. A., E., Rubenstein, D. R., Abernathy, S.M. Seils, and D. P. Sulmasy, 1996. The effect of pharmaceutical benefits managers: is it being evaluated? *Ann Intern Med* 124: 906–913.

Smalley, W. E., M. R., Griffin, R. L., Fought, L. Sullivan, and W. A. Ray, 1995. Effect of a prior-authorization requirement on the use of nonsteroidal anti-inflammatory drugs by Medicaid patients. *N Engl J Med* 332: 1612–1617.

Soumerai, S. B. and H. L. Lipton, 1995. Computer-based drug-utilization review – risk, benefit, or boondoggle? *N Engl J Med* 332: 1641–1645.

Soumerai, S. B., D., Ross-Degnan, S. Gortmaker and J. Avorn, 1990. Withdrawing payment for nonscientific drug therapy: intended and unexpected effects of a large-scale natural experiment. *JAMA* 263: 831–839.

Soumerai, S. B., D., Ross-Degnan, J., Avorn, T. J. McLaughlin, and I. Choodnovskiy, 1991. Effects of Medicaid drug-payment limits on admission to hospitals and nursing homes. *N Engl J Med* 325: 1072–1077.

Soumerai, S. B., T. J., McLaughlin, D., Ross-Degnan, C. S. Casteris, and P. Bollini, 1994. Effects of limiting Medicaid drug-reimbursement benefits on the use of psychotropic agents and acute mental health services by patients with schizophrenia. *New Engl J Med* 331: 650–655.

Taylor, C. L. 1996. The corporate response to rising health care costs. Ottawa: Conference Board of Canada.

Wilson, R. P. H., I. M. Buchan, and T. Walley, 1995. Alterations in prescribing by general practitioner fundholders: an observational study. *BMJ* 311: 1347–1350.

Zammit-Lucia, J. and R. Dasgupta, 1995. *Reference pricing: the European experience.* Health Policy Review Paper No. 10. London: St Mary's Hospital Medical School.

17 Governing health

John Lavis and Terry Sullivan

A growing literature supports the notion that our social environment – our incomes, our work, our social networks – in large part determines why some people are healthy and others not (Evans *et al.*, 1994). Health-care systems play a significant role in why we get well when we are sick; social environments play a significant role in why we are healthy or why we become sick in the first place. There is an emerging consensus that societies with a more equitable income distribution, more employment and better working conditions, and more social cohesion are healthier and generate a virtuous cycle of prosperity and health (Evans *et al.*, 1994; Amick *et al.*, 1995; Blane *et al.*, 1996; Wilkinson, 1996). In the past, experts viewed health as being largely separate from state policies to redistribute the rewards of a productive economy, create employment and ensure good working conditions, and build social cohesion. Many experts no longer hold this view and see health reform as one of the principal avenues redefining the boundaries between states, markets, and civil society (Dahrendorf, 1995).

This chapter addresses the third policy imperative for health reform: to devise social arrangements which engender healthy populations. As such, the chapter represents a departure from previous chapters in which the focal point was health care and market limits *to* health care reform. Here the focus is health and market limits *as* health reform. Unregulated markets can pose a threat to the very social environments that generate prosperity and health. For example, unregulated labour markets can give rise to growing wage inequality and high levels of job insecurity. The state can play an important role in reducing these threats to social environments and in actively improving these social environments.

Table 17.1 provides three dimensions of the social environment that are particularly important for health, one or more examples of health determinants within each of these three dimensions, and potential government actions targeted at these health determinants which could improve health. The list of potential government actions illustrates the range of public policy beyond traditional health-care policy that can be considered when devising social arrangements which engender healthy populations. Of course, businesses, non-governmental organizations and other groups can actively shape our social

Table 17.1 Examples of health determinants and potential government action to address these health determinants

Dimensions of the social environment	Health determinant	Potential government actions to improve health
Income	Income distribution	Use personal taxation and/or social programs to compensate for growing wage inequality
Work	Unemployment	Use trade agreements, industrial policy and labour-market policy to reduce the incidence and duration of unemployment
	Job insecurity	Use labour-market policy to reduce the prevalence of job insecurity
	Job strain (high demands and low decision latitude)	Use corporate taxation and/or experience-rated workers' compensation premia to provide incentives for job redesign strategies that reduce job strain or more specifically increase decision latitude on the job
Social networks	Social support	Use personal taxation to provide incentives for involvement in social organizations and/or use social programs to compensate for a lack of social support among isolated individuals

environments as well, but we restrict our attention in this chapter to the state. Thus far, health-related arguments have rarely informed states' development of public policy in areas other than health care (Lavis, 1997, 1998a).

In a recent study of the role of the determinants-of-health synthesis (i.e. the body of research on the relationship between social environments and health) in policy change in Canada and the United Kingdom, only two cases were identified in which an institutional innovation or policy change may have come about, at least in part, because of the determinants of health synthesis (Lavis, 1997). Even in these two cases, the policy-relevant ideas embodied in the determinants-of-health synthesis played strategic, rather than instrumental, roles. For example, in one case – the move towards a single-management structure for health and human services in Prince Edward Island – an argument that the move would facilitate cross-sectoral re-allocations in line with the determinants of health was used by the side that found it supportive of its position, but the idea did not play a key role in the development of the position. The provincial government's decision was motivated primarily by a desire to reduce the size of the bureaucracy. By invoking a determinants-of-health argument, however, the government attracted the support of some parts of the health-policy community for a large-scale restructuring effort that would otherwise have been largely unpopular.

Two attempts have been made to provide an understanding of the factors that hinder or shape efforts to devise social arrangements that engender healthy populations. These efforts have focused on interests or on barriers put in place by previous policies. Marmor *et al.* (1994) adopted an interest group model and applied it only within the health policy community; that is, within a policy subsystem that has limited if any influence on public policy beyond health policy. According to this formulation, the power of health-care providers explains why the determinants-of-health synthesis has played such a limited role. Lavis and Sullivan (forthcoming) adopted a policy feedback model. Policies designed to increase access to and quality of health care were argued to have long-run effects on bureaucrats and interest groups that were not conducive to change in public policy beyond health policy.

The approach taken in this chapter involves a complementary perspective. We argue that two hurdles must be jumped for health-related arguments to inform the development of public policy in areas other than health care: one hurdle involves getting on the political agenda and the other involves improving state capacity to consider the health consequences of public policy in these other domains. The United States, the United Kingdom and Canada face very different challenges when it comes to the political agenda: the United States has not yet developed policies that ensure universal access to health care at an affordable cost, which makes moving beyond health care difficult; the United Kingdom health bureaucracy has its hands full with the financing and provision of health care; and Canada has a federal health bureaucracy looking for a new challenge but without much leverage to place health consequences on the political agenda in other policy domains. But even if making health-improving changes to our social environments made it to the political agenda, states typically lack the capacity to consider the health consequences of public policies that influence social environments.

The chapter is organized in four parts. First, we build the case for moving beyond health care by providing a brief overview of the literature on health determinants, particularly the literature on employment and working conditions, and by highlighting the need for public policy to address these determinants. Second, we describe the political agenda and state capacity hurdles confronting those interested in seeing health-related arguments used to inform the development of public policy in areas other than health care. Third, we argue that new institutional arrangements are required if states are to consider routinely the social determinants of health in decision-making and we provide two examples of health reform that used cross-sectoral bodies to increase state capacity for improving health. These examples include a cross-sectoral advisory body in Ontario and cross-sectoral consensus building in The Netherlands. Finally, we conclude with some observations on governing health.

BEYOND HEALTH CARE: SOCIAL DETERMINANTS OF HEALTH

The residents of some states are healthier than the residents of others, almost regardless of which measure of health status is used and how much money is spent on health care. In 1990, women in Japan could expect to live on average 81.9 years, while Canadian women could expect to live 80.4 years and American women 78.8 years. More striking were the differences between countries in infant mortality rates: 4.6 infants died for every 1,000 live births in Japan, compared to 6.8 deaths in Canada and 9.1 deaths in the United States (Schieber *et al.*, 1993). Japan, at the bottom of the Organization for Economic Co-operation and Development (OECD) states for health indicators three decades ago, now outperforms other OECD states across a spectrum of health indicators. The pattern of health-care spending in 1991 was the reverse of what one would expect based on life expectancy and infant mortality data: Japan spent only 6.8 per cent of their gross domestic product on health care, while Canada spent 10 per cent and the United States spent 13.2 per cent (Schieber *et al.*, 1993). National comparisons such as these, coupled with more rigorous individual-level studies, have led to a clear and simple conclusion: the determinants of health extend beyond health care.

Several attempts have been made to provide a conceptual framework within which these determinants can be sorted and better understood (Lalonde, 1974; Bunker *et al.*, 1989; Evans and Stoddart, 1990; Hertzman *et al.*, 1994; Whitehead, 1995). Common to all frameworks is the central importance of the social environment – our incomes, our work, our social networks – which is shaped at least in part by public policies. These policies do not just include those with specific health objectives, such as health policy and occupational health and safety policy. Perhaps more important are public policies with unintended health consequences, such as trade, fiscal, and labour-market policy.

Work-related health determinants

In response to globalization, trade competition, and technological innovation, labour markets have changed dramatically in the last decade, perhaps more than any other aspect of the social environment. Many workers in advanced economies face limited employment prospects and poor working conditions. The resulting 'adverse' labour-market experiences – related either to the availability of work (e.g. unemployment, job insecurity, and overwork) or to the nature of work (e.g. increasing job demands, low job position within a firm, and contingent employment) – can have profound health consequences. Moreover, the health consequences of these labour-market experiences may vary according to the context in which they are experienced. For example, the health consequences of unemployment have been found to vary according to local labour-market conditions (e.g. Iversen *et al.*, 1987); they may also vary according to the generosity of unemployment-insurance benefits or the degree of reliance on work-related social supports. Such interactions may suggest possible intervention strategies (e.g. changes to benefit levels) or groups at which interventions should be targeted (e.g. groups in particular labour markets or groups reliant on work-related social supports). The literature on the links between labour-market experiences and health provides an illustrative example of the influence of the social environment on health. Like all research, many of the studies have methodological limitations, most significantly the potential for the results to be attributable to differences at baseline (e.g. in health) between those exposed to a labour-market experience and those not exposed to the labour-market experience *per se*.

Studies have examined a range of labour-market experiences and their health consequences, which may include behavioural and biological responses, professionally diagnosed disease, and patient-reported mental or physical health and function. Many of these studies have used a cohort design, a more rigorous approach than a cross-sectional design because it permits the examination of whether a labour-market experience at one point in time is associated with a health outcome at a later point in time. Only those studies that used a cohort design and for which data on exposure (to a labour-market experience) and outcomes could be extracted will be discussed. Experiences that have been examined in such cohort studies include unemployment (with disease the only health outcome not examined in adults and with health-related behaviours and mental health and function almost the only health outcomes examined in youth), job insecurity (with a mix of health outcomes examined), job characteristics (with a mix of mostly cardiovascular health outcomes examined), job position within the firm (with a mix of mostly cardiovascular system-related individual responses and disease examined), and organizational characteristics of the firm (with only individual biological responses examined and then only in one study). No cohort studies have examined underemployment or overwork (Lavis, 1998b).

'Adverse' labour-market experiences related to the availability of work – unemployment and job insecurity – have been consistently found in cohort studies to be associated with negative health outcomes. The absolute risk of a negative health consequence was consistently higher among unemployed adults compared to employed adults. For example, unemployed adults have been found to have increased blood cholesterol levels (Kasl *et al.*, 1968), gains of over 10 per cent in body mass index (Morris *et al.*, 1992), and earlier deaths (Moser *et al.*, 1984, 1986; Iversen *et al.*, 1987; Costa and Segnan, 1987; Martikainen, 1990; Stefansson, 1991; Morris *et al.*, 1994; Martikainen and Valkonen, 1996; Lavis, 1997) compared to employed adults. One category of exception to the general association between unemployment and negative health outcomes is health-related behaviours like smoking or alcohol consumption (Iversen and Klausen, 1986; Kaprio and Koskenvuo, 1988; Morris *et al.*, 1992), which could be explained by the relatively high cost of such behaviours for unemployed individuals. The health consequences of unemployment vary according to the local unemployment rate: for example, three studies have found that the mortality rate for unemployed adults was higher in areas (Iversen *et al.*, 1987; Lavis, 1997) or periods (Martikainen and Valkonen, 1996) with low unemployment rates. The absolute risks of heart trouble) and sickness absence were higher among individuals with insecure jobs compared to individuals with secure jobs (Ferrie *et al.*, 1998; Owens, 1966). Moreover, many of the negative biological responses associated with unemployment have been found to be concentrated in the anticipatory phase before unemployment; that is, in the period after notification of job loss but before actual job loss occurs (Kasl *et al.*, 1968; Kasl and Cobb, 1970).

'Adverse' labour-market experiences related to job characteristics and job position within the firm have also been found in cohort studies to be associated with a number of negative health outcomes. The absolute risks of a positive coronary heart disease indicator or of mortality within a specified period were higher among individuals with low job decision latitude, low job decision latitude coupled with low job support, or high job strain (i.e. high job demands and low job decision latitude) (Karasek *et al.*, 1982; Astrand *et al.*, 1989; Falk *et al.*, 1992; Alterman *et al.*, 1994). The absolute risks of disease were not in the predicted direction for individuals in the lowest job position within a firm compared with those in the highest job position (Hinkle *et al.*, 1968; Shekelle *et al.*, 1969), which could be explained by the reversal in the gradient of health-related behaviours by job position since these studies were conducted in the late 1960s. The risks of mortality within a specified period were higher for individuals in the lowest job position within a firm compared with those in the highest job position (Marmot *et al.*, 1978; Rose and Marmot, 1981; Marmot *et al.*, 1984). Moreover, a single measure of the social environment – job control – explained more of the variation in health across job positions within a firm than all standard coronary heart disease risk factors taken together (Marmot *et al.*, 1997).

Public policy

If earning a reasonable income in comparison with others, working in a low strain job, and having a social network are associated with improved health (Evans *et al.*, 1994), there is a potential role for health-improving changes in trade, fiscal, labour market and other public policies. For example, Wilkinson (1992) has estimated that if Britain were to adopt an income distribution more like the most egalitarian European countries, about two years might be added to the population's life expectancy. Recent research has found that both inequality and polarization of family disposable income fell in Canada between 1985 and 1995, but rose in the US government social programs, and taxation in Canada buffered the increasing inequality in labour income (Wolfson and Murphy, 1998). By this example, we do not mean to assert a 'healthism' in public policy, that health should be the single, most important consideration in developing public policy. Health, like income or leisure time, is only one determinant of our well being, and we may be willing to sacrifice perfect health for some other advantage brought by public policy or to avoid some disadvantage. None the less, health can be taken as an important measure of the benefits or costs that accrue from public policy, and as such warrants explicit consideration in the development of public policy.

Municipal, state and increasingly supranational levels of governance each represent possible points to influence policy making. However, these levels differ in the availability of critical policy levers, their potential effectiveness in bringing about changes in health determinants and thus in health, and their potential role in policy development and implementation given the policy levers to which they have access and their potential effectiveness. Municipal governments are quite limited as an influence point for many social determinants of health, although this level of governance may play an important role in delivering public policy and programs which have been developed at the state level. Formal supranational levels of governance, such as the European Parliament, as well as those established under regional trade agreements like the North American Free Trade Agreement (NAFTA), have available some critical policy levers like trade, and some recourse to dispute-resolution mechanisms when conflicts arise. International financial institutions and agencies like the World Trade Organization and the World Bank play important roles which affect health, particularly via conditions imposed on the flows of capital and technology. Access to these supranational institutions and their policy levers remains the purview of nation-states and their representatives.

State-level governments have available constitutional levers in policy arenas such as education and labour markets, as well as in economic and social policy, and states provide access to, and themselves constitute, supranational levers. By state government, we mean both the national level of government and the constituent political units of federations (such as provinces, states or *länder*). Case studies from developing countries like Costa Rica and Cuba have demonstrated that state-level public policies such as investments in parental literacy, increased rights for women, and economic policies that benefit people living in poverty can all positively affect health (World Bank, 1993). The economic and social policies of developed countries like Sweden are commonly assumed to have positive effects on health. Lundberg and Fritzell (1994) argue that Swedish income transfer policies during periods of unemployment have been important to maintaining high levels of national health. Conversely, regional areas of growing income inequality in Britain have shown increases in infant and adult mortality (Phillimore *et al.*, 1994) and in the USA widening income gaps between the black and white population have been followed by a widening gap in life expectancy (Rogers, 1992).

But states can no longer act in isolation. Their capacity to develop and implement health-improving changes in public policy, by which we mean their administrative and financial resources available for fashioning policy interventions, is profoundly affected by the supranational institutions noted above. Some policy options are prohibited; others encouraged or discouraged. For example, unilateral trade restrictions imposed by Canada to protect a vulnerable industry, and hence vulnerable jobs, could be met with formal trade disputes via a bi-national panel (under the Canada–US Free Trade Agreement) or informal trade sanctions imposed by domestic US trade legislation. Deficit-financed expansionary government spending by France during an economic downturn could be met with exclusion from European Monetary Union if France's deficit exceeds the size permitted under the criteria for monetary union.

State governments can develop and implement health-improving changes in public policy, support the evaluation of the health outcomes of public policies, and offer opportunities to facilitate the development of health-improving public policy at the supranational level. Thus many of the relevant public policy levers with health consequences operate at the level of state governments or are accessed through them. Our incomes and how they compare with the distribution of income in our local environment are determined in part by fiscal and social policy; the availability and nature of work are determined in part by rapidly changing trade, industry and labour market policies; and our social networks can in turn be affected by our jobs and our incomes.

POLITICAL AGENDAS AND STATE CAPACITIES

Despite the available research evidence and the potentially influential role of the nation-state in altering social environments (e.g., National Forum on Health, 1998), much has been said and little has been done. Few state governments have been able to broaden health reform to include the dimensions of income inequality, employment and working conditions, and social cohesion. Health is all too frequently seen as health care. With so many good ideas on offer, why has there been so little progress by public authorities in addressing the social determinants of health? In part, the answer lies in political agendas and state capacities.

Political agendas

Policy-makers can attend to a limited number of issues at any given time. Those interested in health are no exception. Time spent addressing the social determinants of health necessarily comes at the expense of time spent addressing other health issues, like the financing and provision of health care. Kingdon (1995) has proposed a general model to explain why some issues appear on the political agenda at a given time and others do not. Basically, three things must come together: a problem, a policy (solution), and politics.

The character of the 'problem' has been interpreted in very different ways in the United Kingdom and Canada. The problem has been framed in the United Kingdom as one of persistent or growing inequalities in health status across social groups (e.g. Townsend *et al.*, 1992), but in Canada as one of persistent or increasing inefficiencies in the production of health (Evans and Stoddart, 1990; Lavis and Stoddart, 1994). The former represents an equity-or justice-based perspective: the problem is an 'unfair' distribution of health outcomes with, for example, the wealthy leading longer, healthier lives than the poor. The latter represents an efficiency perspective: the problem is that the marginal health returns to investments in health care are believed to be less than those from investments in the social determinants of health. The character of the policy solution represented by the social determinants of health has been interpreted in more similar ways in the two jurisdictions: social determinants, like employment and working conditions, can be modified to improve health (or reduce health inequalities or improve the returns to investments in health).

The United States, on the other hand, if motivated by a desire to improve health, faces a more immediate problem: ensuring universal access to health care at affordable cost. While the marginal health returns to investments in health care may be low in countries with universal access to high-quality health care, the marginal health returns to investments in health care for uninsured or underinsured Americans may be very large. American policy-makers could therefore not easily invoke an efficiency based argument for action on the social determinants of health. Instead, given the current problems with access to health care in their country, they would have to invoke an equity-based argument, a choice that would be seen as politically unpalatable by most American policy-makers.

Problems and policy solutions aside, political forces have rarely come together in a way that brought the social determinants of health to the top of the political agenda. Health policy-makers in the United Kingdom, for example, have been primarily concerned with the financing and provision of health care because that is their principal responsibility. Canada, on the other hand, has a federal health bureaucracy that has no constitutional authority over health care (Government of Canada, 1984) and a declining role in financing provincial health-care plans. Accordingly, the federal health bureaucracy is constantly looking for greater visibility in the health domain, an electorally popular arena. The political difficulty at the federal level in Canada, therefore, arises not so much from a crowded political agenda on the part of health policy-makers but from the relative weakness of the leverage that the federal health bureaucracy can exert in policy domains other than health care. Health bureaucracies lack the financial clout that Ministries of Finance or Treasury departments can use to bring their own perspectives to the political agenda of other ministries or departments.

A number of different types of political forces could bring about a change. Kingdon (1995) offers possibilities at several levels. First, public opinion about health and the importance of addressing the social determinants of health could change over time. Second, interest groups or social movements could push strongly for a focus on addressing the social determinants of health. Third, these and other factors could bring about the election of a new government takes as a central objective to address these determinants. None of these possibilities can be predicted but all could be capitalized upon if a possibility presents itself.

State capacities

But even if making health-improving changes to our social environments arrived on the political agenda in a meaningful way, states typically lack the capacity to consider the health consequences of public policies that influence social environments. Governing health, rather than health care, poses a significant challenge. With few exceptions, most developed countries have delegated responsibility for each of trade, labour market, fiscal, social and health policy to separate departments or ministries. This horizontal fragmentation of political and bureaucratic authority created the specialized organizations necessary to govern effectively amidst increasing economic and social complexity (Chubb and Peterson, 1989). However, creating jurisdiction-specific lines of authority has profound implications for those seeking to bring about health-improving changes to public policy.

Jurisdiction-specific problem formulation tends to ignore cross-sectoral problems like improving the health status of the population, and jurisdiction-specific considerations of policy alternatives tend to down-play cross-sectoral perspectives. The current push in ministries of health for maximizing the health outcomes associated with health-care interventions can be contrasted with other ministries' disregard for unintended health consequences and their attention to policy outcomes specific to their own bureaucratic jurisdictions. Policy-makers who are developing a policy that requires advance notification of lay-off would typically consider the potential financial consequences for firms and the potential job-search consequences for employees, not the potential health consequences associated with the anticipatory phase of unemployment (i.e., the period after notification of pending job loss and before actual job loss). To the extent that different stakeholders push for a broader perspective on the outcomes relevant to a particular bureaucratic jurisdiction, states with strong corporatist traditions for policy-making may be more likely to consider health or other non-economic outcomes.

Moreover, few health policy-makers are adequately trained to advocate for the explicit consideration of health outcomes in the development of public policy beyond health care, like in financial-services policy or labour-market policy. These jurisdictions are the domain of their own policy experts, not enthusiastic but naïve health amateurs. The highly specialized nature of each jurisdiction's policy domain encourages the involvement of only those social actors who are familiar with its language and policy details. Individuals working in ministries of health are typically not prepared to use cohort studies that demonstrate associations between job insecurity and negative health consequences to argue for job-protection policies in multilateral trade agreements, even though such efforts may have more significant health consequences for the population as a whole than many of the traditional activities of ministries of health.

Policy entrepreneurs capable of bridging these jurisdictions either alone or on behalf of social groups may therefore fulfil an important need: they open up prospects for change in other jurisdictions, increase points of access to policy development, and enhance the power of otherwise isolated social groups through the use of jurisdiction-specific language. British Columbia's Provincial Health Officer and the United Kingdom's new Minister of Public Health (Olson, 1997) provide examples of how governments can create such policy entrepreneurs. These officials, while linked to the traditional health apparatus of the state (i.e. ministries of health), could, for example, take health-related arguments about the negative health consequences of unemployment to ministries of finance when they are reviewing their public policies relating to adjustment relief and retraining opportunities for workers who lose their jobs.

HEALTH REFORM: INCREASING STATE CAPACITY FOR IMPROVING HEALTH

Cross-sectoral bodies present an opportunity to overcome some of the features of state-level institutions that diminish the prospects for improving health through public policy. These bodies can perform advisory, decision-making or consensus-building roles and can comprise officials within semi-autonomous sites of political and bureaucratic authority. Many state-level governments in developed countries have experimented with cross-sectoral bodies. The motivations for these innovations have been mixed: greater rationality in public sector planning for some, like the British Labour government in the 1970s, or more coordination (read 'doing more with less') in social policy making for its more market-oriented replacement under Mrs Thatcher in the 1980s (Challis *et al.*, 1988). Regardless of motivation, most such institutional innovations are likely to improve capacity to improve health through public policy, especially if the innovation involves some degree of leverage over resources, not just the opportunity for moral suasion. To illustrate the potential offered by cross-sectoral innovations, we describe one Canadian innovation and some interesting recent developments in The Netherlands.

A cross-sectoral advisory body in Ontario

The first institutional innovation in Canada involved the development of a cross-sectoral advisory council, the Ontario Premier's Council on Health Strategy, by the Government of Ontario (Spasoff, 1992; Signal, 1994; Lavis, 1997). The Council, established in December 1987, was charged with providing 'leadership and guidance to the whole government in achieving the goal of health for every citizen in Ontario' (Premier's Council on Health Strategy, 1991a: 1). Unlike other advisory councils that have addressed the determinants of health – like the federal Interdepartmental Reference Group on Population Health or the Federal/Provincial/Territorial Advisory Committee on Population Health – this council was truly cross-sectoral in that it was chaired by the Premier and drew its members from the senior political and bureaucratic ranks of a number of different ministries. As well, the Council involved a variety of stakeholder groups – a more corporatist approach than was typical at that time in Ontario politics.

Given its structure, the Council could more easily focus on determinants of health that cut across traditional bureaucratic domains of expertise and authority, and the presence of the Premier and ministers of government meant that the parallel table of Cabinet decisions was informed by a broader framework of health determinants. The Council produced a number of reports, including *Nurturing Health* (Premier's Council on Health Strategy, 1991b), which built a health-related case for government action in early childhood development and labour-market adjustment. The framework development and priority setting process that underpinned these recommendations (described in Sullivan, 1991) successfully engaged the senior policy actors of government. The Premier's Council's reach was limited, however, by its lack of command over resources and its lack of formalized coordinating authority with regard to other line departments. Nevertheless, it served as a model for the development of similar structures in other provinces and at the federal level (e.g. National Forum on Health).

Cross-sectoral consensus building in The Netherlands

In The Netherlands, stimulated in part by the Black Report (Townsend *et al.*, 1992), a cross-sectoral consensus-building approach to policy development was launched in 1987. The initiative involved the Ministries of Welfare, Public Health and Culture, together with the Scientific Council for Government Policy and key decision-makers from political parties, trade unions, employer organizations, and the health professions. The outcome was a five-year research program commissioned by the Ministry to inform policy making led by the combined efforts of the Dutch universities. Studies on the determinants of health were undertaken to document the extent and nature of social inequalities in health in The Netherlands compared to other countries (Machenbach, 1994). Some small demonstration projects were also set up to evaluate how inequalities might be tackled at the local level. Most importantly, there was an agreement reached on the need to assess major policy decisions for their impact on the country's poorest citizens. A second five-year research program, with a focus on policy-relevant research, was agreed upon for 1993–1997. The approach in The Netherlands has been one of slow but careful analysis, trying to keep the main parties on board in building a cross-sectoral consensus for policy making (Whitehead, 1995).

On a related note, Article 129 of the Maastricht Treaty urges member states to encourage the improvement of the public health of member states, and requires that member states consider the health impact of other European Community policies such as agriculture and the environment. This supranational agreement, although limited by the diffuse role of the European Community, could provide some cross-sectoral imperative to strengthen health, if the impact of public policies on the health of the most disadvantaged in society were taken as a measure. Through this policy initiative there may be a firm foothold for reducing health inequalities in the European jurisdiction (White-head, 1995).

CONCLUSION

The general aim of improving state capacity has captured widespread interest. The World Bank (1997) recently devoted its annual World Development Report to the subject and the Canadian federal government recently announced its intent to rebuild the policy research capacity that was lost during years of expenditure reductions. Rarely, however, has any mention been made of state capacity for improving health through public policy; that is, for governing health. Yet in the face of dramatic shifts in the social environment, especially in employment and working conditions and in our improved understanding of how the social environment can affect health, increasing state capacity for improving health may offer great rewards. Health reform is not just about health care; it is also about devising social arrangements which engender healthy populations.

While the United States may continue to be preoccupied with health-care issues, other countries with universal access to high-quality health care can rigorously pursue the development of state capacity for improving health. As suggested in Table 17.1, the range of potential government actions to improve health spans a vast number of policy domains. Acting to reduce income inequality could involve both personal taxation and social programs. Acting to reduce the incidence and duration of unemployment could involve trade agreements, industrial policy and labour-market policy. And acting to reduce job strain could involve corporate taxation and experience-rated workers' compensation premia. Bringing forward information about the health consequences of public policies that have health as an unintended consequence, not an explicit objective, requires far more capacity than currently exists in most states.

One way of building state capacity involves overcoming institutional fragmentation through cross-sectoral initiatives. But the central message of a comprehensive review of cross-sectoral initiatives was simple: 'coordination does not just happen because ministers or top civil servants say that it should. It means creating the right kind of framework and providing the right kind of incentives for the individual actors who alone can make it work' (Challis *et al.*, 1988). Health-improving changes in public policy do not just happen because cross-sectoral governance mechanisms are created. For example, all states are constrained to some degree by supranational institutions like the World Trade Organization or regional trade agreements like NAFTA. The European states and the European Community, with strong corporatist traditions for policy-making, may be more disposed than states with more fragmented and pluralistic models to generate the institutional innovations necessary to improve health through public policy. Increased state capacity through institutional innovation may provide for the possibility that those seeking health-improving changes to public policy may at least be sitting at the table when key decisions are made, and may be able to influence the formulation of the problem. State capacity for improving health may be developed in just such small steps.

REFERENCES

Alterman, T., R. B., Shekelle, S. W. Vernon, and K. D. Burau, (1994). Decision latitude, psychological demand, job strain, and coronary heart disease in the Western Electric Study. *American Journal of Epidemiology* 139 (6): 620–627.

Amick, B., III, S., Levine, A. R. Tarlov, and D. Chapman Walsh, (eds) (1995). *Society and health*. New York: Oxford University Press.

Astrand, N.-E., B. S. Hanson, and S.-O. Isacsson, (1989). Job demands, job decision latitude, job support, and social network factors as predictors of mortality in a Swedish pulp and paper company. *British Journal of Industrial Medicine* 46: 334–340.

Blane, D., E. Brunner, and R. G. Wilkinson, (1996). *Health and social organization: Towards a health policy for the 21st century*. New York: Routledge.

Bunker, J. P., D. F. Gomby, and B. H. Kehrer, (1989). *Pathways to health: The role of social factors*. Menlo Park, CA: The Henry J. Kaiser Family Foundation.

Challis, L., S., Fuller, M. Henwood, *et al.* (1988). *Joint approaches to social policy: Rationality and practice*. Cambridge: Cambridge University Press.

Chubb, J. E. and P. E. Peterson, (1989). American political institutions and the problem of governance. In J. E. Chubb and P. E. Peterson (eds), *Can the government govern?* Washington, DC: Brookings Institution.

Costa, G. and N. Segnan, (1987). Unemployment and mortality. *BMJ* 294: 1550–1551.

Dahrendorf, R. (1995). A precarious balance: Economic opportunity, civil society, and political liberty. *The Responsive Community* 5 (3): 13–39.

Evans, R. G., M. L. Barer, and T. R. Marmor, (1994). *Why are some people healthy and others not? The determinants of health in populations*. New York: Aldine de Gruyter.

Evans, R. G. and G. L. Stoddart, (1990). Producing health, consuming health care. *Social Science and Medicine* 31 (12): 1347–1363.

Falk, A., B. S., Hanson, S.-O. Isacsson, and P.-O. Ostergren, (1992). Job strain and mortality in elderly men: social network, support, and influence as buffers. *American Journal of Public Health* 82: 1136–1139.

Ferrie, J. E., M. J., Shipley, M. G., Marmot, S. Stansfeld, and G. Davey Smith, (1998). The health effects of major organizational change and job insecurity. *Social Science and Medicine* 46 (2): 243–254.

Government of Canada (1984). *Canada Health Act*. Ottawa: Queen's Printer.

Hertzman, C., J. Frank, and R. G. Evans, (1994). Heterogeneities in health status and the determinants of population health. In R. G. Evans, M. L. Barer and

T. R. Marmor, *Why are some people healthy and others not? The determinants of health in populations*. New York: Aldine de Gruyter.

Hinkle, L. E., L. H., Whitney, E. W., Lehman, J., Dunn, B., Benjamin, R., King, A. Plakun, and B. Flehinger, (1968). Occupation, education, and coronary heart disease. *Science* 161 (838): 238–246.

Iversen, L. and H. Klausen, (1986). Alcohol consumption among laid-off workers before and after closure of a Danish ship-yard: A 2-year follow-up study. *Social Science and Medicine* 22 (1): 107–109.

Iversen, L., O., Andersen, P. K., Andersen, K. Christoffersen, and N. Keiding, (1987). Unemployment and mortality in Denmark, 1970–80. *BMJ* 295: 879–884.

Kaprio, J. and M. Koskenvuo, (1988). A prospective study of psychological and socioeconomic characteristics, health behavior and morbidity in cigarette smokers prior to quitting compared to persistent smokers and non-smokers. *Journal of Clinical Epidemiology* 41 (2): 139–150.

Karasek, R. A., T., Theorell, J. E., Schwartz, C. F. Pieper, and L. Alfredsson, (1982). Job, psychological factors and coronary heart disease. *Advances in Cardiology* 29: 62–67.

Kasl, S. V. and S. Cobb, (1970). Blood pressure changes in men undergoing job loss: A preliminary report. *Psychosomatic Medicine* 32 (1): 19–38.

Kasl, S. V., S. Cobb, and G. W. Brooks, (1968). Changes in serum uric acid and cholesterol levels in men undergoing job loss. *JAMA* 206 (7): 1500–1507.

Kingdon, J. W. (1995). *Agendas, alternatives, and public policies* (2nd edn). New York: HarperCollins.

Lalonde, M. (1974). *A new perspective on the health of Canadians*. Ottawa: Government of Canada.

Lavis, J. N. (1997). An inquiry into the links between labour-market experiences and health (dissertation). Cambridge, MA: Harvard University.

Lavis, J. N. (1998a). *Ideas, policy learning, and policy change: The determinants-of-health synthesis in Canada and the United Kingdom*. Hamilton: McMaster University Centre for Health Economics and Policy Analysis, Working Paper.

Lavis, J. N. (1998b). Labour-market experiences and health: A systematic review of cohort studies. In J. E. Hurley, D. Feeny, M. Giacomini, P. Grootendorst, J. N. Lavis, G. Stoddart and G. Torrance (eds), *Health policy in the era of population health: An exploration of changing roles*. Report submitted to Health Canada through the National Health Research and Development Program.

Lavis, J. N. and G. L. Stoddart, (1994). Can we have too much health care? *Daedalus* 123 (4): 43–60.

Lavis, J. N. and T. J. Sullivan, (forthcoming). Health improvement and the state: Past policies, current constraints and the possibility of political change. In B. Poland, L. Green and I. Rootman (eds), *Settings for health promotion: Linking theory and practice*. Newbury Park, CA: Sage Publications.

Lundberg, O. and J. Fritzell, (1994). Income distribution, income change and health: On the importance of absolute and relative income for health status in Europe. In World Health Organization (ed.), *Economic change, social welfare and health in Europe*. Copenhagen: WHO Publications, European Series No. 54: 37–58.

Machenbach, J. (1994). Inequalities in health in The Netherlands: Impact of a five year research program. *BMJ* 309: 1487–1491.

Marmor, T. R., M. L. Barer, and R. G. Evans, (1994). The determinants of a population's health: What can be done to improve a democratic nation's health status? In R. G. Evans, M. L. Barer and T. R. Marmor (eds), *Why are some people healthy and others not? The determinats of health in populations.* New York: Aldine de Gruyter.

Marmot, M. G., G., Rose, M. J. Shipley, and P. J. S. Hamilton, (1978). Employment grade and coronary heart disease in British civil servants. *Journal of Epidemiology and Community Health* 32: 244–249.

Marmot, M. G., M. J. Shipley, and G. Rose, (1984). Inequalities in death – specific explanations of a general pattern? *Lancet*, 5 May: 1003–1006.

Marmot, M. R., H. Bosma, H. Hemingway, H. Brunner, E. Brunner, and S. Stansfeld, (1997). Contribution of job control and other risk factors to social variations in coronary heart disease incidence. *Lancet* 350: 235–239.

Martikainen, P. T. (1990). Unemployment and mortality among Finnish men, 1981–5. *BMJ* 301: 407–411.

Martikainen, P. T. and T. Valkonen, (1996). Excess mortality of unemployed men and women during a period of rapidly increasing unemployment. *Lancet* 348: 909–912.

Morris, J. K., D. G. Cook, and A. G. Shaper, (1992). Non-employment and changes in smoking, drinking and body weight. *BMJ* 304: 536–541.

Morris, J. K., D. G. Cook, and A. G. Shaper, (1994). Loss of employment and mortality. *BMJ* 308: 1135–1139.

Moser, K. A., A. J. Fox, and D. R. Jones, (1984). Unemployment and mortality in the OPCS Longitudinal Study. *Lancet* ii: 1324–1329.

Moser, K. A., A. J. Fox, D. R. Jones, and P. O. Goldblatt, (1986). Unemployment and mortality: Further evidence from the OPCS Longitudinal Study 1971–1981. *Lancet* i: 365–367.

National Forum on Health (1998). *Canada health action: Building on the legacy.* Sainte-Foy, Quebec: Editions Multimondes.

Olson, N. (1997). At last, a public health minister. *BMJ* 314: 1498–1499.

Owens, A. C. (1966). Sick leave among railwaymen threatened by redundancy: A pilot study. *Occupational Pschology* 40: 43–52.

Phillimore, P., A. Beattie, and P. Townsend, (1994). Widening inequality of health in northern England, 1981–1991. *BMJ* 308: 1125–1128.

Premier's Council on Health Strategy (1991a). *Towards a strategic framework for optimizing health.* Toronto: The Queen's Printer for Ontario.

Premier's Council on Health Strategy (1991b). *Nurturing health: A framework on the determinants of health.* Toronto: The Queen's Printer for Ontario.

Rogers, R. (1992) Living and dying in the USA: Sociodemographic determinants of death among blacks and whites. *Demography* 29: 287–303.

Rose, G. and M. G. Marmot, (1981). Social class and coronary heart disease. *British Heart Journal* 45: 13–19.

Schieber, G. J., J.-P. Poullier, and L. M. Greenwald, (1993). Health spending, delivery, and outcomes in OECD countries. *Health Affairs*, Summer: 120–129.

Shekelle, R. B., A. M. Ostfeld, and O. Paul, (1969). Social status and incidence of coronary heart disease. *Journal of Chronic Diseases* 22: 381–394.

Signal, L. N. (1994). The politics of the Ontario Premier's Council on Health Strategy: A case study in the new public health (dissertation). Toronto: University of Toronto.

Spasoff, R. (1992) A new approach to health promotion in Ontario. *Health Promotion International* 7: 129–133.

Stefansson, C.-G. (1991). Long-term unemployment and mortality in Sweden, 1980–1986. *Social Science and Medicine* 32 (4): 419–423.

Sullivan, T. (1991). Strategic planning for health: How to stay on top of the game. *Health Promotion* 30: 2–8, 13.

Townsend, P., M. Whitehead, and N. Davidson, (eds) (1992) *Inequalities in health: The Black Report and the Health Divide*. London: Penguin Books.

Whitehead, M. (1995). Tackling inequalities: A review of policy initiatives. In M. Benzeval, K. Judge and M. Whitehead. *Tackling inequalities in health*. London: The King's Fund, 22–72.

Wilkinson, R. G. (1992). Income distribution and life expectancy. *BMJ* 304: 165–168.

Wilkinson, R. G. (1996). *Unhealthy societies: The afflictions of inequality*. New York: Routledge.

Wolfson, M. C. and B. B. Murphy, (1998). New views on inequality trends in Canada and the United States. *Monthly Labour Review*, April.

World Bank (1993). *World development report 1993: Investing in health*. New York: Oxford University Press.

World Bank (1997). *World development report 1997: The state in a changing world*. New York: Oxford University Press.

18 Health, health care and social cohesion

J. Fraser Mustard

The various chapters in this book have brought out a number of points about health, health care, and social and economic policy. The primary focus has been on publicly and privately funded health care, funding constraints, the role of economics in meeting the needs of sick or injured individuals and the need for new institutional arrangements. What we know is that the total resources available to finance health care services are not infinite and that health care providers who think that more resources will be available through privatization and that markets will make the system more efficient, fail to understand or accept that a nation's total resources have limits. Since health care is not a primary source of wealth creation, the financial limits are set by the wealth a region or nation produces and the societal demands on that wealth (Evans and Stoddart, 1990). Publicly financed systems striving to achieve equity in health services when a nation's real wealth base is not growing, end up restricting the income growth of many health care providers and have difficulty introducing expensive new technologies. This is why two-tiering the system (private and public financing) allows some providers to gain a greater share of the pie while others will get less. It also changes the equity in the system since some patients will be unable to afford care or will have less than desirable service (Evans *et al.*, 1996; Evans, Chapter 2 this volume).

Excess consumption of a nation's wealth by health care can divert resources from investing in the 'real economy', which is important in primary wealth creation (Evans and Stoddart, 1990; Evans, 1994). If the 'real economy' fails to grow (as seen in the new concepts of the determinants of economic growth), it is difficult to increase expenditures in what is not the primary source of wealth creation for a society. Economic beliefs that do not differentiate between what can be considered as primary wealth creation and secondary wealth creation and the strengths and limits of markets in providing health care can create distorted policies in the health care field and create inequities in the provision of health care.

It is imperative that the health care cost debate be set in the broader historical socio-economic framework and the deep and broad technologic change underway currently. Dahrendorf (1995) has pointed out that the developed countries of the West face a precarious balancing act between the new opportunities created by the present technological revolution, and of economic change, and the threats posed by these forces on the factors that contribute to sustaining social cohesion and tolerant democratic societies. Other writers support Dahrendorf's view that major technological and economic changes have the potential to erode equity and the civic qualities of a society and undermine democracy and political liberty, and that major efforts may be needed to prevent this from happening (Hutton, 1995; Kuttner, 1997).

We now understand that transforming technological change affecting all sectors of society has profound effects on how regions create wealth (Lipsey and Bekar, 1994). The changes in an economy produced by these deep and broad technological changes can lead to economies or wealth of a society diverging or converging (*Economist*, 1992) from the per capita wealth of other societies. Recent periods of major deep and broad technological change with great effects on the socio-economic character of societies were the Industrial Revolution (the harnessing of fossil fuels as an energy source) and, later, electricity replacing steam power. The lessons learned from analysis of these changes are that business cycles as measured by changes in gross domestic product do not capture the deeper changes in an economy produced by transforming technological changes. One measure that does capture some aspects of how well an economy is adjusting to major technological change is total factor productivity. In the United States, total factor productivity (an index of the efficiency of all inputs used by the firm rather than just labour productivity) was flat for more than twenty years during the transition from steam to electricity (David, 1991) and this was associated with social changes and a decline in clerical wages. Today we are in an equally powerful technological revolution which can be described as 'chips for neurons' with similar effects on the income of people and its institutions.

In Canada, as in many other developed countries, total factor productivity has been flat for more than twenty years (Helpman and Fortin, 1995; Canada, 1996). In a sense, our primary wealth-creating sector has not been growing at a pace to sustain our public and private expenditures in the secondary wealth-creating sector (Mustard, 1996). This has been associated with increasing unemployment, increasing income inequality, rising levels of poverty and the decreasing ability of the public sector to finance public programs (Canada, 1996). The debate about health care, methods of payment, and how to organize the provision of care are being, in part, driven by the economic forces released by the technological revolution we are in.

The debates about the financing of health care in a changing economy are largely questions of resource availability, resource distribution for providers of care, and social equity in the provision of health care that could have far reaching implications for the long term social cohesion of a society. One of the phenomena that can occur when there is increasing public sector debt as a result of governments trying to sustain income equity in a changing economy through transfer payments and publicly financed programs like health care, is that the self-interests of influential groups will argue against increasing taxes (which tend to increase in periods of major economic change with widening gaps in income and increased unemployment, and increased demand on transfer payments) and push for the dismantling of government programs when they stand to gain from the dismantling (Evans *et al.*, 1996, 1997). Many of the chapters in this volume bring out aspects of these debates. When solutions threaten certain ideological self-interest positions, a variety of strategies are used to protect the economic position of the interest groups. This can lead to substantial distortion of information about health care to serve the groups needs

Publicly financed programs like education and health care are a form of consumer co-operative collectively buying services from providers, whereas most social programs involve taxing one group to pay another (transfer payments). When governments are constraining expenditures, there are more sources of potential conflict with cuts in health care and education because of their universal nature than with cuts in transfer payments.

If a nation or region has considerable power and has elites that wish to promote throughout the world a market-driven society based on individualism with limited social responsibility, it can, as in the case of the United States health care debate, generate sufficient disinformation to try and undermine what other societies, based on a more equitable social philosophy such as no financial barriers to access to health care, are trying to do. Ted Marmor (Chapter 14 this volume) has made this very point. The intensity of the debate during Clinton's attempt to revamp the health care system in the United States highlighted the conflict between the Canadian approach to health care and that in the United States. The *New York Times* (1992) had an editorial based on a series of false statements about the Canadian system, largely generated by narrow, ideologically based policy institutes in Canada premised on deeply flawed studies. These attempts to distort what goes on in Canada illustrate the disruptive effects of groups with strong ideological beliefs coupled with a restricted socio-economic perspective on another society's values.

Some providers of health care like to promote the belief that medicine is the primary determinant of health and well-being. This concept has been a useful device in both publicly financed and privately financed systems to create political climates to help providers capture more resources. This result does not necessarily improve the social cohesion or trust of a society and the health of the population (Evans *et al.*, 1996). The discussion and concerns about social trust or capital in respect of the quality of societies has emerged as a potentially important issue in the health, health care debate (Evans *et al.*, 1996). Social trust or capital has as its focus, the concepts of community, social organization and cohesion (Fukuyama, 1995; Putnam, 1993; Kawachi *et al.*, 1997; Shleifer *et al.*, 1996; Wilkinson, 1996). The terms 'social capital' or 'trust' have been used to describe this quality of societies and a number of studies have examined the relationship between social cohesion on a community's economy, its tolerance, its governance and its health and well-being. This can be defined as the social organization reflected in civic participation, sense of reciprocity and trust in others that facilitates cooperation among citizens for mutual benefit. The characteristics of health and social services in a society, such as how health care is provided (public or private), may influence the social cohesion or trust of a community. A two-tier health care system may weaken a community's sense of trust (Evans *et al.*, 1996).

The economic framework or beliefs that dominate a society influence the quality of social environments (Putnam, 1993; Hutton, 1995; Kuttner, 1997). Capitalism based on individualism with little concern for the social environment and its effect on the life-cycle of individuals will tend to create substantial inequality in income distribution and contribute to erosion of a society's trust or social cohesion. Within the United States, it is the communities with the greatest income inequality that have the least trust and highest mortality rates (Kawachi *et al.*, 1997). When economies that are going through a major technological change are in trouble, income inequality tends to increase (David, 1991; Newman and Attewell, 1995; Bronfenbrenner *et al.*, 1996; Kuttner, 1997). Paradoxically, communities with the highest degree of trust are the ones that tend to do well economically and have better health statistics. It seems likely that societies that know how to use their resources, human and financial, to sustain the quality of their social environments during periods of major socio-economic changes will be the ones that sustain trust and social cohesion.

Since the social environment of a society and the way a society provides health care is influenced by its health and economic beliefs, it is useful to examine these beliefs and their relationship to health care and health and how the beliefs are used by groups in a society.

HEALTH BELIEFS AND HEALTH CARE

In Greek society, health beliefs were expressed by two gods, Aesculapius and Hygeia (Mustard, 1987). If the dominant health belief was that of Aesculapius, the primary health interest of society was in the role of medicine. Today, societies (such as the United States) in which the Aesculapius view dominates will tend to have a strong individualistic philosophy. In contrast, if the belief is in the framework set out by Hygeia, the focus will be how the environments in which we live and work throughout the life course determine the health and well-being of individuals and populations. These societies will, in theory, tend to have a partnership philosophy and higher degree of trust or social capital (Eisler, 1987). Societies in which the belief of Aesculapius dominates will tend to have a more individualistic culture and have as their main health focus, health care and health care policy not health policy. Societies in which the concepts of Hygeia are dominant will tend to focus on the determinants of health and inequalities in health and how policies that affect the economic and social characteristics of society (income equity, provision of social safety nets, etc.) affect the development and health and well-being of individuals and populations. There is a natural tendency to confuse the two health beliefs leading to difficulty in differentiation between policies concerned with health care (health care policy) and those concerned with the determinants of health and the social environment (health policy). The recent report of The National Forum on Health (1997) illustrates this difficulty. Canada is presently caught in a debate about the relative importance of the socio-economic determinants of health (Hygeia) and the role and value of medicine and health care (Aesculapius) in influencing the health of Canadians.

Providing care to individuals in a time of illness is a well-entrenched part of the culture of most societies. The expectations of members of a society for health care range from supportive compassionate care in times of need to medical interventions that stabilize problems and, in some circumstances, provide a cure and improve the quality of life for individuals with chronic health problems. The immediacy of the needs of an individual with a disorder affecting his or her health, creates the need for an immediate response. It is only natural that societies create institutions to meet these needs since all members of a society will require health care at some time during their life. This need has led in developed countries to sophisticated systems of health care available in some form to all members of society that are directly or indirectly publicly regulated and substantially publicly financed through a variety of institutional arrangements (Evans, 1994; Evans, Chapter 2 this volume). The level of funding is, in most systems, related to the wealth of a society and is driven by the work of providers of health care.

The providers of care logically argue the importance of their role in improving the health and well-being of sick and injured individuals and continually develop and bring into the provision of care, new and often improved interventions for the diagnosis and treatment of illness or injury. Since health care services throughout the developed world have a large element of public finance, their growth creates increasing demands on the public purse. As a consequence, governments become increasingly concerned about the efficiency and the nature and appropriateness of health care services, and providers of care become caught between the forces trying to constrain costs and their professional desire to sustain their incomes and to provide new and more effective care. Thus, the health care policy pressures on government in this sector are immediate, focused on the balance between constraining expenditures and the needs and desires of health professionals providing care to individuals and the expectations of sick individuals. These pressures are relatively constant with political implications, leaving little room or incentive for Ministries of Health to focus on the broader and longer term policies relating to the quality of the social environment and its effects on health (health policy).

The economic circumstances and the expectations and beliefs for both providers and consumers of health care, have forced the health belief framework of most developed societies into the Aesculapius mode. Thus most institutions concerned with health (academic, business, and government) are focused on the health care component of health and the needs of individuals who are sick or injured, not on the broader social environment and health issues. It is interesting that the Blair government in the United Kingdom, perhaps to counter the health care pressure, has created a minister with a specific responsibility for the society and health issues and inequalities in health (Tessa Jowell, Minister of State for Public Health, United Kingdom – press release May 1997).

A society that decides to make health care available to all of its citizens through a universal health insurance system, makes provision of health care a potential institutional structure to help sustain social cohesion and trust. These societies may be better able to balance the policy implications for both health care and the determinants of health. Certainly the United Kingdom, Scandinavian countries, and Canada have shown to date stronger initiatives and interest in the social determinants of health than the United States.

The socio-economic issues, relating to social cohesion or trust, that effect the health and well-being of individuals and populations are less visible to individuals, poorly understood, and often blurred by narrow self-interest groups. This subject also comes up against the restricted intellectual framework of medicine and other caring professions and does not have immediate political implications. The belief structures or intellectual framework which determines academic disciplines, influence recognition and rewards and steer the way in which academics and others define and study problems. These factors influence the beliefs and focus of academic institutions, governments, research agencies and the concepts and formation of health policy.

HEALTH BELIEFS AND THE DETERMINANTS OF HEALTH

Most physicians are intuitively aware of the limits to medicine and the importance of the social environment in which people live and work on the effectiveness of medical interventions and on the health of people. Virchow ([1849] 1985), a German pathologist in the last century, who spent many years trying to understand the causes of vascular disease and its thrombotic complications, like heart attacks, in his later years came to the conclusion that the key factor influencing the health and well-being of individuals and populations was the socio-economic conditions in which they lived and worked. In this century, McKeown (1976, 1988a), a British physician, was also interested in how the socio-economic changes associated with the Industrial Revolution affected health in the United Kingdom. His detailed analysis of the changes in mortality in the United Kingdom following the Industrial Revolution led him to conclude by exclusion that the reason for increase in life span was the improved nutrition of the population resulting from improvements in agriculture and food distribution associated with the gradually improving standard of living. His conclusion that public health in its traditional form accounted for only 25 per cent of the decrease in mortality rates following the Industrial Revolution and that medicine's effect was minimal, upset his profession. When he died, the writer of his obituary in the *Lancet*

(McKeown, 1988b) stated, 'There would be no civil honours for a man as forward looking and as disturbing as this.' Interestingly, it was McKeown's work that was the basis for the famous 'Lalonde Report' (1974) from Health Canada in the 1970s. This report set out the reasons for the differences between the health (social environment issues) and the health care agendas and the need for strategies to develop policies for health different from those for health care. For all the reasons that have been discussed, this landmark report was not widely understood and applied in society largely because the health care belief framework (Aesculapius) continued to dominate most sectors of Canadian society.

McKeown's conclusion about what caused the drop in mortality rates following the Industrial Revolution, within the United Kingdom, troubled not only his profession but others such as Fogel, an economic historian, who was also sceptical. Fogel set to work (1991, 1994) to examine whether food production and distribution did improve in western countries in association with the Industrial Revolution, and whether this could be related to the improvements in the health of these populations. He found that the records of agricultural production and distribution following the Industrial Revolution confirmed McKeown's conclusion that the populations in western countries became better nourished, leading to improved health. He did this in part by targeting two measures of the adequacy of population nutrition (height and weight) that were available in the records of most of these countries. The height of a population is primarily determined by its genetic characteristics and how well it is nourished during childhood. Thus, changes in the mean height of a population are a measure of how well children are nourished and, indirectly, the conditions of early childhood. One of the strong associations he found was that as the mean heights of populations in Western countries improved with better production and distribution of nutritious food, so did life expectancy. There was also an association between improved average weight of the population and better health. Many adults were undernourished at the time of the Industrial Revolution and were, therefore, only able to do limited work and were vulnerable to poor health. Fogel also observed that the improvement in the circumstances of children, as estimated by the changes in height, appeared to be related to a lessening of the risk of chronic diseases in adult life. He thus concluded that conditions in early life set the risks for many health problems in adult life. McKeown's earlier analysis did not let him draw this conclusion. The 'Black Report' (Black, 1980) emphasized the importance of early childhood conditions as an important determinant of health. This conclusion, that the conditions of early childhood are a determinant of health in later life, is strongly supported by the results of recent research (Barker, 1992; Hertzman and Wiens, 1996; Power and Hertzman, 1997).

While the historical evidence shows that health improved with the prosperity associated with economic growth following the Industrial Revolution, it is not clear how important socio-economic conditions are in determining health and well-being in today's prosperous western countries. Is health care a more important determinant of health today than the improved prosperity and socio-economic conditions following the Industrial Revolution? There is now a substantial body of evidence that the quality of the environment in which individuals live and work throughout the life cycle is still the major determinant of health and well-being (Kaplan, 1997; Marmot *et al.*, 1995; MacIntyre, 1994; Townsend and Davidson, 1982). Some estimates indicate that in western countries more than 75 per cent of the inequalities in health are determined by the social and work environments in which individuals live and work (Kaplan, 1997; Marmot *et al.*, 1996).

SOCIAL ENVIRONMENT, HEALTH AND HEALTH CARE

A historical example of the tensions between the two health beliefs and public policy comes from initiatives in health in the United Kingdom in the second half of this century. During the Second World War, many social leaders in the UK wanted to narrow the gap in health status between the upper and lower classes. Lord Beveridge (1942) and his colleagues believed that health care was an important determinant of health and convinced the government that the gradients in health as measured by death across the social classes (lowest mortality in the top social class and highest mortality in the bottom social class) was primarily caused by financial barriers to access to health care (see Drache and Sullivan Chapter 1).

The debate in the British Cabinet during the Second World War also revealed another tension in beliefs that is important in relation to economic and health beliefs. This was focused on the recognition by some in the government that in the fifty years before the war began, the British economy had declined substantially compared to other developed nations (Dahrendorf, 1982; Hutton, 1995; Barnett, 1986). British technological and industrial capability was so weak at the start of the war that it was only through the import and application of American technology early in the war that Britain was able to produce the material necessary to at least hold the Germans. Thus, some in the government recognized that Britain had to rebuild its industrial economy after the war if it was to restore its wealth-creating capacity in relation to other countries. These individuals recognized the difficulty of introducing and financing national social programs (secondary wealth creation) if the primary wealth creative capacity of the nation was weak. The debate reflected the chapter in Adam Smith's book ([1776] 1991) that discusses productive and non-productive labour. Smith states that medicine, important as it is, is non-productive labour and a society's expenditures in this sector are dependent on the productive or primary wealth-creating sector. Smith categorizes doctors like a variety of other professional groups, such as opera singers, lawyers, and civil servants, as menial servants. This point, which seems as important today as it was in Smith's time, implies that expenditures on medicine or health bear some relationship to how much a society can afford to spend on what might be called its secondary wealth-creating sector. In the British Cabinet debate during the Second World War, advocates for improving the health of the population by removing the financial barriers to health care, won. Britain, as it has worked to rebuild its economy, has had difficulty sustaining or expanding support for its social programs such as health care.

The story of Britain's socio-economic problems since the Second World War illustrates the effects of socio-economic factors on health and the problem of financing health care when the country's primary wealth-creating capacity is sluggish (Dahrendorf, 1982; Hutton, 1995). Many of the chapters in this book relate directly or indirectly to this dilemma of the limited resources of a country and the consumption of a large portion of them in health care. This issue is relevant to Canada since Canada has had a sluggish economy since 1975, as reflected in our weak growth in total factor productivity and the associated socio-economic changes such as unemployment and poor improvement in the incomes of people under 45 (Helpman and Fortin, 1995; Canada, 1997; Statistics Canada, 1997).

The establishment in the United Kingdom of the National Health Service in 1948, with the belief that this would decrease the slope of the gradient in health across social classes, was a test of the role of medicine in reducing the inequalities in health as measured by mortality. This initiative, along with the emergence of effective medical treatments for some diseases including infectious diseases, reinforced the belief that medicine now had a major influence on the health of individuals and populations. However, the Merrison Royal Commission on the UK (1979) health care system in the 1970s reported that contrary to the expectations set by the Beveridge report for the national health care service, the gradient in health, as measured by death, across the social classes had actually increased since 1948. The life expectancy of the population improved during this period with the greatest improvement in the upper social classes and the least improvement in the lower social classes.

The release of this report led to an intense debate as to whether the widening gap in health status across social classes was due to poor allocation of resources for health care in relation to need, barriers created by health care professionals and other factors or was caused by the changing socio-economic conditions in the United Kingdom affecting the health and well-being of individuals throughout their life course (Allsop, 1984; Illsley and Baker 1991; MacIntyre, 1997). We do not know whether there were changes in social cohesion or trust during this period, but there is evidence of growing income inequality in British society (Wilkinson, 1993; Hutton 1995).

The Labour government of the time set up a commission chaired by Douglas Black, the Chief Medical Officer in the Department of Health and Social Services, to explore why there was a steepening mortality gradient across social classes despite the fact that there was a national health service (Black, 1980). The commission concluded that the primary factor causing the growing inequalities in health was socio-economic, due in a large part to the effects of poor quality social environments on families and children. This report was released when Margaret Thatcher's Conservative government had taken power. Her government, with its strong commitment to individualistic capitalism, restructuring society and its institutions and cutting back on publicly financed social programs, did not want a debate about social issues and health to hamper their goals. They therefore allowed only 260 copies of 'The Black Report' to be printed. It was, however, subsequently published by Penguin Books with the title *Inequalities in Health* (Townsend *et al.*, 1988). Like the earlier Lalonde Report in Canada, nothing substantial was done to implement the recommendations in the 'Black Report'.

This story illustrates that health and economic beliefs and ideological and political forces can hamper a society's attempts through government to address the social environment and health issues. The political philosophy based on the theme of individualism with little societal responsibility believes that the best rise to the top and the less able or fortunate slide down the socio-economic scale partly as a result of poorer health as a result of their own behaviour and that little can be done to help them. Least of all, this philosophy holds that finances should not be used to help these individuals since many will tend to become lazy and dependent on welfare. This point of view clashes with the view that societies should try to sustain quality social environments and equity in health and well-being. One of the forces that influences the quality of social environments is how societies create and distribute wealth and the effects on individuals.

Economists still do not adequately understand the determinants of economic growth and the effects on the environments in which people live and work (*Economist*, 1992; Kreps, 1997; Frank, 1993). There is increasing recognition that standard economic thought does not provide adequate concepts to sustain reasonable opportunities for work and income equality, particularly in times of major economic change. Most of the work of economists does not pick up on Fogel's (1991, 1994) observation about how the improved quality of the population following the Industrial Revolution had a large effect on economic growth. There is a need to link our economic concepts about how we create wealth with our improved understanding of the factors determining the quality of populations such as changes in the environments in which individuals live and work.

The new Labour government in the United Kingdom has reactivated the Black Report under a committee chaired by Sir Donald Acheson, another former Chief Medical Officer of the Department of Health and Social Services (UK, 1997). This time the United Kingdom government has created a new portfolio to deal with the society and health issues, since it is very difficult to get the Ministry concerned with health care to cope with issues around the complex social determinants of health. This initiative could fail, however, because this new department does not have the structure and resources to integrate our new understanding about the determinants of economic growth, health and human development to create and improve social environment for British society.

The Canadian Health Forum report (National Forum on Health, 1997), like the Black Report (Black, 1980), concluded that one of the factors contributing to the inequalities in health were the socio-economic changes affecting Canadian society, particularly the effect on mothers and children. There is growing recognition that conditions of early life set coping skills, behaviour and health risks in adult life (Mustard and Keating, 1993; Mustard, 1996). The recent Throne Speech by the Government of Canada (Canada, 1997) gives a high priority to strategies that could improve support for mothers and children. The socio-economic changes in the United States, Canada, and the United Kingdom driven, in part, by a growing culture of economic individualism, have been associated with a decrease in the quality of social environments and the number of children and families living in adverse circumstances (Picot, 1995; Bronfenbrenner *et al.*, 1996).

Despite the major socio-economic changes affecting societies today, our improved understanding of economic forces, social change, the human life cycle, and health and well-being provides competent societies with an opportunity to cope with major economic social changes better than in the past. A key part of this new understanding is the increased appreciation of how early childhood circumstances affect ability to learn behaviour, and health risks throughout the life cycle.

THE LIFE CYCLE AND SOCIO-ECONOMIC FACTORS

The circumstances in which children are raised during their early years has a major effect on their subsequent development (Power and Hertzman, 1997; Brooks-Gunn, 1994; Young, 1997). A narrow economic focus, with little concern about society, will tend to undermine the quality of social environments with negative effects on those with little political clout, particularly mothers and children. Because the early childhood period sets the basic coping skills, behaviour and competence for the life cycle, this lack of concern has implications in respect to the future quality of a population. We know that societies that invest in mothers and children tend to have better overall performance in measures of literacy and mathematical performance (OECD and Statistics Canada, 1995; Case, in press). They also appear to have better health and well-being in adult life (Caldwell, 1986; Mustard, 1996; Hertzman, 1995).

The government of Canada and several provincial governments, recognizing the importance of the conditions of early childhood and later life events, have issued strong statements about initiatives to prevent adverse circumstances in early childhood. Many have created ministries concerned with mothers and children (British Columbia [1996]), or secretariats concerned with mothers and children and youth (Manitoba [1994], Ontario [1997], New Brunswick [1994]). One presumes that these governments recognize that their present government department structure cannot cope with the issues around children and youth. These developments could mean that Canadians who may have a stronger base of social cohesion or trust than the United States and the United Kingdom are taking steps to minimize the adverse effects of our present socio-economic change on mothers and children. Canada may be moving to implement policies relating to development and the determinants of health that will have a positive effect on the health and well-being of future generations. To be effective, these policies must mobilize communities and strengthen the cohesion and trust of our communities. The most difficult challenge is to increase the understanding of those concerned with economic and social policy about the determinants of health and human development and economic growth.

ECONOMICS, HEALTH AND WELL-BEING

The historical evidence as assessed by McKeown (1976, 1988a) and Fogel (1994) emphasizes that for reasons that are not yet fully understood, how nations create and distribute wealth affects the structure of society and the health and well-being of the population. Both Das Gupta (1993) and Sen (1993) have argued that measures of the health of populations are good indicators of an economy and its effect on society. We now know that societies that get into economic difficulties can have negative effects on income distribution and their social environments with adverse effects on the health and well-being of their population (Fogel, 1994; Kaplan, 1997). Throughout the industrialized world there is a clear split between those who believe the way for the future should be based on greater emphasis on the individual and less concern about people and the social environment and those who want more collective action to sustain the quality of the environment in which we live and work. This difference can be considered as individualistic capitalism versus capitalism in a societal context. (Capitalism in which the private sector has a strong commitment and incentive to invest in its society.)

Economic beliefs, like health beliefs, are important factors influencing how societies cope with socio-economic factors and health and well-being. Despite the historical evidence about the relationship among economies, the social environment, and health, many of today's theoretical economists tend to ignore these relationships in their work. Indeed, Frank (1993) has argued that the education or training of American economists tends to make them insensitive to the people aspect of society. Back in the time of Adam Smith, the social conditions were part of his socio-economic arguments and theories. However, as economics took steps to become a science and use Newtonian mathematics to develop and 'prove' theoretical concepts, the discipline gradually excluded many subjects or issues from its work that were difficult to measure and model (Kreps, 1997). Many of the observations about people, health and well-being and society are difficult if not impossible to include in the theoretical equilibrium mathematical constructs they have developed. Thus, although the more restricted theoretical economic work of today is relevant to concepts such as productivity, labour, capital, inflation and business cycles, it has become largely separated from the world of people and their societies, the quality of populations and major technology innovation and its social effects. Since economics and its theories have had a considerable influence in English-speaking western countries on values and public policy, they have tended to tilt the capitalism and ideology of English-speaking cultures to what can be described as classical libertarianism.

Solow (1970), working from the neo-classical economic framework, characterized the key factors driving the economy today as greed, rationality, and equilibrium. There was no discussion or concern about the environment in which individuals live and work and the factors influencing these conditions and the effects on coping skills, competence and behaviour. In order to do their work and adhere to their mathematical models for evaluating the economy, it has been suggested economists have steered clear of the non quantitative 'saloons of the social science' (Kreps, 1997). By staying away from what many consider the anarchy of sociology, some claim much has been accomplished by pushing ahead with what has been described as the 'scientific canonical principles of neoclassical economists' (Kreps, 1997). Thus, there has been little effective communication between neo-classical economists and scholars in health and the other social sciences concerned with human development and health and well-being. One has only to look at the intense debate between Evans *et al.* (1997) and Rice (1997) and Pauly (1997) and Gaynor and Vogt (1997) over markets and health care to get a sense of this intellectual clash.

Kreps (1997), reviewing the present stage in the evolution of economics, has suggested after discussion with Paul Romer that the mathematical modelling constraint created by neo-classical economics on what is studied in economics, has greatly narrowed the field of study since Adam Smith's day. If today's constrained neo-classical economic framework can broaden out to include measures of technology and economic growth, the social environment and the determinants of human development, health and well-being, this would again place economics in a broader socio-economic framework. Romer, according to Kreps (1997) has likened this potential evolution of economics to an hour-glass. The base of study in Adam Smith's time more than 200 years ago was broad. It then became narrowed with the constraints of Newtonian mathematical modelling and now may move with new analytical approaches to a fuller inclusion of measures of the social environment, human development and health. Until economists can cope more readily with the concepts of the quality of the social environment as measured by social cohesion or trust, and the quality of a population in terms of health and well-being, there will be a sharp conflict between a narrow individualistic form of capitalism versus capitalism within a societal framework.

The potential significance of broadening the intellectual framework of economics in relation to the quality of a population and long term economic growth is brought out by one of the conclusions from Fogel's (1994) historic analysis – 50 per cent of the economic growth in the United Kingdom following the Industrial Revolution was because of the better quality of the population as a result of their improved health and well-being. With a few exceptions, economics has been unable to embrace both the historical evidence and the present evidence about the determinants of health and well-being in relation to economic and societal change.

Many economists use education as an indicator for the quality of a population. Unfortunately, our new understanding of human development, particularly the development of the brain in early life and its effect on cognition and behaviour in later life, shows that standard measures of education do not capture the full story about the quality of populations (Mustard, 1996). Among the problems is the fact that measures of learning (literacy, mathematical skills) when assessed against socio-economic markers show that these indicators, like measures of health, are a gradient (Willms, 1997). Economic theory does not easily cope with the implication of gradients. Some countries have shallow gradients for measures of health and human development when assessed against socio-economic indicators, and a high mean value; others have steep gradients and a lower mean value (MacIntyre, 1994; OECD and Statistics Canada, 1995; Case, in press). These gradients are driven in part by the effects of economic forces on social environments and the conditions of early childhood. A country like the United States, in contrast to Canada, has very steep gradients in measures of literacy and mathematics ability when assessed against socio-economic indicators. Canada's measures show that while we do not have the shallowest gradients, we are doing better than many other developed countries such as the United States.

There is evidence that some provinces have steeper gradients in literacy than other provinces (Willms, 1997). A measure of how well Canada and other countries are coping with the socio-economic changes can be seen starkly in the changing slopes of these gradients.

SOCIAL CAPITAL (TRUST), HUMAN DEVELOPMENT, AND HEALTH

How does the environment in which individuals live and work affect their health and well-being and does this show a relationship to the concepts of social capital or trust? Studies on populations in relation to their socio-economic status or places of work show that health is a gradient when assessed against job hierarchy or place in the social hierarchy. This observation is true for both death and sickness/absence from work (Carstairs and Morris, 1991; Marmot, 1992; Marmot, 1994; MacIntyre, 1994). In the case of the Whitehall civil service, these observations are from a middle class educated population who are well fed, housed and served by a publicly financed health care system. These gradients are not primarily due to variation in the conventional lifestyle risk factors (Marmot et al., 1995). It would appear that these health gradients in the workplace are related to the competence and coping skills of individuals and their job characteristics (Marmot *et al.*, 1997). As well as the effect of job structure, these gradients in health may be influenced by competence and coping skills set in early childhood (Mustard, 1996; Hertzman and Wiens, 1996). There is a growing body of evidence that early life conditions set basic competence and coping skills and many of the risks for the health problems in adult life (mental ill health, blood pressure, accidents, coronary heart disease, strokes) (Barker, 1992; Power and Hertzman, 1997). The development of the brain in the period in which it is most plastic (late in utero to age six) appears to set an individual's basic competence and coping skills which relate to future developments and many of the risks for chronic health problems in adult life (Power and Hertzman, 1997; Hertzman, 1996).

The revolution in neuroscience has now given us substantial insight into the importance of early childhood. The billions of neurons in the brain have to form trillions of connections to give an individual full competence and coping skills (Huttenlocher, 1984; Perry, 1996). The most crucial period for this is late in utero and during the first six, particularly the first three, years. Children who receive inadequate stimulation (such as touch, sound, vision, smell, taste) during this period will not form the optimum connections among their billions of neurons, with poor capability to learn in the school system and antisocial behaviour. We now appreciate the neuroscience basis for why a poor early childhood can lead to difficulties in learning in the school system and coping with the challenges of life throughout the life cycle (Mustard, 1996; Hertzman, 1996; Shore, 1997). We now are beginning to understand that the biological pathways (neuroendocrinology and neuroimmunology) by which we cope with the environment in which we live and work throughout the life cycle influence ability to learn and affect health and well-being (Coe, 1993; Mustard, 1996; Perry, 1996; McEwen, 1998). As discussed earlier, how well a society is coping with socio-economic change can be estimated by the gradients in measures of child development in the early life period and the gradients in health and well-being later in life. We know that adult health risks are related not only to early childhood but also to the kind of social interaction and support individuals have in their daily lives (Kaplan, 1997; Cassel, 1976; Berkman, 1985; Seeman *et al.*, 1987).

One measure that appears to give a reasonable estimate of the quality of the first years of life estimates the cognitive and behavioural characteristics of children when they enter the school system (Doherty, 1997; Fuchs, 1994; Tremblay, 1992). This measurement is often referred to as 'readiness to learn'. We now appreciate that the measurement can predict performance in mathematics in the school system, behaviour in the school system and juvenile delinquency. It has been observed that quality preschool support for children can greatly reduce later events such as unemployment, crime, and mental health problems (Hertzman, 1996; Tremblay, 1992; Kaplan, 1990; Schweinhart, 1993; Young, 1997). Thus, an important early life measure of how well a society is doing is the 'readiness to learn' of its children when they enter the school system. There is now some evidence that this is also a gradient when assessed against socio-economic indicators (Brooks-Gunn, 1994). We do not have good comparative longitudinal Canadian data but many primary school teachers believe that the number of children entering school who cannot cope has increased substantially over the last ten to twenty years. In some schools, they estimate that as many as 30 per cent of the male children cannot cope when they begin school. Since this probably reflects the outcomes of the conditions influencing the preschool period, this may mean it may be an early indication of a deteriorating preschool environment for children.

Many believe that societies with a strong base of social capital or trust will have the smallest negative effect on the conditions for early childhood. However, there has been no direct measure of this. There has, however, been one set of studies looking at the relationship between health and social capital (trust). In the United States, they found that there was a strong correlation between income equality and health (Kennedy, *et al.*, 1996). They also found a strong correlation between trust and income equality. When they examined mortality rates by state against measures of trust by state, they found a very strong correlation (Kawachi *et al.*, 1997). This evidence is in keeping with the other evidence showing that the quality of the social environment in which people live and work affects their health and well-being. The Roseto study (Egolf *et al.*, 1992) illustrates the effect of community relationships on health and what happens when these relationships are eroded. In developed countries, the countries with greater income equality have lower mortality rates than countries with a high degree of income inequality (Wilkinson, 1992; Lynch, 1997).

SOCIO-ECONOMIC CHANGE, HEALTH AND WELL-BEING

Can today's societies cope with the pressures from the economic changes being driven by the 'chips for neurons' technological revolution in an intensively globalized world? Those that do well will be those that can integrate the knowledge we now have about the determinants of health, human development and economic growth, and adjust their institutional and social frameworks. Some of the barriers to making these adjustments have been outlined in several chapters in this book discussing the problems in health care.

The present economic change is affecting all countries and their social structure. All developed countries are going through a very major technological revolution as powerful as the Industrial Revolution – the 'chips for neurons' revolution. For instance, changes in Canada show that since about 1975 our productivity as measured by total factor productivity has been flat (Fortin, 1996; Canada, 1997). Around 1975, our unemployment rate starts to climb, wages cease to improve (particularly for individuals under 40 years of age), more individuals became increasingly dependent on government transfer payments to sustain their income, and more children are in poor economic circumstances (Canada, 1997; Statistics Canada, 1997; Picot, 1995). There is growing evidence that Canada's social well-being, like that of other market societies, has declined since the late 1970s.

This lack of real economic growth (as measured by total factor productivity), and the increased need for government transfer payments to sustain income has led to an increase in taxes on a wealth base that has not been growing. The bottom half of the population as defined by median income has increasingly become dependent on transfer payments over the last twenty years to sustain their incomes (Statistics Canada, 1997) (about 25 per cent from transfer payments in 1972 to nearly 70 per cent in 1992), while the incomes in constant dollars of the population over 45, in contrast to those under 45 (Canada, 1997), have continued to improve (although slowly). During this period, the relative income for the population under 45 has declined. Youth unemployment has remained high, and families with young children have become increasingly dependent on transfer payments rather than earnings from work to sustain their income (Statistics Canada, 1997). As governments have had to cut back on expenditures, they have had to cut transfer payments which tend to hit hardest those with the least political influence, such as mothers and children. There is some evidence that the economic status of mothers and children has been deteriorating recently (Statistics Canada, 1997; Picot, 1995). A society with a strong base of social capital or trust should be able to cope with these changes better than societies based on chaotic individualism.

Communities that share a common understanding appear to produce leaders that can build networks among the different sectors of their community (social capital, trust) and mobilize community resources to buffer some of the problems. Many community groups believe that government programs must be designed to better support what communities can do and not disrupt the partnerships communities can build. There is no good evidence that governments have been able effectively to create policies and strategies to mesh efficiently with these community initiatives. Governments need to assess whether their support for individuals or groups in communities builds or strengthens social capital and the effects on human development, health and well-being.

We do not know how strong social cohesion or trust is in Canada or in other countries, but it may be strong in particular sub-national regions. Part of this is related to our long history of being a society in which individuals accept a responsibility to help their broader community. These values are under considerable stress at the present moment. However, many of our governments are showing an increasing awareness of the issues, although they have yet to develop programs that are compatible with the role of communities in sustaining social cohesion or trust and take into account our improved understanding of the relationship among the economy, human development, and health and well-being. To bring about effective programs and changes, there will have to be better linkages with communities and regions (partnership not control) and measurement tools that will let communities estimate how well they are doing.

Promotion of more interaction among community groups and regions that have taken action could be a very important initiative. Community groups are potential teachers for each other of how to sustain their social environments. It is possible that a national capability along these lines might develop by interaction among groups such as community foundations, early childhood educators, social entrepreneurs, business leadership and community-based policing. Government programs should be designed to support this interaction. If this interaction could be built using the social entrepreneurship present in communities, using modern techniques of communication, it could have a significant effect on the future health of communities and the quality of populations everywhere. If this can be done, it would help countries cope with a world practising capitalism to develop a high quality, healthy population by building strong social environments. This way we would have a strong social capital base, good coping skills, and a healthy population. Only time will tell if we will be able to do this.

REFERENCES

Allsop, J. 1984. *Health Policy and the National Health Service*. London: Longman.

Barker, D. J. P. 1992. *Fetal and Infant Origins of Adult Disease*. Papers written by the Medical Research Council. Environmental Epidemiology Unit. London: British Medical Journal.

Barnett, C. 1986. *The Audit of War*. London: Macmillan Publishers Limited.

Berkman, L. F. 1985. *The Relationship of Social Networks and Social Support to Morbidity and Mortality*. Social Support and Health. Academic Press Inc.

Beveridge, W., Lord. 1942. *Social Insurance and Allied Services*. London: HMSO. Cmnd. 6404.

Black, D. 1980. *Inequalities in Health*. Report of a research working group chaired by Sir Douglas Black. London: DHSS.

Black, Sir Douglas. 1988. *Inequalities in Health: the Black Report*. Edited by Peter Townsend, Nick Davidson and Margaret Whitehead. Harmondsworth, Middlesex: Penguin Books.

British Columbia, 1996. Ministry of Children and Families, September 1996.

Bronfenbrenner, U., P. McCelland, E. Wethington, P. Moen and S. Ceci. 1996. *The State of Americans: This Generation and the Next*. New York: The Free Press.

Brooks-Gunn, J. 1994. Economic Deprivation and Early Childhood Development. *Child Development* 65: 296–318.

Caldwell, J. C. 1986. Routes to Low Mortality in Poor Countries. *Population and Development Review* 12: 171–220.

Canada. 1996. Growth, Human Development, Social Cohesion. Policy Research Committee. PCO, Ottawa.

Canada, 1997. Speech from the Throne to open the first session thirty-sixth parliament of Canada. Governor-General. 23 September.

Case, R. In press. Socioeconomic Gradients in Mathematical Ability and their Responsiveness to Compensatory Education. In *Tomorrow's Children*. New York: Guilford.

Cassel, J. 1976. The Contribution of the Social Environment to Host Resistance: the Fourth Wade Hampton Frost Lecture. *American Journal of Epidemiology* 104, (2): 107–123.

Coe, C. 1993. Psychosocial Factors and Immunity in Nonhuman Primates: a Review. *Psychosomatic Medicine* 55: 298–308.

Dahrendorf, R. 1982. Recent Changes in the Class Structure of European Societies. *Daedalus* 225–270.

Dahrendorf, R. 1995. Precarious Balance: Economic Opportunity, Civil Society, and Political Liberty. *Responsive Community* 5(3).

Das Gupta, P. 1993. *An Inquiry into Well-Being and Destitution*. Oxford: Clarendon Press.

David, P. 1991. Computer and Dynamo: the modern productivity paradox in a not-too-distant mirror. *Technology and Productivity: the Challenge for Economic Policy* 315–347.

Doherty, G. 1997. Zero to six: the basis for school readiness. Applied Research Branch. Strategic Policy. Human Resources Development Canada.

Economist Magazine. 1992. Economic Growth: Explaining the Mystery, 4 January: 15–18.

Egolf, B., J. Lasker, S. Wolf, L. Potvin. 1992. The Roseto Effect: A 50-Year Comparison of Mortality Rates. *American Journal of Public Health* 82: 1089–1092.

Eisler, R. T. 1987. *The Chalice and the Blade*. San Francisco: HarperCollins.

Evans, R. G. 1994. Health Care as a Threat to Health: Defense, Opulence, and the Social Environment. *Daedalus* 123 (4): 21–42.

Evans, R. G. and G. L. Stoddart. 1990. *Producing Health, Consuming Health Care*. Canadian Institute for Advanced Research Population Health Working Paper No. 6.

Evans, R. G., M. L. Barer and T. R. Marmor. 1994. *Why are some people healthy and others not?* New York: Aldine De Gruyter.

Evans, R. G., T. Homer-Dixon, M. Wolfson, A. Maynard, T. Marmor and J. Goldstone. 1996. *Health Care, Social Fragmentation, Economic Change and the Human Ingenuity Gap*. Canadian Institute for Advanced Research.

Evans, R. G., T. Rice, V. Pauly. Gaynor and Vogt W. B. 1997. Assessing Markets: Model and Practice. *Journal of Health Politics, Policy and Law* 22: 383–508.

Fogel, R. W. 1991. The Conquest of High Mortality and Hunger in Europe and America: Timing and Mechanisms. *Favorites of Fortune: Technology, Growth and Economic Development Since the Industrial Revolution*. Harvard University Press.

Fogel, R. W. 1994. *Economic Growth, Population Theory, and Physiology: The Bearing of Long-Term Processes in the Making of Economic Policy*. NBER Working Paper No. 4638. Cambridge, MA: National Bureau of Economic Research.

Fortin, P. 1996. The Great Canadian Slump. *Canadian Journal of Economics* XXIX (4): 761–787.

Frank, R. H. 1993. Does studying economics inhibit cooperation? *Journal of Economic Perspectives* 7 (2): 159–171.

Fuchs, V. 1994. *Mathematical Achievement in Eighth Grade: Interstate and Racial Differences.* NBER Working Paper No. 4784.

Fukuyama, F. 1995. *Trust*. London: Penguin Books Ltd.

Helpman, E. and P. Fortin. 1995. *Endogenous Innovation and Growth: Implications for Canada.* Industry Canada Occasional Paper, No. 10.

Hertzman, C. and M. Wiens. 1996. *Child Development and Long-Term Outcomes: A Population Health Perspective and Summary of Successful Interventions.* Social Sciences and Medicine.

Huttenlocher, P. R. 1984. *Journal of Mental Deficiency* 83: 485.

Hutton, W. 1995. *The State We're In*. London: Jonathan Cape.

Illsley, R. R. and D. Baker. 1991. Contextual Variations in the Meaning of Health Inequality. *Social Science and Medicine* 32: 359.

Kaplan, G. A. 1990. Socioeconomic Conditions in Childhood are Associated with Ischaemic Heart Disease During Middle Age. Human Population Laboratory, California Department of Health Services.

Kaplan, G. A. 1997. Whither studies on the socioeconomic foundations of population health? Editorial. *American Journal of Public Health* 87 (9): 1409–1411.

Kawachi, I., B. Kennedy, K. Lochner and D. Prothrow-Stith. 1997. Social Capital, Income Inequality, and Mortality. *American Journal of Public Health* 87: 1491.

Kennedy, B., I. Kawachi and D. Prothrow-Stith. 1996. Income Distribution and Mortality: Cross Sectional Ecological Study of the Robin Hood Index in the United States. *British Medical Journal* 312: 1004–1007.

Kreps, D. M. 1997. Economics – The Current Position. *Daedalus* 126 (1): 59–85.

Kuttner, R. 1997. *Everything for Sale: The Virtues and Limits of Markets.* New York: Alfred A. Knopf Inc.

Lalonde, M. 1974. *A New Perspective on the Health of Canadians (a working document).* Ottawa: Government of Canada.

Lipsey, R. G. and C. Bekar. 1994. A Structuralist View of Technical Change and Economic Growth. In T. J. Courchene (ed.), *Technology, Information and Public Policy. The Bell Canada Papers on Economic and Public Policy,* Vol. 3. Kingston: John Deutsch Institute, Queen's University.

Lynch, J. W. 1997. Understanding how inequality in the distribution of income affects health. *Journal of Health Psychology* 2 (3): 297–314.

McEwen, B. S. 1998. *New England Journal of Medicine.*

MacIntyre, S. 1994. Understanding the Social Patterning of Health: The Role of the Social Sciences. *Journal of Public Health Medicine* 16: 53.

MacIntyre, S. 1997. The Black Report and Beyond: What are the Issues? *Social Science and Medicine* 44 (6): 723–745.

McKeown, T. 1976. *The Modern Rise of Population*. London: Edward Arnold.

McKeown, T. 1988. *The Origins of Human Disease*. New York: Basil Blackwell.

McKeown, T. 1988. Obituary. *Lancet* ii: 58.

Manitoba. 1994. *Establishment of Manitoba's Children and Youth Secretariat*: p. 1.

Marmot, M., M. Bobak, and G. Davey Smith. 1995. Explanations for Social Inequalities in Health. In *Society and Health*. New York: Oxford University Press.

Marmot, M., Y. Ben-Shlomo and I. White. 1996. Does the Variation in the Socioeconomic Characteristics of an Area Affect Mortality. *British Medical Journal* 312: 1013–1014.

Merrison, Sir Alec. 1979. *Royal Commission on the National Health Service*. London: Her Majesty's Stationery Office.

Mustard, J. F. 1987. Achieving Health for All: implications for Canadian health and social policies. *Canadian Medical Association Journal* 136: 471–473.

Mustard, J. F. 1996. Technology, Information and the Evolution of Social Policy: The Chips for Neurons Revolution and Socio-Economic Change. In T. J. Courchene (ed.), *Policy Frameworks for a Knowledge Economy*. John Deutsch Institute for the Study of Economic Policy, Queen's University, Kingston, Ontario.

Mustard, J. F. and D. P. Keating. 1993. Social Economic Factors and Human Development. In *Family Security in Insecure Times*. National Forum on Family Security. Ottawa: Canadian Council on Social Development Publications.

National Forum on Health. 1997. *Canada Health Action: Building on the Legacy*. Ottawa.

New Brunswick. 1994. The Family Policy Secretariat. 26 October, 1994.

New York Times. 1992. Canada's No Medical Model. Editorials/Letters. Tuesday May 26.

Newman, K. S. and P. Attewell. 1995. *The downsizing epidemic in the United States: toward a cultural analysis of economic dislocation*. Joint effort of Kennedy School of Government, Harvard University and Department of Sociology, City University of New York, Graduate Center.

OECD and Statistics Canada. 1995. *Literacy, Economy and Society: Results of the First International Adult Literacy Survey*. OECD, Paris, and Statistics Canada, Ottawa.

Ontario. 1997. Secretariat for Children and Families.

Perry, B. 1996. Neurodevelopmental aspects of childhood anxiety disorders: neurobiological responses to threat. In *Textbook of Pediatric Neuropsychiatry*. Washington, DC: American Psychiatric Press.

Picot, G. 1995. *Social Transfers, Changing Family Structure, and Low Income Among Children*. Statistics Canada Research Paper Series, No. 82. Ottawa.

Power, C., and C. Hertzman. 1997. Social and biological pathways linking early life and adult disease. *British Medical Bulletin* 53 (1): 210–221.

Power, C. *et al.*, 1997. Social Differences in Health: Life-Cycle Effects between Ages 23 and 33 in the 1958 British Birth Cohort. *American Journal of Public Health* 87 (9): 1499–1503.

Putnam, R. D. 1993. *Making Democracy Work: Civic Traditions in Modern Italy*. Princeton: Princeton University Press.

Schweinhart, L. J. 1993. *Significant Benefits: the High-Scope Perry Preschool Study Through Age 27*. Ypsilanti, MI. High-Scope Press.

Seeman, T. E. *et al.*, 1987. Social Network Ties and Mortality Among the Elderly in the Alameda County Study. *American Journal of Epidemiology* 126 (4): 714–723.

Sen, A. 1993. The Economics of Life and Death. *Scientific American*, 1 May: 40–47.

Shleifer, A., R. La Porta, F. Lopez de Silanes and R. W. Vishny. 1996. *Trust in Large Organizations*. Cambridge, MA: Harvard University Press.

Shore, R. 1997. *Rethinking the Brain: New Insights into Early Development*. New York: Families and Work Institute.

Smith, A. [1776] 1991. *The Wealth of Nations*. New York: Knopf.

Solow, R. M. 1970. *Growth Theory: An Exposition*. New York: Oxford University Press.

Statistics Canada, 1997. Crossing the low income line. Ottawa.

Townsend, P. and N. Daridson 1982. *Inequalities in Health: the Black Report*. Harmondsworth: Penguin Books.

Townsend, P., N. Davidson and M. Whitehead 1988. *Inequalities in Health. The Black Report. The Health Divide*. London, Penguin Books.

Tremblay, R. E. 1992. Early Disruptive Behaviour, Poor School Achievement, Delinquent Behaviour, and Delinquent Personality. *Journal of Consulting and Clinical Psychology* 60 (1): 64–72.

UK. 1997. Labour Highlights Shocking Inequalities in Health – Chris Smith to Announce New Inquiry. *News from Labour*. Issued by the Labour Party media office, London (March).

Virchow, R. [1849] 1985. Translated and issued as *Collected Essays on Public Health and Epidemiology*, Vol. 1. J. L. Rather, ed. Canton, MA: Science History Publications.

Wilkinson, R. G. 1992. National Mortality Rates: the Impact of Inequality. *American Journal of Public Health* 82 (8): 1082–1084.

Wilkinson, R. G. 1993. The Epidemiological Transition: From Material Scarcity to Social Disadvantage? 11th Honda Foundation Discoveries Symposium. Prosperity, Health and Well-Being. October 16–18, 1993. Toronto: Canadian Institute for Advanced Research.

Wilkinson, R. G. 1996. *Unhealthy Societies: The Affections of Inequality*. London: Routledge.

Willms, J. D. 1999. *Quality and Inequality in Children's Literacy: the Effects of Families, Schools and Communities*. In Press. Human Development Program. Canadian Institute for Advanced Research. New York: Guilford.

Young, M. E. 1997. *Early Childhood Development*. Washington, DC: The World Bank Development Department.

Index

increased 164–5; downsizing 229;
efficiency 36, 65, 66–7, 130;
measurements 69; public/private
roles 66; regulation 16, 131; US 132–36
problem-solving 278–80, 285
Problem-Solving Decision-Making
scale 279–80
professional licensing 89–90
property rights 100–1
Pross, A. P. 276
providers 88–9; citizenship 66; devolved
authorities 172, 173–4; funding 333;
NAFTA 88–9; and patients 286;
private 142–3 n12, public 287;
rationalization 183; self-interest 35–7
provinces: debt 228–9; devolution 167–8,
171, 179; drug payments 298–9;
economic growth 240–1; health care
expenditure/revenue 190–1; health care
output 235, *236*; health care
responsibilities 238; NAFTA 96–7;
programs 246; tensions with regions 194
Provincial Health Council 194, 196
Provincial Progressive Conservative Party 49
psychiatric patients 300, 301
public domain 4
public funding for health care 1, 2, 6, 25–7,
29–30, 310–11
public health: Alberta 62–3, 186–7; blood
transfusion system 8; Canadian/US policies
60–1; social determinants 334–6, 337–8
public health insurance 13, 67, 106, 107, 260
public payment system 6
public policy 27–8, 60–1, 247–8, 317–18
public/private mix, health care 26–7, 29–30,
66, 68–71, 98–9, 106–7; Australia
120–21; Britain 2, 6, 70, 132–6;
Canada 5, *70*
public sector spending 149, 228, 287
purchasing power parities 294–5
Putnam, R. D. 169, 178, 331, 332

quality 198–9, 213–15
Quality of Work Life committee 215
quasi-market reforms 3, 6
Quebec: budget allocations 156;
Castonguay-Nepveu Commission 151,
157; *Citizen-Oriented Reform* 152;
community vision 164;
decentralization 16, 161; devolution *167,
168*; Forum national sur la santé/National
Health Forum 149; Gouvernement
du 247; health reforms 152–3, 182; local

community health service centres 151;
non-patented medicine 306;
Orientations 152; private delivery 235,
237; public/private approach 44; regional
boards 153–6, 161–2, 179; Regional
Councils 169; Regional Health and Social
Services Councils 151; Regional Medical
Commission 153, 163 n3; regionalization
147, 150–3; Rochon Commission 152,
153, 157; social change 157–8
queueing: *see* waiting lists

Rachlis, M. 6, 48–9, 254
Rae, Bob 208
Rae administration 217, 218
Ranachan, A. 14
RAND Health Insurance Experiment 75
Rasell, E. 32, *33*
Rasmussen, K. 175, 177, 181
rationalization, health care system 178–80
rationing, medical care 260
razor gangs 115–18, 124 n17
readiness to learn 343–4
Reagan, Ronald 261
redistribution of wealth 67
reference-based pricing 301–2
referral, by physicians 49
regional boards 153–6, 161–2, 168, 179,
180; boards of directors 154, 155–6;
Canada Health Act 155
Regional Councils, Quebec 169
regional delivery service 195–8
regional health authorities 14, 187–9, *191*,
195
Regional Health Authorities Act 189, 195
Regional Health and Social Services
Councils 151
Regional Medical Commission, Quebec
163 n3
regionalization 147, 150–3
regulation 16, 127
Reinhardt, U. E. 27, 41
Relman, A. S. 286
Renaud, Marc 162
Research & Statistics, Maritime Medical Care
Incorporated 299
residualism: health care 201 n1; welfare
policy 186–7
resources: allocation 2–3, 240, 275, 286;
distribution 148; equity 67, 152;
Ontario 210; population 240;
reallocation 67
Rhenberg, Clas 77, 78